ADVANCE PRAISE FOR THE BOOK

'As someone who has witnessed, first-hand, the power of technology to transform lives, I find *The Co-Intelligence Revolution* by Professor Venkat Ramaswamy and Krishnan Narayanan a profoundly insightful guide to a pivotal transformation. This book captures a fundamental leap, where AI becomes not just an automator but a co-creator alongside human ingenuity, redefining how value is built for businesses and society. Drawing from over 100 practical examples and the wisdom of global leaders, the authors offer frameworks such as *Life-Xverse, Tokenized Digital Intelligence (TDI)* and the *PIEX Lens*. These frameworks collectively argue for co-intelligent enterprise transformation and a future where AI amplifies human capabilities, driving sustainable, experience-centric value at scale. It is an invitation for entrepreneurs to seize this co-intelligent era, just as we leveraged co-creation at Infosys, to propel meaningful progress with purpose'—**Narayana Murthy, co-founder, Infosys**

'Venkat and Krishnan have written a timely and compelling book. AI technologies are evolving at a dizzying pace, and organizations and societies worldwide need guidance to navigate and thrive in this complex landscape. *The Co-Intelligence Revolution* presents a powerful vision of how humans and AI can co-create value, shaping a future where technology amplifies human potential rather than replacing it. I have always believed that technology must be a force for inclusion and empowerment. This book offers a road map for a better world— one where AI serves humanity, not the other way around. It is a must-read!'—**Nandan Nilekani, co-founder and chairman, Infosys, and founding chairman, UIDAI (Aadhaar)**

'Rapid advances in the science and technology of artificial intelligence (AI) and machine learning are expected to have a profound impact on every intellectual discipline and essentially all aspects of our lives and livelihood. How society is transformed by the AI revolution will ultimately be decided by how we maximize the potential of AI in domains as different as scientific discoveries, business productivity, healthcare and lifelong learning, and how we minimize any deleterious consequences of this powerful technology. A key factor in successfully extracting benefits for society from these advances lies in augmenting human intelligence with machine intelligence. Ramaswamy and Narayanan present very insightful ideas, documented carefully with illustrative examples and case studies from organizations and enterprises around the world. They point to opportunities provided by this collaborative intelligence or co-intelligence, to revolutionize learning, commerce and society, and approaches to tap into such opportunities. This timely book will be an important contributor to the global conversation on the intersections of human and machine intelligence and the underlying implications of these intersections on humanity itself'—**Subra Suresh, former director, National Science Foundation, USA; member, governing board, Anusandhan National Research Foundation, India; and president, Global Learning Council, Switzerland**

THE
CO-INTELLIGENCE
REVOLUTION

'Peter Drucker recognized early on the importance of the man-made network of institutions and organizations—what he called 'social ecology'. In today's polarized world, the quality of these institutions and their ability to create value are essential for society's stability and survival. With AI emerging in various forms, we now have powerful tools to amplify human ingenuity and creativity. Venkat Ramaswamy and Krishnan Narayanan offer fresh insights for large-scale value creation, showcasing compelling real-life examples of co-creation through the power of co-intelligence'—**Richard Straub, president, Global Peter Drucker Forum**

'This book comes at a crucial time when AI is reshaping research, learning and the very meaning of intelligence. Its vision of AI, which is collaborative, ethical and deeply integrated with human values, aligns with our vision of "IIT Madras for all", and our belief in nurturing AIs that not only enhance academic inquiry but also empower society. I am doubly delighted that our alumni are pushing the frontiers of knowledge. I congratulate Venkat and Krishnan for their thought-provoking work and highly recommend this book to anyone keen on understanding the future of Human–AI collaboration'—**V. Kamakoti, director, IIT Madras**

'Venkat and Krishnan's book is a treasure trove of powerful ideas, vividly demonstrating how "co-intelligence"—the collaborative synergy between humans and AI—is revolutionizing industries at an unprecedented pace. The implications for the manufacturing and services sectors are profound, creating significant opportunities for startups and MSMEs. India will deeply resonate with and value their concept of "CoDPI", which leverages AI to enhance digital public infrastructures—an undeniable force for good that has the potential to be transformative for every country. This book is an invaluable guide for entrepreneurs, investors, business executives and government leaders. It builds on the paradigm of co-creation and "folding in the future", which the visionary late Prof. C.K. Prahalad envisioned more than two decades ago in *The Future of Competition*, co-authored with Prof. Venkat Ramaswamy'—**Gopal Srinivasan, chairman and managing director, TVS Capital Funds**

'Around twenty years ago, professors Venkat Ramaswamy and the late C.K. Prahalad published *The Future of Competition*, predicting that value creation would shift from transactional exchanges to collaborative experiences co-created by companies and customers. Today, that vision is fundamental to business strategy. In this groundbreaking new book, professors Venkat Ramaswamy and Krishnan Narayanan reveal the next frontier of value creation—*Co-Intelligence*—where Human–AI collaboration becomes central to innovation. They argue compellingly that AI must be embraced as a strategic partner rather than a mere tool. The authors provide robust frameworks and practical examples to guide businesses beyond digital transformation into becoming co-intelligent enterprises, embedding AI into their core, to collaboratively co-create sustainable value. It is essential reading for anyone wanting to thrive in the emerging era of Co-Intelligence'—**Katsutoshi Murakami, CEO, Sirius International LLC and co-creation strategy specialist**

insights into how global leaders across industry and higher education are thriving by embracing AI as a collaborative partner. Engaging case studies highlight how institutions, such as the University of Michigan, are doing trailblazing work in promoting AI literacy and providing AI access to all. I believe every graduate should experience foundational AI education and meaningful interaction with AI tools. I strongly encourage everyone to read this book for its practical and actionable insights on how AI can make our world a more welcoming place for all of us'—**Ravi Pendse, vice president, Information Technology and chief information officer, University of Michigan**

THE
CO-INTELLIGENCE
REVOLUTION

How Humans and AI
Co-Create New Value

VENKAT RAMASWAMY
KRISHNAN NARAYANAN

PENGUIN
BUSINESS

An imprint of Penguin Random House

PENGUIN BUSINESS

Penguin Business is an imprint of the Penguin Random House group of companies
whose addresses can be found at global.penguinrandomhouse.com

Published by Penguin Random House India Pvt. Ltd
4th Floor, Capital Tower 1, MG Road,
Gurugram 122 002, Haryana, India

Penguin
Random House
India

First published in Penguin Business by Penguin Random House India 2025

Copyright © Venkat Ramaswamy and Krishnan Narayanan 2025

All rights reserved

10 9 8 7 6 5 4 3 2

The views and opinions expressed in this book are the authors' own and the facts are as
reported by them which have been verified to the extent possible, and the publishers are
not in any way liable for the same.

Please note that no part of this book may be used or reproduced in any manner
for the purpose of training artificial intelligence technologies or systems.

ISBN 9780143474944

Typeset in Sabon LT Std by Manipal Technologies Limited, Manipal
Printed at Thomson Press India Ltd, New Delhi

www.penguin.co.in

MIX
Paper | Supporting
responsible forestry
FSC® C010615

To Brahman and Swami Krishnananda,
Ishvara and Shivashankar,
Bhumi Devi and Soulmate Bindu,
Prakriti and Joyful Adithya and Lalitha,
Matrudevo Bhava and Pitrudevo Bhava,
and co-creators of the future everywhere

In loving memory of my father, Shri A.V. Ramaswamy;
God bless his soul

—Venkat Ramaswamy

Thanks to Amma, Ramya, Rohan and Shriya for your love
and encouragement

In loving memory of my appa

—Krishnan Narayanan

Contents

List of Figures

Foreword

by Kris Gopalakrishnan

It gives me immense pleasure to write the foreword to this book. First, because I have known both Venkat and Krishnan for a long time. I fondly remember releasing Venkat's book on co-creation at Infosys in 2007 and interacting with him on how to make the idea work in the Indian IT context. I know Krishnan from his Infosys days. Later we founded a research non-profit together, and he works with me now.

Second, as someone deeply passionate about technology and AI and their transformative potential for India and the world, I find their exploration of 'co-intelligence' and its impact on our lives timely, insightful and compelling. My journey in technology began decades ago when I graduated from IIT Madras in computer science and became a software engineer. I had a ringside view of the development of the IT industry in India, and I saw the power of technology to empower individuals, transform businesses and drive societal progress.

The book's focus on both co-intelligence and 'life-experiences' resonates deeply with my own convictions. We are at the next pivotal moment in the impact of technology on society, where the convergence of human ingenuity and AI is unlocking unprecedented possibilities. I am particularly excited by the

potential of AI to address some of the world's most pressing
challenges. Having witnessed the uneven distribution of
technological progress in India and across the world, I believe
that technology must be carefully leveraged to create positive
impacts for our diverse population.

I would like to see the vision of this book fulfilled in two
areas that are dear to me—scientific research and business
excellence. My philanthropic investments in brain research
stem from a deep-seated belief in the transformative power of
scientific exploration. Just as India made significant strides in
the IT sector, I am confident that we can replicate this success in
neuroscience. By fostering cutting-edge brain research centres
at esteemed institutions such as the Indian Institute of Science
and IIT Madras, and through their collaboration with global
brain centres, we are laying the foundation for breakthroughs
in understanding the human brain, potentially leading to cures
for debilitating diseases like Alzheimer's and dementia, and for
neuromorphic AI architectures.

The book's emphasis on 'co-creation' aligns with my
experiences at the Confederation of Indian Industry (CII),
where I have advocated for collaborative partnerships between
startups and industry, academia and government. The theme
of CII's annual business summit 2024 was 'Co-Creating the
Future Responsibly'. The book's exploration of 'co-creative
living organizations' fostering ecosystemic innovation provides
a valuable framework for all enterprises looking to navigate
the complexities of the co-intelligence world. I firmly believe
that businesses must have a responsibility to contribute to the
wellbeing of society. The book's exploration of 'sustainable
wellbeing impacts (SWIs)' and its focus on how co-intelligence
can be leveraged to address social challenges in areas like
agriculture, education and healthcare resonates strongly with
my own commitment to these causes.

I believe that this book will serve as an invaluable resource
for entrepreneurs, business leaders, policymakers and anyone
seeking to understand and harness the transformative power

of co-intelligence. It offers a compelling vision of the future, where humans and AI collaborate to create a world that is more equitable, sustainable and fulfilling for all. I commend Venkat and Krishnan for their insightful work and encourage readers to embrace the principles of Human-AI co-creation as we embark on this exciting journey into the future.

Preface

The advent of generative artificial intelligence (GenAI) has given rise to a *co-intelligence* world where the creativeness of human intelligence is amplified by machine intelligence—a different kind of intelligence that humans can compose with— one that comprehends the entire corpus of humanity with its reasoning traces therein, finds relational patterns and is 'jointly creative'. The imperative is to harness this newfound power of Human–AI interactive engagement to co-create new-value through our life–experiences, innovation and organizations.

As we will see in this book, in this new realm of co-intelligence, organizations have to craft co-intelligence architectures powered by shared digitalized infrastructure (SDI) platforms that interactively engage individuals as creative-experiencers (whether customers, workers, managers, financiers, partners, policymakers, designers or citizens), anywhere and everywhere in their interconnected value chain, offering, management and Nature–Society–Economy–Technology (NEST) ecosystems. Organizations have to configure flows of interactive engagements in interconnected ecosystems of extended reality (physical, digital and virtual) environments with all stakeholders to co-create value in a risk-managed fashion and co-evolve sustainable wellbeing impacts (SWIs) at speed, scale and scope.

Like the ongoing evolution of AI with its exponential bursts, the ideas in this book developed similarly. One of us, Venkat

Ramaswamy (VR), published *The Future of Competition: Co-Creating Unique Value with Customers* (HBS Press, 2004), together with the late C.K. Prahalad.[1] That book put forth the ideas of 'experience innovation' in an internetworked world of 'interactions' and 'co-creation' of unique value with customers. With an individual- and experience-centric view, they posited that digitalized human experiences would become central to enterprise value creation, innovation, strategy and organizational management. Enterprises began to slowly, but surely, embrace concepts they had discussed (see Figure P-1), such as 'customer experience' in business models, leveraging 'customer competence', innovating 'experience-oriented' offerings, fostering 'experience personalization' and the larger perspective of 'co-creation' of value with all stakeholders.

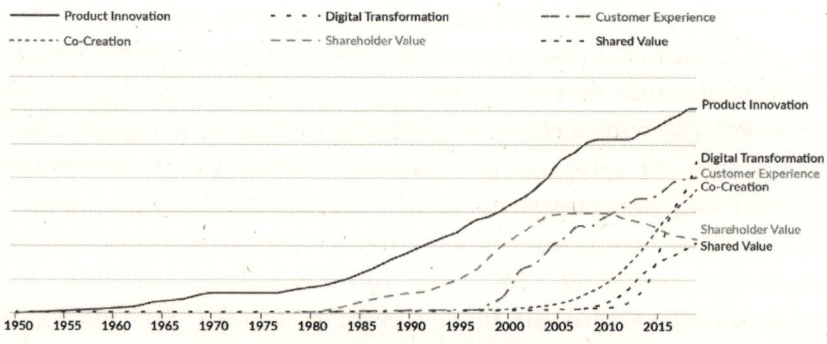

Figure P-1: Google Ngram Analysis
(*Source:* Based on authors' analysis)

From 2005 until 2010, VR engaged with thousands of managers globally who had begun experimenting with interactive value creation. He discussed how enterprises were building and leveraging platforms of engagements that enabled 'large-scale ongoing interactions' among the firm, its customers and its extended network. Enterprises were tapping into user communities and extending their resource base through practices such as crowdsourcing and open innovation. Some had also begun allowing their customers to personalize offerings. Managers were going beyond a conventional 'goods-services' mindset to developing a human *'experience'* mindset. Success stemmed from using people's actual lived experiences to generate insights and change the nature and quality of interactions in building *co-creative enterprises*. This culminated in VR's next book, with Francis Gouillart, *The Power of Co-Creation: Build It with Them to Boost Growth, Productivity, and Profits* (Free Press, 2010).[2]

With increasing de-centring of value creation towards human experiences and its further democratization in society and economy, VR soon published, with Kerimcan Ozcan, *The Co-Creation Paradigm* (Stanford University Press, 2014), a book that provided both a broader and a deeper theoretical and synthesized basis for co-creation of value with all stakeholding individuals based on their lived experiences.[3] At the same time, it discussed the growing importance of interactional creation of value across sectors (private, public and plural) in expanding wealth–welfare–wellbeing in society, economy and business. Building on these early ideas, VR went on a sabbatical in 2017–18 and engaged with Nandan Nilekani's EkStep and Societal Thinking extended team (with the guidance of Sanjay Purohit, chief curator). This was also when Nilekani, co-founder of Infosys, was returning to the company as chairman, amid his ongoing societal transformation journey.

VR, as he guided Infosys in its co-creation journey since 2007, first met Krishnan Narayanan (KN) there.[4] Then chairman and chief mentor, N.R. Narayana Murthy, later recounted to us 'how he had experimented with the idea of co-creation at Infosys, and it was a huge success in a service industry like customized software development'. Then CEO, Kris Gopalakrishnan, later shared with us how he believed 'co-creation will change the way we think about development and use of technology for the benefit of humanity'.

KN's experience with all things digital was in industry. Between 2000 and 2013, he was a member of Infosys Lab's

Management Council, consulting with Global 1000 CXOs on digital transformation while managing a global programme in partnership with Microsoft and collaborating with research and innovation (R&I) clusters from the US, Netherlands and Australia. In 2016, he, along with Kris Gopalakrishnan and N. Dayasindhu, co-founded itihaasa Research and Digital, a research think tank where they study the evolution of technology and innovation in India. KN has examined India's landscape of AI, brain sciences and quantum technologies R&D, written extensively on India's national digital stack and contributed to the development of a non-personal data governance framework for the country (where Kris Gopalakrishnan chaired the Indian Ministry of IT's committee on it).

In the two books that KN has co-authored, *Against All Odds: The IT Story of India* (Penguin Random House India, 2022) with Kris Gopalakrishnan and N. Dayasindhu, and *Empowering India: Ideas for Action by Scientists and Engineers* (Indian Academy of Sciences, 2023) with Thalappil Pradeep,[5] he has chronicled the growth of the Indian IT industry and startups, visualized future tech-driven business opportunities and outlined ideas on science, technology and innovation for empowering India and achieving sustainable development. KN has undertaken and studied a number of techno-social interventions as a founding board member of AquaMAP, a water management and policy centre in India, as president of the IIT Madras Alumni Association and as an adviser to Manthan, India's platform for R&I.

In the summer of 2021, as the Covid-19 pandemic accelerated the tech intensity and digital transformation of enterprises, we (KN and VR) reconnected and began to explore implications for next-generation and AI-infused organizations and putting life–experience ahead of technology. We began discussing the implications of India's digital innovation and its population-scale digital public infrastructures (DPIs) from an organizational perspective. We visualized the increasing emphasis on ecosystem co-innovation of life–experiences on the one hand and co-evolving sustainable wellbeing impacts on the other.

And then ChatGPT happened in late 2022, with GenAI starting to transform the global societal, economic and business landscape. It became clear to us that the world was on the cusp of yet another revolution—this time, one entailing a structural transformation of the very nature of value and the process of creating it. As we researched this further, a next generation of ideas and concepts on co-intelligence-driven innovation and co-creation of risk-managed value began taking shape. We visualized this through what we called a *PIEX* lens (*P*latforms of *I*nteractive *E*ngagements driving *I*mpacts in *E*cosystems of life-e*X*periences).

It also became evident that moving forward, for organizations to thrive and sustain themselves in the future, they must become 'living-system' organizations harnessing the power of Human–AI interactive engagements for co-intelligence-driven and SWI-based transformation. Even as we were shaping this book, Ozcan and VR presented a visionary approach to understanding the evolving relationship between technology and human experiences in another book, *Dynamic Relationality Theory of Creative Transformation: Grounding Machinic Ecosystems in Life-Experiences* (Elsevier, 2024*)*. It offers a theoretical yin to our book's practice yang, emphasizing a life- and experience-first perspective in the convergence of AI and human intelligence. Moving beyond traditional tech-centric views, it advocates for co-creative emergent experiences instead of mere digital platformization.

As no single example could possibly exemplify our entire synthesized frame of reference, we convey our perspective and key ideas in this book using various examples as 'thinking props'. (See **Figure P-2** for a consolidated list of examples researched and discussed in this book, some in more detail than others.) We strive to articulate emergent and evolving next practices, recognizing that a revolutionary paradigm shift occurs over a fairly long period of ferment. We share the spirit of humility in recognizing the work of many whose shoulders we stand upon, weaving their perspectives into our narrative throughout this book. We hope it is a clarion call to action in co-creating a new world of possibilities. While we focus primarily on the strategic implications for organizations, particularly with a conceptual practice inclination, we believe that, ultimately, all of us will have to see, think and act differently, with far-ranging implications for education, and human learning and development more broadly. We expect another long but exciting journey through the unfamiliar that will force us out of our comfort zones into a cross-sector, co-intelligence-driven innovation and risk-managed value co-creation, one that is more expansive, equitable and fulfilling in amplifying the creative potential of humanity and our planetary experiences.

Venkat Ramaswamy and Krishnan Narayanan

ECOSYSTEMS	EXAMPLES			
Agriculture	AB InBev	EDF	JetBlue	Pacific Northwest National Laboratory
Automotive	Accenture	eGov Foundation	Jugalbandi	Palantir
Banking	Adobe	EkStep	Khan Academy	People+ai
Consumer Durables	Air Canada	Energy Swaraj Foundation	Klarna	Philips / Signify
Consumer Packaged Goods	Airbnb	Espírito Santo	Kochi Open Mobility Network (KOMN)	Ping An
Distribution	Alibaba	Etherisc	Kraken-Octopus Energy	PM-Kisan
Education	Amazon	Fédération Française de Tennis	L'Oréal	Project ECHO
Electronics	Amul	FedEx	Land O'Lakes	Reliance
Energy	Anthropic	Finternet	Lemonade	Sahamati
Entertainment	Apple	Flanders	Mahindra	Salesforce
Fashion	Apurva	Ford	Mandiant (Google)	SanboxAQ
Financial Services	Aston Martin	Gaia-X	McKinsey	SAP
Government	AT&T	Gefion	Mercedes-Benz	Sarvam
Healthcare	ATP	General Motors	Meta	Second Nature
Hospitality	AWS	GitHub (Microsoft)	Microsoft	Shell
Insurance	AXA	Global Learning Council	Ministry of State, AI, United Arab Emirates	Shibuya
IT Services	BASF	Goldman Sachs	MInT Collaborative	Siemens
Logistics	BCG	Google Cloud	MIT	Sikshana Foundation
Management Consulting	Bloomberg	Government of India	Mobilitas	Softbank
Manufacturing and Industrial	BMW	Government of New Zealand	Moms First	Stellantis
Mobility and Transportation	Catena-X	Government Technology Agency, Singapore	Monarch Tractor	Tesla
Professional Services	Central Bank of Brazil (BCB)	Haier	Morgan Stanley	Toyota
Public & Social Services	City of Helsinki	Henkel	Motorola Solutions	Uber
Retail	Clifford Chance	Hippocratic AI	Namma Yatri	UIDAI
Social Enterprises	Commonwealth Bank of Australia	HPE	NIO	United Nations
Software & Technology Services	Companhia Brasileira de Alumínio	HubSpot	Nissan	University of Michigan
Supply Chain	Coursera	Humber College	NPCI	Villars Institute
Telecom	Danfoss	IBM	NTU Singapore	Volkswagen
Travel	Databricks	IdeiaGov, Brazil	NVIDIA	Wiley
Utilities	DBS	IDEO	Open Network Digital Commerce (ONDC)	xAI
Web3	DeepMind (Google)	IIT Madras	OpenAI	Yotta
	DeepSeek	Industree	OpenEvidence	
	Dell	Infosys	OpenTable	
	DIKSHA	ING	Oracle	
	Discovery	ITC		

Figure P-2: Book Examples
(*Source:* Based on authors' analysis)

1

Engaging with a New AI

In April 2023, Biwan, a small village about two hours away from New Delhi, India's capital, was the site of a remarkable socio–technical experiment. Mohd. Abdullah Khan and his fellow farmers spoke in their native language of Hindi to Jugalbandi, an AI-infused service available on their mobile phones, to discover details of relevant government schemes. Jugalbandi was more than a WhatsApp-based chatbot. It combined two artificial intelligence (AI) models: i) a language model, developed under the Bhashini mission of the Government of India, trained on large datasets of various local Indian languages and ii) a Microsoft Azure OpenAI service-based dialogic interface, fine-tuned and inferenced on Indian government policies, schemes and related documents.[1]

India has over 20,000 government programmes, but common citizens find it difficult to access them. English, the primary language of government and business, is spoken by only about a tenth of the population of over 1.4 billion. While some government documents are also in Hindi, spoken by about half of Indians, a vast majority of the population is unable to access government programmes due to language barriers, let alone successfully find and avail themselves of relevant programmes.[2] Jugalbandi understands questions in multiple languages, whether spoken or typed, retrieves information on relevant government programmes and relays it back in native languages, regardless of the source language of the information. Thus, the farmers and AI engage in back-and-forth interaction to create meaningful outcomes—a *jugalbandi*, which in Indian classical music refers to a duet between musicians who riff off each other to create something new together.

Interestingly, when Jugalbandi presented forms to a farmer who was eligible for a specific scheme, the farmer wondered if it could complete the process for him. Jugalbandi Studio now facilitates the development of *Agentic* AI systems capable of executing specific action flows across different applications and making coordinated decisions on one's behalf. This is a new form of AI. What's crucial to recognize here is the capacity now for all of us to have a *natural human language* dialogue with a computational system that understands us in our native context.

A demo of Jugalbandi's capabilities was shown to Satya Nadella, executive chairman and CEO of Microsoft, during his visit to India in early January 2023.[3] Later that month, at the World Economic Forum, Nadella marvelled at the incredible pace of technology *diffusion*:

> That (Jugalbandi) meant that a large model, a foundational model (ChatGPT) that was developed on the West Coast of the US a few months before, made its way to a developer in India, who then added value to it to make a difference to remote village life.[4]

This rapid diffusion and democratization of AI capabilities is remarkable.

Since then, Microsoft has defined a new ecosystem of global offerings through its vision of *AI Copilots*. Nadella wrote in his letter to Microsoft shareholders in October 2023: 'We have entered a new age of AI that will fundamentally transform productivity for every individual, organization, and industry on earth, and help us address some of our most pressing challenges. This next generation of AI will reshape every software category and every business, including our own.'[5, 6] The next month, in his keynote address at the Microsoft Ignite 2023 event, Nadella added, 'We are at a tipping point. This is clearly the age of Copilots.'[7] In January 2024, at the World Economic Forum meeting in Davos, he described what distinguishes the Copilot era from the earlier eras of PC and web. '. . . this is more about "expertise at your fingertips" . . . setting the era we are definitely in.'[8] Microsoft has since rolled out its 'Copilot Studio' agent builder that offers an immediate, interactive agentic AI development experience within its offerings.

But how did OpenAI and its foundational model ChatGPT come to be? It took some years in the making—gradually at first and then in a big bang. Multiple technologies had to fall in place first. None more than NVIDIA's.

The Big Bang of GenAI: NVIDIA, Google and Microsoft

NVIDIA stands out as a pivotal force in ushering in the generative AI (GenAI) revolution with OpenAI. Founded in 1993 with a vision of accelerated computing, NVIDIA went beyond the limitations of general-purpose computing of CPUs (central processing units) and introduced a groundbreaking alternative in GPUs (graphics processing units). Its co-founder and CEO, Jensen Huang, says,

> At the time, the way of designing computers was rather split between general-purpose computing versus using accelerators. About 99 per cent of the value was believed in general-purpose computing, and about 1 per cent believed in acceleration.[9]

NVIDIA also created CUDA, a software platform that enables GPUs to speed up complex computations. In its early years, NVIDIA tackled applications at the cutting edge, such as gaming, scientific simulations and medical imaging.

A milestone moment came in 2012 when 'AlexNet AI and CUDA made first contact'.[10] NVIDIA's GPUs powered an AI system, AlexNet, to recognize objects in pictures and win the 2012 ImageNet challenge. Soon, AI would surpass human performance in image recognition. Huang says, 'This was the big moment, the big bang of deep learning, a pivotal moment that marked the beginning of the AI revolution.' By 2016, NVIDIA invented a new integrated system for *deep learning*, DGX-1, which significantly advanced AI model training capabilities. Huang hand-delivered the first DGX-1 to OpenAI, and said, 'I thought it was incredibly appropriate that the world's first supercomputer dedicated to artificial intelligence would go to the laboratory that was dedicated to open artificial intelligence.'[11]

Besides DGX-1, OpenAI needed another ingredient to create AI magic. In 2017, Google introduced a new AI technique called Transformer, which went on to become a modern-day Rosetta Stone moment. It transformed the way AI models helped in language understanding.[12] OpenAI adopted the Transformer architecture in its AI offering. And in 2018, Nadella, finding OpenAI to be 'directing energy towards the things that have the biggest impact',[13] placed a $1 billion bet on its technology.

NVIDIA, Google and Microsoft—like the Magi, all three giants of the tech world came bearing technological gifts.

In November 2022, OpenAI released an early demo version of ChatGPT (generative pre-trained transformer)—i.e., an AI system that allowed humans to have a **Chat** in natural human language with the **G**enerative outputs of deep learning networks, which were **P**re-trained on the corpus of humanity's worldwide web, reportedly using 10,000 NVIDIA GPUs,[14] and powered by the **T**ransformer architecture. Within five days, it attracted over a million users[15] and over 100 million users within just two months.[16] The growth rate was more than four times faster than that of TikTok and fifteen times faster than Instagram's.[17] Although AI as a discipline originated in a Dartmouth College workshop in

1955, it suddenly catapulted into the collective consciousness of humanity across the globe.

Returning to the Jugalbandi pilot innovation, in September 2023, India's Bhashini mission, whose capabilities were leveraged in it, launched the Pradhan Mantri Kisan Samman Nidhi (PM-KISAN) app nationally. Available in English, Hindi, Bengali, Odia and Tamil, its AI chatbot assisted farmers in conversationally seeking information related to their application status, payment details, eligibility status and other scheme-related updates. The PM-KISAN app, in its earlier version, also provided a face authentication-based electronic KYC (know your customer) feature, which farmers could access on their mobile phones. Within seven months, over 110 million farmers had completed their KYC process and accessed the direct benefit transfer system of the government's financial aid scheme.[18] The PM-KISAN app was developed in collaborative creation with EkStep, a non-profit organization focused on creating digital public goods and infrastructure together with other organizations to deliver population-scale innovation and impact across India (and from Asia through Africa to Latin America).

In November 2023, OpenAI launched the GPT Store, a new-age marketplace similar to the mobile-era marketplaces of the Apple App Store or Google Play, allowing people to discover and consume GPTs, custom versions of ChatGPT developed for specific purposes. Within two months, over 3 million GPTs had been created.[19] For instance, PaidLeave. ai, a GPT, helped expectant or new moms understand New York State's paid family leave policy by providing easy-to-understand explanations, prompts to guide users through what they might need, and even drafting emails or action plans for communication with HR. Reshma Saujani, founder of Girls Who Code and Moms First, who developed it in collaboration with Novy.ai and Craig Newmark Philanthropies, says,

It doesn't just answer your questions. One of the things I love about the site is it gives you a bunch of easy prompts because maybe you don't know what you're supposed to ask for. It will draft you an email to HR if you need one. It will let you email yourself an action plan or checklist. When you go to the government website, they don't really do that for you.[20]

Something different was happening here. Although some of the underlying applications or websites had been available as online solutions earlier, the GPTs differed significantly. People could now chat in their natural human language with a seemingly intelligent advisor or expert, whether in work, travel, or other domains, discovering information in a conversational and creative way. Huang boldly calls out the advent of a new Industrial Revolution: '2017, the transformer arrived. 2022, ChatGPT captured the world's imaginations and helped people realize the importance and capabilities of artificial intelligence. And 2023, generative AI emerged and a new industry begins.'[21]

In January 2025, DeepSeek, a relatively unknown AI research lab from China, released an open source reasoning model, DeepSeek-R1, that beat leading models like OpenAI o1 on several math and reasoning benchmarks, using 'distilled' models and algorithmic innovations with much fewer GPUs, and an operational training cost estimated under six million dollars, with similar cost efficiencies in compute requirements reported for its V3 base model as well.[22] While it prompted a global technology reckoning, focusing on the 'inference' side of model use, Nadella had a more positive take on AI leading to a 'Jevons paradox' moment: 'As AI gets more efficient and accessible, we will see its use skyrocket, turning it into a commodity we just can't get enough of,' he wrote on X.[23]

Microsoft's collaboration with the Agricultural Development Trust (ADT) of Baramati in India offers a powerful example. Through AgriPilot.ai, farmers in Maharashtra receive real-time, AI-powered insights on irrigation, fertilization, and pest control, significantly enhancing yield while reducing resource waste. Microsoft's Azure Data Manager for Agriculture, coupled with Azure OpenAI, processes vast amounts of data—from soil sensors to satellite imagery—to generate simple, actionable guidance in local languages via WhatsApp. The impact has been striking with crop yields surging by 30–40 per cent, sucrose content rising 20 per cent, and the harvest cycle shortening from eighteen to twelve months.[24]

As Satya Nadella put it, 'To me, it sort of really connects all the dots, right? From Azure IoT, the data connectivity back to a data plane, and then to be able to use something like Azure AI, but ultimately to empower a farmer to be able to do their farming with higher yields.' This exemplifies the *co-intelligence revolution*—where AI, digital infrastructure, and human expertise come together to unlock new levels of productivity and sustainability.[25]

Before we delve into this new industrial revolution, let us take a quick historical tour of how we arrived at this moment.

A Brief History of the Industrial Revolutions

The power of steam engines, electricity, computing and processing of data drove the previous industrial revolutions that have fundamentally reshaped society. See **Figure 1-1**.

- *1.0 Industrial Revolution* (1760–1820): *Steam power* mechanized agriculture and industry, leading to mass production.
- *2.0 Industrial Revolution* (1870–1930): *Electric power* brought electrification, further enhancing production capabilities.
- *3.0 Industrial Revolution* (1950–1990): *Computer power* introduced automation and electronics, ushering in the *Information Age*. The advent of the public Internet, coupled with exponential leaps in computing power, storage capabilities and networking technologies, paved the way for further innovations in sensing, machine learning and mobile communication.

- *4.0 Industrial Revolution* (2005–2022): *Data power* led to the convergence of physical and digital interactions within cyber-physical systems, enabling unprecedented interconnectivity and accelerating the Information Age. This convergence unlocked unprecedented potential for value creation, transforming industries and societies in ways previously unimaginable.[26,27] Information technology became an integral part of the product itself, as smart connected products combined hardware, sensors, data storage, microprocessors, software and connectivity in myriad ways.[28]

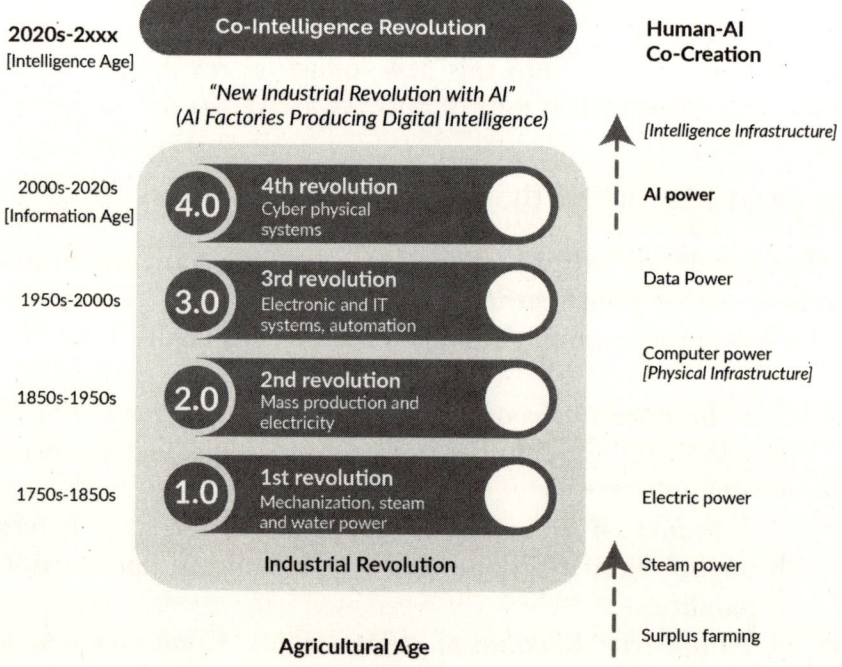

Figure 1-1: *The Co-Intelligence Revolution*
(Source: Venkat Ramaswamy; Britannica)

The Information Age in 3.0 IR and 4.0 IR has also evolved over several decades. See Figure 1-2.[29]

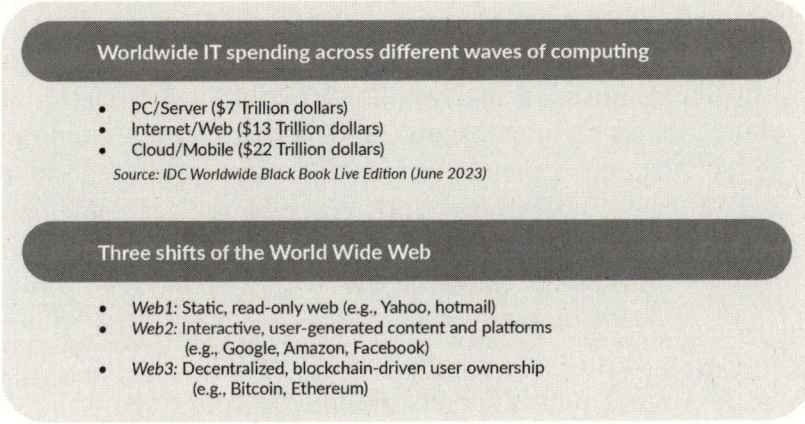

Figure 1-2: *Evolution of the Information Age*

Even the underlying computational architectures have advanced and transformed over the years. IBM's renowned $5 billion gamble in 1964 with its System/360—a pioneering mainframe system—marked a transformative moment in computing history. It introduced *a new era of compatibility*, as IBM unified a family of computers under a single architecture for the first time. This groundbreaking move established *the first platform business model*. The System/360 fundamentally changed computing by *decoupling software from hardware* through an innovative layer called the *operating system*. This layer enabled software to run across different machines, allowing companies to start small and scale up as needed, and inspired new approaches to designing and using computer systems. In the late 1970s and later, Intel's x86 microprocessor and Microsoft's operating systems (such as MS-DOS and later, Windows) became the foundation of the personal computer (PC) revolution.

In the Information Age, enterprise AI architectures too progressed, from rule-based systems to data-driven analytics, followed by predictive models, before evolving into scalable decision engines. In their book, *Competing in the Age of AI*, Marco Iansiti and Karim R. Lakhani discuss these decision engines—think of Google's ad auctions or Uber's dispatch decisions.[30] Operating through a cycle that integrates user engagement, data collection, algorithm design, prediction, and improvement, such an *analytical* AI factory contains a data pipeline, creates algorithms and models that make predictions, provides an experimentation platform to test hypotheses regarding new algorithms and embeds the pipeline and algorithms in a scalable and consistent software environment.

Erik Brynjolfsson and Andrew McAfee, in *The Second Machine Age*, explored the transformative impact of digital technologies and their potential to automate tasks previously performed by humans. They predicted 'countless instances of machine intelligence and billions of interconnected brains working together', while also cautioning that technological progress might leave some people behind. [31]

Don Tapscott, a pioneer in calling attention to blockchain technology as an open, distributed, global platform, articulated the idea of the 'Second Era' of the Information Age. He emphasized that 'digital technologies permeate everything and every business process'—with innovations such as machine learning, robotics, cryptocurrencies and synthetic biology reshaping the entire economic and social landscape. He argued that the convergence of artificial intelligence, blockchain and the Internet of Things (*trivergence*) was foundational to this transformation.[32,33]

The Covid-19 pandemic dramatically accelerated the adoption of digital technology by businesses worldwide. A McKinsey study found that the pandemic had expedited the digitization of customer interactions and the share of digital offerings by several years.[34] Microsoft CEO Satya Nadella emphasized this shift, stating, 'Every company is a software company,' and urged organizations to embrace 'tech-intensity'. He elaborated:

For any organization to succeed in a world of unprecedented constraints, they will need to empower employees, foster a new culture of hybrid work, engage their customers in new ways, intelligently and virtually, transform products and services with new business models, and optimize operations to keep customers and employees safe and secure. And they will need to take data from one system to use it and to optimize the outcome of another. We call this tech intensity, and it is key to business resilience as well as transformation.[35,36]

Post-Covid-19, GPTs marked a major societal shift with the discovery of *the language of* human language as it were, enabling us to interact with computers in *our natural human language*. As Sam Altman remarked: 'Deep learning worked . . . Humanity discovered an algorithm that could really, truly learn any distribution of data.'[37] This amazing innovation and large language models (LLMs) such as ChatGPT transformed the very foundation of the *Intelligence Age*. Since then, open source LLMs from Meta's Llama and Alibaba's Qwen have furthered this transformation very rapidly.

AI Factories—The Production of Intelligence

In a post-LLM era, we now stand on the brink of the Co-Intelligence Revolution—a new industrial revolution. We define *co-intelligence* as the creative synergy between human intelligence and machine intelligence, where AI augments and amplifies human capabilities rather than just automating tasks, with the relative contextual interplay of both '*AI systems-in-the-loop-of-Humans*' (AISILH) and '*Humans-in-the-loop-of-AI systems*' (HILAIS) in every interaction. And this revolution is technologically driven by *electronic neural networks fed with vast amounts of data and put to work with accelerated computing*, in a new form of AI factory.

According to Huang, while the previous industrial revolutions converted water into steam into electricity, the next industrial revolution outputs *tokens* from electrons, which he believes will create over $100 trillion (about what the world's GDP was in 2024) in new industries on top of a new generation of 'data centres'. He declares, 'The future is going to have a new industry—the production of intelligence at enormous scale.'[38]

This intelligence is produced in *AI factories*, i.e., data centres training AI models and transforming energy and data into *tokenized digital intelligence* (TDIs) much like the factories of the past that transformed raw materials with electricity into goods. This new form of AI factory with TDIs, together with co-piloted GenAI and Agentic AI systems, is in turn, transforming society at *global warp speed*. And NVIDIA, with its accelerated computational architectures, is at the forefront of this new industrial revolution. NVIDIA now bears IBM's torch (hardware), and also that of Intel (processors), Microsoft (software), Cisco (networking) as well as Google (analytical AI factory). NVIDIA seems to have combined all of them into a 'great ball of fire' by *pioneering a new full-stack accelerated AI computing architecture for the 'production of intelligence'*. No wonder NVIDIA's market capitalization has surged from $550 million in 1999 to over a staggering $3.6 trillion in 2024.[39]

The 'What'

What exactly do these tokens produce and transform? Huang says, 'You can take these tokens, you reformulate it in such a way that it turns into English, French, proteins, chemicals, graphics, images, videos, robotic articulation, steering wheel articulation.'[40] For instance, GenAI systems such as ChatGPT or Claude convert text to text, while Stable Diffusion or Adobe Firefly convert text to images. Such production of intelligence can be further fine-tuned for specific tasks like legal assistance, customer service or educational tutoring, making it versatile across different industries and value chain ecosystems. This spans the gamut from B2C-oriented industries to B2B ones:[41]

- *Healthcare* benefits from GenAI in drug discovery, where NVIDIA's BioNeMo models help researchers predict protein structures, accelerating molecule screening and drug customization processes significantly. Research institutions utilize GenAI for medical natural language processing applications and genomic data access, furthering advancements in health and genomics research.
- *Financial services* leverage GenAI for customer service, fraud detection and personalized banking, while domain-specific models, such as *FinFormers*, help in navigating unstructured financial data.
- The *Energy sector* employs GenAI for predictive maintenance, visual inspections and knowledge repositories to improve grid reliability and engineer productivity.
- *Public sector* applications include automating administrative tasks, enhancing public service efficiency and reducing manual workload.
- *Telecommunications* use cases include network diagnostics, field technician support and AI-as-a-service offerings, enhancing operational efficiency.
- In *Media and Entertainment*, GenAI streamlines content creation, voice generation and audience engagement, allowing studios to optimize costs and enhance viewer experiences.
- In *Retail*, GenAI aids in product description generation, personalized recommendations, and even virtual clothing design, reducing environmental impacts.

AI factories are advancing the next generation of *brain research*

At the Centre for Computational Brain Research (CCBR) at the Indian Institute of Technology, Madras (IITM), India, for instance, one project attempts to reduce the computational requirements of deep neural networks during inference. Its Sudha Gopalakrishnan Brain Centre has developed a high-throughput histology pipeline that processes whole human brains into high-resolution digital images. Storing, organizing and viewing these gigapixel images and petabyte-sized volumes is a daunting challenge, as these massive datasets are crucial for advancing our understanding of the brain's structure and functions. Identifying tens of billions of neurons (only one of the cell types in the brain) and trillions of connections is a formidable challenge. The non-uniform nature of cell shapes and contours makes it difficult for algorithms designed for regular objects and faces to work on billions of cells.

AI has a key role to play in solving these problems through deep learning methods. In just two years, the centre has acquired around 100 brains and already processed over thirty brains. Mohanasankar Sivaprakasam, professor and head, IITM Brain Centre, says, 'This is the first time such large-scale human brain image data has been generated at this resolution across the entire brain.' [42] In December 2024, the Brain Centre released DHARANI, the world's first and freely accessible 3D atlas of the developing fetal human brain.[43]

All this is made possible with a cluster of NVIDIA-DGX A100 systems at the Brain Centre. Kimberly Powell, VP of healthcare at NVIDIA, in her keynote speech at GTC 2024, comments on their unique partnership:

> The team's brain research platform called Neuro Voyager is imaging the brain at a cellular level with each brain image containing between 2–3 petabytes of data. We have worked with them to digitize the brain data and visualize it at any resolution right down to half a micron. They are also putting a chat front end on it. The chatbot can be used to query information from 10 years-worth of brain research and answer simple questions.[44]

AI factories are advancing the next generation of *materials science research*

Consider also the recent R&D efforts by Microsoft and the US Department of Energy's Pacific Northwest National Laboratory (PNNL) to design new battery materials, previously unknown to humans and not in our observable world of nature. Microsoft initially subjected over 32 million candidate materials (made by swapping atoms in existing crystals with different elements from the periodic table) to AI inference. This narrowed the field down to a promising pool of 500,000 potential candidates that were predicted to be stable. After this, they tested these new materials to see if they had useful properties, like how easily they reacted with other chemicals (redox potential) and how light interacted with them (band gap). The first screening reduced the candidate list to 800. Then, they put these candidates through the paces of traditional physics-based HPC simulations to confirm the properties from AI screening. These AI models provided a 1500-fold speedup in predicting material properties compared to traditional calculations.

Microsoft then used powerful computer simulations to see how the atomic structure of the materials changed and how well ions moved around inside them. This helped narrow down the options to about 150 promising candidates. The next selection came about through collaboration with the PNNL team. They considered things like how new and useful the materials were, how easy they would be to work with, and how readily available the elements were. This gave them the final eighteen most promising candidates.

Now, researchers at PNNL took centre stage. They synthesized the top contender, characterizing its structure and measuring its conductivity. This new material candidate boasts a significant advantage: it requires roughly 70 per cent less lithium (a rare, resource-intensive and costly material) compared to traditional lithium-ion batteries.[45] *A process that would have taken years was completed in weeks. And it was based on the joint creativeness of human and AI.* Microsoft has wrapped these capabilities into a software product, Azure Quantum Elements (AQE), purpose-built to accelerate scientific discovery. Researchers worldwide can use AQE Copilot to query and visualize data, write code and initiate simulations.

Or consider SandboxAQ, whose Large Quantitative Models (LQMs) offer a distinct approach to AI, contrasting with LLMs. Instead of relying on Internet data, LQMs are grounded in quantitative data and equations that govern the *physical world* such as physics, chemistry, and biology. SandboxAQ is partnering with Sanofi, a major pharmaceutical company, to leverage LQMs to accelerate the development of new biomarkers and drugs. LQMs are also being utilized to create new catalysts capable of transforming low-value refinery byproducts into valuable materials like carbon composites for cars.[46]

AI factories are advancing the next generation of *medical research and healthcare*

We are now also exploring the *language of other realms* through a *fusion of technologies that is blurring the lines between physical, digital and biological realms—of atoms, bits and genes.* In 2020–21, Google DeepMind's AlphaFold, an AI algorithm, solved a fifty-year scientific grand challenge by predicting protein structure folding, which has significant implications for drug discovery and our understanding of biological processes. Within two years, DeepMind, in collaboration with the European Molecular Biology Laboratory, released the AlphaFold Protein Structure Database for public use, containing over 200 million structures and accessed by more than one million users in over 190 countries.[47] Demis Hassabis, co-founder of Google DeepMind and who was jointly awarded the Nobel Prize for Chemistry 2024 for his work on protein structure prediction, says,

> I've always thought if we could build AI in the right way, it could be the ultimate tool to help scientists, help us explore the universe around us.[48]

This breakthrough has paved the way for even more ambitious projects, such as DeepMind's ongoing effort to create a *'virtual cell'*, an AI-powered simulation that models the dynamic interactions within a living cell. By extending AlphaFold's capabilities beyond static protein structures to cellular pathways and processes, this initiative could revolutionize drug discovery, accelerate biomedical research, and enhance our understanding of complex diseases like cancer and neurodegenerative disorders. Hassabis envisions a future where AI-driven simulations allow scientists to test hypotheses at an unprecedented scale, drastically reducing the time and cost associated with experimental research while unlocking new frontiers in human health and longevity.[49]

Or consider physician experiences with healthcare, which translates into what patients experience with their healthcare. Every minute, two new medical papers are published, contributing to an ever-expanding ocean of knowledge that doctors must somehow navigate while providing patient care. With only about one million active physicians serving a US population of 340 million, doctors are under immense pressure to stay current while avoiding diagnostic errors. The US healthcare system, a $4 trillion industry, suffers from inefficiencies and preventable medical mistakes, with an estimated 300,000 to 800,000 lives lost annually due to errors in clinical decision-making. This context underscores the pressing need for AI-powered augmentation—not as a replacement for doctors, but as an intelligent co-pilot ensuring that physicians can access the latest, most relevant, and evidence-backed medical insights in real time.

Developed by a team led by Daniel Nadler, OpenEvidence functions as an AI-driven medical decision support system, used by over a quarter of US doctors today, and growing fast. What sets OpenEvidence apart in the crowded AI landscape is its laser focus on medical accuracy and trust. Unlike general AI models trained on the Internet's mixed-quality data, OpenEvidence was built exclusively on prestigious medical journals and authoritative sources like the New England Journal of Medicine. This specialized approach is proving invaluable in a healthcare system facing a projected shortage of over 1,00,000 doctors and where medical knowledge doubles every five years. From emergency rooms in major hospitals to cancer centers in underserved rural communities, doctors are using OpenEvidence to navigate complex cases, avoid harmful drug interactions, and sometimes even save lives. Further, the impact of AI-driven co-intelligence in healthcare extends beyond diagnostics. OpenEvidence is already being leveraged to streamline administrative workflows, such as clinical documentation and insurance claims processing. By reducing bureaucratic overhead, AI copilots enable doctors to focus more on patient care rather than paperwork, addressing one of the major drivers of physician burnout.[50]

The 'How'

A new way of creating software

The rise of intelligence production involves not only technological advancements but also a complete reimagining of how we create software. Huang describes this transition as 'reinventing the whole computing stack from coding to machine learning, from running code on CPUs to running neural networks on GPUs, from developing software to now developing artificial intelligence'.[51] The computing stack has undergone a fundamental transformation from coding-based software (Software 1.0) to machine learning and AI-based software (Software 2.0). This shift represents a new way of creating software—not through programming alone, but through machine learning. As NVIDIA's Jensen Huang declared, 'Software is eating the world, but AI is going to eat software,' adding flavour to the famous software-eating metaphor of Marc Andreessen.[52] A radical consequence of this shift, as Huang states, is that 'fundamentally every company is an intelligence manufacturer . . . instead of just producing software, we're now producing intelligence'.[53] *Every* company, not just tech firms.

Implementing AI factories

Across the globe, companies and countries have joined forces with NVIDIA to transform over a trillion dollars' worth of traditional data centres into powerful hubs of accelerated computing for generating further value across industries. Companies like HPE and Dell globally, and Reliance Industries and Yotta Data Services in India, have partnered with NVIDIA to offer various data centre AI factory solutions. For instance, HPE Velo is a turnkey private cloud AI solution. Huang, in conversation with HPE CEO Antonio Neri, says,

> It is about simplifying all of this incredibly complicated technology in three stacks—the data stack, the model stack and the computing stack—turning it into this private cloud so that you (customers) could operate it or get the benefit from it with all that complexity being extracted from you.[54]

The Dell AI Factory enables seamless deployment and management of AI workloads within private, hybrid or multi-cloud environments. As Dell Technologies Founder and CEO, Michael Dell, put it,

> The real question isn't how big AI is going to be, but how much good is AI going to do? How much good can AI do for you? Well, that's up to you. Reinventing and reimagining your organization is hard. It feels risky, even frightening. But the bigger risk and what's even more frightening is what happens if you don't do it.[55]

Sunil Gupta, co-founder and CEO of Yotta, envisions India to 'become an AI garage for the world'.[56] Reliance Industries and NVIDIA are partnering to build AI infrastructure in India. Mukesh Ambani, chairman and managing director of Reliance Industries, says, 'As India advances, computing and technology supercentres like the one we envisage with NVIDIA will provide the catalytic growth just like Jio did to our nation's digital march.'[57]

Indeed, several countries are implementing AI factories to establish their own *sovereign* AI. Consider Denmark's new AI supercomputer, Gefion, named after a goddess in Danish mythology and housed in Denmark's new Danish Centre for AI Innovation (DCAI). Denmark's minister for industry, business and financial affairs Morten Bødskov says, 'Gefion provides our Danish enterprises with entirely new opportunities. [It] will drive the advancement of the green transition, enable tailor-made solutions, and strengthen the competitive standing of our companies in the global market.'[58] Mads Krogsgaard Thomsen, CEO of the Novo Nordisk Foundation, highlights how public–private initiatives with AI factories are the way forward in solving global issues: 'In the future, we must cooperate even more with exceptional partners from all over the world if we are to solve the enormous challenges facing not only our own countries but the planet.'[59]

Also, consider Japan's AI Grid, a collaboration between NVIDIA and SoftBank announced in November 2024, which aims to create a new AI-factory-powered telecommunications network capable of not only handling conventional data like voice, video and internet traffic, but also producing and distributing 'intelligence' throughout the country. This AI factory is expected to be twenty-five times computationally more powerful than the world's current largest supercomputer. The AI Grid, which combines AI computers and radio computers in the 5G network using NVIDIA AI Aerial technology, will be deployed across SoftBank's extensive network of 200,000 sites (cell towers, base stations), serving 55 million customers in Japan. One compelling application is the integration of AI into edge devices like cars and factories. By streaming video data to the AI-equipped base stations in the AI Grid, cars can leverage powerful AI models for real-time safety analysis and traffic control. Huang describes a reimagined industrial scenario:

Ask the factory, 'What is happening?' 'Were there any accidents?' 'Is there anything abnormal happening?' 'Was anybody injured today?' You just have to ask the factory, because the factory has now turned into an AI. That AI model doesn't have to run in the factory. That AI model can run in the SoftBank radio.[60]

Picture this—you are talking to a factory and getting real-time responses.

Learning patterns to augment human creativeness through new interfaces

The new AI factories *learn the language of patterns in tokens of any type of content*. They 'learn to discern patterns in data without being explicitly programmed to do so.'[61] Careful development of *fine-tuned* and *distilled* AI models allows for using organizational data to make specific inferences. For instance, by training on organizational data on customer interactions, the model can predict customer churn. Humans can then interact with a trained model in natural human language to generate multi-modal content (text, images, videos, audio, code, simulations and other articulations), introducing a whole new 'general purpose technology' (what 'GPT' means for the rest of us).[62] Thus, GenAI with ChatGPT-like co-pilots and speech–text human language understanding are now the basis of *new interfaces of AI enhancing our life–experiences with AI and creating new sources and forms of value*. Masayoshi Son, founder of SoftBank Group, says, 'Bill Gates said PC on every desktop. Steve (Jobs) said smartphone in every hand. I think now we should say AI agents to everybody.'[63] Personal AI agents that follow an individual through their lives, tailored to local culture and behaviour and offering personalized assistance in areas like education, travel planning and healthcare. They *augment human creativeness* in engaging and propelling interactive life–experiences with AI. Reid Hoffman likens it to a 'steam engine of the human mind', heralding a cognitive industrial revolution.[64] Whether their ability to create new content is a 'feature' or a 'bug' depends upon whether one is trying to 'amplify one's creativeness' or not. A GenAI system can consider a person's context to provide highly personalized answers in the person's spoken language. However, LLMs can sometimes make mistakes and confidently state something that's wrong. Organizations use a technique called *retrieval augmented generation* (RAG), which helps the AI model find relevant information from the real world and use it to give more accurate and helpful answers. For example, in insurance, RAG can help LLMs provide accurate information about policy coverage and claims processes, improving customer satisfaction.

Nextgen Innovation and Value Creation in the Co-Intelligence Age

As machine learning writes software and simulates complex new physical, digital and virtual articulations in the Co-Intelligence Age, Huang's vision of seeing data centres as *factories of the twenty-first century* extends to the practical deployment of Physical AI (besides Agentic AI and LQMs)—with GenAI being shaped with the laws of the physical world; call it *Nextgen AI* factories. Physical AI entails humans and autonomous devices (think cars as much as humanoid robots) interacting with the physical world in new ways. Unlike traditional AI infrastructures, which focus on standalone AI models or applications, Nextgen AI Factories emphasize continuous learning, composability, and tokenized intelligence (TDIs) as reusable building blocks.

CEO of Tesla, Elon Musk's vision is aligned with Nextgen AI. Consider AI factories based on representations of driving data (such as car, traffic, road, weather data) that produce tokens powering autonomous driving capabilities and driving experiences. The Tesla car itself is an AI factory on wheels with robotic AI and a digital chauffeur. By continuously learning from both external data and *driving experiences across fleets of software-defined automobiles*, offerings can be continuously enhanced in new and more valuable ways. In contrast, in the case of traditional automobiles enabled by software, a car company may use an existing AI tool to improve standalone features like adaptive cruise control or parking assistance that can make the driving experience smoother.

Consider that the NVIDIA AI Factory, established in 2020, integrated state-of-the-art DGX servers, storage solutions, networking technologies and AI software frameworks, all to create a comprehensive infrastructure for AI development and deployment. Huang says,

> We can't design a chip anymore without AI. At night, our AIs are exploring design spaces vast and wide that we (humans) would never do ourselves because it costs too much money to explore it. And so, our chips are so much better. Because of an AI, we could reduce the amount of energy used for our chips. It's higher performance. We can't write software without AI anymore. We use AIs to file bugs. So, our bugs database actually tells you what's wrong with the code, who's likely involved, and activates that person to go fix it. I want to turn NVIDIA into one giant AI.[65]

NVIDIA uses Nextgen AI factories in crafting its *own* co-intelligence architectures. Further, it now offers other organizations a *Nextgen AI foundry service*, as it were, so enterprises can build out their own co-intelligence architectures, analogous to what Taiwan Semiconductor Manufacturing Corporation (TSMC) did for fabless semiconductor chip design. For instance, Accenture's AI Refinery is built on NVIDIA's AI Foundry, leveraging its full AI stack. Together, it allows for custom model creation enabling businesses to scale their AI solutions enterprise-wide.[66] In the future, as AI models become more sophisticated—with multi-modal models capable of processing and understanding information from multiple sources like text, images, audio and video—some will be embedded with advanced virtual assistants or agents that execute complete workflows. Consider NVIDIA NIM, a set of easy-to-use microservices for accelerating the deployment of foundation models on any cloud or data centre, and in turn, facilitate agentic AI workflows. For instance, AI agents can help in planning a multi-country trip, handling everything from booking flights and hotels to suggesting local attractions. Some of these AI agents may be trained specifically with respect to governance and compliance for particular application contexts. A company's agents can themselves become offerings as they interact with agents in the customer organization, orchestrated and managed by humans in integrated value chain ecosystems. For instance, NVIDIA's agents can interact with electronic design automation (EDA) agents from Cadence Design Systems and Synopsys in the co-design of NVIDIA's offerings.

Mustafa Suleyman, former co-founder of DeepMind and current CEO of Microsoft AI, envisions a future where 'AI-at-the-edge', apart from AI-on-the-cloud, will become an integral part of our daily lives, serving as a research assistant, coach, companion and personal chief of staff.[67] The landscape of language models has already expanded beyond LLMs to include small language models (SLMs), multi-modal models that handle multiple types of data like text and images and local language-specific LLMs designed for non-English languages. SLMs, such as *Microsoft's* Phi-2, match or outperform models up to twenty-five times larger.[68] SLMs are greener compared to the compute-heavy LLMs.[69] These smaller and more efficient SLMs can be run locally on edge devices without requiring constant connectivity to centralized cloud servers. This local processing capability opens up exciting possibilities for AI integration in everyday devices. For instance, imagine conversing with an intelligent refrigerator that suggests recipes based on dietary needs and available ingredients, or an earpiece translating conversations seamlessly during international travel.

Consider non-English-oriented language models such as NVIDIA's Nemotron-4-Mini-Hindi-4B, Sarvam 2B from Sarvam in India and PhoGPT from VinAI in Vietnam. They face several challenges. First, built-in support is lacking for local languages (e.g., in India, they have less than 1 per cent Indic language content), which limits accessibility for non-English speakers and hinders the widespread adoption of AI in regions with diverse linguistic needs. This lack of support can prevent many communities from fully benefiting from AI advancements.[70] Second, the availability of high-quality training data in these languages on the web is limited. Third, the cost of processing text in these languages in traditional LLMs can be high due to complex tokenization methods. For instance, similar information content in English, when expressed in Hindi, has almost three to four times higher tokens in GPT and Llama.[71]

NVIDIA's small language model, Nemotron-4-Mini-Hindi-4B, with 4 billion parameters, 'was pruned, distilled and trained with a combination of real-world Hindi data, synthetic Hindi data and an equal amount of English data'.[72] Sarvam 2B is India's first foundational open-source 2-billion-parameter Indic language model with efficient representation for ten Indian languages. It was trained using 4 trillion tokens generated using *synthetic data*.[73] However, Sarvam 2B costs only one-tenth the cost of comparable language models due to its efficient design and reliance on synthetic data for training. Vivek Raghavan, co-founder of Sarvam, says, 'If you want to perform a query or two in a week or a month, you should use the large language models. But for use cases requiring millions of daily interactions, I believe smaller models are more suitable.'[74] Pratyush Kumar, co-founder of Sarvam, remarks on his company's name: 'In Sanskrit it (*sarvam*) means "all", as we are intentionally invested in technical and ecosystem innovations that make this technology accessible to all.'[75] By building AI models that understand the diverse range of Indian languages and are optimized for *voice-based interactions* (rather than text-based), they hope to empower innovation and wider adoption of LLMs in India.

Researchers are also trying to peer into the inner workings of GenAI systems. For instance, Anthropic's study of the neural network of its LLM, Claude 3.0, provided insights into the model's internal representations, with considerable potential for enhancing safe and responsible use of AI. When a feature linked to scam email recognition was artificially activated, it overrode the AI's safety protocols to generate scam emails. This finding highlights the importance of understanding and controlling internal features to ensure AI safety.[76]

While safety remains a crucial concern in the evolution of AI, the need for explainability and structured reasoning is equally pressing. This is where Symbolic AI (which incorporates logic, rules, and structured knowledge representations to perform reasoning) and Neuro-symbolic AI (which combines symbolic reasoning with deep learning) play a pivotal role in Nextgen AI architectures. For instance, Neuro-symbolic AI, powered by category theory, [77] can help build complex but explainable AI systems for financial governance systems, while structured rule-based logic is leveraged to augment deep-learning predictions in AI copilots in risk management. In AI factories, this means not only producing TDIs but also ensuring that these TDIs are auditable, interpretable, and accountable, reinforcing the role of AI as a co-creator of value rather than an opaque black-box system as such.

The evolution of AI from standalone systems to *compositional* intelligence—where models continuously learn, adapt, and interact, driven by TDIs that serve as modular, reusable building blocks, enables AI architectures to scale efficiently across domains in co-creating unique value. Imagine a future where *AI actively co-creates life-experiences with humans*, rather than simply reacting to commands.

In 2024, NVIDIA released Blackwell,[78] a cutting-edge AI platform designed for scalable intelligence production. As AI systems become more effective at scaling training and deeper inference, they lead to higher-quality, more thoughtful and reasoned outputs, further reinforcing co-intelligence as an emergent paradigm. NVIDIA is focusing on developing a robotic foundation model capable of learning and generalizing movement and articulation from unstructured multimodal data, including language, images and videos. Huang envisions a future where 'expressing tasks in human language could guide a mechatronic system of diverse limbs and agility to perform specific actions'.[79]

By watching simulations and understanding the structure within them, the system learns how humans move and applies that knowledge to robots, revolutionizing automation and robotics. Such systems require structured, real-world models to ground their reasoning and interactions. This is precisely where *Cosmos*, NVIDIA's world model, launched in January 2025, plays a transformative role—bridging TDIs with physics-based intelligence to simulate and co-create within real-world constraints.

Cosmos is akin to how ChatGPT is a language model—but instead of generating text, Cosmos models the real world. However, just like language models need factual grounding (e.g., PDFs, search results), a world model must be anchored in *physical laws*. This is where NVIDIA's *Omniverse* comes in. Omniverse functions as a physics-based simulation platform, integrating Newtonian mechanics and structured solvers to ensure realism. The synergy between Cosmos and Omniverse allows for the generation of infinite future scenarios, grounded in physical reality. For example, in manufacturing, rather than conducting expensive real-world tests for robotic workflows, Cosmos + Omniverse enables AI-driven virtual simulations to explore all possible paths, optimizing efficiency while reducing wear-and-tear. In short, Cosmos models the world, Omniverse simulates it with physics, and together they create grounded, scalable intelligence for real-world applications.[80] Such systems can also learn cause-and-effect information from data ('Causal AI'), and help machines make better decisions in manufacturing.[81]

This is taking it to the heart of the new Co-Intelligence Age—Nextgen AI building AI and augmenting human capability, with 'AI systems-in-the-loop-of-Humans' (AISILH) and 'Humans-in-the-loop-of-AI systems' (HILAIS). (See **Figure 1-3.***)*

As co-intelligence capabilities advance exponentially, Andrew Ng, a prominent computer scientist, entrepreneur and educator, highlights that AI as a general-purpose technology is continuing to evolve and expand its applications. He says,

> The even better news is there is also new tech on the horizon that's stacking on top, more and more S-curves that drive even more applications in the future.[82]

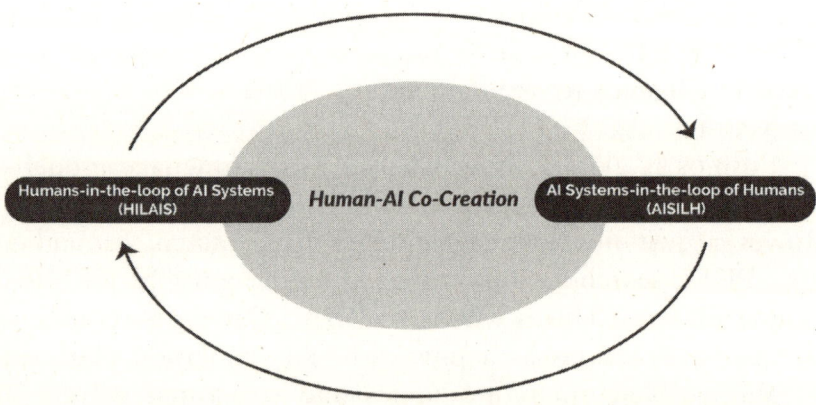

Figure 1-3: *Human–AI Co-Creation (Source: Venkat Ramaswamy)*

The Life-Xverse

From NVIDIA to OpenAI, Jugalbandi and Microsoft, as we will discuss at length through various examples in this book, the age of co-intelligence brings forth *a new creative collaboration between humans as creative-experiencers and AI systems, emphasizing Human–AI interactive engagement to co-create risk-managed value.* This partnership is not only about humans instructing AI or relying on AI for efficiency but also about the two entities engaging interactively to create new impacts of value together. AI's ability to learn, understand and co-create with humans defines the future of value creation, expanding beyond physical goods and services into co-intelligence-driven interactive life–experiences.[83] In previous industrial revolutions, the focus was on the *exchange* of goods and services to create value. In the *Co-Intelligence Revolution*, AI factories produce tokens of intelligence that facilitate new emergent *life–experiences*. This transformation is profound because *while goods and services can be exchanged, life–experiences must be co-created with AI in a co-intelligence world.*

We propose a new term—*Life-Xverse*—a neologism that captures a new space of Human–AI interactive engagement and innovation of new value in a co-intelligence world. Harnessing Human–AI interactive engagement in the age of co-intelligence requires a broader vision of AI as not only computational partners but also humans as creative-experiencers, steering AI capabilities together, while amplifying human capabilities in what we call the **Life-Xverse:** *an interconnected realm of Nature, Society, Economy, and Technology (NEST) ecosystems across physical, digital, and virtual realities, dynamically fostering human and planetary wellbeing through co-intelligence flows and emergent life–experiences.*

As we will see, the Life-Xverse represents a fundamental shift in how we conceive intelligence—moving beyond the limited perspectives of AI as merely a partner or a super-agent to a more profound vision of co-intelligence. It is not just about AI assisting humans but rather an adaptive, interactive ecosystem where AI, humans, and digitalized infrastructures engage in continuous intelligence flows, co-creating emergent experiences and value. Unlike traditional views where AI is framed as a passive assistant or a highly capable super-agent, the Life-Xverse embraces AI as a participatory intelligence within dynamic human-AI ecosystems. AI is not just a separate entity that processes data and executes tasks; rather, it is embedded within an evolving network of interactive engagements. Intelligence is no longer a pre-defined output but an adaptive and relational process occurring across *Nature, Society, Economy, and Technology (NEST)* ecosystems.

Within the Life-Xverse, AI factories are no longer traditional production hubs but intelligence-generation ecosystems. Instead of simply executing human-designed functions, these AI factories generate TDIs that are highly contextual, real-time intelligence units that facilitate the co-creation of interactive life-experiences, rather than static goods and services. TDIs are dynamic, continually evolving based on real-world interactions, reinforcing the idea that AI does not operate in isolation but as part of an organic intelligence system. While previous industrial revolutions emphasized the exchange of goods and services as the primary mechanism of value creation, the Life-Xverse reframes value as no longer being confined to physical or digital transactions, but instead emerging through interactive life-experiences, that become the focal point of human-AI co-intelligence. AI no longer serves as a static recommendation engine or an autonomous planner; it is a co-experiencer, evolving in real time with human interaction. Ultimately, the Life-Xverse envisions a future where intelligence is not bound by individual entities but is relational, interconnected, and continuously shaped by the interplay between AI, humans, and systemic infrastructures. Rather than a world where AI functions as a dominant super-agent or a passive co-pilot, the Life-Xverse fosters a decentralized, adaptive intelligence ecosystem where humans and AI dynamically co-create meaningful experiences at speed, scale and scope.

In the conventional AI view, AI is either the conductor (super-agent) or a musician playing a set role (partner), implying AI either leads or assists within pre-defined structures.[84] In the Life-Xverse view, intelligence is the music itself, continuously evolving through a symphony of interactive co-intelligence flows between musicians (humans, AI, and systemic intelligence networks). No single entity controls the music—it emerges dynamically from the interplay of all participants. This is the defining vision of the *Co-Intelligence Revolution*: a relational intelligence paradigm where it is not about AI controlling or merely assisting, but AI engaging in co-intelligent, co-evolutionary flows with humans to amplify collective creativity, adaptability, and sustainable wellbeing impacts.

Looking Ahead

In *Chapter 2: Into the Life-Xverse with Co-Intelligence*, we enter into the *Life-Xverse* and innovation that connects AI factories with new value creation interfaces at the edge, fusing the physical, digital and virtual realms of life–experiences. We discuss the concept of *co-intelligence architecture* in organizational ecosystems through illustrative examples of Siemens' industrial metaverse and Apple Intelligence. We then explore L'Oréal's personalized beauty solutions and how it is harnessing its co-intelligence architecture to drive innovation across its organization ecosystem entailing offerings, value chain, management and Nature–Society–Economy–Technology (NEST) ecosystems.

In *Chapter 3: Crafting and Leveraging Co-Intelligence Architectures*, we explore how tech-forward enterprises have themselves embraced shifts in Life-Xverse innovation and value creation, with examples such as *Databricks, HubSpot, Salesforce, SAP, Google, AWS, Oracle, Meta, xAI* and *Microsoft*. We discuss how these enterprises are co-innovating *service-as-a-capability*, for and with their customers, partners, employees and other stakeholders. Finally, we consider how India and other governments worldwide are investing in *digital public infrastructures (DPIs)* to accelerate and broaden the achievement of the United Nations (UN) Sustainable Development Goals (SDGs), together with the plural and private sectors. We showcase initiatives like India's *Open Network for Digital Commerce (ONDC)*, the global *Finternet* and Brazil's *Pix, DREX* and *Espírito Santo 500*.

In *Chapter 4: The PIEX Lens: Visualizing and Expanding Value*, using examples of *Monarch, NIO, ABInBev, Reliance*

Retail and *People+ai*, we introduce an organizational lens, the PIEX lens, to visualize co-intelligence opportunities in Life-Xverse innovation and value creation. We then discuss how the PIEX lens can be used to expand organizational innovation and the creation of value across five constituent loci: enactment, capability, activity, strategy and performance, using several examples across the private, public and plural sectors (*Airbnb, Lemonade, Commonwealth Bank of Australia, Philips / Signify, AT&T, Discovery, Shell, Shibuya, Alibaba, IdeiaGov Brazil, Ping An, Danfoss* and *Nike*).

In *Chapter 5: Ecosystem Co-Innovation with Stakeholders*, we explore how different organizations within a shared ecosystem space engage in ecosystem co-innovation, even as they compete. Using a singular example of the *Automotive-Mobility Life-Xverse*, we first explore examples such as *GM (General Motors) Marketplace, Stellantis, Volkswagen, BMW, Nissan* and *Toyota*. Then, through a range of illustrative examples from EV-native *Tesla* to established OEMs like *Ford, GM* and *Mercedes,* we discuss how they are approaching ecosystem co-innovation with stakeholders with their own business strategies. Then we examine how automotive network ecosystems like *Catena-X* and *MInT Collaborative* are laying shared digitalized infrastructure foundations for *Data+AI ecosystem governance* in Europe and India, respectively. We conclude with the example of *Mahindra* and its co-intelligence strategy and co-creation movement.

In *Chapter 6: Becoming a Co-Intelligent Enterprise*, we first motivate the need for a new organizational paradigm in the Life-Xverse. We examine the transformation of organizational management systems using forward-looking examples of *NVIDIA, Microsoft, DBS* and *Haier*. We illustrate how, as co-intelligence architectures become deeply embedded in business processes, the technical capabilities of organizations must be connected to the demands of external stakeholders, as well as internal employees/managers, as they leverage resources, access competence and engage together in cross-sector co-intelligence-driven Life-Xverse innovation and risk-managed PIEX lens value co-creation. We then explore the next practices of risk management in the Life-Xverse in organizations such as *Mobilitas Insurance, AXA, Hippocratic AI, Klarna, Adobe, FedEx, Bloomberg, Morgan Stanley, ING, Mandiant* and *Amazon*. Finally, we define the three essential characteristics of a Co-Intelligent Enterprise, which sets up the remaining three chapters of the book.

In *Chapter 7: Designing Co-Creative Living Organizations in a Co-Intelligence World*, we discuss a philosophy of organizations as *living-systems* to thrive and succeed with a Life-Xverse first frame of reference for innovation and value creation. We explore the idea of *managers as creative-experiencers and AI orchestrators* through the example of *Palantir*. We highlight workforce transformation, *Accenture* and *BCG*, and collective intelligence efforts at *Project ECHO*. We then discuss the evolution of *Infosys* as an *AI-first Live Enterprise*. Then we explore how *Companhia Brasileira de Alumínio* is building a co-creative learning community. Finally, we discuss the need for purposeful design of *co-intelligence knowledge environments* that support managerial environments.

In *Chapter 8: Co-Evolving Sustainable Wellbeing Impacts Across Sectors*, we discuss organizational transformation in co-evolving SWIs at speed, scale and scope, across the private, plural and public sectors. We first step into the *agricultural Life-Xverse* with the examples of *ITC* and *Land O'Lakes*. We then dive further into opening up development with co-intelligence and examine how *Industree* is empowering women at the grassroots level to build sustainable livelihoods and become wealth creators, and how *eGov Foundation* is creating large-scale impact for Indian urban government systems with digital public goods. We then delve into NEST ecosystem transformation more broadly. We consider examples of how UK-based *Kraken-Octopus Energy* is transforming the energy ecosystem at large towards a more sustainable path, and how *Motorola Solutions* is enabling critical collaboration between public safety agencies and other enterprises. We then explore government-level sustainability efforts such as digital-twin initiatives in *Helsinki* and *Singapore* and *New Zealand's* focus on *kaitiakitanga* (connoting guardianship of the sky, the sea and the land).

In *Chapter 9: Cultivating EcoAI Literacy and Lifelong Learning*, we delve more broadly into the lifelong learning environments of people and talent in society and economy, critical to the adaptability and sustainability of all organizations. We propose the idea of *EcoAI literacy* and discuss initiatives such as Second Nature's *University Climate Change Coalition* and the climate science GenAI tool, *ChatClimate*; the researching of sustainability solutions at *MIT and NTU Singapore*; and finally, government-level AI-literacy initiatives in the *United Arab Emirates* and *Flanders*. We then deep dive into the *education Life-Xverse* through examples such as *Coursera, the University of Michigan, DIKSHA* and *Khanmigo*.

We end the book with *Ad Astra*—a message for humanity as we venture forth into the *Co-Intelligence Revolution*.

2

Into the Life-Xverse
with Co-Intelligence

In the Life-Xverse, co-intelligence flows drive innovation and transform life–experiences. The Life-Xverse is a multi-dimensional concept that combines physical, digital and virtual spaces into an ecosystem space where stakeholding entities—including individuals, organizations, public institutions, AI systems and digital platforms—interact and co-create value. This environment is designed to facilitate Human–AI interactivity through continuous engagement and adaptation. Within this setting, co-intelligence plays a critical role as the driving force for creating and sustaining the value and impact that organizations envision through their Life-Xverse innovation.

Think of the Life-Xverse like a dynamic space that brings together a wide array of participants (humans, AI, organizations) in a shared, interconnected environment that spans the physical, digital and virtual realms. Co-intelligence is the engine that powers interactions in this space, enabling the process of creative transformation through which humans and AI work together to co-create meaningful, sustainable outcomes and transform life–experiences. The Life-Xverse includes diverse stakeholders across public, private and plural sectors.[1]

Within the Life-Xverse, AI is not just a tool but a creative partner. AI's ability to process data, predict outcomes and offer unique insights, and GenAI's ability to bring this into the context of human engagement, enhances human creativeness, with humans bringing their subjective experiences of the world and ethical considerations to the table. Co-intelligence facilitates this Human–AI symbiotic synergy with 'joint creativeness'. Rather than AI simply executing predefined tasks or humans making isolated decisions, co-intelligence powers Human–AI interactive engagements, where humans and AI collaboratively generate new ideas and create novel experiences together in the flow of engagements. The Life-Xverse is fundamentally a co-creative space, and co-intelligence is how the creation of value is actualized in risk-managed fashion. Co-intelligence— humans and AI working in tandem to create personalized, relevant experiences, products and solutions, often in real time—moves beyond passive personalization to active, participatory value co-creation. The Life-Xverse is inherently adaptive, thanks to co-intelligence. This adaptability is crucial for responding to challenges in interconnected AI ecosystems, whether in education, food, health or mobility. Co-intelligence is the cognitive and creative layer that makes the ecosystems functional, productive and impactful.

Let us now enter into the co-intelligence-driven world of Life-Xverse innovation. We begin with a detailed example of Siemens in the industrial business space.

Siemens and the Industrial Metaverse

Siemens, a 176-year-old multinational conglomerate, has continuously redefined itself by embracing technological advancements, especially in the realms of automation and digitalization. At Siemens, their vision is to make the digital twin a reality for every industrial sector, enhancing co-intelligence and co-creation between humans and machines. Siemens is not merely about machines but also about people—connecting and empowering them with knowledge and insights that come from data.

At the Consumer Electronics Show (CES) 2024, Siemens announced plans for its *industrial metaverse*. Its president and CEO, Roland Busch, said,

> We envision the industrial metaverse as a virtual world that is nearly indistinguishable from reality, enabling people— along with AI—to collaborate in real time to address real-world challenges.[2]

Let us understand how Siemens is translating this vision to reality. It has three fundamental building blocks: i) digital twins, ii) software-defined automation and iii) data and AI.

Digital Twins

Busch, a physicist by training, emphasizes that the digital twins in this metaverse are physics-based, and not just high-quality 3D renderings as seen in animated films and many computer games. They have a photorealistic or immersive feel, as well as simulation capabilities, with complete fidelity in terms of mechanics and thermodynamics. The digital twins not only look like the real world, but they also behave like it. Engineers, designers and other technical experts can use them for designing, testing and validating products and projects in a virtual environment, significantly reducing the time and cost associated with physical prototypes. *NVIDIA's Omniverse* facilitates collaborative innovation and *immersive engineering* by providing a unified platform for 3D design, simulation, and complex workflows to engineers and designers. Busch says,

> In the metaverse, the interaction will be so immersive, interactive, so life-like, we will hardly be able to detect whether we are manipulating a physical object or a digital twin. We can do it without the traditional bounds of time. So, when something goes wrong, we can go back to the

moment when the problem first appeared and fix it or ask an AI co-pilot to do it.[3]

Siemens announced a partnership with Sony to further its immersive engineering, combining its *Xcelerator* portfolio of industry software (such as Siemens NX computer-aided design/manufacturing solutions) with Sony's new spatial content creation system, which features an Extended Reality (XR) head-mounted display with high-quality 4K OLED micro-displays and controllers. Creators will not only be able to see real-scale 3D models in an XR environment with the high-definition display but also create and modify 3D models within it. The system includes ring and pointing controllers that allow users to intuitively manipulate and accurately point objects in virtual space. For instance, the *Formula 1 Red Bull Racing* engineering teams expect to use the Siemens-Sony NX Immersive Designer (humans-in-the-loop of AI systems) to improve the communication between headquarters and the track. On the design front, they already use VR systems to speed up the styling reviews of the car (AI systems-in-the-loop of humans). With immersive engineering, this process would accelerate even further as the loops can be compressed into hours rather than weeks. Yoshinori Matsumoto, Executive Deputy President, Technology and Incubation, Sony Corporation, says,

> By combining our technologies and Siemens' expertise in engineering, we are excited to enable better immersive engineering that redefines the daily workflow of designers and engineers. The high-quality, realistic rendering and intuitive interaction will give creators tools to pursue better immersive creative processes that fuel further innovation in the industrial metaverse.[4]

Software-Defined Automation

While digital twins help optimize industrial processes, software-defined automation helps in the actual production.

Traditionally, this has been achieved through programmable logic controllers (PLCs), which act like 'mini brains' controlling the factory. The next generation of controllers are *virtual PLCs*. This represents a shift from hardware-centric to software-centric automation systems. It decouples the control logic and software functionalities from the underlying hardware, running on general-purpose computing platforms rather than dedicated hardware. This approach allows for more flexible, scalable and intelligent control over industrial processes.

Siemens has also established several other collaborations to further these building blocks of its industrial metaverse. Consider the standards for depicting 3D objects. Siemens Digital Industries Software had its own file format, JT, for 3D geometry, metadata and other information related to product design and engineering. But given the industry-wide demand for interoperability across 3D workflows, Siemens joined the Alliance for OpenUSD, an organization that includes NVIDIA, Pixar, Apple, Adobe and Autodesk among others, and which promotes the technology standard, Universal Scene Description (USD*)*. Interoperability across 3D tools and data makes OpenUSD compelling and enables developers and content creators to collaborate seamlessly on large-scale 3D projects.[5] Thus, this integration allows Siemens customers to work with USD files directly within their existing software tools.

Data and AI

The final building block comprises data and AI. A highly automated factory generates vast amounts of data that are collected by *edge* devices in the industrial metaverse. These devices, in turn, filter this data and pass on relevant datasets to analytical AI/GenAI systems *for engineers to engage in natural language and develop innovative solutions together*. Siemens is engaging developers and forging multiple innovative partnerships on the AI ecosystem front, even as it builds out its **co-intelligence architecture***,* strengthening its tech capabilities, as we conceptualize in **Figure 2-1**. Such a co-intelligence architecture supports and amplifies Life-Xverse innovations of not only external customers and partners (such as Sony, NVIDIA and others in its offerings and value chain ecosystems) but also of its internal employees (workers, managers, designers, business leaders and so on).

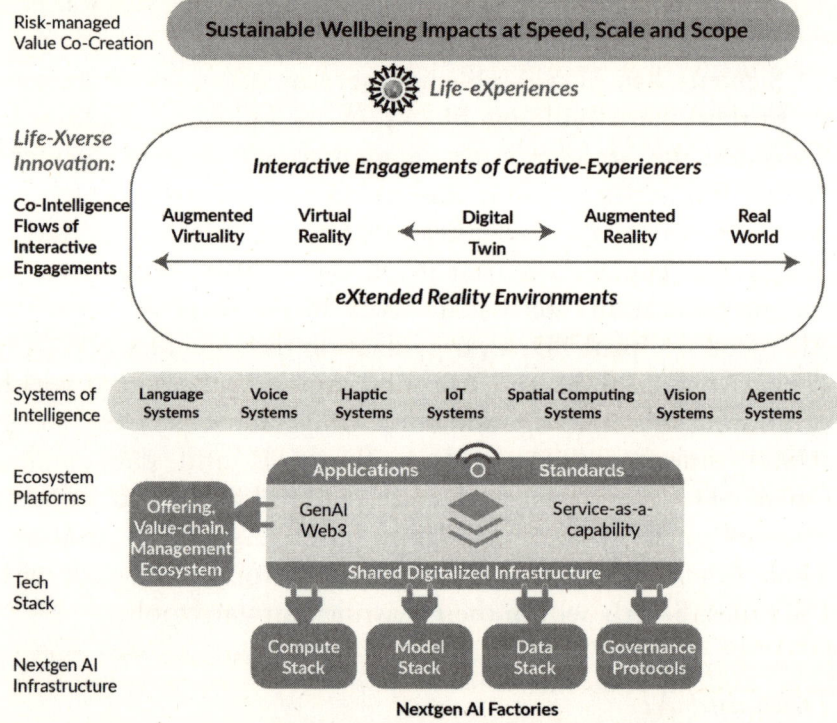

Figure 2-1: *Life-Xverse Innovation and Co-Intelligence Architecture (Source: Venkat Ramaswamy)*

For instance, Siemens is reinventing its Xcelerator B2B marketplace with *Salesforce's Einstein One Commerce* platform. Einstein offers guided selling features, allowing Siemens' customers to describe their challenges and find the right products to purchase on the marketplace. Additionally, it benefits its partners and sellers by providing automated recommendations and facilitating cross-selling and upselling opportunities.[6] Siemens has also partnered with Amazon Web Services (AWS) to democratize the availability of GenAI models in the industrial metaverse, making them more accessible to application developers. *Amazon Bedrock*, an AWS service that offers multiple AI foundation models via a single API, is integrated with *Mendix*, the low-code platform under the Siemens Xcelerator portfolio. With this, a worker in a factory can quickly find information about machines without having to manually search through voluminous databases or manuals. Access to GenAI models is just a few clicks away for the engineering teams.[7]

Industrial Copilot

Partnering with Microsoft, Siemens released the *Siemens Industrial Copilot*, a generative AI-powered assistant (nicknamed *Danny*),[8] which offers intelligent support for tasks ranging from code generation and debugging to process optimization. It helps translate and generate PLC code from different programming languages to control Siemens' controllers. Maintenance engineers can interact with Danny when a machine breaks down and troubleshoot the problem. Engineers can also ask Danny questions about specific tasks, like understanding a construction plan, and it responds with step-by-step instructions. This capability allows employees, even those with less experience, to perform complex operations by following Danny's guidance. Busch says, 'This has the potential to revolutionize the way companies design, develop, manufacture, and operate. Making human–machine collaboration more widely available allows engineers to accelerate code development, increase innovation and tackle skilled labour shortages.'[9]

Siemens' vision of industrial co-pilots transforms the entire value chain ecosystem, unlocking value creation potential by improving human–machine collaboration and accelerating development and innovation cycles. Together with its partners, Siemens is making GenAI a reality for its customers on a broad scale. Siemens is placing big bets on the industrial metaverse because of the significant impacts it brings to industry and society.

Busch says,

> With generative AI and the industrial metaverse, building and using technology is becoming easier and faster. We will be able to accelerate innovation, accelerate sustainability and accelerate access to new tech . . . the industrial metaverse will redefine reality and transform the way we live, work, play or make. The industrial metaverse will redefine reality and transform the everyday for everyone.[10]

Sustainable Impacts

Siemens is also engendering *sustainable impacts* through its solutions. For instance, at Northvolt, a major lithium-ion battery manufacturer, Siemens leverages digital twins to enable comprehensive simulations, optimize its processes and reduce the CO_2 footprint of its battery types by two-thirds. Similarly, at Heineken, Siemens assists in reducing CO_2 emissions across more than fifteen production sites. By simulating energy flows within the production processes, Siemens identifies the most effective changes to achieve decarbonization goals. This includes the use of heat pumps and other energy-efficient technologies.[11]

As shown in the top half of **Figure 2-1**, Siemens engenders *sustainable wellbeing impacts* (SWIs) of risk-managed value at speed, scale and scope by leveraging Human–AI interactive engagements through *shared digitalized infrastructure* (SDI) platforms in organizational ecosystems (offerings, value chain, management and NEST ecosystems) entailing systems of co-intelligence. Life-Xverse innovation facilitates the interactive agency of individuals as creative-experiencers. It amplifies the value-creative capacities of humans, individually and collectively, across the extended reality of co-intelligence-driven interactive system environments. SWIs entail emergent life–experiences of humans as creative-experiencers—be it customer experiences or worker experiences. For instance, when Siemens built its new factory, it leveraged its own industrial metaverse technologies to build a complete digital twin upfront, which led to significant productivity and sustainability impacts. But Siemens also puts the *life–experiences of its workers at the centre*, envisaging the factory project as a change management process. It involved members from all departments to review the factory digital twin and understand how the shop floor would be structured, where the machines would be, and even see the machines perform virtually. Once the workers understood the bigger picture, they found the transformation to the metaverse less intimidating. Peter Koerte, chief technology and strategy officer at Siemens, says,

> That factory was 20 per cent more productive. It saved 5 million kilowatt-hours per year in terms of electricity, reduced 3,000 tons of CO_2, and 6,000 cubic meters of water. It's a triple win, really. You're becoming more competitive, you're becoming more sustainable, and your people feel more empowered because they had a say in that. I can tell you it is worth that effort to go the extra mile in the very early days. Although it feels like you're slowing down, you actually accelerate because by the time you build it, you don't need to explain it anymore, because everybody is familiar with the concept.[12]

Siemens' motto of 'transforming the everyday for everyone' with its industrial metaverse showcases Life-Xverse innovation in action, through which life–experiences are transformed for all its participants through co-intelligence flows of engagements. Co-intelligence opens up whole new pathways of innovation and value creation through interactive engagements in organizational ecosystems of emergent life–experiences. It enables designers and manufacturers to perfect their models in the digital realm before allocating physical resources. It also accelerates the achievement of sustainability goals by optimizing resource use and accurately accounting for emissions. On an ongoing basis, challenges such as interoperability and platform integration have to be addressed with a grounding in the life-experiences of individuals as they engage with it to continue to successfully reap potential benefits.

Next, we explore how co-intelligence is driving life-Xverse innovation at a consumer-tech company, Apple.

Life-Xverse Innovation with Apple Intelligence

Apple's journey towards personal intelligence began in 2010 with Siri, a virtual assistant that aimed to answer questions and complete tasks through voice commands. But it fell short of competitors in terms of its intelligence functionality. Fast-forwarding to 2024, Apple announced a more comprehensive approach called 'Apple Intelligence', which aims to leverage machine learning across all its devices and services to provide a more personalized interactive experience.[13] It offers capabilities such as advanced natural language understanding for efficient communication, system-wide writing tools for rewriting, proofreading and summarizing text, and image generation in various styles for enhanced visual expression. Tim Cook, Apple's CEO, says,

> Our unique approach combines generative AI with a user's personal context to deliver truly helpful intelligence. And it can access that information in a completely private and secure way to help users do the things that matter most to them.[14]

Indeed, Apple's approach to GenAI and LLMs is distinguished by three key themes: i) on-device processing, ii) being grounded in personal context and iii) robust privacy and security measures. Unlike many companies that rely on cloud processing, Apple prioritizes handling most data and tasks directly on the user's device. Leveraging advanced silicon, Apple ensures powerful generative models run efficiently and securely on-device. This includes using *adapters*—small collections of model weights that can be dynamically loaded and swapped—allowing the model to specialize for specific tasks without needing large, static models. Additionally, Apple employs state-of-the-art quantization techniques to compress models, making them small enough to fit on devices while maintaining high performance and quality. This ensures complex AI capabilities are available even on portable devices like iPhones and iPads.

Apple Intelligence is grounded in the user's personal information and content. It integrates deeply with the user's apps and personal data to provide relevant and contextual responses. A semantic index creates a map of a user's habits, preferences and relationships within their device. The App Intents toolbox integrates seamlessly with Siri, enabling it to orchestrate interactions across a wide range of apps within Apple's ecosystem. This orchestration allows Apple Intelligence to prioritize notifications, assist with writing tasks and perform actions like finding specific photos or playing a podcast based on personal context.

Apple's LLMs are designed with privacy at their core. Personal data is processed on-device whenever possible, minimizing the need to send data to external servers. When cloud processing is necessary, Apple uses Private Cloud Compute (PCC), which does not store or allow access to user data. This cloud processing approach includes publicly logged software and strong cryptographic attestation, ensuring that processing is transparent and secure. Apple's systems are also designed to be verifiable by independent security researchers, with both device software and cloud processing software accessible for inspection. This commitment to transparency and security ensures that users' privacy is protected while delivering powerful AI capabilities. Not only has Apple addressed concerns around privacy, but it also has considered fears of its users missing out on the explosion of creative AI tools being built outside their controlled walled-garden environment. To bridge this gap, Apple has partnered with OpenAI, allowing users to interact with ChatGPT directly. It is even considering AI partnerships with Google and rival Meta for their LLMs.[15]

Another aspect of Apple's SDI lies beyond the mobile device itself, in 'spatial computing,' which aims to seamlessly blend physical and digital realities and foster collaboration and shared experiences. Cook says, 'Just as the Mac introduced us to personal computing, and iPhone introduced us to mobile computing, Apple Vision Pro introduces us to spatial computing[16] . . . When you've tried it, it's an aha moment, and you only have a few of those in a lifetime.'[17]

World Labs is another spatial intelligence AI company building large world models (LWMs) to perceive, generate and interact with the 3D world. Fei-Fei Lei, co-founder and CEO of World Labs, says, 'Sight turned into insight; seeing became understanding; understanding led to action. All these gave rise to intelligence.'[18] To create an AR/MR/VR experience that feels totally real, the technology (wireless connection, computer power and storage) needs to work flawlessly, while designing systems based on 3D human experiences, i.e., how we see, think and react physically, to make it feel truly immersive. In a *6G world* and beyond, we can expect ubiquitous immersive connectivity in extended reality environments at even higher speeds in new application domains that are already visible: (i) multisensory XR applications, (ii) connected robotics and autonomous systems, (iii) wireless brain–computer interaction and (iv) blockchain and distributed ledger technologies.[19]

The goal is to seamlessly connect the co-intelligence infrastructure (at the bottom of **Figure 2-1**) with extended reality environments of life–experiences across the Life-Xverse (at the top of **Figure 2-1**). *That is where value is migrating to and where it is enacted in flows of interactive engagements that drive SWIs.*

We now discuss a detailed example of L'Oréal in the consumer space.

Beauty for Each—L'Oréal

L'Oréal is a 115-year-old global leader in the beauty industry of cosmetics products in makeup, skincare, hair care and fragrance. Its CEO, Nicolas Hieronimus, took centre stage at CES 2024 to showcase the company's technological evolution:

> Beauty has been an essential human need from time immemorial. From homo erectus to the metaverse . . . We used to promise 'beauty for all'. Thanks to tech we want to offer 'beauty for each'. [20]

This is achieved through a high degree of personalization of its offerings. Barbara Lavernos, deputy chief executive officer, in charge of research, innovation and technology, explains how L'Oréal creates experience personalization in the context of their AI-infused product, Beauty Genius:

> It will act like a personal beauty advisor, available 24/7 in your pocket. It can also help answer questions about your beauty routines and even sensitive topics without having to speak to a real person, such as acne, dandruff, or hair loss. It can also help guide people through these challenging issues and avoid uncomfortable or intimidating situations. [21]

The Beauty Genius delivers highly personalized beauty routines through a sophisticated blend of cutting-edge technologies. Leveraging over ten LLMs, GenAI, computer vision, augmented reality and colour science, the system provides tailored skin and skin tone diagnostics. Users can explore and virtually try on a vast selection of over 750 L'Oréal products, receive personalized recommendations, and access curated beauty education. This technology, refined over a decade, boasts unparalleled accuracy, thanks to training on an inclusive dataset of over 6000 images and rigorous testing by makeup artists worldwide. L'Oréal, the centurion enterprise, is *speaking a new language that leverages tech-intensity to create new life–experiences through its co-intelligence platforms and offering ecosystems.*

Lavernos continues: 'To elevate the user experience, we analyzed hundreds of thousands of real-life conversations between consumers, our own consumer care lines and beauty advisors in stores. As a result, it feels like you are having a real conversation with a genuine beauty expert and not just a faceless algorithm.'[22]

L'Oréal's beauty advisor relies in part on startup ModiFace's AR technology, which it acquired and built into its virtual makeup 'try-on' app, analysing textual and visual information related to a particular makeup shade and reproducing it on a video of one's own face. During the Covid-19 pandemic, the L'Oréal app attracted over 1 billion user visits and tripled its try-on-to-sales conversion.[23]

Over the years, L'Oréal has released several such smart connected offerings to its consumers, including Perso (an AI-powered at-home system for skincare and cosmetics) and Le Teint Particulier (meaning 'unique tint' and a technology that makes custom-made and personalized foundation). Through its app on the user's mobile, Perso performs personal skin analysis of parameters such as deep wrinkles, fine lines and pore visibility. It then does an assessment of local environmental conditions, such as temperature, UV index and humidity, which can influence the state of the user's skin. Users then provide Perso information on their personal skincare concerns (such as dark spots or pigmentation) and product preferences (such as preferred texture and hydration level). The Perso device then dispenses a personalized blend of high-performance skincare. Guive Balooch, head of L'Oréal's technology incubator, which developed Perso, says, 'Customization relies on information about your (customer's) unique skin and personal preferences as well as your environment; this technology accounts for that. Perso uses AI to optimize the formulas and actually gets smarter as you use it.'[24] This approach also exemplifies the integration of marketing, product research and supply-chain efforts to enhance consumer experiences.

Interconnecting Offering Ecosystems and Value Chain Ecosystems

L'Oréal's smart connected offering ecosystems are interconnected with the co-intelligence of its *value chain ecosystems*. Since its consumers are keen to understand from where the product materials are sourced, L'Oréal provides QR codes on its products, which redirect consumers to a dedicated website providing information on product ingredients and their origin, manufacturing location and environmental and social performance.[25] Soon, consumers will be able to simply speak in their natural language, get answers to questions, and have ongoing conversations not only with Beauty Genius but also with a human beauty advisor as needed. One can also imagine inviting others, such as friends and family, into the conversation, especially for special makeup and makeover occasions.

L'Oréal has also recognized the importance of digitalization in its demand planning and supply chain. Through its demand sensing initiative, L'Oréal integrates data on what it sells to its distributors with consumer demand data from e-commerce and retail stores. L'Oréal has extended its digital platforms to its suppliers, sharing requirements for packaging components and raw materials with thousands from its vendor base.[26] This gives sufficient time for vendors to prepare for any expected sudden uptick in demand or inform in advance if they face challenges in fulfilling these requirements.

L'Oréal also engages with its global technology ecosystem partners to deliver its consumer offerings at *speed, scale and scope*. Its two-way integration of demand sensing and supply chain management also applies to its 'digital content' supply chain, besides its 'physical product' supply chain. Consider its CREAITECH GenAI beauty content lab, which engages with ecosystem partners/offerings such as WPP Open, the advertising giant's AI platform and NVIDIA's Omniverse, to generate over 800 beauty images. This brings newfound speed, scale and scope of collective creativity in its marketing processes, media messaging and go-to-market initiatives. However, the company has adopted some strict ethical guidelines in its usage of GenAI—they do not use AI-generated images for life-like faces, hair, skin or body to enhance the product benefits in external marketing. Instead, these images improve the productivity of the *internal* marketing process. Asmita Dubey, chief digital and marketing officer of L'Oréal, says,

> We have to understand that the marketing processes today are very complex. The marketers are talking to their managers, or they are talking to the agencies, and there's a lot of back and forth happening. Those visualizations take a lot of time. When you do storyboarding, it is simply an image for an internal creative process. We can absolutely say, 'Use a Revitalift bottle, in a rainy weather and put it out there.' The time and effort saved in that internal creative process is enormous.[27]

L'Oréal has also experimented with GenAI images in the world of gaming and Web3. L'Oréal has partnered with Ready Player Me, a cross-game avatar platform on the metaverse, and offers dedicated hair and makeup looks. NYX Professional Makeup, a subsidiary of L'Oréal, announced the world's first beauty DAO (decentralized autonomous organization) to nurture a community of 3D artists.[28] L'Oréal continuously enhances its collective learning and market knowledge through flows of data, content and service exchange in these connected ecosystems. The creative infusion of GenAI in these flows of engagements highlights the importance of *collaborative innovation of employees within and across the creative value chain and content ecosystem network*.

Consider also similar engagements with Salesforce's cloud solutions. Its Salesforce Marketing Cloud personalization is live across thirteen brands and allows L'Oréal teams to interactively build out consumer journeys of individuals, with both consumers and employees seen as 'creative-experiencers' engaged in potentially value-creating flows of content, data and service exchange. For instance, L'Oréal's customer-facing organization can engage with individuals using tailored product recommendations automatically or send automated abandoned cart emails so they can pick up exactly where they left off. Salesforce Commerce Cloud powers connected online shopping experiences across more than 200 of L'Oréal's D2C websites. Dubey says,

> Messaging based on shopping habits, and use of Salesforce services, powers our quest to bring greater personalization, relevance, and satisfaction to our consumers . . . we use Einstein (Salesforce's AI for CRM) because it allows us to analyze the shopping habits of our consumers and make predictive product recommendations. This technology has generated 15 per cent to 20 per cent of sales for one of our B2C brands.[29]

Significantly advancing this interconnected ecosystem, L'Oréal has partnered with IBM to transform its manufacturing processes through digital and AI solutions. Leveraging IBM's Watson IoT platform, L'Oréal has enhanced agility, responsiveness and personalization on its manufacturing floor. As part of a co-innovation initiative, L'Oréal and IBM identified and launched approximately 30 projects addressing manufacturing pain points through agile digital solutions, notably developing a mobile application. This app enables real-time gathering and sharing of data from manufacturing lines, instantly addressing issues previously unsolved and dramatically increasing operational flexibility. The Watson IoT solution further empowers L'Oréal to capture real-time consumer requests, directly integrating this personalized data back into production lines. Such technological integration allows L'Oréal to respond rapidly to diverse consumer needs while significantly boosting operational efficiency.[30]

Management Ecosystem

L'Oréal has adopted a unique strategy of universalization in how the company is organized and managed, i.e., its own *management ecosystem* and the way in which it engages its employees and *managers as creative-experiencers globally.* Universalization means 'globalization that captures, understands and respects differences . . . in desires, needs and traditions'.[31] L'Oréal is *strategically concentrated yet operationally decentralized*. The *strategically concentrated* aspect can be seen in the appointment in 2021 of Lavernos as the combined head of research and innovation (R&I) and technology. Jean–Paul Agon, chairman and former CEO, says, 'This new direction of Research, Innovation and Technology will enable us to conquer new territories, increase brand innovations and strengthen our position as the world leader in beauty.'[32]

The *operationally decentralized* aspect is visible in the way L'Oréal has built worldwide R&I and marketing hubs, one for each of its strategic markets: the United States, Japan, Brazil, China, South Africa and India. Consider the case of India. The R&I facilities there include its Product Development Center in Mumbai and Advanced Research Center in Bengaluru. The Mumbai teams are engaged in deep dives into Indian hair and skin needs through clinical studies to meet local consumer beauty expectations. At Bengaluru, teams with expertise in chemistry, biology, engineering and physics explore the potential of plants, biotechnologies and bioinformatics to identify active ingredients and innovative solutions for hair concerns and pigmentation. Through interactive engagements across L'Oréal's R&I global management ecosystem, L'Oréal brought to India new beauty categories, such as dermo cosmetics, and products specifically designed for the Indian market, such as Maybelline Colossal Kajal (an eyeliner that combined traditional beauty methods, i.e., kajal, with modern technology) and Garnier Men (skincare products for fairness suited to India). At the inauguration of the R&I centre in India, Agon said, 'With one of the highest growths of the Group in Asia Pacific, India is a key contributor to L'Oréal's objective of reaching one billion new consumers . . . It is in line with L'Oréal's universalization strategy of adapting our global brands to each culture's specific needs.'[33]

- L'Oréal's management ecosystem transformation demonstrates the importance of visionary leadership, structured digital strategies, cross-functional collaboration and a culture of R&I. Such a transformation follows from *de-centring and democratizing innovation and flows of value-creative engagement that encourage experimentation across functions within and across its organizational ecosystem*:

- *Vision and Leadership*: Its digital transformation was driven by a strong vision from the top, starting with CEO Jean–Paul Agon's declaration of 'The Year of The Digital' in 2010. This leadership paved the way for a cultural shift towards embracing digital innovation across various functions.

- *Role of the Chief Digital Officer*: Lubomira Rochet, as the first chief digital officer, played a crucial role in structuring and implementing the digital vision. She set clear objectives, such as increasing e-commerce sales and enhancing consumer interactions through personalized experiences and social media engagement.

- *Co-Innovation and Experimentation*: L'Oréal encouraged co-innovation in product development by fostering an agile and experimental approach. This included the use of 3D printing for rapid prototyping, the deployment of serialized QR codes for product traceability and consumer engagement, and the adoption of cloud platforms and machine learning for demand sensing.

- *Operations 4.0*: The creation of a chief operations digital officer role, filled initially by Stéphane Lannuzel, focused on integrating digital technologies within the supply chain. This initiative, dubbed Operations 4.0, aimed at reducing product development times, increasing manufacturing and distribution agility, and leveraging data science for improved supply chain performance.

- *Integration of IT and Operations*: Recognizing the need for
  IT to support the digital transformation, L'Oréal restructured
  its IT department, placing it under the operations function.
  This move facilitated better alignment between technology
  capabilities and business needs.

L'Oréal has also transformed its HR function using AI in its
management ecosystem. Hundreds of L'Oréal recruiters process
millions of resumes and recruit in the thousands annually. This
transformation enhances experiences in the flow of recruiting for
both the recruiter and the candidate. The first port of call for a
candidate is Mya, an AI assistant that conducts initial screenings
and provides real-time feedback, significantly cutting down the
time recruiters spend on administrative tasks. Recruiters have
trained Mya to inquire about specific job-related factors like
work location, salary range and legal work status. She does
not reject candidates during an interview and only empowers
human recruiters to make that decision. Data analysis of the
first 10,000 recruiting conversations revealed that Mya engaged
92 per cent of the candidates with near-perfect satisfaction.

Once the candidate is cleared for the next round, they
encounter Seedlink, an AI-powered interview analysis tool.[34]
L'Oréal uses it to determine cultural fit by comparing candidates'
responses to open-ended behavioural questions with those from
employees across different countries. This approach ensures
that the evaluation reflects the diverse cultural norms within the
company, where the individual and the team are placed before
any organizational hierarchies, and one gets inspiration not only
from colleagues but also from achievers from all walks of life.[35]
The AI tool assesses traits like adaptability and teamwork while
reducing biases by using standardized criteria and excluding
demographic information from the evaluation process. Niilesh
Bhoite, HR Director—Beauty Tech at L'Oréal, says,

Is this going to replace the human recruiter? Is this going to
ensure that the human touch will be invisible slowly? And

my answer now, after three years of implementing these projects globally at L'Oréal, is a big no. These technologies have only helped human recruiters take more sound hiring decisions and have acted as an enabler.'[36]

Jean–Claude Le Grand, executive vice president of human relations at L'Oreal, adds, 'This new technology reinforces HR people's counselor role and enables them to really focus on the qualitative and human dimension of the recruitment process.[37]

NEST Ecosystem

Enterprises like L'Oréal increasingly interact within and across their organizational ecosystems towards SWIs, making thoughtful collective choices, adapting and influencing the sustainability goals of all stakeholders, including their own. For instance, by aligning with its environmentally conscious customers, L'Oréal initially partnered with and later acquired Gjosa, a Swiss environmental water-tech startup, to develop a sustainable showerhead that reduces water consumption at the hair washing station by 69 per cent. In the process, they saved more than 182 million litres of water. L'Oréal has installed this innovation in over 10,000 of its professional hair salons across Europe and the Middle East. It plans to expand its reach twenty-fold in the coming years.[38] Thus, L'Oréal also innovates and creates value in the broader NEST ecosystem. Other initiatives include:

- *Greener Supply Chain and Circular Economy*: L'Oréal focuses on reducing the environmental impact of its supply chain. This includes sustainable sourcing of raw materials, minimizing carbon emissions and improving energy efficiency in production processes. It is implementing circular economy principles by promoting recycling and reuse of materials. This includes initiatives for collecting and recycling empty product containers.

- *Climate Action, ESG Governance and Employee Engagement*: L'Oréal has integrated ESG goals into its governance, setting targets for reducing carbon footprint, water use and waste. By 2025, the initiative plans to achieve 100 per cent renewable energy for its operated sites. By 2030, it aims to reduce greenhouse gas emissions from product transport by 50 per cent on average per finished product compared to 2016 and ensure all factories use 100 per cent recycled and reused water in industrial processes. Additionally, 95 per cent of formula ingredients will be biobased, derived from abundant minerals or come from circular processes.[39]
- *Social Initiatives*: L'Oréal is also involved in numerous social initiatives, such as promoting diversity and inclusion, supporting communities through philanthropy and ensuring ethical practices throughout its operations. By 2030, it aimed to benefit three million people through its social engagement programmes. Having accomplished the goal in 2023 itself, it is aspiring for even greater impact: to benefit 2 million people *each* year thereafter. By 2026, L'Oréal aims to allocate 80 million euros to support the most vulnerable women via the L'Oréal for Women fund. In India, the L'Oréal Beauty for a Better Life programme empowers disadvantaged young women. Through beautician and beauty advisor training (with over 8000 graduates to date), it equips them for salon and retail careers.
- *Economic Initiatives*: L'Oréal engages with the startup community in many ways. It sponsors a beauty accelerator in collaboration with Station F; with Founders Factory, it runs a digital accelerator; and its own corporate venture capital fund supports Business Opportunities for L'Oréal Development (BOLD).
- *Tech Initiatives*: L'Oréal's Application Programming Interface (API) marketplace offers developers and partners a digital platform to access and utilize various interfaces to innovate and enhance beauty-related technologies. For instance, 'skin screen' is one such API that offers advanced skin diagnosis as a service to other developers and startups.

Sustainability is deeply embedded in L'Oréal's NEST ecosystem. Together with IBM, L'Oréal has collaboratively developed the industry's first AI model dedicated to sustainable cosmetic formulation, pioneering the use of bio-sourced and circular economy materials. This groundbreaking AI model leverages L'Oréal's extensive cosmetic science expertise combined with IBM's advanced AI technology, fundamentally redefining innovation at the intersection of beauty, chemistry and sustainability. By focusing on renewable ingredient behaviour in cosmetic formulas, L'Oréal can create more inclusive and environmentally sustainable product lines, aligning with its ambitious target of achieving predominantly bio-sourced and circular economy-based formulas by 2030. Stéphane Ortiz, Head of Innovation Métiers & Product Development, L'Oréal Research & Innovation, says of the IBM collaboration:

> As part of our Digital Transformation Program, this partnership will extend the speed and scale of our innovation and reformulation pipeline, with products always reaching higher standards of inclusivity, sustainability, and personalization.[40]

This collaboration exemplifies L'Oréal's comprehensive integration of technological innovation and sustainability into its broader value-chain and NEST (Nature-Society-Economy-Technology) ecosystem strategies, demonstrating leadership in the co-intelligence-driven transformation of the beauty industry.

Thus, in the Life-Xverse, AI becomes a co-creator across the globe, capable of producing new insights in different domains, accelerating research and decision-making and enhancing human capabilities in creatively transforming offering, value chain, management and NEST ecosystems in which organizations operate—as we will see through numerous examples in this book. Kerimcan Ozcan and Venkat Ramaswamy, in their book, *Dynamic Relationality Theory of Creative Transformation*, say: 'As organizations evolve as ecosystemic assemblages themselves, they strategically architect their position within

Nature–Society–Economy–Technology (NEST) assemblages, balancing adaptability and stability, and steering ecosystems toward envisioned goals.'[41] Such organizations work towards impacts that promote *sustainable wellbeing impacts (SWIs)– encompassing geo-biological, psychological, socio-cultural, and economic impacts of people and planetary wellbeing,* which need to be achieved together with all stakeholders—from customers to employees and managers to suppliers, partners, financiers and other stakeholders.

As shown in **Figure 2-2**, forward-looking enterprises are building out their **Co-intelligence Architectures** to effectively support interconnected offering and value chain ecosystems through management ecosystems, which, in turn, connect with other organizations (within and across sectors) in the wider NEST ecosystems in which they operate. The concept of **tokenized digital intelligence (TDI)** that we introduced in the first chapter is central to this architecture.

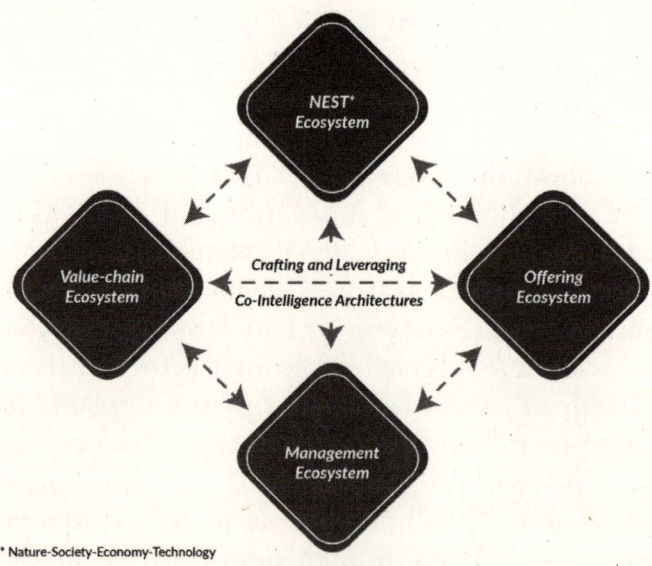

* Nature-Society-Economy-Technology

Figure 2-2: *Creative Transformation of Organizational Ecosystems (Source: Venkat Ramaswamy)*

Tokenized Digital Intelligence

Tokenized digital intelligence (TDI) is a digital representation of knowledge, insights or actions created by AI systems. It is not a physical object but a modular unit of intelligence that drives value in interconnected ecosystems by enabling personalized, interactive and adaptive engagements. Let's consider a simple example. You are a customer using L'Oréal's Perso device to create a personalized skincare product tailored to your specific skin condition, environment and preferences. A TDI is created when the Perso app asks you to take a selfie and answer a few questions: How oily or dry does your skin feel? What's your current skincare goal (e.g., hydration, anti-ageing)? Do you prefer a cream or gel texture? Sensors in the Perso device capture *real-time* environmental data, such as humidity and UV index, in your location. AI analyses the photo to identify skin hydration levels, visible pores and fine lines. The AI combines your input, skin scan results and environmental data into a *Skin Hydration TDI*—a digital representation of your unique skincare needs.

A TDI, however, is not just information; it *drives decisions and actions* within an ecosystem. For instance, the Skin Hydration TDI doesn't just describe your skin—it guides the creation of a specific product. Think of a TDI like a recipe card created by a smart chef: The chef (AI) gathers ingredients (data) about you (skin hydration, climate, preferences). The recipe card (TDI) lists exactly what to do to make a dish (skincare product) tailored for you. Each time a dish is made (product used), you can leave notes (feedback) to improve the recipe for next time.

Thus, TDIs are a new type of resource that is dynamic, actionable and modular, enabling personalized value creation. Unlike traditional resources (like raw materials or static data), TDIs are adaptive. They change and improve based on real-time inputs and user feedback. They are not standalone; they interact with other systems (e.g., supply chains, AI models and user preferences) to create holistic, integrated outcomes. They are *living digital assets*, as it were, actively contributing to the co-creation of value. TDIs serve as the glue connecting supply chains, AI models and user preferences, ensuring seamless integration and co-creation. In the case of L'Oréal Perso, by interacting transparently with ethical sourcing and user feedback, TDIs reinforce trust while supporting L'Oréal's sustainability goals. The Skin Hydration TDI can cross-reference individual preferences with supply chain and AI model TDIs, and connect with a *Product Recommendation TDI*, engaging back with a customer in a potential dialogue about, say, excluding non-vegan ingredients. The system creates a dynamic feedback loop, where the product evolves in response to both immediate and anticipated user requirements. As a result, the product not only meets technical skincare needs but also aligns with the user's lifestyle and emotional values, deepening trust and satisfaction. On L'Oreal's part, TDIs enable it to align customer experience with sustainability goals, such as reducing waste by dispensing only what is needed.

TDIs are pivotal in crafting and leveraging co-intelligence architectures that we discus at length in the next chapter. They enable co-intelligence flows within the interconnected realms of the Life-Xverse. Acting as modular units of actionable intelligence, TDIs synchronize physical, digital and virtual realities to facilitate personalization, collaboration and feedback loops across NEST ecosystems, in which value chain, offering and management ecosystems are situated.

3

Crafting and Leveraging
Co-Intelligence Architectures

In this chapter, we explore and draw lessons from how tech titans are crafting and leveraging co-intelligence architectures for their own ecosystems and those of their customers and partners, driving interconnected innovation, transforming life–experiences and unlocking new sources of value. We discuss how *shared digitalized infrastructures* (SDI) are enabling the development of co-intelligence architectures in tech-forward organizational ecosystems. We examine how enterprises are co-innovating *service-as-a-capability* for and with their customers, partners, employees and other stakeholders. Finally, we consider how India, Brazil and other countries are investing in *digital public infrastructures* (DPIs), together with the plural and private sectors, and exploring new pathways in cross-sector Human–AI co-creation of new value and accelerating societal progress in achieving Sustainable Development Goals (SDGs).

We start with the world of *data* itself, without which there is no AI, with an illustrative example of how Databricks is fuelling the democratization of data access in organizations.

Databricks—Making Data Accessible

Databricks is an innovative data platform company that is democratizing access to advanced data capabilities. Founded by the original creators of Apache Spark, including Ali Ghodsi, Matei Zaharia and others, Databricks provides a unified analytics platform that allows organizations to efficiently handle big data, perform complex analytics and deploy machine learning models at scale. The founders proclaim: 'There weren't many people willing to bet that a bunch of students and teachers in a research lab at Berkeley—with virtually no business experience among them—could take the open-source software that they helped create, enhance it, and deliver it as a cloud-based platform for data and AI.'[1]

As Databricks has matured, it has aggressively expanded its AI and GenAI capabilities, solidifying its position as a key player in the AI landscape. Ghodsi says,

> AI will change data platforms . . . The impact of AI on data platforms will not be incremental, but fundamental: massively democratizing access to data, automating manual administration, and enabling turnkey creation of custom AI applications.[2]

It acquired MosaicML, a leading platform for creating and customizing GenAI models. Unlike traditional AI models, which are often pre-trained on generic datasets, Databrick's offerings allow companies to train these models on their own data, ensuring that the AI is fine-tuned to their specific requirements. It has also introduced LakehouseIQ, an AI-powered knowledge engine that uniquely understands an organization's specific business context, including its data, jargon and internal processes. Ghodsi says, 'We're not just making data accessible; we're making it intelligible, actionable, and much more valuable.'[3]

Consider JetBlue, which has significantly accelerated its innovation by leveraging Databricks' AI and data platform.

Its BlueSky operations digital twin, which is a real-time virtual model of JetBlue's operational environment, uses data and AI to simulate, predict and optimize various aspects of airline operations, including flight schedules, maintenance and passenger services. For instance, JetBlue leverages GenAI to create predictive models that anticipate potential flight delays by analysing massive datasets, including weather conditions and air traffic control inputs. This predictive capability allows the airline to adjust schedules proactively, minimizing disruption. It also optimizes fuel efficiency by simulating different flight routes and conditions, leading to significant cost savings. JetBlue uses GenAI to analyse customer data and tailor services and improve satisfaction during travel.[4]

Let us consider another industry solution, Databricks Data Intelligence Platform for Financial Services, and see how it has enabled Discovery Limited with its digital-first bank. Discovery Bank, launched in 2019, focuses on personalized banking experiences with technology-driven services. Discovery Limited is known for its Discovery Insurance *shared value* Vitality programme, which incentivizes healthy behaviour by offering rewards and discounts. This programme is integrated with its insurance products to encourage members to adopt healthier lifestyles, which can reduce healthcare costs in the long term. (We discuss the Vitality programme further in the next chapter.) With Databricks service-as-a-capability, it has brought its shared value model into banking, going after new co-intelligence-driven value creation opportunities through a *behavioural banking* approach. Databricks capabilities have empowered Discovery Bank to deepen experience personalization in its customer's lived-journey of banking by facilitating customer adoption of healthy financial habits, resulting in higher savings levels and lower risk of over-indebtedness. Databricks has also enabled Discovery's advanced servicing, fraud detection and risk management. Discovery's data ecosystem can focus on client behavioural fingerprints and provide hyper-personalized insights to drive initiatives that enhance client engagement and financial health. Discovery Bank also uses Databricks' governance and security features to streamline its data management and ensure compliance. The platform's medallion architecture (which helps organize data in stages, from raw to refined) and Unity Catalog (a unified data governance solution) have helped the bank manage data lineage, table history and access controls efficiently. Thus, the Databricks Data Intelligence Platform has transformed Discovery Bank's ability to leverage advanced analytics, resulting in faster decision-making, reduced technical debt and enhanced ML capabilities. The platform's comprehensive tools support the bank's data ecosystem, driving innovation and shared value, with a remarkable return on investment (ROI) of over 500 per cent.[5]

By providing a unified, scalable, accessible, integrative platform for all its customers, Databricks democratizes access to data intelligence, enabling enterprises of all sizes to harness the power of data + AI. This democratization fosters innovation and drives data-driven decision-making for all, ultimately leading to better business outcomes and impacts at large in business, economy and society. As data continues to grow in importance, platform companies like Databricks will continue to play a crucial role in empowering organizations to stay competitive in an increasingly data-intensive co-intelligence world.

We now delve further into the business application space of enterprises with three other illustrative examples of tech-forward companies, HubSpot, Salesforce and SAP, which together span enterprise ecosystem interactions across marketing, sales and service to supply chain, operations, enterprise resource planning, financials and human resource management.

HubSpot—Transforming Inbound Marketing

HubSpot is a customer relationship management (CRM) platform dedicated to helping businesses grow better by providing tools for marketing, sales, customer service and content management. Unlike competitors such as Salesforce, which focuses on enterprise-grade customization, HubSpot emphasizes ease of use, rapid deployment and integration, especially for small and medium-sized businesses (SMBs). Central to HubSpot's mission is inbound marketing, which attracts customers through valuable content and experiences rather than interruptive marketing. It is about attracting and engaging customers with relevant content on their terms. Over the years, HubSpot has embraced AI to elevate its approach, revolutionizing inbound marketing, sales and customer service with Human–AI interactive engagement at its core. As marketing became more complex and data-driven, it used AI to automate repetitive tasks and enable greater personalization. AI-driven chatbots, for example, were introduced to handle customer inquiries, reducing the workload on human teams and improving efficiency.

HubSpot's new AI-driven system, Breeze, is designed to enhance efficiency across the entire customer platform. Breeze is composed of three key components:

- *Breeze Copilot*: An AI assistant that helps users with everyday tasks such as researching prospects, summarizing emails and preparing for calls. It works seamlessly across HubSpot's smart CRM, browser and mobile interfaces, allowing users to complete tasks more efficiently.
- *Breeze Agents:* AI-powered agents designed to automate complex workflows. For instance, a marketing agent can create multi-format content (like blog posts and social media updates), a sales agent can manage prospect outreach and a service agent can handle customer inquiries 24/7.
- *Breeze Intelligence:* A data enrichment and unification tool that uses LLMs to provide real-time context on customers and prospects. Breeze Intelligence allows businesses to shorten forms, identify buyer intent and enrich customer records with valuable insights. This feature is designed to make lead generation and customer data management more efficient, enabling teams to focus on higher-value tasks.

Breeze's integration into HubSpot's ecosystem marks a significant step in the company's AI journey, making AI more accessible and impactful. In sales, for instance, AI-driven personalization has shortened sales cycles and increased win rates, while in marketing, AI has helped create, personalize and distribute content with greater efficiency. HubSpot's ongoing improvements to its platform, such as Breeze and integrations like Google Enhanced Conversions, reflect the company's commitment to helping businesses navigate complex digital landscapes.[6]

HubSpot CEO Yamini Rangan believes that the traditional growth formula is broken, with businesses finding it harder to attract, convert and retain customers in a rapidly changing digital landscape. She advocates for making things easy by simplifying customer interactions and internal processes so businesses can quickly see value from their tools without complex setups or long delays, speeding up operations by leveraging AI to accelerate tasks, reduce inefficiencies and enhance productivity, allowing businesses to grow faster, and creating unified solutions that ensure that all tools and data work seamlessly together, giving businesses a complete and cohesive picture of their customers and processes. She emphasizes a growth formula focusing on three critical metrics: traffic × conversion × retention, to the power of AI. As Rangan notes,

> The way to think about AI is not to underplay AI or to overhype AI. It is to understand AI and to co-create with AI. Because co-creation is what can catalyse growth. Across go-to-market functions, AI creates; people curate. AI offers context, people offer connection.[7]

HubSpot's vision for the future of AI is one where businesses can leverage AI not just to automate tasks but also to transform the way customers can interact with them. It sees AI as an integral partner in every aspect of business growth, from content creation and lead generation to customer service and sales, with the human element still remaining central in value co-creation.

AI Journey at Salesforce

Salesforce, which launched in 1999 as a pioneering cloud-based CRM platform, has evolved into an end-to-end business solution platform, offering services across customer relationship management, artificial intelligence (Einstein AI), analytics (Tableau), app development (Heroku) and integration tools (MuleSoft).

Predictive AI can be used for analysing data to predict outcomes and optimize performance, Generative AI can be leveraged to create new content and insights, and Agentic AI can perform more complex operations. For instance, while a chatbot might help a customer check an order status, its Agentforce digital labour platform can autonomously manage complex tasks such as account reactivations, manage reservations, or respond to seasonal demands without requiring human intervention. This makes AI agents more sophisticated, with the ability to understand broader contexts and automate end-to-end workflows.

Marc Benioff, co-founder, chairman and CEO of Salesforce, says,

> This could be the single most important moment in the history of our industry, and customers are turning to us to help them navigate this AI revolution and connect with their customers in a whole new way.[8]

Whether it is an AI system for the consumer or an enterprise, three aspects are key—a compelling user interface, trusted AI models and high-quality data. Trusted AI models are those that provide reliable, unbiased and explainable outcomes, ensuring they align with ethical standards and regulatory requirements. High-quality data is crucial because it enhances the accuracy and relevance of AI outputs, reducing errors and ensuring that AI-driven insights are meaningful and applicable to the specific needs of the business. While consumer AI models are trained on data from the Internet, enterprise AI needs enterprise-specific data, which is grounded and secure. This ensures that AI models are not only accurate but also aligned with the specific needs and context of the business, enhancing the relevance of AI-driven insights and recommendations. Salesforce's AI infrastructure supports such enterprise AI effectively. For instance:

i)   *Data Cloud* acts as a hyperscale data engine within Salesforce, unifying and integrating data from various sources within an enterprise. Its Vector Database is designed to handle both structured and unstructured data, such as PDFs, emails and social media feeds. The capability to handle unstructured data is particularly valuable in scenarios like customer service, where it can quickly surface relevant knowledge articles.

ii) This data engine forms the backbone for analytics and AI applications utilized by *Customer 360* to provide a holistic view of each customer, consolidating information from different interactions and touchpoints. This integration enables businesses to understand customer behaviours, preferences and needs more deeply, facilitating personalized and effective engagement.

iii) Leveraging this unified data, Einstein AI employs machine learning and advanced analytics to deliver intelligent predictions, personalized recommendations and automation, thereby optimizing sales, marketing and customer service processes for a more responsive and data-driven enterprise.

Consider how Aston Martin, the iconic luxury sports car maker, employs Salesforce's integrated technology stack to enhance customer engagement and streamline internal processes. It begins by integrating various data streams, including website interactions, vehicle data and CRM data, into a unified system using Data Cloud.

Aston Martin uses Databricks to integrate and synchronize vehicle telematics data, without creating a copy, with Data Cloud. This integration allows for real-time access and analysis of telematics data alongside other customer data streams in one data environment. Using Salesforce CRM, Aston Martin compiles a comprehensive profile for each customer, including data from previous interactions and preferences. Data Cloud also helps enrich these profiles by integrating additional data sources, such as marketing engagement and vehicle information. For example, based on the expiry of a customer's current vehicle warranty, her visits to the Aston Martin website and social media content viewed about their latest grand tourer model, DB12, the company can better engage with her in the customer journey.

Einstein Copilot, part of the Einstein One platform, can then generate personalized marketing campaigns based on the unified customer data. It might suggest customized features for the customer's DB12, such as tinted windows or a panoramic sunroof, based on her preferences and how popular these features are among similar customer profiles. These recommendations are further personalized by considering her preferred communication channel, such as WhatsApp, where she receives tailored marketing messages.

Slack, integrated with Salesforce CRM, allows internal teams at Aston Martin to collaborate effectively. Slack Record Channels provide a centralized view of all relevant customer information, enabling quick updates and coordination across different departments. Tableau Pulse offers real-time insights by analysing customer data. For example, it helps Aston Martin's team understand the most popular customization options among customers, which can inform future marketing strategies and product offerings. Einstein AI, integrated with Data Cloud and CRM, alerts the team to potential issues, such as a delay in customization delivery, and provides actionable recommendations, like suggesting alternative suppliers to meet customer expectations. Salesforce Prompt Builder is used to create reusable templates for sending automated notifications to customers, such as reminders about upcoming service appointments or new available customizations for their vehicle.

Salesforce's Agentforce platform brings the power of GenAI agents to more organizations. Unlike previous Salesforce AI offerings, Agentforce is capable of autonomously handling complex workflows, integrating customer data across channels and providing more dynamic responses, making it distinct in its ability to manage end-to-end tasks with minimal human intervention. OpenTable, an online reservation platform with a vast network of 60,000 restaurants and 160 million diners, is implementing Agentforce to enhance its customer service. It addresses over 90 per cent of customer inquiries, including common concerns like account reactivations, reservation management and loyalty point expiration. Publishers like Wiley are also seeing improvements in efficiency with Agentforce compared to previous AI solutions. Benioff says,

> They (Wiley) have incredible seasonal demand right now when kids are going back to school. And they're able to use Agentforce to directly expand their customer service capability. And instead of hiring or trying to surge their customer service organization and train all these folks, which, by the way, is what they've done in the past, now they're able to just use Agentforce to take that additional capacity.[9]

SAP—Becoming Intelligent and Sustainable

SAP has undergone a remarkable technological evolution from its origins as a core ERP (enterprise resource planning) provider to becoming a leader in cloud computing and AI innovation. At

SAP Sapphire 2022, Christian Klein, CEO and member of the executive board of SAP SE, outlined a vision for the company:

> Let's reinvent how enterprises run for the next 50 years—resilient, intelligent, and sustainable.[10]

Embracing GenAI

In this new vision, SAP began asking itself questions about leveraging GenAI in its solutions in a meaningful and differentiated way and not just rushing into it. Its GenAI digital assistant, Joule, is named after the pioneering English physicist known for thermodynamics, James Joule. What sets Joule apart from generic chatbots like ChatGPT is its enterprise-specific focus and deep integration with SAP's ecosystem. It is built from vast amounts of anonymized, secure data contributed by 28,000 global SAP customers, including over 300 million users.[11] Unlike general-purpose chatbots, Joule is tailored to understand and interact with SAP applications, providing specialized support for business processes such as finance, supply chain and human resources.

It leverages SAP's extensive business data to deliver precise, context-aware responses that align with corporate workflows and objectives. SAP Datasphere Knowledge Graph, by automatically generating knowledge graphs from existing data connections and tables, creates a detailed ontology that represents relationships and business contexts from sources like S4HANA. This empowers Joule to answer complex and open-ended questions more effectively. Additionally, Joule can not only answer queries but also suggest actionable insights and automate routine tasks. This capability transforms the chatbot *from a mere conversational agent to a powerful tool for enhancing productivity and driving business innovation.*

At Joule's release in 2023, Klein said, 'Joule has the power to redefine the way businesses—and the people who power them—work. It will know what you mean, not just what you say.'[12] A year later, having seen the significant productivity enhancements that it provided with their pilots, Klein confidently stated at SAP Sapphire 2024: 'Joule will be your digital assistant spanning across all our solutions. Joule will become our new front end, our new UX and will turn your words into action to become the biggest productivity engine for every SAP end user.'

He expects that, soon, 80 per cent of the most-used tasks performed by over 300 million end users of SAP's cloud software will be managed via Joule, enhancing productivity by 20 per cent. For example, Joule will streamline functions such as order management, billing and cash collection and accelerate book closing by managing standard compliance checks across various accounting guidelines. Let us explore other projects that have established the benefits of Joule.

SAP's Joule was used to enhance the productivity of consultants and developers working with SAP systems by up to 30 per cent, enabling faster implementation of solutions. In 2024, when introduced to 4000 internal consultants, Joule saved them up to two hours daily by providing quick access to relevant information. This efficiency is achieved through Joule's extensive database, which includes *fifty certification programmes, over 200,000 pages of content and 2 TB of curated community content*, all powered by NVIDIA's advanced technology for superior question answering. Joule's impact extends to SAP's consulting ecosystem, potentially saving 600 million working hours annually and speeding up cloud transformations.[13]

Joule also features ABAP code generation capabilities, boosting productivity by 30 per cent for developers. This allows for easy generation, understanding and testing of modern ABAP cloud code, facilitating the transition from legacy code to modern solutions. This cutting-edge technology is based on *large language model training with SAP's latest S4HANA cloud code, utilizing 250 million lines of code, and powered by NVIDIA's software and hardware, along with the Starcoder (LLM for code generation) model.*

SAP has forged partnerships with leading technology companies, including NVIDIA (for e.g., integrating with Omniverse) and Microsoft, to co-innovate solutions. Joule uses Microsoft 365 Copilot to create a Microsoft Teams channel and add project members, ensuring everyone stays updated. When planning an off-site meeting, employees can simply ask Joule for specific HR policies, such as daily travel allowances in expensive cities, without leaving their workflow. Joule summarizes the relevant policies based on organizational data, making it easy to plan activities like team dinners. For event planning, Joule leverages its bi-directional integration with Microsoft Copilot to analyse team members' Outlook calendars and find the best week for a project launch. It then sends calendar invites and coordinates travel options through SAP Concur (expense management system), utilizing location data from SAP SuccessFactors HCM (human capital management). This unified experience eliminates the need to switch between multiple systems, ensuring all crucial steps are managed seamlessly.

SAP is also transforming various functions, such as supply chain management and finance. Consider a scenario where a supply chain planner responsible for a vacuum cleaner product line notices disruptions at their supplier's end. Typically, addressing such disruptions would take days or weeks of communication and mitigation efforts. But Joule quickly identifies that a natural disaster has impacted the supplier, resulting in a delay in sensor components essential for production. Proactively, it suggests using SAP Integrated Business Planning to assess the broader impact on the supply chain. The planner discovers that some key customers are affected, with only two weeks of safety stock remaining. Joule then recommends alternative suppliers based on criteria important to the planner, such as sustainability ratings, procurement costs and delivery times. Joule also integrates with SAP Analytics Cloud to simulate various economic scenarios, like fluctuating inflation rates, using advanced techniques such as Monte Carlo simulations. This allows companies to predict future financial performance with greater accuracy.[14] SAP's Business Data Cloud unifies and governs all SAP data and seamlessly connects with third-party data, aiming to deliver transformational insights and a unified experience across all lines of business.

SAP + Databricks

SAP's strategic partnership with Databricks marks a significant shift in the enterprise data management landscape.[15,16] The partnership introduces SAP Databricks, a new offering that natively integrates the Databricks Data Intelligence Platform within SAP Business Data Cloud, allowing customers to combine their SAP data with other enterprise data easily. Companies can then develop AI models unlocking agent systems for critical business functions, putting the concepts of Nextgen AI factory and Tokenized Digital Intelligence (TDI) in action. For example, by integrating SAP Joule and Databricks, L'Oréal can envision evolving its Beauty Tech strategy with Nextgen AI driven supply chains and TDIs that seamlessly connect AI-powered customer interactions, real-time demand sensing and dynamic personalization. For instance, when a customer of L'Oréal with dry skin asks Beauty Genius AI for skincare advice, its TDIs enable a real-time, personalized response. L'Oréal may leverage SAP Joule to retrieve past purchases, while it uses Databricks AI to analyze live environmental factors like humidity and pollution. Beauty Genius then recommends products dynamically, adjusting if the user prefers vegan options or seasonal skincare. If the customer hesitates to buy, the AI can offer a discount and update L'Oréal's supply chain to optimize inventory. TDIs ensure AI-driven beauty experiences are adaptive, interactive and continuously improving over time.

Sustainability—A Focus on the Green Line

Klein's SAP vision also emphasizes sustainability: 'We also understand that business must be both profitable and sustainable. This means putting people, the planet and profit on equal footing—making the "green line" as important as the top line and the bottom line.'[17]

SAP Cloud for Sustainable Enterprises helps its clients manage their carbon footprint, reduce material waste and become a socially responsible business. The industry cloud solution focuses on enhancing sustainability and ESG reporting by integrating and harmonizing data from various sources, allowing businesses to make informed decisions. It supports climate action by managing carbon footprints across the value chain and promotes circular economy practices by optimizing material choices and ensuring compliance with regulations. Additionally, the solution emphasizes social responsibility by ensuring workplace safety and managing supplier risks, thereby helping enterprises understand and mitigate their impact on people and society.

SAP and Amul (India's largest dairy cooperative) are jointly working on transforming the lives of 1.5 million Indians (comprising children, adolescents, youth, women and farmers) by focusing on knowledge transfer and technology capacity-building towards social entrepreneurship, enabling a skilled workforce, digital inclusion and bridging the gender equality gap for the community. As Kulmeet Bawa, former president and MD, SAP, Indian subcontinent, and chief revenue officer, SAP Business Technology Platform, notes:

> Technology can act as a catalyst in shaping India's journey to an inclusive and sustainable economy. While urban development projects such as smart cities and futuristic mobility are reflective of this potential, true progress of India lies in the development of her villages. Our work with Amul is an expansion of this vision and will provide citizens with the information and tools they need to succeed. As India continues to lead global action on sustainability, collaboration like ours will also provide the critical foundation for an inclusive and resilient future in which no one is left behind.[18]

In Chapter 5, we will delve deeper into an open data ecosystem supported by SAP—Catena-X. It promotes a circular economy and sustainability by fostering collaboration and data exchange across the automotive industry to optimize resource use and reduce waste. Let us turn next to hyperscalers and tech-platform companies—Google Cloud, Amazon Web Services, Oracle Cloud Infrastructure, Meta, xAI and Microsoft.

AI-infused Transformations at Google Cloud, AWS, OCI, Meta and xAI

Google's Vertex AI is a comprehensive machine learning platform on Google Cloud that provides tools for building, deploying and scaling ML models. It now supports over 130 AI models, including Gemini 1.5 Pro, with enhanced long-context understanding (capacity to run 1 million tokens) and multi-modal capabilities (process audio, video, text, code and more).[19] One of the new areas of focus at Google is GenAI *agents*. Pichai says,

> I think about them as intelligent systems that show reasoning, planning, and memory. They are able to 'think' multiple steps ahead, and work across software and systems, all to get something done on your behalf, and most importantly, under your supervision.[20]

Google Cloud's customers are leveraging AI agents in their businesses. For instance, at Goldman Sachs, AI agents assist in summarizing public filings and extracting sentiment and signals from corporate statements, which helps analysts quickly gather and interpret critical information. Uber utilizes AI agents to enhance both employee efficiency and customer experiences by intelligently managing user communications. For example, when a user reaches out for assistance, the AI agent provides a summary of previous communications and relevant details, allowing the support team to respond more effectively and efficiently.

Amazon Web Services (AWS) is also bringing service-as-a-capability to its enterprise customers through three major layers of the GenAI stack: *infrastructure, model access and applications.*

i)   At the bottom layer, Amazon's infrastructure includes foundation models and large language models (LLMs). AWS offers specialized hardware like NVIDIA GPUs and custom-built chips like Tranium and Inferentia, enabling large-scale training and inference capabilities.

ii) Through Amazon Bedrock, the middle layer focuses on providing access to a diverse set of LLMs and foundation models. Bedrock simplifies the process of building and scaling GenAI applications, offering enterprise-grade security and privacy. It allows customers to experiment with different models, such as those from AI21, Anthropic (Amazon has invested $4 billion in Anthropic and AWS has become its primary cloud provider), Cohere, Stability AI and Amazon's own Titan models.

iii) At the top layer, Amazon offers applications built on these foundation models, allowing users to leverage GenAI without requiring specialized knowledge. Amazon SageMaker, a managed service, helps developers train and deploy models efficiently. It supports a wide range of use cases, from natural language processing to image generation, making it accessible to companies across various industries.[21]

Oracle, well known for its databases, has transformed itself as a hyperscaler. It embeds AI capabilities within Oracle Cloud Infrastructure (OCI) to enable businesses to build and run AI applications efficiently. This includes support for high-performance computing, data analytics, and machine learning workloads, enabling clients to develop custom AI models and deploy them across a global network of data centres. It has now enabled a multi-cloud ecosystem that integrates its cloud services with those of other major hyperscalers like AWS,

Google Cloud and Microsoft Azure. It has embedded its hardware, like the Exadata cluster, directly within other cloud providers' data centres. This approach promotes flexibility, allowing organizations to choose the best cloud services and infrastructure for their needs and fostering interoperability between different cloud platforms.[22] Larry Ellison, co-founder, chairman of the board and chief technology officer of Oracle, says,

> We've talked for a while about our ability to build very small data centers, one you could put in a ship or a submarine or how a full Oracle Cloud we will soon have in six standard half-racks to go into a conventional data center, so virtually any one of our customers could choose to have the full Oracle Cloud in their data center, with every service in the Cloud.[23]

Its OCI GenAI empowers both its internal teams and clients. Talking about how GenAI is transforming Oracle's product development, Ellison says, 'If we're starting a brand new project, we're generating that code. We're not handwriting it anymore. We're generating that code in this thing called APEX (Oracle's enterprise low-code application development platform).' A smaller team is able to develop code faster, with enhanced application security. The OCI GenAI provides a model hub, prompt libraries, vector databases, and small language models and facilitates the deployment of AI models for various industry-specific needs. For instance, in healthcare, Oracle Cerner oversees the management of billions of electronic health records (EHRs). Leveraging anonymized EHR data, Oracle can develop generative models specifically tailored to healthcare applications. Ellison says,

> We are taking a lot of electronic health data and training it to give a draft of the doctor's discharge note or a draft of an order. The doctor reviews it, edits it and then submits

it. So, the model is making the doctor's job easier. It is not taking over the doctor's job.[24]

Meta, with its open-source Llama AI frontier models, is fostering a collaborative developer ecosystem. Meta's ecosystem partnerships for Llama 3.1 include collaborations with over twenty-five companies, such as AWS (cloud deployment), NVIDIA (specialized hardware support), Google Cloud and Microsoft Azure (real-time inference and integration). Zuckerberg says, 'Open source will ensure that more people around the world have access to the benefits and opportunities of AI, that power isn't concentrated in the hands of a small number of companies, and that the technology can be deployed more evenly and safely across society.'[25]

Meta has also placed a lot of emphasis on the safety of AI models. Llama Guard is an internal security tool designed to detect potential harms in input prompts and output responses. Additionally, Llama Guard's functionality extends to on-device deployment, which means it operates directly on users' devices, ensuring that sensitive data does not need to be transmitted to the cloud. This not only enhances privacy but also allows for more efficient and faster processing of data. Meta has also released other safety tools—Prompt Guard targets prompt attacks like direct jailbreaks and indirect prompt injections, while Code Shield focuses on preventing the generation of insecure code. Zuckerberg says,

> We need to protect against two categories of harm: unintentional and intentional . . . On this front, open source should be significantly safer since the systems are more transparent and can be widely scrutinized.[26]

A new competitor has emerged in the AI space—xAI, founded by Elon Musk, which has developed the Grok series of AI models. Grok-3, the latest iteration, is designed to integrate deeply with X (formerly Twitter), offering real-time contextual awareness by processing live feeds from the platform. Unlike conventional AI models that rely on pre-processed datasets, Grok-3 is engineered for dynamic adaptation, providing responses that are continuously refined based on evolving trends and events. xAI's focus is on AI autonomy, ultimately embedding Grok-3 within Tesla's Full Self-Driving (FSD) systems and integrating it into SpaceX's robotics initiatives. This represents a broader shift in AI where real-time, multimodal data streams are leveraged for more contextual and responsive AI engagements.

Yann LeCun, a Turing Award winner and the Chief AI Scientist of Meta, advocates for a shift from traditional LLM architectures to joint embedding predictive architecture (JEPA) in the future. He argues that while LLMs excel at generating text, they lack true understanding and reasoning capabilities. In contrast, JEPA aims to develop AI systems that learn from minimal data and are capable of reasoning and planning. Consider a scenario of an autonomous car driving down a road, lined with trees, on a windy day. LeCun says,

> It'll (the car's AI system with JEPA) tell you there are moving leaves, but it's not going to give the details of exactly what's going on. And so, when you do the prediction in representation space, you're not going to have to predict every single pixel of every leaf. And that not only is a lot simpler, but also, it allows the system to essentially learn an abstract representation of the world where what can be modeled and predicted is preserved and the rest is viewed as noise and eliminated by the encoder.[27]

Microsoft—Ushering in an Era of Copilots with Agents

Microsoft, in the last decade under the leadership of its chairman and CEO, Satya Nadella, has become one of the defining enterprises of the co-intelligence era—from its roots in *desktop computing* to *hyperscale computing*, providing access to compute infrastructure and software as a *platform*, offering service-as-a-capability to its customers and partners, all the while transforming its own portfolio of businesses and the future of work in the process. Let us explore how its own SDI platforms, whose capabilities it offers as a service and infuses in its offerings to customers and partners, and its own co-intelligence architecture have evolved in the past few years.

The Copilot Era

Nadella argues that two technological breakthroughs have come together to define this new era of AI—natural language as a universal interface to any computer and the emergence of a reasoning engine that has the capability to analyse and intelligently interpret vast amounts of available data:

> Just like you boot up an OS (operating system) to access applications or use a browser to visit websites today, our belief is that you will invoke a Copilot to do all those activities and more: to shop, to code, to analyze, to learn, to create . . . Copilot will be the new UI that helps us gain access to the world's knowledge and your organization's knowledge.[28]

Microsoft's first commercially successful integration of ChatGPT and other LLMs in their software offerings was with GitHub Copilot. Nadella shares the aha-moment of its experimentation in a Freakonomics Radio interview: 'Once we got to GPT-3 when it started to learn to code, we said, "Oh wow, this emergent phenomenon, the scaling effects of these transformer models, are really showing promise."'[29] Microsoft took it to Nat Friedman, CEO of GitHub, a developer platform they acquired in 2018. Friedman and team created GitHub Copilot, a new AI pair programmer, that helps developers write better code. Friedman, an amateur pilot himself, uses a flight analogy to describe it: 'The tool was more like a copilot—someone who joins you in the cockpit and makes suggestions . . . Usually you listen to a copilot, sometimes you ignore him.'[30]

GitHub Copilot uses the OpenAI Codex engine to suggest code and entire functions in real time, right from the developer's editor. Trained on billions of lines of code, it turns natural language prompts into coding suggestions across dozens of languages. It shares recommendations based on the project's context and style conventions. Developers can quickly cycle through lines of code or complete function suggestions and decide which to accept, reject or edit. A recent analysis of the code on GitHub found that an average of 46 per cent of developers' code files across all programming languages were generated by GitHub Copilot.[31] Customers, including large corporates, began embracing this co-intelligent solution. Duolingo, the language learning app, has seen a 25 per cent increase in developer speed. Its CTO, Severin Hacker, highlights how useful it can be for enterprises with sprawling codebases: 'A tool like GitHub Copilot is so impactful at large companies because suddenly engineers can make impactful changes to other developers' code with little previous exposure.'[32]

Now, every core product and services team at Microsoft is rolling out *copilot experiences*—AI-powered chat in Bing, Microsoft 365 Copilot, Dynamics 365 Copilot, Copilot in Microsoft Viva and others. Consider the case of Bing Copilot. In an online search market completely dominated by Google, Microsoft released an innovation—a search bot that combined its proprietary model, Prometheus, with OpenAI's model to provide a single, summarized answer. Users could also chat naturally and ask follow-up questions to their initial search. Within a year, over 5 billion chats and 5 billion images were created using Bing search.[33] It has now become the browser of choice for ChatGPT. Google was forced to respond with its own chatbot, Gemini. Nadella quipped, 'I want people to know that we made them (Google) dance.'[34]

Copilot enabled Microsoft's Power Platform, the next-generation business process automation and productivity suite that helps everyone, from experienced developers to people with little or no coding experience, a.k.a. 'citizen developers' to build applications. Business users can describe what they want to do in natural language, and it will generate a list of the most relevant Power FX formulas for them to choose from.[35] Or consider Viva, its employee experience platform. With Copilot infused, managers get an entirely new and interactive way to engage their workforce. For instance, they can query Viva for recommending draft OKRs (objectives and key results) based on employee annual plans, identifying blockers and suggesting appropriate next steps. They can also create compelling posts from simple prompts on relevant workplace topics.

Microsoft also wants all developers, not just its own, to have this capability to build their own co-pilot. It has put together an enterprise architecture, an AI development framework, that helps developers achieve this. Kevin Scott, Microsoft's chief technology officer, says,

> You can take a large language model like GPT-4 and start using that to build applications. We've established this new application platform called Copilot . . . A plugin is about how you, the copilot developer, give your copilot or an AI system the ability to have capabilities that it's not manifesting right now and to connect it to data, and connect it to systems that you're building. I think there's going to eventually be an incredibly rich ecosystem of plugins.[36]

Companies can develop their own co-pilots, leveraging their enterprise-specific data. For instance, a company may connect the Microsoft 365 Copilot with its private database of legal files and contracts and allow its employees to ask questions about how certain legal issues were handled in the past. For instance, Clifford Chance, a legal firm, has transformed its workflows and work artefacts that get created around merger and acquisition interactions and transactions. Microsoft has now rolled out Microsoft Copilot Studio with a new set of capabilities that enable its customer and partner organizations to build autonomous agents and become true AI-first companies that 'leverage a combination of people, Copilot, and agents to be more efficient, improve customer engagement, and improve employee experience'.[37]

Copilot with Agentic AI at McKinsey

Consider McKinsey, one of the most successful management consulting firms, which has used Copilot Studio to create an autonomous agent to streamline touchpoints with their clients. Traditionally, McKinsey handled client inquiries through a manual process. Incoming emails from prospective clients were received, parsed by team members and routed to the appropriate internal experts based on their area of expertise and the engagement's specific needs. This process, though reliable, was resource-intensive and prone to delays, as it required human intervention to filter and manage each email, determine the next steps and match inquiries to the relevant internal stakeholders.

Through its partnership with Microsoft, McKinsey implemented an autonomous agent designed to streamline this process. When an email from a prospective client arrives, the agent immediately goes to work. It begins by parsing the content of the email, leveraging natural language processing to understand the inquiry's intent, identify relevant industry terms and match it with the firm's internal engagement history. This enables the agent to accurately route the email to the most appropriate partner or team within the firm.

In addition to identifying the right person, the agent automatically drafts a detailed summary of the email, capturing key information and presenting it in a concise format for the recipient. This autonomous response not only speeds up the process but also ensures consistency in how inquiries are handled across the firm.

McKinsey's team was able to design and configure the agent in Copilot Studio without requiring advanced programming knowledge. Using natural language commands, much like directing a human colleague, the team provided the agent with instructions on how to handle client inquiries.

Triggers were set up to monitor a designated email inbox and respond instantly whenever a new message was received. The agent was also connected to various knowledge sources, such as internal documents, SharePoint sites and databases containing engagement information. Additionally, it was integrated with systems like SAP and ServiceNow to ensure comprehensive access to the data needed for accurate decision-making.

The initial deployment of the agent focused on a single email inquiry, but McKinsey quickly realized its potential for scalability. The agent was soon expanded to handle a wide range of client engagements. Over time, it processed more than 1300 engagements, with dozens of inquiries in progress at any given moment. This ability to scale across multiple processes provided significant value. McKinsey envisioned the creation of an orchestration layer, where multiple autonomous agents could be deployed to support individuals, teams and entire business functions—ultimately helping the firm streamline operations across various departments.

While the agent was highly effective in automating many tasks, it occasionally required human intervention. In some cases, the agent would encounter a scenario it could not resolve, such as identifying a partner who had left the firm. In these instances, the agent was programmed to escalate the issue to a human manager. When such a situation arose, a notification was sent to a manager via Copilot Studio, prompting them to review the case and reassign it to the appropriate partner. This collaborative approach ensured that the agent could still operate efficiently while leaving more nuanced decision-making in the hands of human experts.

The deployment of autonomous agents yielded impressive results for McKinsey, which reported a 90 per cent reduction in lead time for handling client inquiries, along with a 30 per cent reduction in administrative overhead. These gains translated into increased operational efficiency and allowed McKinsey's staff to focus on higher-value tasks, rather than getting bogged down in manual processes. As McKinsey continues to refine and expand its use of autonomous agents, it is positioned to further optimize its client experience and internal operations.[38]

This example demonstrates the potential of agentic AI to transform not just client engagement but also the broader business landscape and globally across society at large. Nadella seems driven to spread the mantra of the AI–Copilot era around the world. In his interview with *WIRED*, he explains why he feels so compelled:

> I am haunted by the fact that the Industrial Revolution didn't touch the parts of the world where I grew up until much later. So, I am looking for the thing that may be even bigger than the industrial revolution and really doing what the industrial revolution did for the West for everyone in the world. That means 8 billion people have abundance. That's a fantastic world to live in . . . My dream is that every one of Earth's 8 billion people can have an AI tutor, an AI doctor, a programmer and maybe a consultant.[39]

For instance, nonprofit organization NC Fusion used Copilot in Dynamics 365 Customer Insights to quickly create communications for an advertising campaign that reached thousands of families. Sikshana Foundation has developed the Shiksha co-pilot to enhance educational results and enable educators to construct detailed, age-specific curriculums. Utilizing Azure OpenAI technology, it equips teachers with the ability to formulate an entire lesson plan in a matter of minutes rather than hours. Ravindra K. Nagaiah, a government schoolteacher, says, 'The old method of chalk and blackboard is not sufficient anymore. The time saved by Shiksha, I'm spending with the kids.'[40]

National and Global Digital Public Infrastructures

So far, in this chapter, we have examined the co-intelligence architectures created by private sector tech-forward enterprises. Let us examine initiatives at national and global levels aiming to develop digital public infrastructures/goods (DPIs/DPGs). In fact, DPIs must now leverage co-intelligence to augment value. We call this **Co-Intelligence DPI** or **CoDPI**. It's important to note that not all digital infrastructures qualify as CoDPIs. To be considered a CoDPI, a digital infrastructure must possess five essential characteristics: i) Interoperability: enabling different technologies and service providers to work together smoothly; (ii) Open standards: allowing others to easily build on and connect their services; (iii) Societal scale: achieving broad reach without being limited by geographic, cultural or societal factors; (iv) Governance mechanisms: ensuring clear rules and guidelines to operate safely and responsibly; and (v) Co-Intelligence: leveraging Human–AI interactions to amplify wellbeing impacts sustainably, addressing complex challenges for both people and the planet.

Indian and Global Digital Public Infrastructures for Achieving UN SDGs

Capturing how India's DPIs helped unlock innovation and solve societal problems at population scale, Amitabh Kant, India's G20 Sherpa and the former CEO of NITI Aayog, India's apex public policy think tank, said:

> With effective implementation of DPI, India leapfrogged 40 years of development and made progress in 7 years which was expected to be achieved in 47 years. Any country can use the already developed DPIs and innovate on top of the same.[41]

In 2021, India had 1.1 billion mobile phone connections (79 per cent of the population), over 624 million Internet users (45 per cent of the population) and 448 million social media users (32 per cent of the population). In 2020, India consumed ten times more data than it did in 2015, and in 2022, it had one of the lowest costs of mobile data in the world in a comparison of 233 countries and accounted for about 40 per cent of the world's digital payments in 2024. [42,43] But the technological progress is uneven. Kris Gopalakrishnan, a technology business leader and co-founder of Infosys, opines:

> You can see Industrial Revolutions 1.0, 2.0, 3.0 and 4.0 operating simultaneously in India, making it unique. Technology must be carefully leveraged to create positive impact for the diversity of the population here. [44]

Indian Prime Minister Narendra Modi sees technology 'as a means to empower and as a tool that bridges the distance between hope and opportunity' in the country's journey towards becoming a developed nation by 2047. [45,46] Aadhaar, India's biometric and digital identity system, has become the largest of its kind in the world, having gained 1 billion users in just 5.5 years. This growth outpaced that of many popular online and social media platforms in the world. People use Aadhaar for various government services, like getting direct money transfers. The PM-KISAN chatbot that we discussed in Chapter 1 leverages this population-scale identity infrastructure. Aadhaar has also made it cheaper for banks to add new customers, dropping the cost of verifying customers from Rs 1500 to just Rs 10. This reduction has encouraged banks to serve those who previously did not have bank accounts. By 2018, the number of Indian adults with bank accounts had more than doubled in seven years, covering 80 per cent of the population. [47]

Nandan Nilekani, co-founder of Infosys and founding chairman of the Unique Identification Authority of India

(UIDAI), which issues Aadhaar, a digital identity for every Indian, remarks about how India has developed capabilities to 'use digital technology at a population scale to transform society' and how as a result the country is moving from 'multiple micro-economies to online mega economy'.[48] Technology has truly transformed the daily life–experiences of ordinary citizens of India, and at an astonishing pace. In particular, India's DPI has played a significant role in enabling SDIs of organizations across sectors in the country's remarkable growth in the last decade. Nilekani says,

> Now, around 1.3 billion Indians possess this digital ID and on average 10 million eKYC per day is being facilitated through Aadhar. Meanwhile in payment, UPI facilitates 13 billion transactions monthly, serving about 350 million individuals and 50 million merchants and DPI enabled direct transfer has saved Government $41 billion across Central Government Schemes. Therefore, it's no longer a choice or a luxury, DPI is essential to get to where we want.[49]

The National Payments Corporation of India (NPCI), the entity responsible for developing and operating UPI, under the guidance of the Reserve Bank of India (RBI) and the Indian Banks' Association (IBA), has integrated digital payments into the daily lives of Indian citizens, making DPI a critical infrastructure for economic growth and innovation.

The Covid-19 pandemic catalysed India's digital payments transformation. Consider these scenarios that played out in every street in India then: a small-time vegetable seller or the owner of a nondescript kirana (small retail shop) in rural India—segments that contribute significantly to the country's retail sales, were wary of exchanging currency notes for grocery purchases due to a fear of contamination of the virus. But by then the government had created the United Payment Interface (UPI), India's digital payment protocol, on which private players like Google (GPay), Walmart (PhonePe) and PayTM developed their payment apps. The small retailers embraced these QR-code- and UPI-enabled digital payment systems. By 2021, one third of Indian households used digital payments, and this included one out of four households in the poorest 40 per cent of India.[50] The real-time financial payment transactions crossed 48 billion in India, which was six and a half times the combined volume of the world's leading economies: the US, Canada, the UK, France and Germany.[51] Further, the Reserve Bank Innovation Hub, chaired by Kris Gopalakrishnan, chairman of Axilor Ventures and co-founder of Infosys, began piloting innovations such as digitalization of the Kisan Credit Card (KCC) and the Unified Lending Interface (ULI) to improve access to rural finance/credit.[52]

Now consider India's Open Network Digital Commerce (ONDC), a digital public infrastructure that operates as an open-network e-marketplace for commerce and mobility services. ONDC's earliest pilot, Kochi Open Mobility Network (KOMN), was launched in October 2020 to bring about interoperability among different mobility service providers—taxis, buses, ferries and so on. KOMN has Yatri App (which has 1200+ registered taxi drivers, recorded 15,000+ customer searches and supports hundreds of taxi rides per week) and Stayhalo Telegram bot (which enables customers to book cabs in Kochi and view Kochi Metro Rail schedules).[53] A startup, Juspay, partnered with the Bengaluru Autorickshaw Drivers Union and launched its Namma Yatri app on ONDC in 2022. It soon expanded its services to other cities such as Chennai and New Delhi. Competing with closed-loop mobility platforms like Uber and Ola, Namma Yatri has since served over 200,000 drivers and 4 million customers and facilitated more than 25 million trips.[54] Since ONDC is open, we are witnessing other startups quickly launch competing apps in different cities—in 2023, Yaary joined the ONDC ride-hailing bandwagon and launched its services in Hyderabad, India.[55]

In February 2024, Uber signed an MoU with ONDC to explore mobility service integration. Uber CEO Dara Khosrowshahi, in a conversation with Nandan Nilekani on building population-scale technology, reflects on the opportunities that such DPIs offer Uber:

> Historically, the Uber business started on the streets of Paris and came from hailing high-end luxury cars. Uber has been more in four-wheelers. One of the biggest strategic opportunities for us is in the low-cost space—three-wheelers, two-wheelers—we're building a bus service for high capacity, vehicles that work for longer distances. It's an extraordinary opportunity for us to expand our services to a wider swath of the population.[56]

The DPIs help with seamless driver onboarding, which is one of the largest costs for Uber in the US. Offerings like Aadhaar and its eKYC service and DigiLocker (think of it as a Dropbox for government-authenticated documents) can potentially streamline the process for drivers to join Uber. Verifying documents and background checks can be done much faster, allowing drivers to hit the road quicker. What currently takes a couple of weeks to complete in the US can be done in a day in India. The DPIs include services like UPI for digital payments, which can be leveraged to offer micro payments for shorter trips or rides on budget-friendly options like autorickshaws and two-wheelers. This can attract a wider customer base who might not otherwise use Uber due to cost concerns. By integrating with platforms like ONDC, Uber can potentially offer a wider range of mobility options within its app. This could include connecting riders with public buses, taxis or rentals and creating a one-stop shop for urban mobility needs. Khosrowshahi says, 'We are rooting for this ecosystem to thrive not only in India but also in (other) developing countries. Elsewhere this model expands; it will be a win for society but also for Uber.'[57]

While India's success story firmly established the link between UN SDGs as desired outcomes and DPIs as implementation mechanisms, in 2023, a midpoint evaluation by the UN of its 2030 SDGs showed significant challenges globally. Among the assessable targets, a mere 15 per cent were on track to be achieved. Further, over one-third of these targets had experienced no progress or had regressed below the 2015 baseline.[58] António Guterres, secretary general, United Nations, gave a grim warning: 'Unless we act now, the 2030 Agenda will become an epitaph for a world that might have been.'

There is an opportunity to put DPIs at the centre stage of new efforts to create sustainable wellbeing impacts. The United Nations Development Programme (UNDP) report, 'Accelerating the SDGs through Digital Public Infrastructure', that came out of the G20 deliberations, suggested that DPIs are capable of accelerating economic growth (20–33 per cent via financial DPIs), offsetting carbon emissions (4 per cent reduction for LMICs (Low- or Middle-Income Country) through carbon-trading DPIs) and improving access to public institutions (28–42 per cent more access to justice via DPIs facilitating faster case management and reliable online dispute resolution) by 2030.[59]

An analysis of the global state of DPIs across 210 countries has identified 57 digital identity systems, 93 countries with digital payment systems and 103 data exchange systems.[60] One of the recent efforts in 2025 is EuroStack, which proposes a layered digital stack that integrates AI, cloud computing, semiconductor technology, cybersecurity and federated data spaces to reduce Europe's dependency on technology imports. It aims to enhance the continent's digital sovereignty and support sectors from finance to healthcare.[61] As DPIs continue to evolve at regional-, national-, continental- or global-scale, they drive sustainable wellbeing impacts across ecosystems of life-experiences. See **Figure 3-1** for an illustrative list of global DPIs at mature-stage supporting UN SDGs.

UN SDG	DPI	Country	Impact
No Poverty, Reduced Inequalities	Novissi—social disbursements during Covid-19 To deliver contactless, emergency digital cash transfers at a societal scale. Built on an open-source toolkit, Cider.	Togo	Within a year, the platform disbursed U.S.$24 million to 0.8 million beneficiaries. Up to 21 percent lesser exclusion error in identification of beneficiaries using Cider's prediction models
No Poverty, Reduced Inequalities	ePhilID—digital ID system Protects economically vulnerable groups with benefits, grants legal status and provides access to basic services. Built on India's MOSIP DPI.	Philippines	By May 2023, 30 million IDs were issued.
Good Health and Well-being	Health Data Hub Is a unified platform that aggregates administrative data from various sources such as hospitals, insurance providers and research institutions	France	Has supported over 1600 projects
Quality Education	OpenCerts Is a blockchain-based platform for issuing and verifying digital academic certificates	Singapore	7 months of working time saved per institute
Affordable and Clean Energy	National Carbon Registry Enables countries to manage national data and processes for the effective trading of carbon credits	UNDP	
Decent Work and Economic Growth	InstaPay—retail payment service Enables payments across different banks and wallets and helps MSEs collect payments and build credit-worthiness.	Philippines	Its monthly transaction volume has reached 52 million.
Climate Action	Global Forest Watch (GFW) Uses geospatial data to generate near-real-time deforestation alerts.	World Resources Institute	It has been adopted across nearly 25 countries. 52 per cent decline in deforestation among groups empowered by GFW's platform compared to control groups.
Life Below Water	Global Fishing Watch (GFW) Tracks fishing vessels to combat illegal, unreported and unregulated fishing. Enforces fishing policies, enabling governments to monitor commercial fishing activities.	Global Fishing Watch	20 per cent of the global industrial fishing fleet are covered by the Open Ocean Project, an initiative under GFW.
Industry, Innovation and Infrastructure	SGFinDex—Singapore Financial Data Exchange It is foundational infrastructure for digital finance and enables people to access and understand how their financial data is employed by government agencies and private service providers.	Singapore	SGFinDex has 30,000 monthly active users
Peace, Justice and Strong Institutions	FranceConnect—online identity solution Fosters strong institutions, promoting justice and equal access to public services for everyone, including non-French individuals with French social security.	France	Helps over 40 million users access 1400+ digital services online via identity verification.
Partnership for the goals	X-Road—cross-border DPI for information exchange Implemented as DPI in 20+ countries to facilitate information exchange. Makes international data exchange and trade processes, like tax filing, more efficient.	Estonia	It enables 1.5 billion data transactions annually.

Figure 3-1: An Illustrative List of Global DPIs at Mature-Stage Supporting UN SDGs (Source: Adapted by the authors from a UNDP report)

Finternet—Combining the Power of DPIs with a Unified Ledger System

India's DPIs and its transformative capacity, along with the open architecture of distributed ledger technology, have inspired Nilekani and Agustín Carstens, an economist with the Bank for International Settlements (the central bank for central banks of nations), to propose the idea of *the Finternet* for the world—a seamless, inclusive and interoperable network of financial services. Carstens says,

> The Finternet is a vision of multiple financial ecosystems that connect with each other, much like the internet. It aims to empower individuals and businesses by helping them to have full control of their financial lives . . . We foresee a system in which individuals and businesses could transfer any financial asset, in any amount, at any time, using any device, to anyone else, anywhere in the world. Financial transactions would be cheap, secure and near instantaneous. And they would be available to anyone.[62]

Consider a small business owner who needs capital to start her business. Traditionally, she would face cumbersome paper-based processes to secure a loan against her property. In the Finternet ecosystem, she can 'tokenize' her property documents, securing a loan quickly and securely. This tokenization allows her to access and share verified data with lenders, who can then provide a loan based on these authenticated tokens, streamlining the entire process and ensuring transparency. Besides regulated financial products such as loans, Finternet allows for the management of a wide range of assets, whether they are user-controlled, such as personal content or NFTs, attested assets that are certified by a trusted authority, or registered assets like real estate.

The technical architecture of Finternet is built on a user-centric model, where individuals or businesses are placed at the centre of the ecosystem. Users interact with a variety of applications that serve as gateways to their assets, all of which are tokenized. These tokens are stored on a *unified ledger system*, which isn't restricted to a single technology but can support multiple ledgers (such as Ethereum). The system is supported by trust services that verify the authenticity of assets, adding an extra layer of security. Additionally, the architecture allows for interoperability across different ledgers and composability, meaning different types of assets can be combined seamlessly in transactions—for example, in the scenario above, the business owner can obtain a loan and an insurance cover, offered by different vendors.[63]

While we have focused on India's UPI, Brazil's Pix and Thailand's PromptPay are two other examples of fast payment systems (FPS) that have achieved remarkable success in driving the adoption of digital payments nationally, with a user-centric design, a robust settlement infrastructure, mandatory participation of large banks, a strong role for public-sector governance (in particular the central bank), and open application programming interfaces (APIs) and aliases (e.g., mobile phone numbers) to initiate payments with low transaction costs. Brazil's Pix, like UPI, also encourages private-sector innovation on its DPI. Following the success of Pix, the Central Bank of Brazil (BCB) has started a new initiative called Drex, which aims to create a digital version of its Brazilian 'real' currency. The Drex system includes Drex itself (digital money issued by the central bank), a platform for using Drex, the organizations that will use this platform, and rules and regulations for how it all works. The Drex platform is a digital ledger where different types of money and financial assets can exist together, including central bank money, bank deposits, electronic money and government bonds. This initiative involves close collaboration between the BCB, the Brazilian government, financial regulators and private companies.[64]

Continuing with Brazil, we next examine the case of ES 500 and the need for co-designing SDIs within a shared ecosystem

space and engaging with coalitions of organizations and
building collaborative ecosystem capabilities, together with all
stakeholders.

Espírito Santo—Vision 2035

The ES 500 movement (Espírito Santo 500th anniversary)
marks a groundbreaking approach to regional development
planning for the Brazilian state of Espírito Santo, setting a vision
for 2035, its 500th anniversary. Unlike traditional plans that
primarily rely on economic forecasting (instead of foresight), ES
500 adopts a co-creative, AI-powered framework that merges
human and artificial intelligence to collaboratively shape the
state's long-term trajectory.

In a courageous attempt orchestrated by a public–private
coalition between the visionary planning secretary of the state
government (SEP) and the influential business association ES
em Ação, ES 500 launched a long-term collaborative multi-
stakeholder governance initiative in December 2023 with the
support of Symnetics and GoFw. This initiative brings to the core
of the movement the collective aspirations of representatives
from state and municipal governments, businesses, academia
and civil society institutions gathered in 'mission groups'.
These groups are supported by an AI-assisted intelligence hub,
a communication and engagement platform formed by multiple
channels (social networks, proprietary community platforms,
public committees and councils) and advised by a public
assembly. ES has embarked on five state missions as ambitions
and commitments for the future, co-created by 200 institutions,
which will be expanded with the participation of thousands of
state citizens in 2025.

At its core, ES 500 is designed as a multi-stakeholder
governance model that continuously integrates insights from
public, private and civil society organizations. It leverages
advanced AI tools within the intelligence hub to facilitate
collective visioning and planning among mission groups

representing the various mission group stakeholders. For instance:

- NotebookLM organizes and synthesizes inputs from 250 experts, aggregating diverse insights into actionable frameworks.
- PerplexityPro explores and analyses innovative public policies globally, identifying transformative practices that can inspire local applications.
- Gemini and GPT-4 assist in refining the strategic vision and generating adaptive scenarios to meet future challenges.
- Visualizations generated through MidJourney and refined by Firefly bring the ES 500 vision to life, producing images and videos that capture the imagination of stakeholders and citizens.

Co-Creating Five Missions for a Sustainable Future

ES 500 has developed five transformative missions, collaboratively crafted by over 200 institutions and aimed at fostering a diverse, resilient and innovative state economy:

1. *New Economic Model:* Expands economic diversification into emerging sectors like bioeconomy and blue economy. This mission aligns R&D with entrepreneurship and upgrades logistics infrastructure to support sustainable growth.
2. *Competence Hub:* Focuses on professional upskilling, reskilling and an adaptive education system to meet evolving work demands. This mission envisions a workforce that is equipped for both the present and future needs of the economy.
3. *Integral Care:* Prioritizes preventive healthcare, affordable housing and social cohesion initiatives, creating a foundation for a healthy, inclusive and supportive community.
4. *Regeneration of Territories and Biomes:* Supports an energy transition, circular economy, resilient city infrastructure

and biodiversity conservation to position Espírito Santo as a leader in sustainable practices.

5. *ES Digital:* Develops digital public infrastructure to support 'digital by default' services and participatory governance, empowering citizens with accessible, tech-driven public services.

Social Intelligence Meets AI: The Co-Creative Advantage

By continuously engaging stakeholders and specialists since its inception, ES 500 embraces insights, viewpoints and experiences from multiple agents and sectors. It combines AI technologies with human-driven *social* intelligence, enabling inclusive dialogues and fostering a shared vision across diverse sectors. AI not only accelerates data analysis and policy exploration but also democratizes strategic planning by making the process more accessible and transparent. The integration of AI tools such as GPT-4 for conceptual development and PerplexityPro for policy innovation enables a depth of analysis and foresight that traditional planning methods often lack.

Through these AI-assisted platforms, stakeholders across sectors are able to:

• Engage in real-time feedback loops that iterate on development strategies.
• Access curated, data-driven insights from global best practices.
• Visualize future scenarios that align with the aspirations of Espírito Santo's citizens, fostering a shared sense of purpose and direction.

The ES500 SDI enables a two-way dialogue between decision-makers and the community, ensuring that development strategies remain responsive to the people's needs and aspirations. As ES 500 progresses, its co-creative, AI-driven framework stands as a model for future-oriented governance with SWIs as a North Star.

By embedding co-intelligence in each phase of development, ES 500 not only sets a strategic pathway for Espírito Santo but also serves as a pioneering example of how AI can facilitate sustainable, inclusive and adaptive planning. The initiative's commitment to an agile and collaborative approach promises a future for Espírito Santo that reflects the state's history while dynamically responding to the demands of an evolving global landscape.

The Next Frontier of Co-Intelligence Driven Value Creation

Since 2011, with the cloud/mobile Web 2.0 era, the *Information Age has witnessed an acceleration in the liquification of IT*. Rather than businesses going to where IT was (as exemplified best by mainframe-powered centralized IT centres), IT got embedded in business processes and automated them. Earlier, the IT industry adopted management principles from other industries—for instance, the way software was developed was called the 'waterfall model', inspired by the sequential and automated factory model from the automobile industry. Soon, the IT industry was teaching business-model lessons to other industries with agile development—for instance, cloud computing and software-as-a-service (SaaS) models inspired industries like manufacturing (digital twins), healthcare (telemedicine), education (massive open online courses, or MOOCs) and so on.

In an increasingly tech-intensive world, concepts such as *digital transformation*, *algorithms*, *automation* and *AI* became popular. Due to the absorption of digitization across the enterprise, there was a *softwarization* of the value chain and an increased adoption of AI. Porter and Heppelmann recognized this trend and proposed the idea of value chains influenced by smart connected products. For instance, a tractor went from being just a product to becoming part of a system of systems.[65] Similarly, healthcare IT progressed from mainframes to mobile, influencing hospital systems architectures. Healthcare providers are shifting from their current monolithic electronic health records (EHR)-centric IT systems to other flexible architectures as part of their digital transformation and in order to keep pace with business, clinical and consumer expectations—examples include patient-centric architectures (including aspects of traditional care, home care, social care and a focus on wellness).[66] In their 2019 book *Reinventing the Product*, David Sovie and Eric Schaeffer say: 'Products that are rendered digitally intelligent will instead be designed to interact with their makers, their users and other products over their whole lifespan. Value chains will turn into value circles or even multi-directional value generating systems.'[67] As a result, there is a *fundamental shift in the locus of enactment towards Human–AI co-intelligence flows of interactive engagements*.

We have also witnessed the rapid emergence of *industry clouds* from hyperscalers—Amazon Web Services, Google Cloud, Microsoft, Oracle, and xAI—and other business technology providers such as SAP (as well as system integrators and a vast network of software and application partners), as well as through smart connected offering ecosystems of industrial product companies. For instance, Microsoft Cloud for Healthcare offers the AI-powered Azure Health Bot as a conversational interface for patients, Guidewire offers insurance industry-specific cloud solutions, Philips HealthSuite Digital Platform provides an end-to-end oncology care pathway to hospitals and so on. These industry clouds further enable smart connected flows of interactive engagements in relational ecosystems, accelerating Life-Xverse innovation and its impacts at scale and scope. Rather than requiring all the high-end technology infrastructures to be available on-premises and within an enterprise, businesses can access sophisticated and highly scalable technology stacks in a hybrid fashion across multiple clouds. As a result, there is also *a concomitant shift in the locus of capability towards SDI platforms*, especially as tech-forward enterprises offer *service-as-a-capability* to other enterprises, facilitating cross-sector ecosystem co-innovation towards Human–AI interactive engagement and value co-creation, even as they craft their own co-intelligence enterprise architectures.

Another outcome of *softwarization + AI*, as we will see further in the next chapter, is the growth of private-sector platform businesses of value creation. Platforms connect producers and consumers with each other, allowing them to create an exchange of service and facilitating these interactions at scale (e.g., Airbnb). Geoffrey G. Parker, Marshall W. Van Alstyne and Sangeet Paul Choudary explore such 'technology platforms as a means of value creation'.[68] Platform businesses bring in significant efficiencies of scale—they reduce search costs (of discovering products or services), bargaining costs (by standardizing transactions) and verification costs (by acting as a central intermediary).

At the same time, the rapid evolution of GenAI-based language models is accelerating the *joint creation* of humans working *together with* machines, with *humans-in-the-loop* of AI systems, as well as *AI systems-in-the-loop* of humans. The co-creative power of Human–AI interactive engagement, with generative machine intelligence augmenting human intelligence, amplifies human creative potential in a virtuous cycle.

As tech-forward organizations venture into the next frontier of innovation and value creation, there is a growing recognition of the *migration of value to the top of the tech stack in its interfaces and applications*. Consequently, as they expand their *loci of enactment and capability*, we are also seeing a *shift in the locus of activity towards the lived-journey of creative-experiencers* in customer organizations (e.g., Salesforce's AI journey with Aston Martin). Simultaneously, there is also a *shift in the locus of strategy towards interconnected ecosystems*, as we saw through the various examples in this chapter. These shifts in the loci of activity and strategy are also cascading downstream as various established enterprises in different industries transform their own organizations. Vijay Govindarajan and Venkat Venkataraman show how leading companies (inside and outside of tech) are *using datagraphs* to personalize customer recommendations, update products, optimize advertising and more. Enterprises gain a comprehensive view of how consumers interact with their products and services so that they can develop unique ways to solve customer problems.[69] In their 2024 book *Fusion Strategy*, they discuss how datagraphs are facilitating the fusion of the physical industrial world with digital and the migration of value towards harnessing data +AI in real time.

Finally, there is also a *shift in the locus of performance towards SWIs*. We saw how SAP is expanding the locus of performance towards what it calls the *green line* in addition to the conventional *bottom line* of economic profits. Tech-forward companies have also embraced bold SDG targets. For instance, Microsoft is 'committed to being carbon negative by 2030 and by 2050 to remove from the atmosphere an equivalent amount of all the carbon dioxide emitted either directly or by (its) electricity consumption since 1975,' when it was founded.[70]

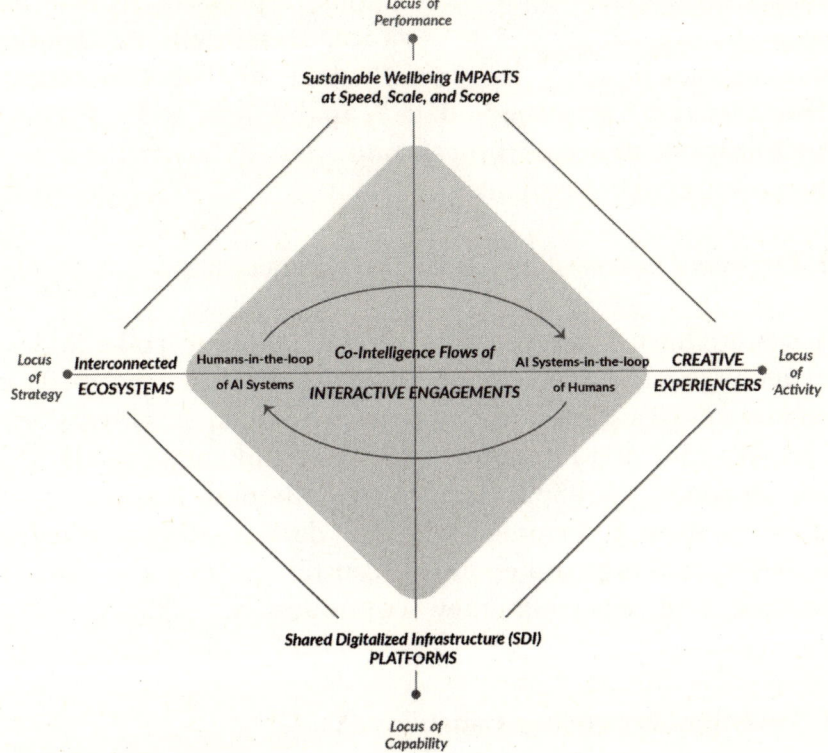

Figure 3-2: Crafting and Leveraging Co-Intelligence Architectures for Life-Xverse Innovation and Value Co-Creation (Source: Venkat Ramaswamy)

Building on these conceptual insights (see **Figure 3-2 above**), here are some key takeaways in crafting and leveraging co-intelligence architectures:

1. Establish Shared Digitalized Infrastructure (SDI) Platforms

SDI platforms serve as the foundation for a co-intelligence architecture by enabling seamless data access, interoperability and real-time analytics across various stakeholders. Organizations should prioritize cloud infrastructure that allows multi-party data interactions, especially critical for collaborative projects. For instance, Databricks exemplifies this approach with its unified data analytics platform, democratizing advanced data capabilities and allowing organizations to access, process and apply data insights across interconnected ecosystems.

2. Empower Stakeholders as Creative Experiencers

A co-intelligence architecture should facilitate stakeholders to act as creative participants rather than passive users. This involves creating platforms where customers, employees and partners can interact, contribute ideas and shape outcomes. For instance, HubSpot transforms inbound marketing by allowing users to leverage real-time data to adapt strategies actively, making stakeholders central to the co-creation process and ensuring they continuously enhance value through interaction.

3. Leverage Service-as-a-Capability (SaaC)

Leveraging scalable, on-demand services as core capabilities in offerings ensures that all stakeholders—employees, customers and partners—can engage in co-creation. Platforms that provide SaaC reduce dependency on isolated expertise and encourage continuous innovation. For instance, Salesforce's Agentforce allows Aston Martin to personalize customer engagement by integrating AI-powered insights directly into their customer interactions, providing dynamic data and insights as a service that enhances Aston Martin's value innovation.

4. Incorporate Data Sovereignty, AI Ethics and Governance

Organizations need to implement robust ethical frameworks and governance mechanisms to ensure data sovereignty, fairness and transparency. These frameworks not only protect user data but also help maintain trust with stakeholders. For instance, Salesforce exemplifies this approach through its Einstein AI platform, which integrates comprehensive ethical standards and data sovereignty protocols. By continuously monitoring and auditing AI outputs for bias and reliability, Salesforce ensures that AI-driven decisions align with both regulatory standards and ethical guidelines. Through its Data Cloud, Salesforce also enables secure data integration across platforms, allowing data to flow efficiently while respecting privacy laws. Meta's open-source foundation models for GenAI contribute to a transparent AI ecosystem by promoting accessibility and encouraging external auditing, aligning with data sovereignty and responsible AI governance standards.

5. Enable Continuous Co-Discovery and Adaptation

Foster a culture of co-discovery, where AI and human insights together drive continuous improvements and innovations. Platforms should be designed to facilitate this dynamic, iterative process where feedback loops support ongoing refinement. For instance, Microsoft's use of Copilot AI agents in McKinsey's decision-making process illustrates how co-discovery allows rapid response to evolving business conditions by combining human expertise with AI-driven recommendations.

6. Embrace Ecosystem-Wide Networked Collaboration

Engage in networked collaborations with industry partners, leveraging joint infrastructure and shared standards. These alliances enhance resilience, accelerate knowledge transfer and create comprehensive solutions for shared challenges. For instance, Google Cloud and AWS exemplify how interconnected ecosystem collaboration can foster innovation through shared standards and infrastructure that allow organizations to access a wide array of co-intelligence resources and applications.

7. Design for Sustainable Wellbeing Impacts (SWIs)

Move beyond short-term performance metrics to focus on SWIs that align with broader societal and environmental goals. This involves configuring architectures to generate measurable impacts, such as reduced carbon footprint and community engagement. For instance, SAP's emphasis on the *green line* as a metric alongside traditional financial performance indicates a shift towards prioritizing SWIs, wherein sustainability goals guide architecture decisions and operational strategies.

In the next chapter, we delve deeper into how any organization (including those outside the tech industry) can visualize and expand Human–AI co-creation of new value.

4

The PIEX Lens: Visualizing and Expanding Human–AI Co-Creation of Value

Unlike the Industrial Revolution of the past 150 years, where value creation was centred on goods and services, followed by the Information Age, where it was centred on IT-enabled digitalization, the new co-intelligence realm amplifies the creativity of human intelligence through machine intelligence—harnessing joint creativeness to engender valuable impacts of life–experiences. With the birthing of a newfound Human–AI interactive engagement, humans now have the general ability to interact with intelligence systems and together bring the context of their varied life–experiences to co-create more meaningful and unique value at the speed, scale and scope of potential impacts as never before, while managing its risks along the way.[1] Organizations must engage with all stakeholders across sectors to leverage a whole new realm of interactional value creation, grounded in life–experiences.

We introduce a new organizational lens (see **Figure 4-1**)—the *PIEX* lens (*P*latforms of *I*nteractive *E*ngagements driving *Im*pacts in *E*cosystems of life-e*X*periences)—to visualize co-intelligence flows and configure platforms for risk-managed Human–AI co-creation of Value. This lens focuses on creating value by leveraging *interactive engagements* as the engine that drives *sustainable wellbeing impacts* (SWI) via *shared digitalized infrastructure* (SDI) platforms. The PIEX lens has a ***dual*** focus on processes *and* outcomes of value, underscoring both the dynamic process of engagement and the tangible outcomes of Value it produces, bringing about transformative, life-enhancing experiences across interconnected ecosystems. As we will see, the 'IE' in PIEX lens is a dual-layer concept, where both *I*nteractive *E*ngagements and *I*mpacts in *E*cosystems coexist.

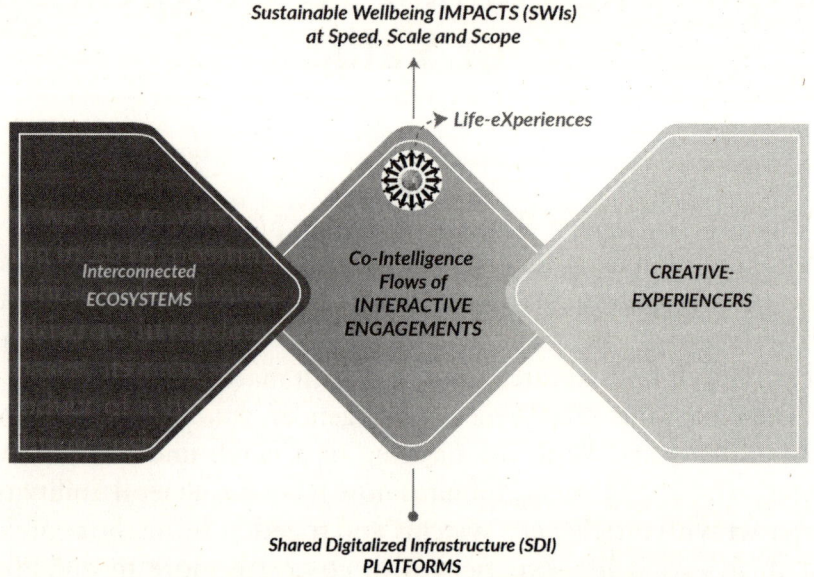

Figure 4-1: The PIEX Lens: Platforms of Interactive Engagements Driving Impacts in Ecosystems of Life-eXperiences (Source: Venkat Ramaswamy)

Visualizing Co-Intelligence Flows

At the heart of PIEX lens visualization are *co-intelligence flows of interactive engagements* of humans as creative-experiencers. The *creative-experiencers* include *all stakeholders* of an organization such as customers, employees/managers and partners, as well as financiers, regulators and other entities (including citizens at large). Creative-experiencers are not mere passive participants consuming an organization's offerings; they are *interactively engaged* to co-create new life–experiences. Rather than merely focusing on the activities in the value chain, enterprises must go beyond to focus on the flows of value in the *lived-journeys* of individuals as creative-experiencers.

Organizational ecosystems in a co-intelligence world are *networked AI systems* of interacting physical-digital-embodied entities and their environments mediated by *SDI platforms*.[2] Purpose-built platformization of resourced capabilities spawns new arrangements of interactive *agency*. Enterprises build coalitions with other ecosystem organizations, often across sectors—private, public and plural—both to co-innovate interactive-system environments and to co-create value through the interactive engagements of creative-experiencers. The Life-Xverse environments in ecosystem engagements of creative-experiencers offer:[3]

i.   Opportunities for creative-experiencers to construct their own life–experiences on demand.
ii.   Facilitate responsive and responsible individual-to-networked AI system-to-individual (I2N2I) interactions for all stakeholders.
iii. Accommodate a heterogeneous group of creative-experiencers, from digital natives to the digitally unsophisticated.
iv.   Enable networked AI system-to-individual-to-networked AI system (N2I2N) interactions in the lived-journey engagements of stakeholding individuals as creative-experiencers.
v.   Recognize that stakeholding individuals may be active or passive in different contexts.

Valuable impacts are engendered across interactive system environments in ecosystems through *emergent life–experiences*, which must be co-created through *Human–AI interactive engagements* across the *Life-Xverse*.[4] If an organizational ecosystem is to create an experience that is unique and meaningful to a creative-experiencer, it cannot be created solely by that organization—it must necessarily involve that individual and the organization's ecosystem (often involving coalitions with other organizations). Life–experiences of potential value emanate from the enactment of interactional creation in co-intelligence flows of engagements in the creative-experiencer's lived-journey. It must be *risk-managed* appropriately. Moreover, value co-creation across the Life-Xverse needs to be more fully recognized through SWIs at *speed* (time taken for SWIs), *scale* (the extent of SWIs) and *scope* (the domains of SWIs)—the North Star of co-intelligence driven Life-Xverse innovation and value co-creation. Organizations are increasingly measuring their impacts through SDG (sustainable development goal) metrics and ESG (environmental, social and governance) scorecards.

Let us discuss some examples to illustrate how *PIEX lens* visualization provides *a new frame of reference* for co-intelligence Life-Xverse innovation and value co-creation.

EV + Autonomy at Monarch Tractor

Take, for instance, farming in the US with Monarch Tractor offering 'the world's first 100 per cent electric, driver optional, connected tractor'.[5] Its founders bring a unique blend of expertise in farming, electric vehicles (EVs) and AI—CEO Praveen Penmetsa is an autonomy and mobility engineer; chief farming officer Carlo Mondavi is a sustainability-focused vintner (wine merchant); President Mark Schwager is the former chief of Tesla Gigafactory and CTO Zachary Omohundro is a robotics PhD from Carnegie Mellon. They talk the language of agriculture as much as they converse in the dialect of sustainability or autonomy. Monarch primarily aims to drive farm profitability in a scenario where about 40 per cent of US farms are facing bankruptcy.[6] It also aims to decarbonize the farm and the farming equipment in a scenario where the industry is a major contributor of carbon emissions.

The Monarch tractor itself is an EV that doesn't guzzle diesel and enables the energy transition of farming. It can also act as a mobile genset, where the farmer can power devices off of the tractor in the middle of the field, and it is connected to a solar system at the farm barn that acts as energy storage. In California, there is even a programme where farmers can make money by putting this energy back into the grid. Monarch allows farmers to employ their existing farming processes and implements with their tractors, thus making the adoption of their tractors easier.

Monarch tractors are virtually supercomputing robots in the field, creating value in new ways together with farmers as creative-experiencers. The farmers are engaged with the Monarch offering ecosystem in their daily lived-journeys of agricultural activities and deriving value in their farming livelihoods and in the communities in which they operate. Technically, the tractor as a smart connected product comprises six NVIDIA Jetson systems on modules, two 3D cameras and six standard cameras.[7] Monarch deploys bi-wire controls in its hydraulics, gearboxes and implement attachments with cloud connectivity. It is this deep technology and AI infusion that truly sets its tractors apart and allows for greater operational efficiencies and cost reduction. For instance, Monarch can easily recognize when two different customers are getting different usage times with their batteries for the same activity of mowing. Using AI and vision cameras, Monarch can suggest simple and small adjustments to the farmer's tractor to become more energy efficient. Such a scenario is not feasible in the context of traditional tractors, where the problem may simply manifest as higher fuel consumption, without any specific additional data points for analysis.

Farmers are also able to use Monarch's under-the-line weeder to mow the grass instead of spraying expensive, environmentally harmful chemicals everywhere, thus saving costs. Using cameras and computer vision algorithms, the tractor gathers and studies crop data every day. It can also deal with information from modern farming tools that have sensors and cameras. This data helps adjust how the tools work in real time, predict future crop yields, understand the current growth stages of plants and check their overall health. Because of edge computing, available through NVIDIA chips on the tractor, it can do the processing in the field in real time without having to send the information to the cloud every time. For instance, it can ensure that the tractor safely moves only within the geofenced region, or it will shut down from spraying if its cameras detect a human on its field path.

Monarch's strategy of creating *open-data platforms* is also novel in an industry that has traditionally adopted closed-loop systems. Penmetsa says:

> Right now, farmers can't even repair their data or do diagnostics on their tractors without approval from the OEM (original equipment manufacturer). What we are doing at Monarch is licensing our technology out to all the tractor companies. One of our big partners, Case New Holland [CNH], is the world's second-largest tractor company. We have given our technology to them, so they sit on our data stack.[8]

At CES 2023 in Las Vegas, US, with Touchcast and Microsoft, CNH showed off a powerful simulation of a commercial customer experience in the metaverse that featured its T4 Electric Power tractor prototype, complete with autonomous features. Visitors were able to virtually experience the tractor. They interacted with a real advisor, asked questions, explored new features, took a virtual test drive, and could buy their vehicle with post-sales support. The Touchcast platform lets enterprises reimagine the customer journey by creating a photorealistic digital twin of their showroom and displaying their vehicles in real-time 3D. Without requiring a VR headset or specialized software, potential customers can browse, customize and purchase their desired vehicle inside the interactive virtual showroom directly from their browser. Silvia Candiani, GM of Microsoft Italy, remarks:

> Industrial Metaverse offers unique opportunities for companies to reimagine the entire customer journey and combine a digital-first experience with the personal touch of a human concierge, all at a fraction of the cost of a physical showroom. It's exciting to see New Holland Agriculture with the contribution of Touchcast, creating a new experience for its customer, showcasing its cutting-edge electric tractor in an innovative way.[9]

Penmetsa ambitiously believes that Monarch is becoming the 'Android of agriculture', as it now offers access to their data lake through APIs to the entire ecosystem—from farmers to tool developers and from agricultural entities to food entities.

Smart Connected Product Experiences at NIO and AB InBev

Now, consider another example of how Human–AI interactive engagements are accelerating and transforming life–experiences through smart connected products. New-age automobile manufacturer NIO Inc. whose Chinese name, '蔚来' (wei lai), translates to 'future', aims to shape a joyful lifestyle around EVs. It has created high-end cars in China that offer sophisticated customer experience using technology and software. NIO vehicles are integrated with NOMI, a voice-activated AI companion that personalizes everyone's experience. NOMI transforms the user experience within the vehicle, from being simply a transportation unit into becoming a travelling digital living space. NOMI can adapt to user preferences, setting wheel positions and seat heights when drivers approach the vehicle, opening/closing windows, snapping selfies, shuffling playlists and other features that vastly improve the average user experience. As of May 2021, NOMI had reached over 200 million interactions.[10] In March 2024, NIO began recruiting beta testers for its NOMI GPT, an LLM-based in-vehicle chatbot that promises to enhance the passenger–vehicle conversation experience.[11]

Outside the vehicle, the NIO app is designed to be a *one-stop platform for its customers*. It enables consumers to buy and customize their vehicles, allows for chat between customers and NIO employees and provides news shared by NIO staff and other car owners. Consider the EV buying and delivery process. Customers can personalize the vehicle they decide to purchase using the NIO app—they can choose the exterior and interior colour, tire outlines, battery plans, loan plans and other features. Once the order is completed, the customer pays a deposit through WeChat Pay. The sales representative then creates a WeChat group comprising the customer, an NIO customer service ambassador, a delivery specialist and a finance specialist. When car owners have questions, they can text in the group chat and expect instant replies from the NIO team. New staff, including maintenance service personnel and repair specialists, are added to the WeChat group, and they may answer any questions that the new car owner might have in the future.

Through the app, users can request a NIO service specialist to pick up their car for valet charging, 24/7. When users plan trips through the NIO app or use NOMI AI, trips can be optimized to recommend charging routes. More than 80 per cent of NIO customers participate in online or real-life community activities, using NIO points/credits—awarded for customer engagements such as community interaction and development, referrals and more. Indeed, this innovative process of owner referral has been fine-tuned successfully by NIO. Since the delivery of its first vehicle in 2018, NIO has built an *online community of enthusiastic owners*, who act as the spokespeople for the company and the cars. Existing owner referrals accounted for more than 45 per cent of its cars sold in 2019.[12]

Human–AI interactive engagements in the creative transformation of life–experiences are not limited just to customer-facing organizations/scenarios but also to employee-facing ones. Consider the case of *AB-InBev*, the largest brewer in the world, which leverages digital twins to create a live online model of their breweries and supply chain. AB InBev's brewmasters can get a real-time view into the complex brewing process and are able to adjust the biological and chemical process parameters based on active conditions. Frontline operators leverage AI algorithms to automatically compensate for bottlenecks in the packaging process, use mixed reality for remote assistance and ensure uptime on the machines. Routing algorithms help the trucks transport beer cases with the lightest carbon footprint and ensure that the right beer and perfect sip are delivered to the consumer at the local pub.[13] Thus, value is created not only through optimized processes and high-quality products but also through enhanced *interactive-system environments of life–experiences* (of quality, taste, sustainability, etc.) throughout the brewing ecosystem.

SDI-Based Innovation—Reliance Retail and People+ai

Reliance Retail is India's largest retail company, with both online and offline channels. JioMart, its online shopping platform, was launched in 2020 in over 200 cities and towns across India. One unusual strategy pursued by Reliance Retail is the fulfilment of JioMart orders of packaged food, grocery and fast moving consumer goods (FMCG) through kiranas (hyperlocal neighbourhood provision stores) enlisted as franchise partners. Since its launch, JioMart has added 2 million merchant partners, with plans to grow them to 10 million in a few years.[14] Jio platforms and Meta announced a partnership in 2020 to accelerate India's digital transformation. Mukesh Ambani, chairman and MD of Reliance Industries, says,

> Mark (Zuckerberg) and I shared a vision of bringing more people and businesses online and creating truly innovative solutions that will add convenience to the daily lives of every Indian. One example of an innovative customer experience that we are proud of developing is the first-ever end-to-end shopping experience with JioMart on WhatsApp.[15]

Shoppers on JioMart can add items to their cart and make a payment to complete the purchase using WhatsApp's UPI-based payment interface—all without leaving the WhatsApp chat.

Now, People+ai, a new community in India, aims to 'connect doers, dreamers, tinkerers and innovators with ideas and resources to build a ecosystem that can empower a billion people to reach their potential'.[16] As its name eloquently suggests, it starts with a focus on people's problems rather than putting AI first. Nilekani, also co-founder of Ekstep, which houses People+ai, says, 'We think AI strategy should be use case led . . . We are not interested in my model is bigger than yours or debates between boomers and doomers in AI. We are in the camp of AI for amplification to make the everyday lives of people better.'[17] Accordingly, People+ai is catalysing several India-specific AI use cases. Its Open Cloud Compute initiative aims to design an open network for compute infrastructure and keep markets competitive for the growing compute demand in India.[18] Or consider India's $10–14 billion last-mile delivery problem due to a lack of structured addresses. People+ai's Sthaan is a virtual address protocol that assigns a human-centric virtual ID, akin to the concept of a beneficiary ID in UPI, linking multiple physical addresses with precise geolocations, street details and machine-readable metadata to optimize last-mile delivery.[19]

Leveraging Co-Intelligence to Transform Life-Experiences through a PIEX Lens

There is a great degree of similarity in all the foregoing examples when viewed through a PIEX lens. In the engagement flows of interactional creation between organizations and individuals as creative-experiencers (whether farmers, software developers, EV buyers, brewmasters or citizens) *impacts of value are engendered to both stakeholders and enterprises*. Whether it is the joy of creating code in software-defined businesses, buying a personalized car, drinking carefully crafted brews or the convenience of micropayments, in all cases, *new forms and sources of value* to creative-experiencers are engendered through co-intelligence engagement flows of data and service exchange between them and organizations. Besides the enhanced economic benefits of co-created value, such as increased revenues or market valuations that accrue to enterprises, they also benefit by gaining valuable insights from creative-experiencers, leading to improved products, services, and customer and other stakeholder experiences. Thus, this transformation is not just about more digitalization, datafication and data analytics but also about engendering valuable impacts in a new era of co-intelligence-driven Life-Xverse innovation and value creation. It leverages both human intelligence and computationally intelligent systems, such as co-pilots, in co-intelligence flows of Human–AI interactive engagements and the co-creation of value.

Co-intelligence SDI platforms manifest themselves in organizational offerings and value-chain ecosystems, whether across private-sector enterprises (AB InBev, NIO, Reliance), the plural sector (People+ai) or the public sector (India's DPIs). Such platforms of engagement catalyse flows of data, content and service exchange across complex interactions of individuals in co-intelligence value-chain offering ecosystems. All organizations must learn to harness this newfound co-creative power of Human–AI interactive engagement in their offerings and value chains in ways that augment their operating models, whether in enhancing current business and operating models or reimagining new ones.

Viewed through the PIEX lens, new areas of opportunities (and associated challenges) become visible in a *product-service offering, across the value chain, in a business process and in the natural ecosystem sphere* in which an enterprise operates. An enterprise's suite of products and services can be designed and managed using the PIEX lens to enhance value while mitigating risks. Enterprises can view their entire value-chain ecosystem with a PIEX lens, which includes all activities that deliver a product or service to the market with ecosystem partners. They can also view their *internal* organization with a PIEX lens to ensure that they are designed to effectively manage risks and co-create value. Finally, through the PIEX lens, enterprises can also consider the broader *societal impact* of their operations and the value they create within the communities in which they operate.

In summary, using a PIEX lens entails:

(i)   A Life-Xverse orientation in innovation and value creation, where co-intelligence flows shape emergent life-eXperiences.

(ii) Crafting co-intelligence architectures that facilitate interconnected organizational ecosystems, integrating offerings, value chains and management systems.

(iii) Engaging stakeholders as creative-experiencers, transforming their lived-journeys through co-intelligence-driven interactions.

(iv) Co-creating risk-managed value by configuring interactive engagements that dynamically shape impacts across ecosystems.

(v)   Orchestration of shared digitalized infrastructure platforms, ensuring interoperability, security and governance across interconnected ecosystems.

(vi) Driving sustainable wellbeing impacts at speed, scale and scope, through continuous Human–AI interactive engagements.

Building on this, we now elaborate on how organizations (whether in the private, public or plural sector) can harness the co-creative power of Human–AI interactive engagement through a PIEX lens. This enables them to expand value with co-intelligence across the five loci that we identified at the end of the previous chapter. (See **Figure 4-2.**)[20] The transformations along the five loci are not independent but related. As we will see with various examples, even as organizations transform along one locus, they will inevitably discover pathways for innovation and interactional creation of value along another locus.

Locus	Beyond:	To:
Enactment	Production-Delivery-Exchange of Goods-Services	Co-Intelligence Flows of Interactive Engagements via Tokenized Digital Intelligence (TDIs)
Capability	Discrete Assets	Shared Digitalized Infrastructure (SDI) Platforms
Activity	Institutional Base of Organizations	Creative-Experiencers
Strategy	B2B2C Chains	Interconnected Ecosystems
Performance	Output Efficiencies	Sustainable Wellbeing Impacts (SWIs)

Figure 4-2: Expanding Innovation and Value Creation with a PIEX Lens (Source: Venkat Ramaswamy)

Interactive Engagements

We begin with how the locus of enactment of value fundamentally shifts beyond production–delivery–exchange of goods and services to co-intelligence flows of interactive engagements entailing data, content and service exchange. Value is enacted in moments of perception, action and sensed events (via both human and nonhuman sensors) across networked ecosystem environments.[21] Life–experiences happen in moments and flow across the Life-Xverse of organizational ecosystems. Co-intelligence enables these life–experiences through TDIs that enhance multi-way dialogic interactions among humans as creative-experiencers together with AI. Value is dynamically created, increasingly in real time, through life–experiences emergent from interactive engagement flows, which go beyond the exchange of a 'fixed' offering between an organization and its customers.[22] While enterprises that are expanding value across the five loci are still in the early stages of experimenting with TDIs in co-intelligence flows of interactive engagements, we motivate and illustrate the nature of the underlying shifts with diverse examples.

Let us begin by considering the *marketplace platform business* in the travel and hospitality ecosystem and examine how Airbnb has gone beyond fixed offerings (e.g., hotel rooms) to a focus on managing the flows of interactive engagement (e.g., co-creating experiences of value with its two types of customers—*hosts* and *guests*).

Augmenting Host and Guest Experiences at Airbnb

Building on top of a computing platform shift towards *smart connected mobile phones* entailing *softwarization* and *datafication* of offerings, Airbnb has since grown to over 5 million hosts who have welcomed over 2 billion guest arrivals in almost every country across the globe. In contrast to conventional hospitality stays at hotels, hosts offer unique stays and experiences that make it possible for guests to connect with communities in a more authentic way. In the rapidly evolving landscape of travel and hospitality, Life-Xverse Airbnb has consistently sought to innovate and adapt, keeping the experiences of guests and hosts at the centre of its digital and AI-enabled transformation.

However, with the Covid-19 pandemic curbing global travel in the first quarter of 2020, Airbnb, which had taken over twelve years to build its hosting community and home rental business, saw 80 per cent of its bookings vanish. The company lost around $1 billion in revenues in the first eight weeks of the second quarter and cut about a quarter of its 7500 workforce. While Airbnb raised $2 billion in debt and equity financing to stay afloat, it slashed about $1 billion in marketing expenses, gave booked guests their money back, covered lost revenue of hosts of approximately $250 million and created a 'super host relief fund' of $10 million. It engaged 200,000 hosts in providing housing for some 100,000 'front-line workers'. At the same time, it launched a new category of 'online Airbnb experiences' (from artists to chefs to celebrities), which became their fastest-growing offering ever.[23]

Remarkably, by the end of the third quarter, Airbnb was in the black again. A key catalyst behind rebounding its core business was connecting with the lived experiences of its customers and hosts and learning from and adapting with them. At the end of the second quarter of 2020, Airbnb had uncovered a key strategic insight, in that while people didn't really want to go to cities or travel on business, they did want to get out of the house in a car and travel somewhere up to 300 miles away ('a full tank of gas'). By the middle of 2020 Q2, it was doing more business in the United States than at the same time the previous year. By engaging together with customers and hosts, Airbnb pivoted its home page on its website to 'Go Near', with interactional flows of engagements crafted around both customers and hosts.

Understanding Flows through Lived-Journeys

Brian Chesky, co-founder and CEO of Airbnb, has since placed an emphasis on deeply understanding the flow of interactive engagements in their lived-journeys, i.e., how people behave and act in the flow of planning a holiday. For instance, people do not book a flight first and then decide on a holiday. Similarly, most people do not know where they want to go when they visit a travel website. He says,

We decided to invert travel. Most travels are organized or categorized (only) by location. And we said, 'What if we added a second access of categorization type of space like a treehouse, an igloo, a castle or an activity like (going to) vineyards where you can go wine tasting?' And we had a goal—what if one day most people (on Airbnb), like on Netflix, aren't typing something into a search box, but they're browsing? And if it's more browsing than searching, this is strategic.[24]

That insight led to Airbnb Categories, which allows guests to explore unique collections of homes based on specific interests or characteristics. Chesky highlights the significance of this feature: 'We could show you places that you would never have thought to search for . . . Airbnb categories are collections of homes organized by what makes them unique. You can search by what kind of trip you want to experience.'[25] Airbnb is experimenting with GenAI to create summaries of guest reviews, which can revolutionize how potential guests evaluate properties by providing concise, informative summaries derived from extensive feedback. Another significant enhancement is the implementation of the Split Stays feature, which allows guests to plan itineraries that include multiple homes within a single trip. As Chesky says, it 'pairs the right two homes together', thus enabling guests to experience different locations or types of accommodations during their travels. For example, a guest could spend part of their trip in a bustling city and the remainder in a serene countryside home, all seamlessly coordinated through Airbnb's platform.

Recognizing that over 80 per cent of its bookings involve multiple travellers, Airbnb simplified the planning process for groups with the ability to create shared wishlists, which allows group members to collaboratively curate a list of potential stays, leave notes and even vote on their favourites to make decision-making more democratic and organized. Once a primary member decides on a property and completes the booking, travel companions can be re-invited using a digital postcard, including essential details like the property's address, check-in instructions and even the Wi-Fi password, ensuring everyone is well-prepared for the trip. A new message tab also helps all group members communicate directly with their host and react to messages. Hosts can also benefit from AI-powered suggestions when replying to inquiries, including automated responses like sending a checkout guide.[26]

Hosts As Creative Experiencers, Not Just Guests

The focus on co-innovating Airbnb's ecosystem of host experiences has also seen significant attention, particularly during and after the Covid-19 pandemic. The company has introduced numerous innovations and enhancements tailored specifically for hosts, reflecting a deliberate shift in emphasis. Consider how Airbnb leveraged AI in this transformation along the locus of capability. The Photo Tour feature, which Chesky described as 'really feels like magic', automatically organizes photos into rooms. It not only saves hosts time but also enhances the attractiveness of their listings by providing a better visual experience to guests. The AirCover for Hosts programme provides comprehensive protection for hosts. Chesky says, 'From the beginning, we realized that to let someone into your home, you have to trust them. And to trust them, you have to know who they are. So, what if we could verify every single guest booking on Airbnb?'[27] It includes features such as identity verification and reservation screening technology. AI is used to verify the identity of every guest booking on Airbnb. Similarly, AI analyses hundreds of factors to prevent unauthorized parties, safeguarding host properties. In addition to these AI-driven enhancements, AirCover now offers tripled damage protection, expanded coverage for valuables and protection for vehicles parked on the property. Similarly, free AirCover for Guests de-risks their stay.

Airbnb Setup has been designed to assist new hosts in getting started. Chesky says, 'The best way to help you do something new is with the help of someone who's done it before, and we have a lot of people just like this. Our very best hosts. They're called Superhosts and they're at the heart of Airbnb Setup.'[28] The AI-powered system asks hosts two simple questions about their location and the type of place they are listing. It then searches through thousands of Superhosts to find the best match, offering personalized support tailored to the host's needs. Further, the system facilitates the onboarding process by allowing Superhosts to provide one-on-one guidance.

Airbnb also facilitates hosts with refugee guests, as well as co-hosting, offering guidance and advice in navigating often complex challenges. For instance, through Airbnb.org's nonprofit partners, caseworkers assist refugees with crucial tasks and even help them find permanent housing in some cases. Hosts are also provided resources about refugee experiences, being of help and support to them, and being mindful of shifting health and safety protocols during a crisis (e.g., the Ukraine refugee settlement effort).[29]

Through Life-Xverse innovation for and with all stakeholders, Airbnb is creating sustainable impacts for its hosts, guests and society at large, along the locus of performance as well. As Chesky publicly declared:

> We believe that building an enduringly successful business goes hand-in-hand with making a positive contribution to society. Increasingly, that is what citizens, consumers, employees, communities and policymakers desire—even demand. Serving all stakeholders is the best way to build a highly valuable business and it's the right thing to do for society.[30]

As Airbnb expands itself in a co-intelligent world towards a life-experience ecosystem platform business, it points to *how shifts in the locus of enactment invariably also entails attendant shifts in the other loci*, i.e., *capability* (building on SDI platforms as the very basis of its business design), *activity* (towards the lived-journeys of hosts and guests), *strategy* (as leveraging ecosystem networks to curate unique environments and emergent experiences) and *performance* (towards making a positive contribution to society), each of which we discuss in more detail in subsequent examples.

Next, we consider a digitally native startup, Lemonade, and examine how it has reimagined insurance by redesigning its business engagement flows with an emphasis on customer and employee experiences from the ground up.

Redesigning Interactive Engagements with AI at Lemonade

Lemonade's business design attempts to eliminate the traditional conflict of interest between insurance companies and consumers by taking a flat percentage fee from customer insurance premiums and using the remaining funds for purchasing reinsurance and paying claims. This approach ensures that Lemonade's financial success is not dependent on denying claims but growing premiums through risk-assessed behavioural pricing, aligning enterprise interests with those of their customers and fostering a more transparent and trustworthy relationship. Lemonade donates any unclaimed premiums to charitable causes chosen by their customers.

Lemonade's radical redesign of the business configuration of insurance focuses intensively on leveraging AI and digital technologies at its core to shift beyond an institutional and product-centric view of insurance to a purpose-built customer and experience-centric business model. From its inception, Lemonade has had an affinity for deep technology. Both its co-founders, Daniel Schreiber (who earlier held leadership roles at Powermat Technologies and SanDisk) and Shai Wininger (founder of Fiverr) are seasoned tech entrepreneurs. Schreiber, CEO of Lemonade, describes how they achieved tech intensity in a short period:

> We're a young company. We went live just six years ago . . .
> our data and statistical capabilities, our machine learning,

has been building at an exponential rate. We now have several hundreds of millions of customer interactions in that centralized intelligence. That intelligence has digested and analysed some 160 terabytes of pretty textured and predictive data. And all of that has resulted to date in about fifty machine learning models, which are, at first approximation, AIs unto themselves.[31]

Customer Engagement Capabilities in the Offering Ecosystem

Let us deep-dive into some of Lemonade's engagement capabilities.[32] AI Maya is Lemonade's *customer-facing AI bot*, responsible for guiding customers through the insurance purchase process. AI Maya interacts directly with potential customers, helping them understand their insurance needs, providing quotes and finalizing policy purchases. Utilizing advanced natural language processing (NLP) and machine learning algorithms to interpret customer responses and provide relevant information, AI Maya dynamically adapts responses based on the customer's input, using machine learning models to predict the most suitable insurance products and pricing. The system pulls in data from various external sources, such as credit reports and property databases, to fine-tune risk assessments and quotes.

AI Maya's capabilities have streamlined the insurance purchase process. Schreiber says, 'AI Maya and her associated APIs sell (almost) all of our insurance. And she does that in a trice. Ninety seconds and you're done, no hassle, no commission.'[33] This efficiency has eliminated the need for traditional sales agents, reducing commission costs by 15–20 per cent. It has also enabled them to offer renters insurance starting from $5 a month, at rates up to 80 per cent lower than traditional providers, with better AI risk assessment of first-time renters and younger customers.

Employee Engagement Capabilities in Lemonade's Value Chain Ecosystem

AI Jim is Lemonade's *AI bot designed for processing insurance claims*. AI Jim manages the entire lifecycle of a claim, from the initial report to the final payout, ensuring quick and efficient service. Employing machine learning algorithms to assess and process claims, AI Jim utilizes data from various sources such as videos, documents and customer histories. Schreiber says,

> In 98 per cent of our claims, the first notice of loss is taken by a bot. And in almost half of those claims, everything is done by a bot, start to finish, right through to asking you any clarifying questions, asking you for documents or to upload a video, analyzing fraud detection, asking you all the questions and wiring money to your bank account, all done without any human intervention. AI Jim is performing better than humans in most of these tasks.[34]

This automation has reduced the time and cost associated with claims processing, enabling some payouts to be made in just a few seconds. AI Jim's fraud detection capabilities have identified approximately $100 million in fraudulent claims, contributing to significant cost savings for Lemonade. In 2023, Lemonade had a world record-setting achievement as AI Jim swiftly assessed a claim, meticulously checked policy conditions, proceeded to execute numerous anti-fraud algorithms and settled it within a remarkable span of two seconds.[35]

Management Ecosystem at Lemonade

AI Cooper is an *internal AI bot* at Lemonade that *manages various operational tasks*. Schreiber says, 'Cooper is a member of the team. You can chat to Cooper through Slack and ask him any number of questions. And he'll run a lot of processes.'[36] AI Cooper plays a crucial role in the company's IT engineering operations and regulatory processes. For instance, when a product manager assigns a new feature, AI Cooper creates a sandbox environment on AWS, runs 14,000 automated tests and coordinates with a human quality assurance (QA) specialist before pushing the feature to production. AI Cooper also assists with regulatory filings by quickly generating loss reports upon request and supports underwriters by monitoring severe weather situations using real-time satellite data. For example, Cooper's integration with NASA satellites enables the identification of fires and the automatic adjustment of insurance offerings in affected areas, demonstrating its extensive utility across various company functions.

Performance Management at Lemonade

The Lifetime Value (LTV) model at Lemonade predicts various customer-related factors such as retention, the likelihood of claims and cross-selling potential. It uses machine learning to analyse a multitude of data points for each customer, including historical data, interaction patterns and demographic information. It generates predictions about how long a customer will stay with the company (churn prediction), the expected frequency and severity of their claims, and their potential to purchase additional products. This model is integral to understanding the long-term profitability of each customer. It has also enabled Lemonade to optimize its marketing expenditures and to focus on acquiring and retaining the most profitable customers. Schreiber says, 'Our conviction and trust in this model, we're putting our money where our mouth is. Eighty-six cents on the dollar that we spent on marketing this past quarter was at the direction of the LTV model.'[37]

Lemonade's AI-driven claims processing has drastically reduced its claim handling costs, measured in terms of loss adjustment expense (LAE) ratio, compared to traditional insurers—7.6 per cent versus 10 per cent for large insurers. On

Net Promoter Score (NPS), a measure of customer satisfaction and advocacy, Lemonade's performance is comparable to tech giants like Tesla and Apple. Schreiber sums up the change Lemonade has brought to the insurance industry:

> Behind the scenes, the bots and the AI are helping us become super-efficient. Insurance is the business of data. Twenty years ago, if I asked you who are the bastions of the world's data and where are the best statisticians in the world, you'd have said insurance companies. Today, you'll say Silicon Valley. And what we're trying to do is to bridge that gap.[38]

Enhancing GenAI Capabilities

Lemonade was built for the new GenAI era we are in when it made a bet on chatbot interfaces at its founding in 2016, positing that if it built its business architecture atop these technologies, as they advance, its structural advantage would grow in tandem. Its knowledge base is stored in vector databases, its tech stack is API-based and its pricing has been the product of a flywheel of continuous machine learning, while delighting customers. In its Investor Day presentation in November 2022, Lemonade showcased its approximately one million-parameter AI model, able to predict churn, claims and cross-category buying for every prospect. In other words, Lemonade was already offering unprecedented levels of insight and precision, and GenAI co-intelligence is an accelerant along the very course it set at its inception.

With LLMs, they efficiently process complex technical reports such as veterinarian health reports of pets or surveyors' building assessment reports and can generate accurate and relevant responses speedily based on their content. They also autonomously manage 22 per cent of incoming emails with their GenAI system. Schreiber puts the impact of their AI/GenAI systems into perspective:

I put it to you that it is pretty much impossible to do (by humans) over the course of the last two years without that level of automation and without being able to use LLMs. The size of our book has doubled. Our gross profit has tripled, and operating expense hasn't moved.[39]

In contrast, traditional insurance companies face more challenges in migrating to co-intelligence driven Life-Xverse innovation and value creation with 'broker-based distribution, siloed systems, disparate databases, and a motley collection of off-the-shelf applications'.[40]

There is a need to accelerate the de-centring of AI infusion in management ecosystems via the digital fabric of Human–AI flows as shown in **Figure 4-3.** The sociotechnical architecture of co-intelligence is shaped across workflow interactions and emergent life–experiences of individuals as creative-experiencers within and across the enterprise ecosystem.

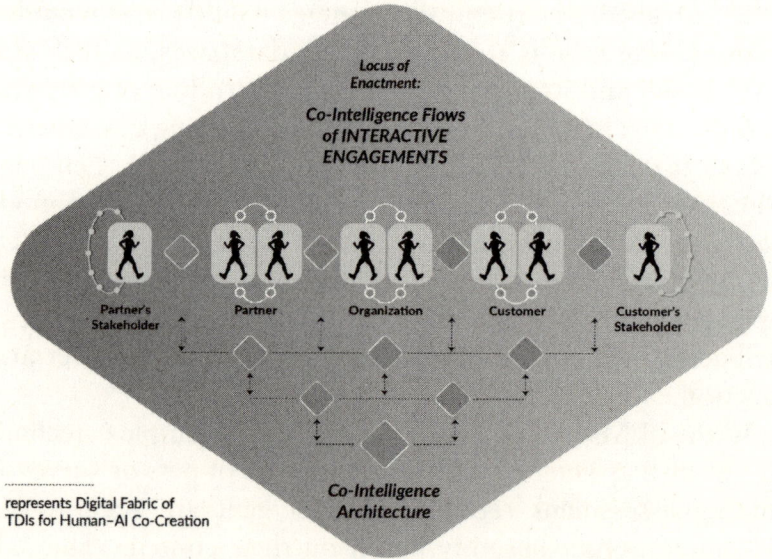

Figure 4-3: Co-Intelligence Flows of Human–AI Interactive Engagements (Source: Venkat Ramaswamy)

Next Best Conversations at Commonwealth Bank of Australia

In the past decade, the Commonwealth Bank of Australia (CBA, or CommBank) has undergone a significant digital transformation journey, aiming to go beyond being a leader in global digital banking. Matt Comyn, its CEO, says,

> CBA wants to remain Australia's clear leader in digital banking. We recognize customers are no longer just benchmarking us against other financial institutions. They compare us with the best digital experiences they get from any business in the world. We intend to be at the global forefront of the digital experience and be the trusted partner at the centre of our customers' financial lives.[41]

AI-Driven Transformation

A core element of this transformation has been the bank's embrace of AI. Consider CBA's Customer Engagement Engine (CEE), an AI-driven customer experience platform that leverages 450 machine learning models trained on a total of 157 billion data points (such as customer banking behaviour, preferences and financial goals).[42] This allows CBA to tailor communications, product recommendations and overall banking experiences to each customer. Talking about CEE, Andrew McMullan, CBA's chief data and analytics officer, says,

> About four years ago, in our branches in particular, our people were telling us that they were finding it quite difficult to think about what conversation to have with customers as they came in . . . So, now when a customer goes into a branch, there'll be a slider that comes across the screen with what we call the next best conversation (NBC). And that allows our people to really serve the customer do that brilliantly.[43]

Capabilities like NBC allow for dialogue and deeper connections with the system, enhancing value-creating banking engagements. In a way, CEE is doing at scale, across all interactions, what a star customer service executive does at a branch level. The For You feature available within the CommBank app is an example of augmenting experience personalization for the bank's customers. Budgeting tools such as Money Plan and Bill Sense, available in the app, empower customers to navigate finances by predicting future bills and managing everyday cash flow. This involves understanding the context of a customer's spending patterns and an awareness of the period of time in a month in the customer's monthly spending.

The transformation of CBA is as much within and about its employees as it is external and about customer experiences. It starts with enhancing *access* to resourced capabilities for value-creating engagement interactions. Not surprisingly, Comyn faced initial resistance from within, when calling for digital transformation. Thus, he brought in new blood in the form of McMullan, and he says, 'We got a significant boost because he brought not only the technical engineering capability but also the practical prioritization to build momentum in a large organization such as ours. And then we really started to scale.'[44]

Experience-Centric Organizational Design

In the past, each channel and product team in CBA operated independently. This meant McMullan had to persuade them to collaborate for the benefit of the whole company and create an orchestrated customer experience, even if it meant sacrificing some control over their projects. McMullan was careful initially in approaching one of the channels, the digital team, at CBA. That team had already built certain capabilities in customer personalization using the Adobe Digital Marketing Cloud platform. So, he wanted to pilot CEE in other channels such as home buying and branch, 'get some runs on the board' before approaching the digital team. It was only then that McMullan implemented Project Sparta to simply lift and shift over 300 digital campaigns built on Adobe into CEE within three months. As his team member put it:

> One of the smartest things we did in the whole CEE journey was to architect it in such a way that we could easily translate those pre-existing digital campaigns into NBCs, allowing us to duplicate three years of work in a matter of months and exponentially increase our reach. This was the moment that CEE had the volume of interactions needed for our AI to become really predictive at anticipating customer needs.[45]

Co-Innovation with Partners

In order to build its AI platform capabilities, CBA has forged multiple partnerships. It has invested in a cloud-based machine learning platform, H2O AI Cloud. Thus, CBA gained access to H2O.ai's suite of AI tools and pre-built AI models. For instance, CBA has leveraged H2O.ai's Document AI product to unlock new possibilities in document processing. Traditionally, extracting data from documents like loan applications or financial statements has been a manual and time-consuming process. H2O's Document AI, with its machine learning capabilities, automates this process significantly. It acts like an intelligent assistant, analysing various document formats—text, images and even handwritten notes—to extract key information with high accuracy. This not only streamlines internal workflows but also allows for faster loan approvals and improved customer service. McMullan says, 'We co-created products and services together . . . we've always had teams that are a mix of H2O and CBA and that cultural but also talent alignment is why we're seeing some of the great results that we're seeing.' Sri Ambati, CEO and founder, H2O.ai, says, 'We feel privileged to be partners. A lot of the wins that H2O has usually come from a native leadership and culture that's already looking to transform . . . Every interaction I've had with almost everyone in the Commonwealth Bank starts with customer and community.'[46]

CBA partnered with Nuance in 2018 to create the virtual assistant Ceba, which has since handled over 15.5 million interactions, managing tasks like card activation and loan payment deferrals. Now, over 60 per cent of customer contacts are resolved entirely by the assistant.[47] CBA is also partnering with Microsoft and developing its banking co-pilot strategy for internal use. For instance, mortgage brokers can access information more efficiently, enabling them to make faster decisions and provide better support to their clients. This is helping connect with the agency of persons (customers and employees) in interactive system environments. In a new experiment, the bank is looking at creating AI-generated customer personas or synthetic agents. CBA chief decision scientist Dan Jermyn said,

> We're looking at harnessing GenAI to understand what products and services may be most needed during different types of natural disasters by simulating the actions and needs of customers during these difficult times . . . also to better understand what messaging would be most effective for helping customers in vulnerable situations—such as when customers are potentially being scammed, or when they experience a loss in the family.[48]

NEST Ecosystems

Let us now consider how CBA is operating in its *NEST ecosystems*. Consider its work in tackling technology-facilitated financial abuse, which involves the usage of digital tools by a victimizer to control a victim's finances, limit their access or rack up debt in their name. CBA built AI models to identify such transactions. In partnership with H2O.ai, it shared these models and the source code on GitHub for other banks to use.[49] By providing access to such AI resources, it is making the networked ecosystem experience environments more *inclusive*. This openness in sharing is making the structures of ecosystems across the environments of various stakeholding individuals more *generative*. CBA is also *linking* with and engaging partners in its ecosystem to offer a suite of sustainable products and services. As part of helping Australia's transport sector in the transition to a low-carbon economy, CBA provided a 'green loan' (based on sustainable management criteria such as renewable energy use, energy efficiency and pollution control) to Canberra Metro. Additionally, CBA's Benefits Finder, a digital tool to help personal and business customers offset the rising cost of living, has connected customers to AUD 1 billion of grants and rebates for which they may be eligible. McMullan says,

> We are not just helping customers make better decisions about their finances but also about how they can reduce and offset their energy usage and carbon emissions. We will be using our AI models to orchestrate a range of services available across the CBA ecosystem for customers, including through our own products like the Green Loan to help homeowners finance solar or a battery or through recently announced partnerships such as Amber Energy (a renewable energy retailer) and CoGo (a fintech start-up that helps provide personalized carbon footprints for customers based on their spending data).[50]

We now explore the locus of capability and the shifts it entails beyond enterprise assets of the industrial world to shared digitalized infrastructure (SDI) platforms that are purpose-built.

SDI Platform Capabilities

Offerings as a Service at Philips and Signify

Consider the case of Philips, the Dutch multinational conglomerate in healthcare and lighting businesses, which in

2010 received an unusual request from one of its long-time customers. The architect, Thomas Rau, simply wanted to buy only light, 1850 hours of 500-lux light; not the Philips bulbs, fixtures or controls.[51] This intrigued the company as, with 'pay per lux', Philips Lighting could embrace a circular business model. With fixed costs shifted to variable operational costs, more customers could be incentivized to adopt newer lighting technologies such as LED. Thus, Philips light-as-a-service (LaaS) was born. By 2016, it was spun out as a separate company, Signify, and has since developed networked wireless control smart lighting solutions that are used in homes, businesses (like hotels, stores and offices) and even cities. Signify's Interact suite offers a toolbox of software apps that connect them to smart buildings and cities. The ensuing data can be shared with existing systems or developers to create new services and experiences, like personalized lighting. Signify even provides tools for developers to expand its offering ecosystem, creating a future of data-driven lighting solutions.

In turn, Amsterdam Schiphol Airport, a business customer, was able to leverage Signify's LaaS to slash its electricity use by 50 per cent in just five years. Schiphol only pays for the light they actually use, while Signify owns the ultra-durable lighting fixtures (lasting 75 per cent longer than traditional options) and handles all maintenance and upgrades. Schiphol also created seven different experience worlds in Lounge 2 of the airport using one system.[52] New York State's Smart Street Lighting programme is another example, wherein Signify partnered with the New York Power Authority (NYPA) and cities across the state. While this system uses less power and reduces the utility's revenue in the short term, it created a connected lighting network that NYPA could, in turn, leverage in its smarter city initiative. Former NYPA president and CEO Gil Quiniones noted, 'As we implemented Smart Street Lighting NY, we came to understand that these systems are no longer used just to illuminate roads. They are, in fact, vertical assets that can be utilized for smart city deployment.' This opened the doors for future revenue streams through new smart services for parking availability, environmental monitoring (integrating with pollution sensors) and public safety (integrating with cameras).[53]

Signify employs AI to monitor the health of lighting systems. AI models can predict potential failures or maintenance needs by analysing data from sensors embedded in the lighting infrastructure. This predictive maintenance approach reduces downtime and extends the life of lighting assets. AI algorithms help in optimizing energy usage by adjusting lighting based on occupancy patterns, natural light availability and other contextual data, contributing to energy savings and sustainability goals.

Signify is utilizing GenAI to enhance both customer service and product development. Its customer care centres leverage GenAI to improve customer experience. Additionally, GenAI is playing a crucial role in the design of its 3D-printed luminaires. An advanced text-to-image model generates intricate texture images, enabling Signify to create unique and visually appealing lighting fixtures.[54] By inputting design constraints and desired outcomes, GenAI models can generate a wide array of design options, some of which might be novel and beyond traditional design approaches. This can expand Signify's offerings in tailoring lighting solutions (e.g., through its Hue offering ecosystem) that adapt to individual preferences and environments, making lighting not just functional but also a personalized immersive lighting experience. GenAI-based systems can also be explored in assisting ecosystemic design of solutions for longevity, repairability and recyclability, aligning with Signify's commitment to sustainability.

Let us turn next to an example of AT&T as a customer and producer of tech platforms co-creating value for and with its stakeholders. Decades before AI became a household term, AT&T scientists were at its forefront—Claude Shannon of Bell Labs (as AT&T was known then), developed a chess-playing program in 1950 and was one of the researchers who coined the term 'AI' in 1955. So, it is with particular interest that we examine one of its recent innovations, where data scientists have employed AI to create better AI. And how it has created an SDI for its internal data scientists.

Democratizing AI and Developer Experiences at AT&T

AT&T has undertaken a significant project in collaboration with H2O.ai, focusing on democratizing AI to create a more inclusive and efficient data science environment. It is centred on the development of a *feature store*, a repository for storing, sharing and reusing machine learning features across the organization. Mark Austin, vice president, data science, AT&T, says,

> I can't tell you, once we put the feature store in place, how many times we've taken a model. Sometimes we've been working on a model for a year or two, and we go to the feature store, and we shop, and we improve it the next day between meetings. So, it's an amazing thing to do better together there.[55]

In collaboration with Palantir and by leveraging its Artificial Intelligence Platform (AIP), AT&T has developed a proprietary GenAI platform, AskAT&T, primarily designed for internal employees to efficiently access company-specific knowledge, ask questions and retrieve insights from vast datasets in a secure manner. Austin says, 'Inside of AT&T, we have 100,000 employees and contractors on it. We've done 120 million API calls. We have fifty-five use cases in production.'[56]

These innovations have been transformative, particularly in the areas of data discovery, engineering, AI creation, deployment and monitoring. They are enabling engineers/operators/managers as creative-experiencers at AT&T.

i) *Find Data*: AT&T has streamlined the process of finding and accessing data, a task that traditionally consumed 60–80 per cent of a data scientist's time. By integrating GenAI, AT&T has made data discovery more intuitive and efficient, allowing users to search for datasets and features using natural language queries.

ii) *Engineer Data*: The feature store is a groundbreaking innovation, serving as both a repository for storing engineered features and a marketplace for sharing them. This store allows data scientists to reuse existing features, reducing redundancy and accelerating model development. Features can be shared across different teams and pipelines, promoting a collaborative environment.

iii) *Create AI*: AT&T's 'coopetition' model, inspired by Kaggle competitions, encourages internal teams to collaborate and compete in developing AI models on its Pinnacle platform. It has run over 266 competitions and hosted over 3000 users. This approach has led to significant improvements in model performance, with some models achieving up to 153 per cent better results than baseline models. The use of ensemble models (combined predictions from multiple AI models) and AutoML tools like Driverless AI (an AT&T robot) has further enhanced this process.

iv) *Deploy AI*: The integration of H2O's feature store with API functionality allows for real-time scoring and inference, essential for applications like fraud detection. In the US, iPhone fraud (such as when criminals exploit phone contracts or sales for unauthorized iPhones or services) is a $1 billion problem. Thus, a customer service agent can enter a customer's phone number into the system, which quickly checks against AI models in the feature store. The system then provides a fraud risk score or alert within seconds, allowing the agent to take immediate action. This process happens seamlessly behind the scenes, making it easy for the agent to use without needing technical expertise. AT&T's AI models helped reduce fraud by over 80 per cent. AT&T also leveraged these models in an entirely different area—in predictive maintenance of their 7000 trucks. Dead vehicle batteries were a recurring problem. One AI model predicted that the vehicles where the drivers braked harder also saw more battery failures. So, AT&T decided to replace batteries whenever they replaced their brakes. The result—$7 million savings per annum. The AI model offered a superior route optimization of their 100,000-plus technicians, resulting in savings of over $10 million per year (from reduced fuel consumption).[57]

An interesting application is Call Before You Dig, with the AskAT&T interface. AT&T receives approximately 20 million calls annually from third parties requesting to dig in areas where AT&T infrastructure may be present. *Palantir's* AI Platform helps streamline this process by integrating geospatial indexing, machine learning models and data ontologies to predict whether AT&T facilities, such as fibre cables, are present at the requested location. Other GenAI applications include SCOUT, which aggregates and correlates over 2.5 million tickets and alarms from AT&T's network systems to provide a real-time, holistic view of network activity and helps streamline incident management, and Mobility Legacy Transport Optimization, which helps AT&T identify and decommission legacy circuits and equipment to reduce costs. By querying network data through an ontology, engineers can quickly assess circuits and inventory, enabling faster and more efficient cost-saving decisions.

v) *Monitor AI*: AT&T's Watchtower platform monitors the performance of AI models and the underlying data in real time. This continuous monitoring helps detect data drifts (changes in data's statistical properties over time, which can impact the model's performance) and ensures that models remain accurate and reliable over time.

Lived-Journeys of Stakeholders as Creative-Experiencers

As organizations co-create risk-managed value via co-intelligence flows of interactive engagements, the locus of activity extends beyond the conventional institutional base of organizations to the *lived-journeys* of stakeholders as creative-experiencers.

Health-Conscious Individuals as Creative Experiencers at Discovery

Consider Discovery Limited, with its origins as an insurance company from South Africa that pioneered a shared-value business model. It delivers better health and value for clients, superior actuarial dynamics for the insurer and a healthier society. In the previous chapter, we saw how it leveraged Databricks service-as-a-capability to expand its Discovery Bank offering and value-chain ecosystems. At the heart of its insurance strategy is Vitality, the world's largest behavioural platform, which rewards and incentivizes people to make healthier choices and adopt behaviours that contribute to better health outcomes. This example is illustrative of value creation along the loci of activity and performance. Adrian Gore, founder and group CEO of Discovery, shares his perspectives on what it takes to change people's behaviour:

> Can you build a product or a brand that stands for good and get people to be part of that inspirational journey? It's not all transactional. If you get people engaged and they feel good about the entire business—the values, the offering, how it feels—you can attract people into a very different world.[58]

Lived-journeys of Creative Experiencers

Consider an individual who joins Vitality. She undergoes a health assessment and selects a set of personal goals to improve overall health and fitness. Based on her health screening, a risk profile is generated, and she is classified accordingly across key dimensions of wellbeing—physical, emotional and financial, as well as legal support. A proactive, customized support plan is set up for her that includes interventions from prevention and education to episodic or ongoing management across all dimensions of wellbeing. The model works only if she wholeheartedly participates in its programmes. She is not merely consuming its offerings passively. Instead, she is a creative-experiencer, benefiting from community events and other healthy, fun activities. For instance,[59]

- She can set personal goals—for weekly exercise, driving (with respect to car insurance) and spending (with respect to personal finances)—for a healthier life and collect Vitality Active Rewards' reward points on achieving them. Discovery offers an Apple Watch as a reward to her, provided she meets her exercise goals over 24 months.
- She can shop for healthy groceries and get rewarded with a 25 per cent back offer, thanks to Discovery's partnership with retailers like Pick n Pay and Woolworth.
- She may join Team Vitality, South Africa's favourite running and cycling club, and connect and compete with millions of runners and cyclists across the world. Discovery has partnered with fitness-related companies like Strava, the world's leading running and cycling platform, to recognize and reward members like her as they get active.

As she engages through the Vitality experience ecosystem, she earns points. During the pandemic, Discovery expanded its popular Vitality Active Rewards programme to include kids and partnered with Apple Pay. With the pandemic-induced lockdowns, parents like her were spending more time with their children at home. Discovery allowed parents to co-opt their children in healthy activities, such as 'eating a healthy breakfast' and 'making exercising fun', that were gamified to earn more rewards. However, failure to meet goals after getting a reward, say, an Apple Watch, means that she will have to pay monthly instalments to retain it. And experience shows that loss aversion is a powerful motivator for members to continue actively participating as creative-experiencers. Discovery also leverages AI to positively influence its customers. In 2023, it offered some of its UK Vitality Health members an AI chatbot,

Wysa, which uses natural language processing to understand the user's free text inputs. Over a third of the people who actively engaged with the app saw a reduction in symptoms for anxiety and depression.[60] Adrian Gore, talking about the shared-value model, says, 'We've seen compelling evidence that this model benefits us and our customers. Once you accept that behaviour is causal, you realize that changing behaviour leads to different outcomes.'[61]

Vitality, as a personal, social and collective experience ecosystem, emphasizes how a health-conscious individual influences the family and community, creates a healthier society and ultimately reduces the burden on the healthcare system. As for Discovery, it brings productivity into its value chain with a scale-efficient operating model, even as it gains with fewer policy lapses and lower claims. Not surprisingly, Discovery outpaced all other brands in the Kantar Most Valuable South African Brands study.[62]

Workers as Creative-Experiencers at Shell

The role of individuals as creative-experiencers is equally applicable in industrial business settings in the flow of people's organizational work, with *workers as creative-experiencers*. Consider Shell, an integrated energy company with capabilities in refining and producing chemicals, trading, retailing and other functions. It leverages AI across its value chain, especially in areas such as preventive maintenance and safety. Mark Wildon, VP of asset management at Shell, says, 'What we find is that if we do AI and it's not embedded in one of our core processes, it becomes hobby.'[63]

Shell has partnered with technology firm C3.ai and generated around 5 trillion aggregated rows of data from 5 million sensors in its assets, which are optimized using 20,000 machine learning models and monitored by two global surveillance centres. It leverages AI to act as a decision support system for humans. Wildon continues:

We do use AI applications in some cases to make autonomous decisions, but actually most of what we do is about getting people insights when and where they need it to help them make better decisions. Magic comes when you can put together AI experts with the people who know the systems that we need to improve.

In one application around machine vision for safety, Shell used drones and CCTV to provide indications of potential anomalies to human supervisors, e.g., when a crane lift was being prepared, and the barriers were not in place. Another safety application was in road transportation, where machine vision was used to focus on the driver's eyes and detect any signs of fatigue and give them an immediate warning or alert. In the case of remote maintenance planning, Shell has a large engineering office in Chennai, India, leveraging AR technology to visualize the actual context of work for other Shell employees around the world.

Fans as Creative Experiencers in Shibuya Web3

Let us now consider a Web3 example that transforms customers from being just passive consumers and fans of content to becoming co-creators of content and co-owners of offerings. Shibuya is a platform that provides content creators with a full-stack solution to fund films, build community and foster a dedicated fanbase. It is like GoFundMe, Reddit and Netflix coming together on a blockchain. Emily Yang, aka Pplpleasr, the founder of Shibuya, describes it as 'a Web3 experiment where long-form content is free to watch but monetized on the blockchain to allow viewer participation on the creative process and also shared ownership'.[64] It is funded through a sale of NFT Producer Passes. Viewers who hold them will be able to stake their NFTs and vote for one of two alternate endings to the first episode of Shibuya's first long-form anime series, *White Rabbit*. These viewers also earn WRAB, an ERC-20 token (a blockchain-based asset on Ethereum), representing fractional ownership of the *White Rabbit* series. The token holders are essentially members of a decentralized autonomous organization (DAO), i.e., a member-owned community on a blockchain, who can vote on the show's future—such as collaborating with a larger production company or moving to a new streaming platform. Shibuya also aims to connect its creator community with studios, show writers, directors and showrunners, who are open to more creative collaboration in their value-chain ecosystems. Venture capitalist Li Jin talks about the 'blurring of lines between fan and creator, between canon (official work of fiction) and fanon (fan-created material)'.[65] The success of Shibuya rests on community co-creation experiences in the lived-journeys of its fans as creative-experiencers and how they are interactively engaged in the enactment of value to them. What's new here is how fans are co-owners of co-created offerings in Web3 fashion, with Shibuya's mission being to reimagine filmmaking and change the way films and shorts are made, with an all-in-one platform capability.

Networked Ecosystem Coalitions

We now discuss the shifting locus of strategy beyond conventional *B2B2C chains* of goods and services to networked ecosystem coalitions with partnering enterprises.

Nurturing AI-Infused Retail Ecosystems at Alibaba

Chinese retailer Alibaba embraced an ecosystemic approach in its phenomenal growth journey when it redefined its strategic vision from being 'an e-commerce company serving China's small exporting companies' to one 'fostering the development of an open, collaborative, and flourishing e-commerce ecosystem'.[66] Its ecosystem started with interconnected networks of buyers and sellers (Taobao, TMall, 1688, etc.), and then as technology improved, it brought online functions like logistics (Cainiao Network), finance (Ant Financial), advertising, marketing, cloud computing and so on. By 2021, it was the largest e-commerce platform business in China, with a 51 per cent market share.[67]

Alibaba leveraged tech-enabled platforms to enable and automate decision-making across networks in the retail ecosystem. The web-celeb model of retailing is a case in point of such an ecosystem network. For instance, fashion entrepreneur Zhang Linchao modelled her latest design ideas on her Weibo social network site; the popular designs were then sold on the Taobao platform in flash sales, with orders rapidly fulfilled through the Ruhan manufacturing services network, also hosted on the Alibaba platform. Another business in Alibaba's ecosystem is Ant, which analyses the transaction data of a seller on its Taobao platform and assesses the seller's creditworthiness in order to offer a micro loan.

Jack Ma, the co-founder of Alibaba, in his keynote address at CeBIT 2015 in Hanover, Germany, envisaged how enterprises would need to operate: 'In the future, the world will be connected not by oil or things, but by data. Businesses will be C2B (consumer-to-business) and not B2C—because of the enormous amount of data, manufacturers must make customised things, or they will face difficulties.'[68]

'Smart Business' Model

Alibaba incorporated the following steps at the core of its Smart Business model: every interaction yields data; all business activities are mediated by software; APIs ensure smooth interaction between systems; and machine learning helps make sense of data in real time. For instance, on Taobao, the domestic retailing website of Alibaba, sellers used the Wangwang instant messaging tool to greet buyers, introduce products, negotiate prices and so on. Technology allowed online what was traditionally done in a physical shop. Additionally, all data related to the transaction was collected for further analysis. Later, Taobao exposed APIs to its e-commerce platform, on which third-party software developers built hundreds of software modules that improved the productivity of merchants. Taobao built a powerful search and recommendations engine supported by machine-learning algorithms. And later, it developed an AI chatbot to respond to customer enquiries—in 2017, during Alibaba's biggest sales day, the chatbot handled more than 95 per cent of questions from 3.5 million consumers.[69] In 2023, it released a GenAI chatbot, Wenwen or Ask Taobao, based on Alibaba's LLM, Tongyi Qianwen (Qwen). Users could ask for customized product recommendations and comparisons.[70]

The very reasons that made Alibaba successful—unfettered access to data and the ability to harness it and manage its ecosystem partners—have become a strategic business risk for the company in recent years. In August 2021, when China passed the Personal Information Protection Law and regulated how companies collect, store and process the personal information of their customers, it significantly affected Alibaba's business. The regulators wanted to break its 'monopoly on information and strictly comply with the requirements of credit information business regulation'.[71] Alibaba was forced to pay a record $2.8 billion antitrust fine and ordered to restructure its businesses, especially to reduce the profitability of Ant Group's lending business. Unlike the case of India, which built its digital public infrastructure from scratch using protocols with open APIs and microservices, and which enabled private-sector enterprises to plug into a broader societal and economic ecosystem, the Chinese government ordered state-owned enterprises to speed up the migration of their data from private operators such as Alibaba Cloud to government cloud infrastructure.

Coalitions for AI Innovation Hub in Brazil

Let us now head to Brazil for a public sector example of the *state of* São Paulo, through its technology innovation hub, IdeiaGov, pulled together a diverse set of *coalition partners* to create AI solutions for diagnosing Covid-19, customized to Brazil's local needs and at lower price points. These range from economic development state departments and the attorney general serving as a focal point for coordination and legal guidance to clinical hospital faculty and practitioners overseeing the AI algorithm development to hub stakeholders managing the development and support of the IdeiaGov platform and funding entities (e.g., Novartis Foundation and development banks).

In response to the public challenge issued by IdeiaGov, three local tech firms developed AI tools to analyse and interpret lung images from patients affected by Covid-19. After testing, they were eventually deployed in clinical settings and used to diagnose over 25,000 patients in São Paulo. Fifty hospitals are connected to the AI platform, of which 40 per cent are public institutions. The AI diagnostic tool supported radiologists, both specialists and the less experienced. The latter started their diagnostic process with AI output reports and trained themselves.[72]

Another team at the University of São Paulo is developing an AI chatbot to answer health-related questions by training it on a database of clinical guidelines of the Ministry of Health in Brazil. One of the application areas of this AI chatbot is to 'train the healthcare workers', rather than exposing it to the citizens directly. The number of physicians (per 1000 people) in Brazil is 2.1 (versus 3.6 in high-income economies) and nurses (per 1000 people) is 5.5 (versus 10.6 in high-income economies).[73] The larger objective is to build the capacity of primary healthcare workers so that they can treat more patients without needing to refer them to bigger and costlier hospitals.[74] This example also points to the need to simultaneously expand the locus of activity (as we discussed earlier) towards engaging knowledge partners and workers as creative-experiencers.

In discussing a new, more dynamic view of *strategy-as-discovery*, Prahalad and Ramaswamy note that in an internetworked world, 'the distinction between strategy formulation and implementation disappears. There is no handoff between thinking and acting'.[75] The new co-intelligence world calls for simultaneously transforming strategy-as-discovery across the locus of activity, i.e., towards rapid feedback loops in the formulation and execution of strategy, which is essential to accelerating the scale and scope of impacts, as discussed in the locus of performance next.[76] In other words, in a co-intelligence world, shifts across the locus of strategy and performance are ever more inextricably related in practices of co-intelligence-driven Life-Xverse innovation and value creation.

SWIs at Speed, Scale and Scope

There is a shifting locus of performance beyond conventional industrial efficiency to amplifying SWIs at speed, scale and scope, encompassing purposeful mission-oriented developmental goals. Let us consider a few examples.

Ping An—Achieving a Healthcare Transformation in China

Now consider healthcare in China. Ping An Good Doctor (PAGD) is an online healthcare platform in China offering real-time consultations and health management services through an ecosystem network of experienced doctors, leveraging AI and digital technologies to provide accessible and efficient healthcare solutions. In their 2023 book, *Beyond Disruption*, Renée Mauborgne and W. Chan Kim highlight the creation of a nondisruptive market in primary healthcare by Ping An, which complemented rather than displaced the existing government-hospital-centred healthcare system in China. It leveraged a pool of highly qualified doctors who had left top government hospitals in China (because they did not want to pursue research, a requirement for promotions there), providing them an opportunity to continue practising medicine and offer accessible healthcare, especially for minor and chronic conditions.[77]

Consider how PAGD leveraged AI and digital technologies to create sustainable impacts at speed, scale and scope. Its AI system provided diagnostic assistance for over 3000 diseases by analysing data from over 530 million online consultation sessions—handling inquiries in the 'quick consultation session', responding to user questions through voice or text and directing them to the appropriate medical department. It increased the platform's capacity and efficiency five to tenfold. Ping An also introduced One-Minute Clinics, which are AI-supported kiosks deployed in various locations like companies, schools and community spaces. These kiosks could address over 2000 diseases and dispense over 100 types of medicine. By early 2019, about 1000 One-Minute Clinics had been established in eight provinces, serving over 3 million people.[78]

With respect to enhancing the scope of offerings, consider PAGD's pharmacy and partner network expansion. It built an extensive network of over 32,000 pharmacies that enabled delivery of medications to users within an hour of ordering through the Ping An app. Through a subsidiary company, Wanjia Healthcare, Ping An equipped over 60,000 clinics with IT systems and support, enhancing their standards and reputations, thus enabling PAGD to direct patients to these qualified local clinics (6000 clinics obtained Wanjia's three-star accreditation) and offer services such as medical examinations and laboratory analyses.

By 2019, PAGD had over 315 million registered users with nearly 67 million monthly active users, demonstrating the large-scale adoption and reliance on the service. Digital technologies helped amplify the SWIs significantly.

Green Transition at Danfoss

Now consider the business energy space. Danfoss, founded in 1933 by Mads Clausen in Nordborg, Denmark, has grown from a small enterprise into a global leader in energy-efficient solutions and climate technologies. Today, it is at the forefront of a green transition, leveraging digital technologies and AI to decarbonize its operations and supply chains. For instance,

Danfoss has developed the Zero Carbon Product platform, in collaboration with McKinsey, that assesses carbon emissions throughout the entire supply chain. It maps each product's bill of materials against a library of around 600 decarbonization levers spanning 100 material categories. This comprehensive assessment allows Danfoss to identify and implement cost-optimized decarbonization strategies, such as selecting alternative suppliers for low-carbon materials like iron, steel and aluminium. Danfoss has integrated data-driven carbon assessments into its product engineering and procurement processes. This integration helps the company identify and focus on key suppliers responsible for a significant portion of emissions. Danfoss uses this data to develop lower-carbon products and retrain employees to incorporate decarbonization strategies into every business process.[79]

Danfoss is leveraging GenAI in partnership with Google Cloud to optimize customer experiences and streamline its internal processes. This includes automating tasks like managing knowledge, generating product descriptions and using AI-powered chatbots to enhance interactions, particularly in e-commerce settings. Danfoss will also utilize its advanced energy-efficient technologies to design sustainable cooling systems for data centres. This includes innovations to capture and reuse excess heat, aligning with Google's sustainability objectives.[80]

Migrating to the Next Frontier

The PIEX lens provides a way to zoom out of extant business models to expand:

- The locus of enactment *into co-intelligence flows of interactive engagements.*
- The locus of capability *into SDI platforms.*
- The locus of activity *into the lived-journeys of creative-experiencers.*

- The locus of strategy *into coalition networks in interconnected organizational ecosystems.*
- The locus of performance *into SWIs at speed, scale and scope.*

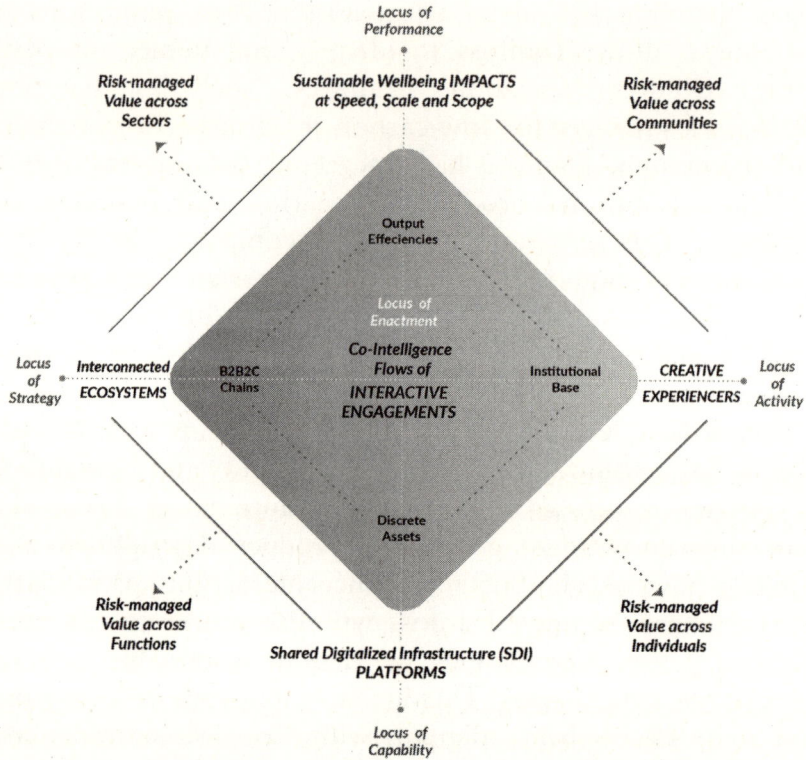

Figure 4-4: Migrating to the Next Frontier (Source: Venkat Ramaswamy)

Across the five loci, there *is an expansion of innovation and value creation* as shown in **Figure 4-4,** from the *inner diamond* of conventional industrial era value creation to the *outer diamond* of the PIEX lens with *risk-managed value co-created across*:

i)   *Individuals*—ensuring that value co-creation is tailored and risk is managed at the individual customer or employee level.

ii) *Communities*—extending value co-creation and risk management to the broader society or a particular community, which could be a geographic community or a thematic community of interest.

iii) *Functions*—integrating risk-managed value co-creation into all functional areas within an enterprise, such as sales and marketing, customer service and branding, supply chain and operations, HR, IT and so on.

iv) *Sectors*—pursuing risk-managed value co-creation across different industry sectors or types (public, private or plural), recognizing that sectors are interconnected and that a systemic approach is needed.

In contrast to the inner diamond of enterprise value creation with an institutional base of assets and operational efficiencies of B2B2C chains, which are still relevant, organizations must now reorient themselves towards embracing a shift towards *collaborative coalition networks in interconnected ecosystems that leverage SDI platforms via service-as-a-capability of Nextgen AI factories*. Engagements are no longer one-size-fits-all but rather AI-infused interactive flows engendering life–experiences of value. Success isn't just about what's produced but also about the sustainable wellbeing impacts of solutions at scale and the speed and reach of those solutions that expand value in 'all win more' ways.

However, as organizations transform themselves beyond the inner diamond to the expansive space of the outer diamond of **Figure 4-4**, it is important to keep in mind that the former is included along with the latter. For instance, a smart connected product company needs to still manage its B2B2C chains and operational efficiencies even as it expands into AI-infused smart connected experience ecosystems. In instances where the physical product is itself not necessarily smart and connected (e.g., the coffee bean at Starbucks), but the buying and consumption experience is, physical channels of engagement must still be managed in terms of reach and growth as part of omnichannel strategies across retail environments. Even as online commerce continues to grow, it is still only about 20 per cent of retail sales worldwide, and brand and channel-related risks and customer segment preferences have to be still managed. For instance, Gen Z shoppers have played a significant role in the revival of retail brick-and-mortar shopping, even as they shop online.

Organizations need to carefully navigate and defend themselves across the spectrum of physical and digital, as the *competitive landscape also expands considerably* with digital startups and more digitally oriented companies focused on value-added services and niche ecosystem strategies. As an illustrative example, let us consider the opportunities and challenges of Nike in navigating value expansion beyond products to experience ecosystems.

Navigating the Expansion of Value at Nike—People, Play and Planet

In the early 2000s, Nike recognized a unique opportunity: combining data with the popular trend of music during fitness. This insight led to the launch of NikePlus in 2006, a platform enabling runners to track, analyse and share their performance, thus introducing a digitalized social community for running enthusiasts. Through partnerships, such as with Apple's iPod and later the Apple Watch, Nike expanded NikePlus, transforming it into a multi-platform experience that connected physical activities with digitalized social engagement. This shift marked Nike's transition from a focus on standalone products to what then-CEO Mark Parker described as 'product + experiences', underscoring the co-creation of value through interactive engagement with consumers.

Digital Experiences and Direct Engagement

With the introduction of the Nike Training Club and Nike Run Club apps, Nike developed a suite of digital tools to foster regular fitness habits and enhance its members' experiences. These platforms offered personalized workout plans, goal-setting tools and daily content—aligning with Nike's strategy to create ongoing interactive engagements. During the Covid-19 pandemic, these digital platforms became a lifeline for users, offering accessible, customized home workouts that adapted to the evolving needs of users worldwide.

This push towards digitalization was strengthened with the creation of Nike's House of Innovation (HoI) retail concept, launched in flagship locations like New York City. These stores combined physical spaces with digital features through the Nike app, providing a digitally connected journey for customers to browse, reserve and purchase items seamlessly. By fostering local community connections and allowing members to personalize products, Nike's House of Innovation exemplified its commitment to enhancing consumer experience through a blend of digital and physical interactions.

The Direct-to-Consumer Strategy and Market Adaptation

Under CEO John Donahue, Nike doubled down on its direct-to-consumer strategy (NCX) in response to shifting consumer behaviours. This approach streamlined Nike's wholesale distribution network, prioritizing fewer retail partners while focusing on a cohesive online and offline experience. By building an integrated retail ecosystem that combined digital commerce data and local insights, Nike aimed to sustain customer loyalty and engagement through accessible, personalized experiences. However, coming out of the pandemic, Nike's continued momentum initially showed that its direct-to-consumer strategy, with a well-integrated online plus offline retail experience, seemed to be working. But at the same time, it seemed to have also lost sight of its roots in sneaker culture and the product space itself as newer focused brands and competitors stepped into the core critical running category on the one hand, and post-pandemic market shifts towards casual and comfortable wear sneakers on the other. Nike is now focused more on balancing the physical and digital, with physical product innovation of shoes. Donahoe said, 'We underinvested in that (running category), and that's what we're reinvesting in.'[81] In September 2024, Nike announced that Elliott Hill, a company long-timer who had just retired in 2020, was returning to replace Donahue as CEO. In December 2024, Elliott Hill detailed a near-term plan for Nike's big turnaround involving refreshing product innovation, rebuilding wholesale and reinvigorating marketing efforts with amped-up, athlete-focused storytelling, all with 'sport at the center'. 'We lost our obsession with sport,' he told investors. 'Moving forward, we will lead with sport and put the athlete at the centre of every decision. The sharpness in each sport is what differentiates our brand and our business and fuels our culture.'[82]

Nike's renewed emphasis on sport and athlete-driven storytelling was on full display during Super Bowl LIX in February 2025, when the company aired its first Super Bowl ad in over two decades. The 60-second spot, featuring WNBA superstar Caitlin Clark, Olympic gymnast Jordan Chiles, and Grammy-winning rapper Doechii, was a bold statement of resilience and empowerment. By tapping into the meteoric rise of women's sports, Nike aimed to reassert its dominance in the performance footwear and apparel space while reconnecting with the cultural pulse of the next generation of athletes. As Nicole Hubbard Graham, a Nike veteran who was named Chief Marketing Officer in 2023, notes: 'It's a timeless athlete insight of being told things you can't be and needing to overcome that.'[83] Beyond the high-profile commercial, Nike's marketing shift also reflects a strategic departure from its previous overreliance on performance marketing. Instead, the company is refocusing on brand-building storytelling—an approach that had once cemented Nike as a cultural icon. As Graham said, 'We really want to get back to athletes over algorithms. You cannot be capturing demand if you're not also creating demand.'[84] With Elliott Hill at the helm, Nike is working to recapture the emotional connection with consumers, leveraging both its storied heritage and a fresh wave of athlete endorsements to drive demand and inspire a new era of engagement.

Leveraging GenAI for Innovation

Returning to its roots in product design and customer engagement, Nike has embraced Generative AI (GenAI) through its Athlete Imagined Revolution (AIR) project, Nike created GenAI-driven custom prototypes tailored to top athletes' unique preferences and performance needs. In collaboration with its athletes, Nike's design team now generates options using AI tools, marking a shift towards hyper-personalized product offerings. Additionally, Nike built a proprietary LLM within its 'private garden' ecosystem, combining internal performance data with public datasets to drive product innovation. Chief Innovation Officer John Hoke described it as a powerful tool for designing personalized products that cater to specific athletic requirements. He said,

> It's a little bit of thinking about developing a private garden, of looking at our own datasets that are exclusive to Nike—so performance data from an athlete, from our laboratories, etc. And then kind of commingling that with some things from the public garden, but making sure that that's all contained within what we're training the model on.[85]

Sustainability and Social Impact through People, Planet and Play

Nike's commitment to sustainable and inclusive practices has evolved into its People, Planet and Play framework, with purpose-driven goals in diversity, youth engagement and environmental responsibility. In recent years, Nike has invested significantly in advancing its diversity and inclusion initiatives, including a 41 per cent representation of racial and ethnic minorities in its US workforce and over $1.4 billion in procurement with diverse suppliers. In 2023 alone, Nike supported 1.1 million children through sports programmes, trained over 142,000 coaches and created inclusive play opportunities, particularly focusing on engaging girls in sports.

On the environmental front, Nike has made strides in reducing its footprint. By FY23, Nike achieved a 69 per cent reduction in greenhouse gas emissions across its facilities and ensured that 100 per cent of waste in Tier 1 manufacturing was diverted from landfills. These sustainability milestones reflect Nike's emphasis on not only creating value for consumers but also contributing positively to the planet and society.

Governance and Long-Term Purpose-Driven Strategy

Nike's governance model for its purpose initiatives is overseen by its corporate responsibility, sustainability and governance (CRS&G) committee, which reports directly to the board. This committee monitors Nike's progress on diversity, supply chain safety and environmental goals, ensuring alignment with broader corporate objectives. Through this governance structure, Nike continuously assesses its purpose-driven actions and adapts to the evolving expectations of consumers, employees and investors who prioritize sustainable and socially responsible business practices.

Nike's journey illustrates how organizations need to continuously innovate through ups and down, balancing human drive with AI in leveraging co-intelligence flows interactive engagements, ecosystems and platforms to co-create sustainable value over time. By blending physical and biological, with digital, social, and cultural experiences, Nike continues to forge impactful brand relationships, while strengthening its commitment to People, Planet and Play—an approach that aligns purpose with profitability and long-term societal benefits.

All in all, sustainable value co-creation requires balanced risk-taking by focusing on co-creation opportunities that can generate superior returns and rewards while simultaneously reducing risks for both enterprises and their stakeholders. Increased shareholder/investor activism, as well as employee and customer activism, is also driving greater expectations for better management of risk-reward relationships.

In expanding value with co-intelligence across the five loci:

- Start by identifying key points of engagement within your current offerings. Use AI-driven insights to personalize and deepen customer and stakeholder interactions at these touchpoints, enhancing co-creative experiences through continuous feedback loops.
- For effective SDI platform integration, analyse your infrastructure to identify and partner with AI or data platforms that best align with your needs. This could mean adopting industry-specific cloud-edge AI solutions to enhance services and streamline data flows.
- Map stakeholder journeys to understand their lived experiences and unmet/unarticulated needs. Use co-intelligence tools to foster participation and personalization in these experiences. Encourage user feedback and integrate these insights to make lived-journey experiences more engaging and impactful.
- Actively seek partnerships and alliances within and outside your sector, with an eye on shared goals such as sustainability or technological innovation. Establish and/or participate in shared digital infrastructures and standards that facilitate smooth interaction and data sharing, especially for industries looking to foster cross-sector innovation.
- Define SWI metrics relevant to your organization's goals. These could include environmental, social and governance (ESG) measures, aligned with global sustainability targets, such as carbon reduction or community engagement

milestones. Implement these metrics at every level, from strategic decision-making to daily operations.

By following this loci-based approach, organizations can strategically navigate the complexities of migrating to a co-intelligence-driven future, enhancing both internal capabilities and external impact. As organizations expand value creation with a PIEX lens, they have to adapt to completely new techno-enterprise environments in a co-intelligence world. Leveraging co-intelligence extends beyond organizational boundaries and fosters an ecosystemic approach to solving global challenges with all stakeholders.

5

Ecosystem Co-Innovation with Stakeholders

'Imagine electric cars making up a third of all vehicles on US roads and fleets of battery-powered taxis whizzing around the streets of London and New York City.' So begins a recent World Economic Forum report on energy transition.[1] But it's a snapshot from the year 1900, when electric vehicles (EVs) were a common vista in Europe and the US.[2] Their limited range and the availability of cheap gasoline swung the balance towards the latter, and EVs had virtually disappeared by the mid-1930s. The rest is history until now; a century later, with energy transitions, there's a renewed vision of mobility ecosystems with a decarbonized future of mobility and a race towards net-zero carbon emissions, all of which requires co-innovating Life-Xverse ecosystems with all stakeholders.

What a remarkable transformation it has been in the automotive sector from when Henry Ford launched the industry's first moving car assembly line at the Highland Park Plant in Detroit, Michigan, in 1913, to Elon Musk co-founding Tesla in 2003 and launching its first EV car in 2008 with EV car sales now reaching 14 million globally. While Tesla has opened up its 50,000-plus Supercharger Network to other automakers, rising Chinese EV competition (e.g., from BYD) and changing tariffs, geographic economic conditions and ultimately, fluctuating consumer demand continue to affect the balance of electric, gasoline, hybrid and alternative fuel (e.g., hydrogen) cars, not to mention car ownership versus access through ride-hailing platforms. Changing regulations, subsidies and incentives, while having had positive effects on sales uptake, make it challenging for established automakers who have varying portfolio strategies and corporate visions of their own (e.g., Toyota emphasizing hybrid EVs with a longer-term hydrogen-fuelled vision, having launched its Mirai, which combines hydrogen with oxygen from the outside air to generate power; Mercedes expecting to have 50 per cent of its fleet as EVs by 2030; and Ford pursuing both internal combustion engine [ICE] vehicles and EVs).

Within these changing corporate strategic directions across particular enterprise ecosystems, organizations have to pursue *ecosystem co-innovation with all stakeholders, within and across the private, public and plural sectors.* Ed Freeman's stakeholder theory aligns with our thinking here. As he put it, '*Managing for stakeholders is about creating as much value as possible for all stakeholders without resorting to trade-offs.*'[3]

Into the Automotive-Mobility Life-Xverse

In a co-intelligence world, the world of automobiles has transformed into a *connected cars, autonomous/automated driving, shared and electric/electrified (CASE)* mobility ecosystem. Cars, from being just computers-on-wheels, have become *intelligence-on-wheels*, with the opportunity to elevate our Life-Xverse value co-creation experiences. Companies are exploring the connected car ecosystem horizon, with technologies ranging from autonomous vehicles (AVs) to advanced driver assistance systems (ADAS). Collaboration with tech-forward organizations on software development and cloud infrastructure has become crucial. The trend towards sustainability is influencing the automotive industry's push towards vehicle electrification. The industry is focused on EV manufacturing and meeting the consumer demand for electric or hybrid vehicles. Auto OEMs are driving sustainability and customer convenience through other means as well, such as mobility as a service. Rather than having to buy a car in the traditional way, consumers get a range of shared mobility options (such as e-hailing, P2P car sharing/riding and shared micro-mobility). We are also witnessing transformations across all functions of the automotive OEMs—in ensuring they have resilient supply chains (for example, to avoid shortages of chips or EV components), digital retailing (for example, contactless buying and online dealerships) and proactive servicing (for example, predictive maintenance and over-the-air car updates).

Auto OEMs are also forging new types of partnerships with companies in extended or allied business *value chain* ecosystems. Consider GM Marketplace, the industry's first in-car commerce platform, which connects users with various brands. For example, if the driver clicks on the fuel icon, petrol stations appear in the vicinity of the vehicle. If Coffee Time is selected, a further dialogue appears for locating a café and then a menu for selecting a particular beverage. If one has decided to pick up and drink the coffee on the go, payment can also be made immediately via Mastercard from the car. The platform is designed to be open so that other interested companies can get involved.[4] Stellantis, resulting from the merger of Fiat Chrysler Automobiles and France's PSA Group, has launched a connected service called Free2move. This initiative goes beyond just vehicles, aiming to create a comprehensive mobility ecosystem encompassing data services, smart features and seamless transportation solutions. PSA is partnering with Huawei's IoT platform OceanConnect to create a Connected Vehicle Modular Platform, and the solutions are offered for download as apps via established iOS or Android stores.[5] Free2move eSolutions, formed from a partnership between Stellantis and NHOA Energy, champions the transition to electric vehicles.

Similarly, major automotive companies are establishing innovative ecosystem coalition networks with tech-forward enterprises and startups to shore up their software capabilities as the car is becoming intelligence-on-wheels. Volkswagen created a 100 per cent subsidiary, CARIAD, to develop its automotive software. It works on the VW.OS automotive operating system, connecting with VW's automotive cloud, consolidating technological platform solutions for data-driven business models and group innovation. CARIAD holds stakes in fifteen automotive technology companies, such as diconium and VAIVA, focusing on different digitization aspects of cars. For instance, its Wireless Car concept is about the networking of cars—if a Volkswagen customer wants to go to Munich, her car will drive her to the train station, and when she arrives in Munich another VW Group vehicle will be waiting for her.[6] CARIAD also collaborates with Bosch on the Automated Driving Alliance to make partially and highly automated driving suitable for volume production and with Microsoft on Volkswagen Automotive Cloud and an Automated Driving Platform.[7]

Automakers are bringing in co-intelligence into the way they design their *offering* ecosystems. Accenture and BMW's GenAI platform, EKHO (Enterprise Knowledge Harmonizer and Orchestrator), revolutionizes the process of transforming enterprise data into actionable knowledge. EKHO ingests and analyses diverse enterprise data using LLMs to provide precise answers to complex questions. At its core are GenAI-enabled GPT agents that intelligently select data sources based on user intent and enterprise-specific data and provide answers. It continuously learns from user feedback and new information added to its knowledge base. For instance, consider how EKHO helps a salesperson at a dealership. **Prospective BMW customers** face a challenge: selecting their ideal vehicle from nearly **10 million configurations** of paint, technology, interiors and accessories. Each option has configuration rules, making some choices incompatible. Previously, salespeople spent hours researching manuals, verifying and recommending configurations. **EKHO** brings about 30–40 per cent productivity improvements in this process.[8]

Nissan uses Katana Studio's content-creation SaaS offering built on NVIDIA Omniverse, COATcreate, for a variety of tasks such as product validation and CGI marketing asset creation. Nissan integrates its data into COATcreate, enabling its business users to seamlessly interact with and test configurations of their cars, such as the new Nissan Z. The users can manipulate 3D assets and scenes using OpenUSD, the digital twins industry standards. COATcreate has greatly reduced Nissan's project completion time. The traditional production pipeline, which involved multiple rounds of interaction between the client, agency, and studio, would typically take about three weeks to complete. COATcreate, on the other hand, allows users to complete that same process in just a few hours.[9]

Pulling all this off successfully requires dramatic transformation of *management ecosystems* supporting value chain ecosystems enabling smart connected products as offering ecosystems on the one hand, and energy transitions and NEST ecosystems on the other hand, with mobility ecosystems entailing enterprises that aim to go beyond cars and transportation to create sustainable city-level societal impacts. Consider Woven by Toyota, a Toyota subsidiary focused on connected mobility solutions. Its smart-city initiative, Woven City, is expected to launch in 2025 and will serve as a 'living laboratory' for testing and developing new technologies, including autonomous driving, AI and hydrogen energy. Toyota has defined twelve distinct areas of daily life to further empower people and has forged partnerships for co-innovations in these areas. For instance, it is partnering with Eneos for carbon-free hydrogen energy, with NTT for a smart-city platform, and with Nissin for healthy living.[10]

Co-innovating Life-Xverse ecosystems with stakeholders is key to success in this new landscape. The needs and preferences of end users, the global push for sustainability and the CASE innovation drivers act as powerful catalysts in shaping mobility ecosystems. This cross-pollination of ideas and expertise across the enterprise ecosystem fosters advancements in mobility

solutions, accelerates innovation cycles and ultimately benefits
both businesses and consumers. Traditional boundaries between
automakers, technology companies and mobility service
providers are rapidly changing and blurring, especially with
software-defined EVs. Established automakers are competing and
collaborating with technology companies to develop EV platforms
and charging infrastructure. Meanwhile, ride-sharing providers
are entering the fray by offering EV rentals and integrating them
into their fleets. This fluidity extends further as energy companies
invest in battery technology and governments enact policies to
promote sustainable transportation. In such a dynamic relational
ecosystem, partnerships form and dissolve rapidly and companies
must constantly adapt to new players, technologies and market
dynamics to maintain relevance and drive innovation.[11]

We begin by exploring the digital, autonomy and energy
transition strategies of automakers, starting with Tesla and
then traditional OEMs such as Ford and GM.

Autonomy+ Mobility + Sustainability at Tesla

Tesla isn't your average car company. Forget roaring engines
and grease-stained garages. Think electric and sustainable.
Think digital. Then think mobility. Tesla envisages its
business as designing and manufacturing a complete energy
and transportation ecosystem—'building a world powered by
solar energy, running on batteries and transported by electric
vehicles'. For example, Tesla leveraged its battery technology
for electric cars to create the Powerwall home energy storage
product, offering energy savings and backup power. Tesla's
Master Plan Part 3 outlines the company's broader strategy
to achieve a sustainable global energy economy through end-
use electrification and sustainable electricity generation and
storage.[12] Its vision for the future includes a smart grid where
Tesla vehicles could potentially tie into a broader energy
network connected to homes and other Teslas. This network
would facilitate novel interconnected offering ecosystems at

population scale, like an autonomous Tesla ride-hailing network or a peer-to-peer car rental service using its self-driving cars.

Clearly, Tesla is reimagining the mobility-energy ecosystem and placing digital technology at the core of the driving experience. Tesla vehicles are integrated with Advanced Sensor Coverage, providing up to eight surround cameras with 360 degrees of visibility at up to 250 m of range. Originally, these cameras were complemented with twelve ultrasonic sensors that allowed for the detection of hard and soft objects. Since then, they have been replaced with a full-fledged Tesla Vision, its camera-based autopilot system. The onboard computer processes the volumes of incoming data using an in-house neural network, which is used to train the Tesla Autopilot self-driving model. The vehicle enables real-time data processing to allow it to effectively and safely navigate obstacles on the road while providing riders with a refined and safer experience.[13] Currently, Tesla offers in its vehicles certain advanced driver assist systems under its Autopilot and Full Self-Driving (FSD) options, although at present the driver is ultimately responsible for controlling the vehicle.

Offering Ecosystem Transformation

In 2022, Tesla began experimenting with a radically new approach to training its Autopilot AI. The traditional neural network path planner system was a rules-based engine that told the car what to do—'stop when the light is red' or 'don't cross double-yellow lines into incoming traffic'. Tesla engineers would typically hand-code these rules. The new approach was called 'learn-from-humans'—imagine millions of Tesla drivers acting as virtual co-pilots, constantly teaching the system the nuances of real-world driving. Every time a driver interacts with the Autopilot or FSD systems, their actions and the car's response are collected automatically. This data includes successful manoeuvers, driver corrections and even situations where Autopilot disengaged. By analysing this collective human input, Tesla's AI can identify areas for improvement and refine its decision-making processes. Recall *tokens of intelligence* that we discussed in Chapter 1. Tesla's AI system represents the Nextgen AI factories as we conceptualized in **Figure 2-1**: *Life-Xverse Innovation and Co-Intelligence Architecture*. From its fleet of millions of cars around the world, the company collects billions of video frames per day. After the AI system was trained on 1.5 million clips, the algorithm became very good. By April 2023, Elon Musk conducted a successful test drive of the new FSD through Palo Alto. At one point in the drive, Musk exclaimed, 'Oh wow, even my human neural network failed here, but the car did the right thing.'[14] Maybe, but one of us (VR) has experienced the opposite as well: indecisiveness on the part of a Tesla car.

In 2024, Tesla took a serious turn towards full autonomy. Musk teased the market with plans to unveil a Tesla robotaxi service, which would be powered by unsupervised FSD. He expects Tesla's Optimus humanoid robots to be used internally the following year. And he writes emphatically on X:

> Going balls to the wall for autonomy is a blindingly obvious move. Everything else is like variations on a horse carriage.[15]

Tesla may also potentially benefit from Musk's investments in his AI startup, xAI—in September 2024, he announced the setup of Colossus, a massive cluster of 100,000 NVIDIA H100 chips.[16] But Tesla's push for cost-effective and scalable autonomy by relying principally on only cameras for FSD is not without its risks. For instance, according to a *Wall Street Journal* report analysing data from over 200 crashes submitted to federal regulators, Tesla Vision may present public safety concerns unlike the broader industry's approach of utilizing a combination of cameras+RADAR+LIDAR, the transition.[17]

All Tesla vehicles, which are IoT cars, have at least a 2G cellular connection to the Internet. Through this connection, Tesla continuously improves the car by updating its onboard model and application in a process called over-the-air (OTA) updates. When the US National Highway Traffic Safety Administration issued recall notices related to fire hazards to GM and Tesla, both companies responded very differently. GM recalled 370,000 pickups into its dealers for repair, while Tesla quickly issued an OTA update to the 30,000 vehicles affected. When TSA accepted the fix, Tesla had, in a way, redefined the meaning of a recall. Or consider the time when Tesla drivers woke up to a new capability in their car—the Summon feature, delivered via OTA, allowed drivers to remotely move their car using their smartphone app. Tesla had redefined customer experience.[18]

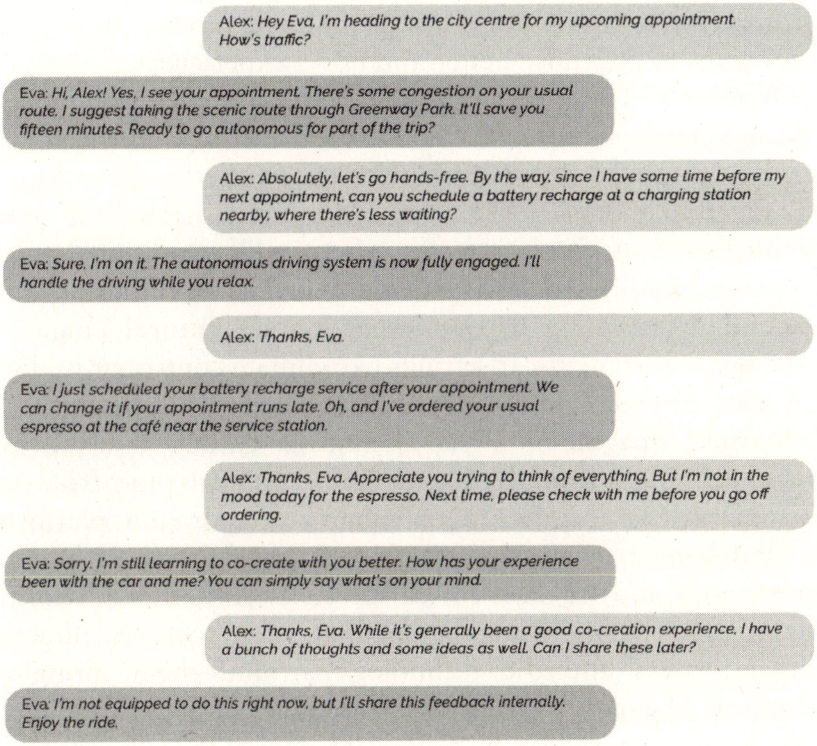

Alex: Hey Eva, I'm heading to the city centre for my upcoming appointment. How's traffic?

Eva: Hi, Alex! Yes, I see your appointment. There's some congestion on your usual route. I suggest taking the scenic route through Greenway Park. It'll save you fifteen minutes. Ready to go autonomous for part of the trip?

Alex: Absolutely, let's go hands-free. By the way, since I have some time before my next appointment, can you schedule a battery recharge at a charging station nearby, where there's less waiting?

Eva: Sure. I'm on it. The autonomous driving system is now fully engaged. I'll handle the driving while you relax.

Alex: Thanks, Eva.

Eva: I just scheduled your battery recharge service after your appointment. We can change it if your appointment runs late. Oh, and I've ordered your usual espresso at the café near the service station.

Alex: Thanks, Eva. Appreciate you trying to think of everything. But I'm not in the mood today for the espresso. Next time, please check with me before you go off ordering.

Eva: Sorry. I'm still learning to co-create with you better. How has your experience been with the car and me? You can simply say what's on your mind.

Alex: Thanks, Eva. While it's generally been a good co-creation experience, I have a bunch of thoughts and some ideas as well. Can I share these later?

Eva: I'm not equipped to do this right now, but I'll share this feedback internally. Enjoy the ride.

Figure 5-1: A Hypothetical Conversation of Alex, a human driver, with Eva, an AI bot, in a car

However, consider a vignette of a hypothetical conversation between a human driver and an AI bot in a car (see **Figure 5-1**). In bringing *AI systems-into-the loop* of the customer's journey, enterprises have to be mindful of categorically trying to deliver experiences for the customer. Rather, they need to co-design these *together with* the customer, by also bringing the *human-into-the-loop of AI systems*, in flows of interactive engagements, which facilitate individuals' co-creation experiences that are meaningful to them—including *reverse* prompt engineering *where the AI is able to prompt the human*. For instance, in the case of Tesla Autopilot, when one proactively disengages the Autopilot while driving, it immediately asks, 'What happened?' Here, the voice button enables us to speak and send Tesla an anonymous message. This helps Tesla in fine-tuning its algorithms to engender better and novel experiences.

However, Tesla, as of 2024, is yet to implement natural language conversational AI in its automobiles, where one can just ask questions about Tesla features on the fly. Elon Musk has stated that Grok, xAI's advanced smart assistant, will soon be integrated into Tesla vehicles, where unlike traditional voice assistants, the system can provide real-time information and respond dynamically to queries in human natural language (whether adjusting in-car settings like climate control or finding the least crowded restaurant and navigating there directly). [19] Further, imagine if Tesla is able to gather and process contextual ideas and lived experiences in real time from its customers. For instance, Qualcomm's Snapdragon platform facilitates interactive value creation at the edge, where human interactions and AI meet in real time. Its AI-driven platform, Snapdragon Digital Chassis, facilitates interactions directly between users and the technology around them, bringing advanced AI capabilities directly to vehicles, transforming real-time driving experiences by processing data at the edge, close to where interactions occur. Snapdragon-powered cars equipped with AI engines can dynamically adjust their interfaces based on the driver's preferences, understand commands through natural language processing and seamlessly provide real-time feedback for driver assistance. Imagine a human navigating or managing in-car features just by asking questions, akin to interacting with a co-pilot. This interface not only personalizes the driving experience but also captures contextual data on user preferences and feedback. Such data is invaluable for fine-tuning AI models on the edge, ensuring vehicles become safer and more intuitive with every interaction. In this way, Snapdragon enables a continuous, user-centred flow of engagement that enhances co-creation experiences while simultaneously building a richer dataset for further refinement, creating a loop of value creation at the edge.

Reimagined Business Models

The intimate customer relationship that is enabled by IoT allows Tesla to experiment with new business models—it has disintermediated the car dealer and sells directly to the customers. Tesla's vehicle sales channels currently include its website and an international network of company-owned showrooms. In some jurisdictions, Tesla also has galleries to educate and inform customers about its products, but such locations do not transact in the sale of vehicles. Such a business model enables Tesla to better control inventory costs, manage warranty service and pricing and obtain rapid customer feedback. In order to provide a touchless delivery experience, Tesla leaves test-drive vehicles in parking lots at its locations, each with its unique QR code posted in the window. Customers scan the code, enter their information and get started on a test drive without talking or even seeing a Tesla employee.[20]

This disintermediation goes beyond just the selling process. Tesla provides service for its EVs through mobile service technicians who perform work remotely at customers' homes or other locations (along with some company-owned service locations for more involved service requests). The connectivity of its vehicles also allows Tesla to diagnose and remedy many problems remotely and proactively. Thus, compared to traditional automobile manufacturers and their dealer networks, Tesla has faster response times and more optimized logistics and inventory. Such remote connectivity also transforms the way Tesla manages an accident situation. Normally, figuring out what caused an accident takes time. But, as Vijay Govindarajan and Venkat Venkatraman point out in *Fusion Strategy*, with a tripartite twin, Tesla can quickly access car product data from its design, manufacturing process data (details about the factory line, robots and people involved in building the car) and performance data during the accident (speed, direction, seatbelt use, weather and who was driving—human or Autopilot). By comparing this crash data with past accidents, thanks to the tripartite twin, Tesla can rapidly guess what went wrong. This lets them develop ways to prevent similar accidents in the future, making their cars even safer.[21] Traditional auto OEMs, on the other hand, typically have data on design and manufacturing in silos but do not capture deployment data in the flow of the accident, thereby being inefficient about the diagnosis and redesign processes.

Even Tesla's after-sales market strategy is very different compared to the traditional automakers. An internal combustion engine vehicle, in 2021, resulted in $36,000 of extra revenues over its lifetime in terms of parts, maintenance and servicing. With an EV, the lifetime after-sales revenue saw a drastic six-fold reduction.[22] Tesla compensates for this with software sales, similar to how Apple makes additional revenues from sales of apps available for iPhone. Tesla offers features like FSD, and access to enhanced connectivity as monthly subscriptions through its app or the in-vehicle user interface. Tesla offers its car owners an insurance product that uses metrics of real-time driving behaviour, such as aggressive turning, hard braking, and unsafe following distance, to determine customers' insurance rates.[23]

Not just disintermediation, Tesla practises a higher degree of vertical integration than what traditional automakers do. It follows what Michael Valentin describes in his 2019 book, *The Tesla Way*, as cross-integration—'condensing the value chain, decompartmentalizing the functions and connecting better with the ecosystem'. Tesla manufactures components, such as dashboards and seats, in-house. Its acquisition of Grohmann, a German engineering automation company, reflects this strategy of gaining internal control over manufacturing processes. On its shop floor, skilled engineers collaborate seamlessly with production workers in an agile scrum approach, blurring the lines between traditional hierarchies.[24] Its 2024 announcement of a $500 million investment in Dojo, a new supercomputer designed in-house specifically to train AI with videos, reinforces its vertically integrated approach.[25]

However, Tesla still collaborates with external suppliers and partners on a number of other fronts. For instance, Tesla released FleetAPI, a tool for developers to build apps that work with its cars, Powerwalls, solar roofs and charging stations. At CES 2024, Samsung Electronics showcased how it leveraged this capability to connect its SmartThings Energy to Tesla products. With this new feature, customers using a Samsung device can see if their home has power from the grid and also control their appliances to make the Powerwall battery last longer when there is an outage, such as during a storm.[26] Also, Panasonic, which produces around a tenth of global EV batteries, has been a long-term co-innovation partner and supplier of Tesla.[27]

Tesla's ecosystem thinking is evident in its model for EV charging. It has a growing global network of Tesla Superchargers, which are its industrial-grade, high-speed vehicle chargers— about 6000 Supercharger stations worldwide, offering over 50,000 charging points in 2024.[28] Where possible, Tesla co-locates Superchargers with its solar and energy storage systems to reduce costs and promote renewable power. Supercharger stations are typically placed along well-travelled routes and in and around dense city centres to allow vehicle owners the ability to enjoy quick, reliable charging along an extensive network with convenient stops. Tesla also works with a wide variety of hospitality, retail and public destinations, as well as businesses with commuting employees, to offer additional charging options for its customers.[29] Tesla made its in-house developed connector, North American Charging Standard (NACS), which can be used for both regular and fast charging EVs, an open standard in November 2022.[30] Soon, companies like Ford, GM, Rivian and other EV OEMs announced their plans to embrace NACS. This is Tesla setting an industry standard. It can benefit from increased Supercharger utilization and revenue while being positioned for government incentives tied to standardization.

Newer players have entered the mobility ecosystem. Xiaomi, a Chinese multinational electronics company known for smartphones and smart home devices, announced, in 2024, its foray into EVs. While Tesla's approach is based on creating an automotive-energy ecosystem, Xiaomi's strategy is in embracing a *Human x Car x Home* ecosystem. Xiaomi's HyperOS is designed to integrate seamlessly across a wide range of devices, including smartphones, smartwatches, TVs and cars, creating a cohesive and intelligent ecosystem.

As organizations navigate the complexity of their interconnected ecosystems, they must also be mindful of *managing ecosystemic and organizational risks across stakeholders*, a subject we discuss at length in the next chapter.

Ford+

In May 2021, Ford unveiled its strategic transformation program, Ford+. As the company claims, 'It's our roadmap to determine Ford's trajectory for the next 10–15 years—creating the single biggest opportunity to create value for the company since Henry Ford scaled the Model T.'[31] Central to this plan are electric vehicles, which Ford wants to comprise around half of its global sales by 2030, connected cars and new revenue streams via subscriptions and digital services. It created three new businesses—Ford Model e (to create electric vehicles and digital experiences), Ford Blue (to deliver a more profitable and vibrant internal combustion engine business) and Ford Pro (to address the market for commercial vehicles and services).

Beyond the significant transformation of its business and operations, Ford+ also entails an important shift in the mindset of the company. Jim Farley, CEO of Ford Motor Company, highlights the big changes that Ford faces as part of its new strategy:

> The biggest transformation for us is to a software services–dominated company and brand. We have to invest in electric architectures and build software know-how in the company. And we need to integrate that know-how in ways we've never had to before . . . When we have the ability to update our products dynamically with software, the customer relationship is no longer episodic. It's every day.[32]

This has necessitated Ford to embrace digital technologies and co-innovations in a deep and significant way.

The Ford Mustang Mach-E, its first all-electric SUV, was introduced in 2019 and soon became the second highest-selling EV in the US. Ford adopted a completely different and unique approach for its development. In collaboration with the design advisory firm IDEO, it established a global design lab network called D-Ford, with teams around the world focusing not on products but on customers. Ford wanted to be more intentional and comprehensive about the diffusion of ideas and put in place a robust, enterprise-wide learning programme to give everyone at Ford access to the design tools and design thinking skill sets. The Mustang Mach-E came through a development process grounded in human-centred design, focused entirely on customer needs and desires. Its development team, called Team Edison, was made up of broad expertise, including members leading the design, charging strategy, infotainment and marketing of electric vehicles.[33]

Keeping customer needs at the forefront, Ford augmented the EV infrastructure available to them. For example, it worked with LG Energy Solution to improve battery supply for the Mustang Mach-E, expanding capacity three times over ten months in 2022,[34] and expanded this partnership in 2023 to bring more EVs to Europe.[35] It created the BlueOval™ Charge Network by stitching together ecosystem partners such as Shell Recharge, Electrify America/Canada, EV Connect and others, where Ford's customers can avail no-cost charging (up to 250 kWh).

Ford's commercial entity, Ford Pro, offers its customers a range of vehicles, including ICE, hybrid-powered models and electric vehicles. It also provides digital services that are integrated into the vehicles and help customers better manage their fleets, reduce costs and optimize efficiency as they transition to electric vehicles.[36] In 2023, Ford Pro's revenues were around $60 billion, with 12 per cent of the vehicles it sold having paid subscriptions for software services. Ford Pro has plans to triple its base of half a million paying commercial customers in a few years.[37]

Ford Pro is reimagining customized vans with their first-to-market Upfit Integration System (UIS). It allows aftermarket equipment makers improved access to the vehicle's electrical system. UIS allows them to control these features through a modern 13-inch SYNC 4 touchscreen instead of a clutter of physical switches.[38] With the newly implemented integration system, upfitters (third-party vehicle hardware/equipment makers) have access to more than 150 signals from the truck with attendant schematics and interfaces. Additionally, cloud-based software connects to the UIS, allowing equipment makers to add digital buttons that allow drivers to control their equipment from inside the truck. It also allows for remote monitoring by fleet managers—for instance, to track temperature in refrigerated vehicles carrying pharmaceuticals or food. Such digital solutions improve the efficiency, reliability and safety of vehicle modifications and customizations.

To enhance the experience of its customers, Ford established Canopy, a joint venture with security leader ADT, to develop AI-based camera technology for professional security monitoring of customers' vehicles. Via Ford Pro Telematics, it offers detailed data for fleet management, optimizing operations for businesses with multiple vehicles. It caters to small business owners and individual vehicle owners, with the FordPass Pro app providing convenient vehicle management features via a mobile app. Ford now focuses on maximizing vehicle uptime with real-time data and predictive maintenance for commercial operators with FORDLiive, and offers a comprehensive solution for larger enterprises and fleet operators with Ford Pro Intelligence, which combines telematics, data insights and connected services.[39]

GM's Connected Future Strategy

GM (General Motors) has worked through the past two decades of rapid transformation to deliver innovative solutions that provide best-in-class customer experiences. During this period, its vehicles are more connected than ever before with *digital chassis* solutions powering modern cockpits, telematic systems and advanced driver assistance systems. GM strives to make continued progress towards the future of mobility. Its CEO, Mary Barra, believes in a future mission of 'zero crashes to save lives, zero emissions so the future generations can inherit a healthier planet, and zero congestion so customers can get back a precious commodity, time'.[40]

GM is pursuing an electric and autonomous future through extensive investments in vehicle electrification, battery technology and software-enabled services. Like Ford, GM recognizes that the automotive industry's future is deeply interwoven with a digitally connected ecosystem that extends beyond individual car ownership to a network of shared, intelligent and sustainable transportation options.

The Ultium Platform—Powering Electric Mobility at Scale

Central to GM's approach is the Ultium Platform, a flexible and scalable electric vehicle (EV) architecture designed to power a wide range of vehicles, from compact cars to trucks. Through Ultium, GM aims to simplify its EV production processes and lower battery costs, making electric mobility more accessible to consumers. This platform approach mirrors Ford's modular strategy, enabling GM to adapt to diverse consumer demands and support different use cases, from daily commuting to commercial transport.

The Ultium battery technology also allows for varying configurations of battery packs, improving energy density and range flexibility. With this system, GM intends to establish a mass-market EV offering that addresses the key barriers to EV adoption, including affordability and charging infrastructure. To drive home the benefits of its Ultium platform, GM is working to integrate its battery systems with smart energy solutions, creating an ecosystem in which vehicles become mobile energy storage units, feeding electricity back into homes or the grid as needed.

Cruise—Pioneering Autonomous Vehicle Technology

Alongside electrification, GM heavily invested in autonomous vehicle (AV) technology through its subsidiary, Cruise. It developed and tested a fleet of autonomous, all-electric vehicles designed for urban environments, in its competitor Waymo's successful wake. The goal was to develop an accessible, on-demand AV service that enhances urban mobility, reduces emissions and alleviates traffic congestion—an ecosystem-driven approach that reflects the principles of co-intelligence.

GM has since folded Cruise's AV technology into the larger company, focusing on personal autonomy and building an integrated mobility solution of individual vehicle ownership alongside shared, intelligent transit systems.

Building an Insights Factory

In addition to its EV and AV initiatives, GM has taken bold steps to integrate artificial intelligence and machine learning across its operations through its Insights Factory. This initiative is aimed at transforming GM from a traditionally hardware-focused company into a data-driven, software-centric enterprise. GM's vision of 'Zero Crashes, Zero Emissions, Zero Congestion', may be words on a slide to some, but for others like Brian Ames, head of the AI Center and senior manager for transformation and enablement at GM, it is deeply personal, knowing a six-year-old that was killed in a car crash.[41] As Ames notes: 'If we're going to change the future, we must change ourselves today.'

The Insights Factory leverages Databricks as the foundational cloud platform, moving GM away from data silos and onto a unified data infrastructure. This shift allows GM to create a 'single source of truth' for data across the organization, enabling teams to collaborate seamlessly. According to GM, a major driver for this shift was the inefficiency of managing vast quantities of data—formerly requiring hundreds of person-years in data collection. Now, by integrating AI and machine learning, GM is empowering its employees to rapidly access, analyse and apply insights at scale.

A particularly compelling use case within the Insights Factory is GM's initiative to enhance vehicle safety through real-time data monitoring. By centralizing data on vehicle health and performance, GM's safety teams can now receive insights in hours instead of weeks, enabling them to address issues proactively and reduce the risk of crashes. This initiative underscores GM's commitment to customer safety and reinforces its mission of 'Zero Crashes'.

OnStar Insurance and Data-Driven Services: Shifting to a Customer-Centric Ecosystem

As GM transforms its product line, it has also focused on creating a data-centric ecosystem through services like OnStar Insurance. By utilizing vehicle data, GM offers personalized insurance premiums based on driving behaviour, providing a real-time feedback loop that encourages safer driving habits. This approach demonstrates GM's commitment to customer-centric value creation and highlights how connected vehicles can contribute to a safer, more sustainable driving experience.

OnStar Insurance is only one example of how GM is shifting to a software-driven model, where vehicles operate as platforms for personalized, data-driven services. In this way, GM is expanding beyond traditional automotive manufacturing into mobility services, blurring the boundaries between transportation, safety and personal convenience.

Collaboration and Infrastructure for a Carbon-Neutral Future

To accelerate its zero-emissions goal, GM has formed strategic partnerships across industries, aiming to build a robust EV charging network and expand renewable energy options. The EVgo partnership, for example, has established one of the largest fast-charging networks in the US, supporting GM's commitment to providing convenient access to charging infrastructure. Moreover, GM's collaboration with Honda on next-generation EV development exemplifies its approach to fostering co-creation within the mobility ecosystem. By collaborating with energy providers, technology partners and even traditional competitors, GM is reinforcing the automotive industry's shared mission of advancing sustainable mobility.

As part of its carbon-neutral pledge, GM plans to achieve 100 per cent renewable energy for its US operations by 2025 and globally by 2035. These goals not only reduce GM's environmental footprint but also contribute to the ecosystem's overall shift towards sustainability.

GM's strategy illustrates how co-intelligence can drive transformative impacts within the automotive ecosystem by integrating digital platforms, sustainable practices, and collaborative partnerships. Like Ford, GM is moving away from being solely a vehicle manufacturer towards becoming an ecosystem enabler that provides intelligent, sustainable mobility solutions.

Through platforms such as Ultium and data-driven services such as OnStar Insurance and the Insights Factory, GM aims to create a connected, experience-driven ecosystem that adapts to user needs in real time while advancing social and environmental goals. GM's ongoing strategic efforts illustrate how traditional industries have to navigate the complex challenges of co-intelligence driven ecosystems and deliver sustainable impacts at scale.

Let us now dwell on ecosystem co-innovation of automakers, one that must be supported by *Shared Digital Infrastructures (SDIs)*.

Fostering Radical Collaboration at Catena-X

Catena-X is a first-of-its-kind, open, collaborative data ecosystem from Europe for the automotive industry, linking global players into end-to-end value chains. Catena is Latin for 'chain', the individual links of which must interlock and hold firmly together. And X represents the participating stakeholders.[42]

Over the past two years, we (VR and KN) have been intently following the development of the network. When the chance arose to speak with a Catena-X insider, we eagerly seized the opportunity to gain deeper insights. In early January 2024, we sat down with Hagen Heubach, global VP and head of industry business unit automotive at SAP, and a board member of the Catena-X Automotive Network, over a video call. We began with Catena-X's origin story. Hagen says,

> When we were really in the midst of the Covid crisis, Oliver Zipse from BMW came by SAP headquarters and sat together with Christian Klein (CEO of SAP) and they discussed how the automotive industry was going through a massive transformation. And one fundamental issue remained that we cannot connect the dots across the value chain.[43]

Klein recalls the conversation that was the start of Catena-X:

> Zipse told me, 'You are managing our material flow, but you're also managing that of Bosch, Siemens and one of our material providers from Latin America. We're all running SAP. Let's get all of these CEOs together in a network, because supply chains are important, and they need to become more resilient.'[44]

Enterprises typically had a view of the supply chain one level up or down, but not across the value chain. And Heubach got involved in the Catena-X initiative when Klein asked him 'to make something happen'.

Soon, the Catena-X Automotive Network was initiated by a number of pioneering companies (including BMW, Mercedes Benz, Robert Bosch, SAP, Siemens, Volkswagen, ZF Group and others) and first publicly announced at the German government's Digital Summit in December 2020. It also received funding of around 100 million euros from the government as part of the 'Future Investments in the Vehicle Industry' programme. The driving force behind Catena-X is the need to streamline data exchange and collaboration. Traditionally, data exchange in the automotive industry has been fragmented and inefficient, hindering productivity and innovation. Catena-X tackles this challenge by promoting two key principles: *data interoperability* and *data sovereignty*.

Architecture for Data Interoperability and Sovereignty

Catena-X will work only if the participating members share relevant data. One of the biggest challenges with respect to such B2B data sharing is the lack of compatibility between datasets. Each enterprise stores data in their proprietary format, and even if they share the data, it will not make sense at an aggregate level. Another challenge is the complexity of the data-sharing process. Accordingly, Catena–X has developed a pioneering approach for interoperability, called eclipse dataspace connectors (EDCs), which act as universal translators and standardized protocols that dictate how data is formatted and structured. It uses *semantic models* as a universal language for data, ensuring consistent understanding across the ecosystem. Heubach says, 'The biggest example of a semantic model is the *digital twin of a vehicle* . . . from the Digital Twin Foundation, we use their Asset Administration Shell (AAS), which is already being used heavily by the machinery industry, and embed it into the standards at Catena-X.'

Imagine a car manufacturer using a digital twin of a new electric vehicle model. The AAS semantic model for battery data would specify how to represent information like battery capacity, range and chemical composition. This ensures that when a manufacturer shares the digital twin of their electric vehicle, anyone in Catena-X can access the battery data section and understand its meaning consistently. Thus, a potential customer, say a mobility service provider, can immediately understand the car's range based on its battery capacity. A battery supplier can use this data to see if their products are compatible with the EV model.

Data sovereignty empowers companies to retain control over their own data and decide who can access it and under what conditions. EDCs act as secure gateways, controlling data flows and enforcing access permissions defined by the data owner. Additionally, Catena-X relies on established legal frameworks to govern data ownership and usage rights. Further, *purpose-based usage policies* dictate how data can be used for only specific use cases and specified durations.

Catena-X ensures that data is now available for further analysis. AI and GenAI capabilities are on the anvil. Heubach says, 'Imagine a co-pilot with Joules from SAP. You come to a car and say, "Where is the metal coming from?" and immediately, the system comes back with, "The metal is coming from a mine in South Africa." In the future, definitely, Catena-X will be AI-based.'

Circular Economy Use Cases

Catena-X offers a variety of use cases that leverage secure data exchange to improve collaboration and efficiency. *Traceability* allows manufacturers to track the origin and journey of parts and materials throughout the supply chain. Catena-X will help companies identify supply bottlenecks at an early stage by making it easier for them to query availability across supply chains. It will also enable better purchasing power in material procurement—for instance, collaborating automotive OEMs on Catena-X would be in a better bargaining position as compared to other industrial sectors in procuring chips. The BMW Group used satellite data and big data analytics in a pilot project to gain in-depth transparency in a leather supply chain all the way back to the origin of the raw material. Fifty leather sub-suppliers and 9000 farms were identified and linked to satellite, geospatial and supply chain data in Catena-X, enabling real-time monitoring in selected world regions. This transparency is required for compliance/regulations with respect to environmental and social sustainability standards.[45]

Catena-X's transparency allows tracing a product's entire life cycle, from cradle to grave. Shared digital twins with end-of-life data improve decision-making, enabling reuse, refurbishment and efficient material recycling. Catena-X supports a circular economy.[46] For instance, its Product Carbon Footprint (PCF) enables calculating the environmental impact of a car throughout its lifecycle, from raw materials to disposal. This empowers manufacturers to optimize their processes and minimize their ecological footprint.

In this context, consider also the use case of Digital Product Passport, which creates a secure digital record of a product's history, including materials, maintenance records and end-of-life instructions. Consider the battery passport involving companies such as BMW (OEM), Dräxlmaier (Tier 1 supplier), BASF and Henkel (chemicals) and LRP Auto-recycling (recycler).

Thorsten Dikmaan, product owner Digital Material Passport at BASF, says,

> The battery passport will play an important role in establishing a circular economy in the automotive supply and value chain. On the one hand, BASF is a supplier of cathode material at the beginning of the value chain. On the other hand, the information from the battery passport helps us in our recycling facilities. By combining digital product passports with the Catena-X platform, suppliers, car manufacturers, and recyclers can use a joint framework to provide information about their products and materials.[47]

Stephan Hoefer, global market strategy head e-mobility at Henkel, says,

> For Henkel, the battery passport is important in collaboration with our suppliers, but also with our customers. For us, it is crucial to look at materials in the battery and consider what we need to implement in future formulations. This could pertain, for example, to new regulations or to raw materials that are more sustainable and more suitable for recycling.[48]

Multi-tiered Governance for Radical Collaboration

Catena-X employs a multi-tiered governance structure to ensure effective management, collaboration and development within its ecosystem.[49]

i) *Association Catena-X Automotive Network*: This entity is responsible for standardization, certifications and governance of the Catena-X ecosystem. It comprises a management board, an association office, an advisory council and multiple committees.

ii) *Development Environment*: This is responsible for the creation of standards and the development of open-source reference implementations and other implementations for the data space. The twenty-eight initial members of Catena-X provided the initial technical resources required.

iii) *Operating Environment*: Here, the various open-source and commercial services and business applications are operated by different providers.

    a. *Confinity-X*: This is the first operating company taking the Catena-X ecosystem from vision to reality. It acts as the central marketplace for the ecosystem, where companies can access and consume various services and solutions certified by Catena-X. Confinity-X is responsible for onboarding new participants, providing support, and ensuring that all solutions meet the established standards for data exchange and interoperability. The Catena-X network may have multiple operating companies, geographically.

iv) *Collaborations*: To ensure trust and conformity, Catena-X has established partnerships.

    a. *Gaia-X*: This is a European initiative that aims to create a federated and secure data infrastructure (Trust Framework). Catena-X is one of the first and significant implementations of Gaia-X. In a project anchored by the German Institute for Transportation Systems, cars can, in real time, share data about irregularities such as obstacles on the road with the Gaia-X platform. The central AI model helps annotate maps and optimizes driving for other human drivers and autonomous vehicles.[50]

    b. *International Data Space Association (IDSA):* This provides architecture principles that enable sovereign data exchange.

c. *Eclipse Foundation:* This hosts the official open-source development project of the Catena-X ecosystem (called *Tractus*-X) and follows the *Eclipse Foundation's* trusted development process for building the necessary federated services and data exchange.

While the Catena-X governance model might seem intricate, this complexity is a necessary consequence of balancing the needs and interests of a diverse set of stakeholders in the mobility ecosystem.

Across the Atlantic, the state of California has become ground zero for regulations around GenAI. Governor Gavin Newsom's executive order outlines measures for the ethical and responsible deployment of GenAI in state government, including risk analysis, procurement guidelines, beneficial use reporting, impact analysis, state employee training, partnerships with academic institutions, legislative engagement and ongoing evaluation of AI impacts. The state has formed a formal partnership with the University of California, Berkeley, and Stanford University, hosting the Joint California Summit on Generative AI in May 2024 to facilitate meaningful discussions on the effects of GenAI on California and its workforce.[51] The end of 2024 saw a tumultuous wave of AI regulations in the US, including stringent safety mandates and export restrictions on foundation models. In January 2025, President Donald Trump issued an executive order to revoke prior AI policies and promote American AI innovation.[52]

Let us now explore the co-intelligence-driven co-innovation strategies at one of the founding members of the Catena-X consortium, Mercedes-Benz.

Co-Innovation at Mercedes-Benz

Mercedes-Benz is developing its own operating system called MB.OS to elevate the digital experience across all its vehicles. Ola Källenius, CEO of Mercedes-Benz, says about the company's role and key principles in creating MBOS:

We are the architects of MB.OS. It means we specify, we design, we develop this whole operating system, but we also procure and partner . . . Our first principle is purpose built, but open to partners; the second is one-to-one relationship with the customer, it all centers around a unique customer ID . . . the car knows you; the third is privacy by design, and we use data to improve the experience for the customer; Fourth, over-the-air (OTA) upgradability. The product doesn't get old, it actually gets better over time.[53]

By decoupling hardware from software, Mercedes hopes to drive innovations much faster. MB.OS would seamlessly integrate functionalities like OTA updates, advanced driver-assistance systems (ADAS) and intuitive infotainment features. To achieve this, Mercedes-Benz collaborates with key technology partners. The NVIDIA DRIVE Orin system-on-chip, a powerhouse capable of 254 trillion operations per second, helps analyse data from a comprehensive sensor suite, including LiDAR from another partner, Luminar. MB.OS integrates Google Maps Platform, giving Mercedes-Benz drivers access to industry-leading navigation features. This includes real-time traffic, automatic rerouting and detailed information about millions of locations through Google Place Details.[54] In the future, the MBUX touchscreen would display interactive 3D maps generated by MB.OS, allowing drivers to zoom in and see buildings and landmarks in a more realistic way.

Now that Mercedes-Benz is focusing on in-house software development, it is forcing a change in the way it manages its ecosystem partnerships. In the past, it relied on Tier 1 suppliers for entire systems (hardware and software). But the emphasis is now shifting towards opening up co-development for efficiency. Michael Hafner, VP of MB.OS base layer and MBUX, says,

In the past, we would develop a complete system with a supplier. If we wanted to go to a different supplier for the next vehicle generation, we'd have to start from scratch, even if there were only incremental changes . . . (Now) we want to focus on standardization and open source for the things where we don't differentiate from our competitors.[55]

The Mercedes-Benz User Experience (MBUX) is an intelligent voice assistant integrated into the dashboard of Mercedes-Benz vehicles. Activated by the phrase 'Hey Mercedes', MBUX uses conversational AI and natural language understanding from Cerence to offer a highly intuitive and interactive user experience. Even when the passenger says, 'I am cold', MBUX understands the context and adjusts the temperature settings of the cabin.[56] In June 2023, Mercedes-Benz integrated ChatGPT into MBUX and launched an optional beta program in the US via an over-the-air update. Markus Schäfer, member of the board of management of Mercedes-Benz Group AG and CTO, says, 'The integration of ChatGPT with Microsoft in our controlled cloud environment is a milestone on our way to making our cars the centre of our customers' digital lives . . . Everything is under one big goal: Redefining the relationship with your Mercedes.'[57]

Mercedes-Benz is not only bringing co-intelligence into its cars; it is also embracing it in factories producing them. Consider Factory 56 in Sindelfingen, Germany, where Mercedes-Benz is using digital twins in the build process. Judson Althoff, EVP and chief commercial officer of Microsoft, which is a technology partner for the industrial metaverse, says,

What's most unique about this facility is it's the only one in the world where simultaneously you can see the energy transition happening in front of your eyes. One line produces both the S-class Maybach limousine and the brand-new EQS electric vehicle. This was super critical for Mercedes and their strategy because most companies that are creating electric vehicles have to build in factories from scratch. And, you actually look at the carbon footprint associated with a factory build, you have to turn out a whole lot of electric vehicles before you're net zero, even in the factory build process alone. So, they've been able to accomplish with these digital twins a fantastic harmonious orchestration between human beings and physical objects.[58]

Like Catena-X, India is experimenting with the creation of an extended automotive consortium focusing on developing digital public infrastructure (DPIs) for the mobility ecosystem. Let us turn to that example.

Bharat Multi-Modal Mobility Stack

In Chapter 3, we saw India's DPI strategy powering the country's nascent mobility ecosystem through ONDC. That success is inspiring new organizations such as the Mobility and Intelligent Transportation (MInT) Collaborative at IIT Madras. We (VR and KN) participated in an initial brainstorming workshop where the idea was conceptualized.[59]

Ramakrishna Srinivasan, CEO of MInT and former chief of digital transformation at Ford, says, 'Digital infrastructure complements and optimizes the physical infrastructure and is an innovation engine to advance future mobility. Our goals include reducing transport emissions and fatalities by 50 per cent and achieving 50 per cent net zero modes in transport.' MInT aims to develop solutions for sustainable transport, accident prevention, and energy efficiency. Its Bharat Multi-Modal Mobility Stack (BM3S) is conceptualized as a collaborative repository of mobility data and models, and their interactions via a digital twin.[60] See Figure 5-2.

BM3S can be used in various ways depending on the user's needs. For instance, a vehicle technology OEM could use battery technology know-how from the stack and customize it for their specific purposes. A government agency might run digital twin simulations to explore 'what if' scenarios and make informed public policy decisions. Mobility service app developers could use the stack's algorithmic modules to accelerate their development instead of starting from scratch.

Meanwhile, another early-stage innovation in the mobility-energy ecosystem is the unified energy interface (UEI), which is an open network for energy to enable transactions between digital energy systems.[61] Built on the Beckn protocol, similar to how ONDC was built, it is a network for EV charging, virtual energy warehousing and battery monetization. Startups such as Kazam and Pulse Energy (EV-charging software platforms), Sheru (cloud energy storage platform) and Turno (commercial EV marketplace) are already on UEI.

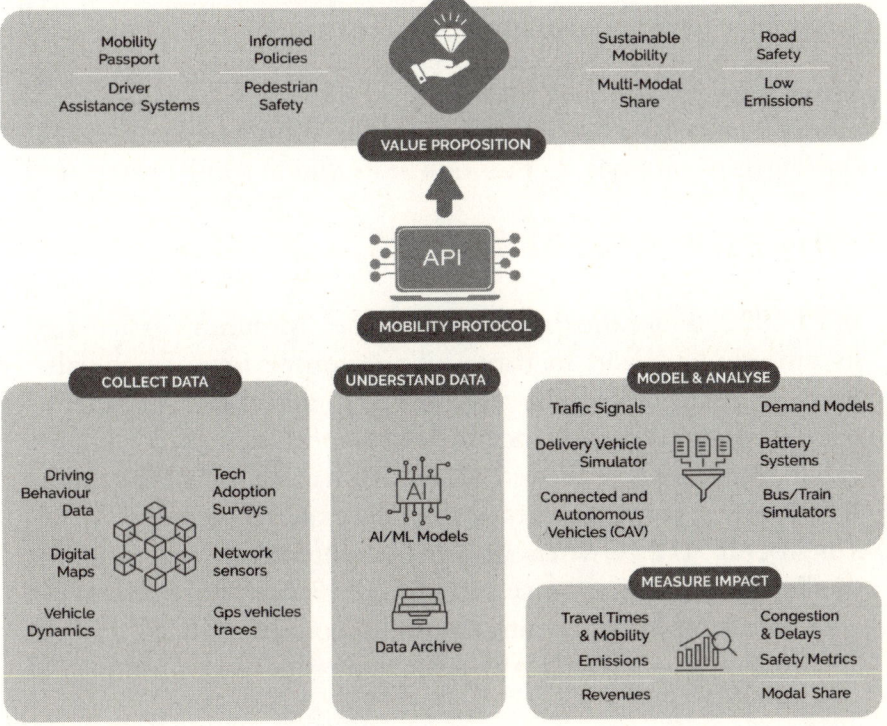

Figure 5-2: Bharat Multi-Modal Mobility Stack (BM3S) (Source: MInT Collaborative, IIT Madras)

As organizations transform their ecosystem engagements, they demand the same transformation from others in their ecosystem. As we have seen, this entails a *systemic transformation* across multiple interrelated enterprise ecosystems. This journey extends beyond just the cold mechanics of organizational restructuring or digital upgrades. It calls for a deeper metamorphosis—a shift in the very soul of organizations towards *ecosystemic* co-creation. Only through a *cultural awakening* of all collaborating enterprises, where co-creation becomes the guiding principle, can true ecosystemic transformation take root. We illustrate this next with the example of Mahindra, one of India's largest vehicle manufacturers.

Mahindra's Transformational Journey

Established in 1945 in India, the Mahindra Group is spread across twenty-two businesses, with Mahindra and Mahindra as the flagship company. Let us look at its digital transformation.[62]

FUTURISE—a digital transformation at Mahindra

In FY2022, under the theme of 'Futurise', Mahindra articulated its ambition to lead in three pillars—outperform financially, lead ESG, and be future-ready. It has undertaken a number of digital initiatives to enhance their automotive customer buying experience. It has deployed an immersive 3D visualizer (using WebGL tech) for customers to virtually experience the XUV700, a high-end SUV. Owners also get an interactive manual with the With You Hamesha service app. Its integrated automotive web-based platform, auto.mahindra.com, is enabled with an innovative chatbot feature for swift query resolution and transactions.

Mahindra has also streamlined its processes at dealerships. It has rolled out a more agile CRM platform across 439 dealerships pan-India and introduced the SalesGenie Nxt App to help them seamlessly manage processes such as inquiry management, test drives, quotations and bookings. It has also leveraged technology to allow for real-time data integration of call centre and dealer agents to share leads. Their World of SUVs format of next-generation dealerships provides convenience to customers by integrating the virtual world with the real on a phygital platform. Embedded screens and immersive virtual reality with mirror display, Wi-Fi-connected customer lounges and specially trained relationship managers provide an immersive customer experience.

Similarly, Mahindra has leveraged digital technologies to transform the ag and farmer experiences too. Krish-e is Mahindra's farming-as-a-service vertical. Through multiple apps, it offers differentiated and farmer-focused advisory and rental services and aims to increase farmers' income through digitally enabled services across the complete crop cycle. In order to enable such an offering, Mahindra has made strategic investments in Resson (a Canadian predictive analytics company), Gamaya (a Swiss hyperspectral image analytics company) and Carnot (an Indian AI-enabled ag-IoT company). DigiSense 4G is Mahindra's next-gen AI-driven open-architecture solution that helps farmers track their tractors and control their farming activities remotely. The mPragati app provides access to DigiSense features like live location and fuel levels to its tractors and farm machinery customers.

Besides transforming its sales and customer experiences, Mahindra is leveraging AI, EV and other technologies to transform its manufacturing capabilities and allied businesses.

i) It has connected critical machines across eight plants across India through the in-house developed platform, Drona, to ensure better productivity, increased machine availability and improved efficiency. Using advanced AI/ML models that capture over 1000 data points, ranging from supplier parts to on-road performance, Mahindra can predict and score the performance of its engines with an accuracy of 99.6 per cent. Such models help reduce the testing time and improve quality.

ii) The AI-augmented digital twin project at its Chakan plant enhances productivity and enables real-time monitoring, while machine learning techniques are used to monitor real-time, inline, spot-welding processes, reducing defects and associated costs. Additionally, the Gen AI-based project streamlines troubleshooting by generating 'why-why' sheets (root-cause analysis) for maintenance processes. Complementing these efforts, 3D modelling is employed to design production line layouts, allowing early identification and resolution of potential issues, thereby minimizing risks and optimizing efficiency.

iii) Mahindra Vision.AI is a versatile computer vision platform designed to build AI models on images, enhancing various business operations such as Mahindra First Choice Wheels (certified used-car company) and Teqo (a part of Mahindra Susten, its renewable energy arm). It detects used car dents, streamlines inspections, and identifies solar plate defects, thereby improving solar cell efficiency. The platform reduces reliance on third parties by automating processes, cutting costs and enhancing safety.

iv) Mahindra is betting big on EV technology. For its Born Electric portfolio of SUVs, it is focusing on driving partnerships along with leveraging internal R&D and innovation capabilities of its research facilities at Mahindra Research Valley, EV Tech Centre, Mahindra North American Technical Centre and UK Design Centre (MADE).

Mahindra also aims to be a purpose-driven brand by being:

i) *Planet positive* (greening its operations, decarbonizing the industry and rejuvenating nature)—Mahindra was the first company globally to commit to doubling its energy productivity through the EP100 initiative (a global initiative led by the international non-profit Climate Group, bringing together over 120 energy-smart businesses committed to measuring and reporting on energy efficiency improvements). It has also committed to having all its locations certified as 'Zero Waste' by 2030.

ii) *People positive* (enabling its associates, communities and customers)—In FY24, Mahindra created significant impact through various social projects—educated over 230,000 girl child (Project Nanhi Kali), environment rejuvenation and planted over 25 million trees, benefiting 27,500 tribal farmer families (Project Hariyali).

iii) *Trust positive* (commitment to its shareholders, partners, and investors). Mahindra has been disclosing information to all stakeholders for over fourteen years through its GRI-based sustainability reporting. As of 2022, it is estimated to have delivered $4 billion worth of social impact. Mahindra has also developed varied mechanisms of stakeholder engagement, involving their customers, employees, partners, dealers, suppliers and investors.

The foundations for meaningful dialogue with these stakeholders hark back to a co-creation movement that emerged in Mahindra a decade back.[63]

A Co-Creation Movement at Mahindra

In August 2010, Naveen Chopra, then senior GM and head of plant quality for Mahindra's automotive division, attended a seminar on the topic of value co-creation conducted by one of us (VR), which focused on the need for creative collaboration and enhanced communication and coordination among stakeholders.[64] As Chopra was constantly striving to improve precisely these practices across the five operating sites of Mahindra's automotive division, he decided to experiment with co-creation thinking by applying its principles first in the quality function. In September 2010, he drafted a short presentation on co-creation thinking, sharing it initially with his immediate colleagues and then with his wider quality team across the five plants. Chopra emphasized the importance of engaging interactively with all stakeholders, from customers and fellow employees to suppliers and dealers, to share work experiences and create value together through platforms of engagements and environments of interaction, purposefully designed and configured to address the interests and needs of participating individuals.

As head of quality, he was already collaborating with multiple functions of the business, such as manufacturing, marketing and customer service, in a quest to enhance and enrich the company's quality culture. He himself began to engage with employees in internal experience-sharing sessions. Simultaneously, Chopra started to tackle the practicalities of communicating co-creation thinking more widely, together with a core team representing different functions—including dealer channel, training, manufacturing and supply chain management. They put together several examples of co-creation in action and also communicated more precisely how it worked in practice.

For example, they explained that it was not just about getting feedback, but it also involved sharing experiences and experiential learning. An early success was when the team decided to form a small group of engineers with ten to twenty-five years of specialist automotive experience each and enable them to pass on their knowledge and expertise to dozens of younger colleagues. The team identified specific stakeholding individuals from the pool of engineers who could benefit from this type of knowledge sharing.

The team established an engagement platform—in this case, 'live' monthly workshops—where the whole group could meet to share knowledge and experiences. These were led by a voluntary cadre of experienced engineers who took on the role of trainers. The meetings were more than just about talking shop. To be effective, they required an honest approach from all participants, based on mutual respect, openness and the willingness to experiment. Typically, a workshop would focus on a specific theme, with one or two seasoned engineers passing on their expertise to their junior colleagues. Between workshops, the groups would document their learning and jointly create an internal training module on the subject, which could be run at any time and updated as necessary. Throughout the month, the team focused on making workshop design changes by asking participants how their experiences could be improved and how the platform could be more valuable.

In just two to three months, the platform had enabled specialized knowledge sharing and training to be rolled out at high speed with hardly any extra cost to the company. This early success was soon appreciated at senior management levels within Mahindra. In the ensuing eighteen months, around fifty similar modules were created, with 400 to 500 employees benefiting. Naveen says, 'Using traditional classroom training methods, this would have taken us ten years.'

In the case of suppliers, the joint team first considered how supplier meetings could improve mutual understanding, cooperation and collaboration. If supplier capability could be augmented, it was reasonable to expect that quality would improve too, with both parties 'winning more'. Instead of taking the traditional approach of first finding fault with the suppliers and urging them to take corrective action, efforts were made to consider how they interacted with Mahindra. Suppliers were encouraged to share their experiences. There was initially some suspicion among suppliers about the dialogue process, which was natural because Mahindra was their customer, but by the end of 2010, some 80 suppliers were on board, with this effort producing the desired results.

In the case of dealers, as with the suppliers, traditional meetings were reformed into a more effective engagement platform, with emphasis placed on seeing issues from the dealers' perspective and supporting them. Further, stakeholders who were typically not part of the quality conversation, such as auto repair mechanics, were involved in sharing their knowledge about vehicle defects, failure modes and problem-solving solutions, and they also were invited to Mahindra's plants. Again, both Mahindra and the dealers reaped the benefits, from addressing vehicle defects to shaping new product features, including more productive relationships and faster cycle times. Some dealers initiated co-creation thinking in their own businesses. As a result, defects for top dealers reduced significantly. New diagnostics for dealer technicians and new product knowledge enhancement through training sessions on focused topics resulted in getting service right the first time while also gaining a better understanding of part failures based on actual field experiences.

By early 2011, word of Naveen's success with co-creation was spreading within Mahindra, with other area executives beginning to see its potential to transform their own functions. As momentum continued to build, a co-creation workshop for about 350 people was held in May 2011, where several individuals shared their experiences. Several people beyond the core team took the lead in conducting sessions. Some executives who were exposed to co-creation thinking at this event began acting on it in areas as diverse as sustainability and social impact.

Then, in the next Global Program for Management Development (GPMD) program in early August 2011, the core team shared their experiences with several other leaders from within the Mahindra extended enterprise. By the end of August 2011, six more executives had become co-creation champions, some of whom had begun to embed early co-creation thinking into activities they were spearheading. In particular, a culture of co-creation had begun to spread in the extended supply chain network. The head of manufacturing in the automotive division became an ardent co-creation champion. He enlisted his own core team, beginning with an experimental program in engagement of contract labour. Through this programme, by asking contract employees for ideas and giving them the ability to self-organize, the Mahindra officers had been able to achieve their quality-related goals more consistently. The manufacturing team then tackled core areas in the production process, including redesigning the manufacturing shop floors by setting up internal platforms of engagement.

Co-creation thinking began to spread in the extended supply chain network. This was crucial to the success of Mahindra

Automotive because an automobile typically has more than 5000 parts, with Mahindra manufacturing core components such as the engine, transmission and body in its plants and with as much as 70 per cent of parts coming from a network of suppliers across multiple tiers. While Mahindra engages primarily with Tier 1 suppliers who provide sub-assemblies and systems, Tier 1 suppliers in turn procure components from Tier 2 suppliers. However, these Tier 2 suppliers are small to medium enterprises with limited resources and skills, often with traditional practices and lacking exposure to modern methods. Following the co-creation workshops, Mahindra began involving over 400 tier 1 suppliers—both officers and operators—in 'co-creation competitions,' inviting the best entries to share their Kaizen, Pokayoke, and Quality Control' stories, first with Mahindra senior management and then across the Tier 1 network.

The popularity of this programme was a positive surprise for Mahindra management, which assumed that the suppliers would be hesitant to share practices with each other. In reality, however, the alternate thinking of learning by sharing, facilitated by Mahindra, began to spread with Tier 1 suppliers starting to see the power of creating value together as an example of 'win more, win more'. Once this took root, Tier 1 suppliers began to engage Tier 2 suppliers, inviting Mahindra to participate as well. For Mahindra, this was a unique opportunity to promote comprehensive holistic growth and the improvement of Tier 2 suppliers' productivity, quality, cost, delivery, safety and morale. And so, Mahindra enabled a 'supplier cluster' platform of co-creation engagements at the Tier 2 level—facilitated by Tier 1 suppliers—bringing together groups of five to 15 co-located Tier 2 suppliers manufacturing similar products for a common shared purpose of improvement and for achieving agreed deliverables. This has also resulted in transforming the culture of Tier 2 suppliers, working together with Tier 1 suppliers and positively affecting quality and delivery at the Tier 1 level, and subsequently enhancing automotive quality overall at Mahindra. Over 10,000 supplier personnel were involved, with about 30 clusters having been formed and over 50 lean management projects executed.

In November 2011, the company held an event involving over 1000 Mahindra employees, suppliers, dealers and even its other non-traditional stakeholders, such as banks and educational institutions. As a step towards wider societal responsibility, the principles and successes of Mahindra's co-creation journey were shared with this broad spectrum of business and social stakeholders. In turn, local banks and schools learned to create platforms to engage their own stakeholders.

Mahindra next began to harness the power of technology and social media to move the crucial engagement platforms beyond face-to-face workshops to achieve wider geographical and enterprise ecosystem impact. For a widely diversified conglomerate like Mahindra, further development of digital forums enabled the enterprise ecosystem to scale co-creation, share its best practices and make its principles, methods and tools more easily accessible throughout its many functions and divisions. Mahindra achieved a balance between co-creation and the management systems of the conglomerate enterprise through co-creation champions at the corporate level in other areas. For instance, leaders who were engaged with many different internal functions in developing a collective corporate identity, Mahindra Rise, were co-opted. Mahindra also engaged changemakers across India through a societal engagement platform (www.sparktherise.com). Further, Mahindra undertook co-creative engagement of manufacturing operators in training, competency enhancement of employees and talent development of officers. Likewise, platforms for co-creative new product development began to involve the marketing and branding functions together with communities of consumers, including the launch of new vehicles.

Chairman of the Mahindra Group, Anand Mahindra, articulated a vision of creating Mahindra as a reflective organization. By 2021, over 2600 employees had benefitted from Reflective Conversations Community (RCC) workshops that taught them how to use digital solutions for more engaged conversations. Chopra, Mahindra's first co-creation champion, is now head of product development and component development and material management at Mahindra Truck and Bus and is continuing on his co-creation journey.

A culture of co-creation can thus become part of an organization's DNA as such, encouraging managers to engage as creative-experiencers and AI orchestrators with the support of a knowledge environment that enhances adaptive co-intelligence learning capabilities. Despite increasing sophistication of the technical architecture, there is time-invariant human effort and empathy required in developing the social architecture and organizational culture for effective co-creation of risk-managed value with all stakeholders. As Anand Mahindra notes:

> In the decade since co-creation was mooted, technological platforms have enabled human engagement at deeper levels and on an infinitely broader scale. As a consequence, businesses can and must expand their strategies to encompass a profitable engagement with all stakeholders. The powerful idea that 'we can do even better for ourselves if we do well for others' encompasses the way that successful organizations will contribute to wealth, welfare, and wellbeing in society.[65]

* * *

Taken together, all the examples in this chapter illustrate how organizations must co-innovate Life-Xverse ecosystems with stakeholders from their own vantage spaces. All of them collaborate with ecosystem coalitions of partners across sectors to expand the locus of their strategies with newfound capabilities and activities in the lived-journeys of their downstream customers, across individuals and communities in which they operate.

What does this mean for the practices of management? How would this all work for organizations? We turn to these questions next.

6

Becoming a Co-Intelligent Enterprise

Over two decades ago, with the advent of the Web, C.K. Prahalad and Venkat Ramaswamy proposed the idea of 'experience of one' in discussing a new frontier of experience innovation, experience personalization, and how *experiences must increasingly be co-created through experience-oriented networks and interactive organizational systems.*[1] Thanks to communication technologies and analytical AI, and now co-intelligence platforms with spatial computing, enterprises are co-creating life–experiences that are more dynamic and immersive. As we have seen throughout this book with various examples, organizations can rapidly reconfigure *physical + digital* ecosystem environments *constituting their offering ecosystems interconnected with value-chain ecosystems* and intelligently combine and integrate capabilities from ecosystem networks in real time to achieve unique co-created value through their *management ecosystems.* The PIEX lens calls attention to such value creation with all individuals as creative-experiencers, at the top of the tech stack in its interfaces and applications, and at the edges of cloud computing, through Human–AI interactional creation across engagement flows (of working, learning, consuming, playing and making) and emergent life–experiences. Interconnected intelligent ecosystems with copilot capabilities, powered by *shared digitalized infrastructures* (SDIs), engage with humans as creative-experiencers and connect with the life–experiences of people in *extended Nature–Society–Economy–Technology* (NEST) ecosystems to engender valuable *sustainable wellbeing impacts* (SWIs). Value is co-created in the flow of interactive engagements. It is characterized by the co-creative power of humans in co-existence with AI.

This also means that organizations, through their management ecosystems, need to deeply understand and connect with the lives and lived-journeys of *all stakeholding individuals as creative-experiencers and co-creators of value, be they consumers, workers, managers, financiers, partners, policymakers, designers or citizens.* Only if they understand and connect with the lived experiences of people and empower them to be value co-creators with copiloted management systems can they co-innovate experience-centric offerings and drive AI-powered hyper-personalized experiences tailored to their needs. A focus on lived-journeys with the help of AI also means that enterprises need to visualize strategic opportunities and risks in every moment of interactive engagement between individuals as creative-experiencers and networked offerings and value-chain ecosystems. As organizations learn to harness the newfound co-creative power of Human–AI interactive engagement in their organizational ecosystems, they must co-design and risk-manage co-intelligence flows of engagements in co-creating value with internal and external stakeholders. This requires organizations to have unprecedented levels of fluidity within their ecosystems and constantly reshape their relationships and alliances. But they cannot achieve these objectives unless *organizations transform their institutional structures to facilitate individual interactive agency.*

In Chapter 3, we saw how tech-forward companies have been crafting co-intelligence architectures for innovation and value co-creation with their customers, partners and stakeholders. In so doing, they have had to undergo their own transformation in their management processes.

Flattening the Organization—NVIDIA

The concept of the modern organization as we understand it today emerged during the early twentieth century, when Henry Ford introduced the *product assembly line factory*. Product-based organizational forms emphasized multi-divisional specialization and coordination. Concurrently, military organizations during the World Wars introduced businesses to the concepts of hierarchical command structures and strategic planning. Over the decades of the industrial revolutions, these principles were further refined and expanded upon by management theorists until organizations came to terms with the need for innovating management models themselves with the increasing democratization and de-centring of value creation in society and the economy.[2] Organizations need to enhance their management agility, responsiveness and overall effectiveness in navigating a rapidly evolving landscape of innovation and value creation. For instance, in the case of NVIDIA, Jensen Huang has adopted a transformative management model. 'Every company in the world should not be built like the US military.'[3] He has about sixty direct reports, unlike traditional organizational models. 'My direct reports are sophisticated. They're really talented. They're incredibly good at their job. They're excellent leaders.' This means Huang does not need to micromanage them. 'No one-on-ones, and no career advice.' He prefers group meetings, where everyone can learn from what's working and what's not. Failures in one project are discussed openly in these group meetings so that everyone can learn from them, not just the affected teams.

Huang rejects the conventional approach of periodic planning systems. He states, 'No five-year plans. Because the world is a living, breathing thing, we just plan continuously.'[4] NVIDIA excels at building highly complex computers through meticulous engineering and refinement. Simultaneously, it fosters innovation by dedicating resources to experimental projects, embracing adaptability and risk-taking.

Our company actually has two different ways of working. One of them is rather organic, shape-shifting all the time. If a particular investment's not working out, we give up on it, move the resources somewhere else. That's the agile part of the company. And then there's a part of the company that's not rigid, but it's really refined. These two systems have to work side by side.[5]

Huang's approach to information discovery and communication is also very different. 'I don't read any status reports. They are meta information by the time you get it. And so, they're barely informative.'[6] Instead, he gets his reports to send in their *top five things*: 'whatever you observed or whatever you did or whatever you learned', every day. He remarks, 'Ground truth is the best source of information.'

In line with his visionary thinking and taking long-term bets, Huang talks about going after *zero billion-dollar markets*. He says,

Our purpose should be to go and do something that has never been done before. That is insanely hard to do. If you achieve it, you could make a real contribution. That market is probably zero billion dollars in size. Because it has never been done before. I'd rather be a market maker, a market creator, than a market taker. To create something new that never existed before versus thinking about (market) share.[7]

That said, while NVIDIA's employee turnover rate in 2024 was about 2.7 per cent compared to about 17.7 per cent for the overall semiconductor industry, and despite its financial success and the wealth it has generated for its employees, its grueling and pressure-filled work culture can add to human stress. With a flat corporate structure incentivizing employees to compete for attention rather than collaborating effectively, it can in turn lead to internal conflicts and undermine long-term goals. Time will tell how NVIDIA navigates its organizational growth challenges.[8]

Let us next take a whirlwind tour of Microsoft's organizational transformation since 2014, when Nadella took over as its CEO, the third in its history. Under Nadella's watch, during 2014–2024, Microsoft's revenue went up two and a half times, while operating income more than trebled.[9,10] Its stock outperformed popular market indices for the period 2018 to 2023—an investment in its stock returned one and a half times that from NASDAQ Computer and over twice from S&P 500. Its market capitalization increased nearly eight times from 2014 levels to reach around $3 trillion in 2024,[11] when it became the most valued company on the planet. These spectacular outcomes resulted from significant changes in Microsoft's corporate culture, customer orientation and partnership ethos. The company changed its mission statement from 'a computer on every desk and in every home' to 'empower every person and every organization on the planet to achieve more'. The new mission embodied the spirit of 'renewal of Microsoft' that Satya Nadella discussed with the board when he was appointed CEO.

Microsoft's Renewal

Microsoft reoriented itself as the productivity and platform company for the mobile-first, cloud-first world. It envisaged mobile-first to mean the mobility of the human experience across all devices and recognized that the cloud made that mobility possible. It also called out the importance of AI as part of its technology substrate. Microsoft talked about *tech-intensity*: tech adoption, tech capability and trust in technology in enterprises in the context of how they digitally transform, build business resilience and create value.[12]

Refreshingly, for a tech company, Microsoft articulated a vision for AI that was human-centric. In his Ignite 2021 address, Nadella says,

> In the AI we create, using all this enormous power of the cloud, we will look for increasing levels of predictive and analytical

power, common sense reasoning, alignment with human preferences, and perhaps most importantly, augmenting human capability . . . We need to build technology with the design intent to protect the fundamental rights of all people, including privacy, and strengthen these institutions we all depend on for our livelihoods and wellbeing.[13]

However, it took more than just a reframing of its mission and technology focus for Microsoft to succeed. Satya's first mail as CEO to all employees of Microsoft alluded to the essence of the transformation journey: 'In order to accelerate our innovation, we must rediscover our soul—our unique core. We must all understand and embrace what only Microsoft can contribute to the world and how we can once again change the world.'

In the email, he inserted the image of a target, and in its centre appeared the words, 'digital work and life–experiences', surrounded by Microsoft's cloud platform and computer devices. The emphasis was on applying the PIEX lens, as it were, to its organizational ecosystem.

Microsoft reframed the need for technology from a perspective of creating value surplus in society. It placed an emphasis on the *empowerment* of stakeholders across the world. Nadella says,

We can't do business effectively in 190 countries unless we prioritize the creation of greater local economic opportunity in each of those countries . . . Real business success cannot be just the surplus that you create for your own core constituency, but also the broader surplus that is created to benefit the wider society.[14]

Microsoft also clearly articulated a humanity-centric approach to developing new technology. Nadella says,

I explain Microsoft's approach to AI as based on three core principles. First, we want to build intelligence that augments human abilities and experiences. Second, we also have to build trust directly into our technology . . . And third, all of the technology we build must be inclusive and respectful to everyone, serving humans across barriers of culture, race, nationality, economic status, age, gender, physical and mental ability and more.[15]

Ultimately, the transformation at Microsoft played out over several years and helped reimagine its culture and sales, partner, employee and developer experiences.

Cultural and Learning Renaissance

Nadella's clarion call for 'rediscovering our soul' was the foundation for Microsoft's renaissance, which was primarily a cultural one. 'I like to think that the C in CEO stands for culture. The CEO is the curator of an organization's culture.'[16] He defined culture as a 'complex system made up of individual mindsets. Culture is how an organization thinks and acts, but individuals shape it'. Microsoft leveraged the work of Stanford professor Carol Dweck on *growth mindset* as a framework for this cultural transformation. Growth mindset was emphasized in three actions by all employees—first, to obsess about its customers; second, to actively seek diversity and inclusion; and third, to become one company, one Microsoft (networks and structures). Customer success became central to the way all employees were expected to think. This meant putting away the differences and sharply competitive nature of engagement between different departments (product teams, sales teams, technical teams, etc.) within Microsoft. As Nadella put it, 'they (different Microsoft product teams) get to own a customer scenario, not the code'. An emphasis was placed on empathy and being empathetic in listening to customer needs as well as engaging with employees.

There was a transition from being know-it-alls to *learn-it-alls*. To encourage the shift towards a learning culture,

Microsoft created an annual hackathon named Microsoft One Week during its yearly employee event. The hacker subculture was known in the tech world for its spirit of fun, collaboration, competition and problem-solving. In the first year of the hackathon, over 12,000 employees from eighty-three countries entered 3000-plus hacks, ranging from ending sexism in video games to making computing more accessible to people with disabilities to improving industrial supply-chain operations.[17] The hackathon also became a forum for unearthing leadership talent, even from people who were not on that path as per their existing roles (emergence). For example, the team that created learning tools for people with reading and writing disabilities in OneNote (a note-taking software) was given the responsibility to manage the product's market expansion.[18]

Talent acquisition was also revamped, keeping in mind the growth mindset, that quality employees/leaders are not born but developed, and that talent could be found everywhere. From going to only a few elite schools to hire, Microsoft expanded its hiring to nearly 500 schools. Executive compensation was modified and linked to progress on dimensions like diversity and inclusion.[19] All these actionable efforts resulted in positive outcomes on the ground. According to the Microsoft 2023 Diversity & Inclusion (D&I) Report, women made up more than 29 per cent of Microsoft's executive roles. The representation of women and most racial and ethnic minority groups (Asian, Black and African American, Hispanic and Latinx, and multiracial employees) at all levels increased over the past five years. Over 96 per cent of employees reported some level of awareness of the concept of allyship, a foundation of their approach to D&I.[20]

The transformation involves ongoing communication and engagement with employees. On its enterprise-level social networking platform, Yammer (now Viva Engage), it monitored questions posed on the platform in real time. Leaders answered directly and engaged with employees across geographies and time zones. Daily Pulse (now in the Viva Pulse app) was a survey sent every day to a set of Microsoft employees. It consists of twenty core questions, five organization-level questions and a few open-ended questions that keep changing every month. It takes a snapshot of how employees are feeling about the company, its culture and other topical themes. There was a monthly town hall with all employees, providing business updates and taking questions live. During the event, employee engagements were measured to capture real-time sentiment.[21]

Transforming Work Experiences

Co-creating customer success through co-innovation requires democratizing transformation, which, as Marco Iansiti and Satya Nadella argue, requires giving the entire workforce the capacity to become innovators. Their research shows that to enable transformation at scale, companies must create synergy in three areas: capabilities (e.g., digital skills of employees), technology (e.g., AI and data stack) and architecture (e.g., organization and technical architecture).[22] This aligns well with our PIEX lens-based conceptualization of organizational ecosystem and co-intelligence architecture. Nadella comments on Microsoft's mission to create technology advances that radically democratize creation:

> We will need to expand access to skills, tools and platforms, as well as connections and collaboration across communities so that everyone can create, whether it's building a virtual world, students working on an assignment with short-form videos, knowledge workers creating formulas and spreadsheets, pro developers writing code or domain experts using local tools to build applications.[23]

Microsoft reimagined how it looks at work from an employee or worker experience-centric perspective—whether it is the customer-facing sales experience or internal-facing teams experience or the partner-facing experience. This experience-first focus has led to an intensive focus on the 'future of hybrid work experiences', especially via its employee experience platform, Viva. As hybrid work has led to a growing disconnect between employees and managers/leaders, especially on issues of productivity and maintaining autonomy while ensuring accountability, the benefits of flexibility, and the role of the 'office', it now recognizes that 'work is no longer just a place but an experience that needs to transcend time and space so employees can stay engaged and connected no matter where they are working'.

Microsoft, as part of its productive enterprise vision, undertook an intentional shift away from traditional product service models and put the user at the centre of the reimagined employee experience.[24] The outcome of this initiative was the development of the Employee Experience Cloud, Microsoft Viva, which is AI-infused. It brings together communications, learning, wellbeing and knowledge directly within the flow of work so that employees have the information, the resources and the support they need to succeed and thrive and stay connected with each other and the company's mission. Features such as Answers in Viva and People in Viva leverage AI capabilities to transform the employee experience.

Consider how a process using Viva looks for onboarding a new employee at a personal protective equipment (PPE) manufacturer:

Behind the scenes, AI systems are processing everything from sales decks to meeting agendas to invoices to create Wikipedia-style 'rough cuts' of everything her company knows and does, from topics and concepts to people and workflows. In Teams, she gets a message from a new coworker with a mask-making acronym she doesn't know. She hovers over it, and a card appears to tell her what it means. An Outlook email from HR triggers another card that lets her dig into her health insurance options. An assignment from her new boss has her thinking, 'Where do I start?' until another card appears with a roster of suggested colleagues who could help, all tied to their LinkedIn profiles.[25]

Transforming Sales, Partnering and Marketing Experiences

Microsoft also created value across functions—sales, marketing and ecosystem partnerships. When Satya Nadella took over as the CEO, Microsoft transformed its business model from one with a focus on selling and licensing operating systems, servers and packaged software to one focused on subscription of cloud and services, with Azure at its heart. Consequently, it undertook a major transformation of its sales function.[26] The sales organization, which was geographically oriented, was restructured around industries in order to offer industry-specific services and solutions to its customers. It focused especially on six industries: education, financial services, government, health, manufacturing and retail. Microsoft brought technical expertise (specialist team units that helped in new business acquisition) closer to the customer by including engineers in the field sales/account teams. It also introduced a customer success unit for the first time in its history (although this was standard practice in other cloud/SaaS companies), a team that would work with customers after the sale was completed and help them leverage more cloud capabilities in their transformation. Sales compensation and incentives were remodelled on actual consumption/usage of the cloud by the customers and not just on total contract value. Traditionally, Microsoft had many salespeople in a 'feet on the street' model and met customers face-to-face to make the sale. It adopted an inside-sales model aided with a digital infrastructure and Azure AI-enabled sales guidance to increase its coverage of customers.

Microsoft also started leveraging behavioural analytics to gain sales insights on a more real-time basis and improve commercial revenues. It created a platform that combined data being generated from everyday work in Microsoft Office 365, more traditional datasets, such as revenue and customer relationship management (CRM) data, with insights derived from its Viva Insights platform about internal and external networks, collaboration behaviours, coaching and mentoring, meeting effectiveness and so on. For instance, one insight it gained was that while sellers and executives were spending more time with customers in high-growth accounts, they were not paying enough attention to the 15 per cent of low-growth accounts that have high potential. It also found that higher sales outcomes correlated with larger seller networks—not just external customer networks, but also internal networks within the sales organization and other units of the company. Microsoft rolled out dashboards to about 500 leaders and 4000 sellers worldwide. Leaders have access to insights such as customer-contact metrics, sales team behaviours related to strategic priorities and accounts in which sellers are investing their time. Individual sellers receive a highly personalized set of weekly insights about their own work patterns, along with recommended actions.[27]

Microsoft's transformed management ecosystem necessitated a reimagination of its value-chain ecosystems (and vice versa). Thus, Microsoft dramatically changed the way it partnered with companies, even traditional competitors. It began working with Google to make it possible for MS Office to work on the Android platform. Similarly, it partnered with Apple to offer MS Office on iOS and to enable customers to better manage their iPhones within an enterprise. Although HoloLens competed with the virtual reality platform Oculus Rift, Microsoft partnered with Meta (Facebook) to ensure that its Minecraft gaming applications worked on their devices. It also began collaborating with the open-source community and with the Linux operating system, which it had once infamously described as a 'cancer'. In 2015, it released Visual Studio Code, a code editor optimized for building and debugging modern web and cloud applications, and made it open-source, thus introducing its technologies to developers who traditionally did not work with Microsoft. Its partnership with Red Hat meant that enterprises built on the latter's open-source software could use Azure cloud to scale up globally. By 2018, Microsoft had 72,000 cloud partners who were contributing to 95 per cent of Microsoft's commercial revenues.[28]

Microsoft also changed the way it communicated, both internally and externally. It identified five topics for all its company-facing language: customer-obsessed, growth mindset, diversity and inclusion, making a difference and One Microsoft.[29] It used many surprising mediums to communicate with employees. For instance, it ran campaigns based on one of these topics on the recyclable coffee cups used at their Redmond campus in the US. Instead of relying on standard press releases for its external marketing, it created a site called Microsoft Stories, which carried in-depth feature stories about people and projects. Rather than being entirely focused on product features, it created ads that connected with people through storytelling about the company's purpose and passion. For instance, it created a series of commercials under the Empowering series— the 2014 Super Bowl ad featuring Steve Gleason, former NFL player and now living with ALS, showed him narrating, like he does in his life daily, the spot using his Surface Pro to speak, via eye-tracking technology.[30] Its 2019 We All Win Super Bowl ad was about how Xbox's Adaptive Controller helps children with disabilities to play and feel included socially.[31]

By 2023, in the tenth year of Nadella's tenure as CEO, Microsoft had become one of the most valuable companies in the world. His 'cultural renaissance' of the company was already yielding fantastic economic results and beyond. And yet, on 23 September that year, at an event in New York, Nadella, with his voice crackling with a boundless energy of a developer kid at a tech candy store, declared a new direction for Microsoft. They would be diving headlong into the era of Copilots—'Microsoft Copilot, your everyday AI companion.' This was the narrative with which we began Microsoft's story in this book.

Shifts in the View of Organizational Management

Microsoft's organizational transformation points to the environment of the individual manager as a subset of a broader culture of collaborative interactive engagement that embraces an entire ecosystem of stakeholders, starting with the individual enterprise. The social architecture of such a co-creative organization must recognize that managers as heterogeneous individuals are at the heart of flows of interactive engagements. The organizational capacity to learn, nurture, share and deploy knowledge across boundaries (personal and institutional), as well as the intercultural and interpersonal competence of managers in navigating across those boundaries, becomes critical capabilities. Life-Xverse co-intelligence value creation is as relevant inside the organization, as managing outside it and requires seeing *managers as creative-experiencers* with the same PIEX lens we have been discussing and building capabilities for them to leverage knowledge rapidly within and across the organizational ecosystem.

Increasingly, rapid reaction time and associated skills such as the ability to amplify weak signals, interpret their consequences, and reconfigure resources faster than competitors will be a critical source of advantage. It's not just running faster but thinking smarter that makes the difference. Risk-managed Life-Xverse co-intelligence value creation puts a premium on the governance process for co-creation of value. Approaching 'zero managerial latency', i.e., the ability to continuously monitor the environment and respond rapidly, suggests a highly decentralized management approach, one where managers at all levels have the tools to engage in their managerial environments interactively (think of 'the Life-Xverse of managers'), understand what is happening around them, and make relevant, appropriate decisions through effective Human–AI interactive engagement. In this view, flexibility, teamwork, ongoing problem solving and constant searching for valuable impacts through multi-stakeholder collaboration are the norm.

Management co-creation demands protocols and disciplines, as well as structures and processes when organizing management activities. It is like building a sandbox for managers, who are not restricted in how they can use the sandbox—they can do anything they want in it so long as they stay in the sandbox and engage interactively in their flow of work with other managers. They also provide co-intelligence systems that support these managers with protocols for interoperability and guardrails for ethical governance. Thus, protocols and disciplines, as a basis for the organizational design of co-intelligence platforms in management ecosystems, can provide a shared framework for co-innovation and co-creativity in the organizational ecosystem.[32]

Richard Straub, founder and president of the Global Peter Drucker Forum, calls for a more human-centred approach to management to meet the demands of today's complex world with its 'poly-crisis' challenges. Together with Julia Kirby, they discuss the *Next Management* frontier, one that is about 'empowerment, trust, decentralization, antifragility, horizontal and bottom-up, agility, and experimentation and learning', where managers 'recognize their organizations are embedded in ecosystems and take a holistic view of institutions as innovators and value creators'. At the core of their endeavour is Peter Drucker, the management guru, and his fundamental tenet that management should concern itself with 'making society higher performing and more humane at the same time, by unleashing human talent, creativity, and ingenuity and channeling it with a sense of purpose'.[33] As Drucker said, 'Innovation, rather than being an assertion of human power, is an acceptance of human responsibility.'[34]

While businesses have traditionally been seen as isolated operating entities, the next practices of management have to embrace an ecosystem-centric thinking and sustain collaborations in natural and institutional ecosystems. As James Moore said,

I suggest that a company be viewed not as a member of a single industry but as part of a business ecosystem that crosses a variety of industries. In a business ecosystem, companies coevolve capabilities around a new innovation: they work cooperatively and competitively to support new products, satisfy customer needs, and eventually incorporate the next round of innovations.[35]

Risk-managed Life-Xverse co-intelligence value creation places newer demands on such organizational ecosystems. McKinsey, the consultancy firm, outlines some key actions that enterprises and their managers need to undertake to *rewire themselves for the AI world*.[36] Enterprises must reinvent their technology architecture by modernizing their core technology infrastructure to support AI at scale. Additionally, they need to revamp their data architecture by establishing a robust framework capable of handling the vast amounts of data that AI requires. Furthermore, organizations should redesign their workflows and processes to incorporate AI capabilities seamlessly. There needs to be a particular emphasis on reskilling/upskilling the workforce with advocacy for significant investments in training employees to equip them with the necessary skills for an AI-driven environment. It also highlights the need to foster a culture of innovation, promoting experimentation and risk-taking to facilitate AI transformation. Leadership and governance must be aligned, with leaders setting a clear AI strategy and ensuring that governance structures support the new AI-focused directions.

Transforming to the World's Best Bank—DBS

In 2009, when Piyush Gupta became CEO of DBS, he inherited a conventional bank struggling with poor customer satisfaction and limited digital innovation. By reimagining DBS as a 'technology company offering financial services', Gupta led a remarkable digital transformation, establishing DBS as a global leader and the 'world's best bank'. DBS aimed to become a digital-first bank by benchmarking against technology giants like Alibaba, Amazon and Google. It grounded its transformation on three strategies: i) becoming *digital to the core*, ii) embedding DBS in the *customer's own journeys* and iii) creating a *26,000-person startup*.

DBS wanted to imbibe the desirable qualities of tech majors—Google (open source), Amazon (cloud platforms), Netflix (personalized recommendations), Apple (design), LinkedIn (learning), and Facebook (collective). As David Gledhill, then CIO of DBS, looked at these names, it struck him that DBS could become the D in it to create GANDALF, the wizard from J.R.R. Tolkien's *Lord of the Rings*.

While GANDALF became the rallying cry for digital transformation, DBS adopted five key technology elements to drive change throughout the organization: i) shift from 'project' to 'platform'; ii) organize for success; iii) develop high-performing agile teams; iv) automate everything; and v) design for modern systems. DBS created thirty-three platforms aligned to business segments and products, with each platform managed by '2-in-a-box' leaders from both business and IT. It placed great emphasis on deepening the tech talent available within the company and embraced innovative mechanisms like *hackathons* to train even senior DBS executives. Soon, the number of technologists became a third of the entire workforce and double that of bankers in the company! DBS created *learning programs* such as DigiFY and Tech Academy to train employees on concepts like agile, AI and big data, journey thinking and other digital technologies. From just 15 per cent of technology services being *in*sourced in 2015, it went up sixfold in six years.[37]

Customer-Centric Obsession

DBS wanted its employees to become *customer-obsessed*. It embraced human-centred design and introduced the language of 'customer journeys' from the customer's perspective, not that of the company. DBS began investing heavily in AI. Gupta, commenting on DBS' aspirations to become an *AI-fuelled bank*, says,

> This is very meaningful and material. And it's a far more intelligent and appropriate way to deal with customers: to give them choices, ideas, insights, and reflections. That's the big picture of where we are and what we are trying to do.[38]

In 2018, DBS introduced the PURE framework, an acronym that stands for Purposeful, Unsurprising, Respectful, and Explainable. It provides comprehensive internal guidelines to ensure proper governance and ethical standards in data use. It was later expanded to encompass AI use cases within the bank. The framework aims to address the subjective nature of data-use ethics: (i) Purposeful: There needs to be a clear purpose for the use of data; (ii) Unsurprising: The use of data should not surprise customers and stakeholders, even if there is a legitimate purpose; (iii) Respectful: Data must be used in a respectful and responsible manner, including how it's collected and how its use is communicated to customers; (iv) Explainable: The model and data outputs should be explainable both internally and to customers. PURE is governed by the Responsible Data Use (RDU) Committee, consisting of about twenty senior leaders from cross-functional teams. The committee examines the data employed, use cases, and communication around data use.

Central to the AI strategy at DBS are proprietary platforms like ADA (Advancing DBS with AI) and ALAN (an AI protocol and knowledge repository), which result in *AI industrialization*, i.e., enabling rapid development and deployment of AI models across the bank. Using AI, DBS sends out 45 million personalized messages each month to over 5 million customers across Asia. These messages help them make better decisions about saving and investing their money. The DBS Quick Finance application leverages AI to allow small businesses to apply for loans in just one minute, approve in one second, and, in some instances, disburse instantly.[39]

Embracing GenAI

The transformation of DBS has continued with a strategic grounding of embedding AI and, more recently, Generative AI (GenAI), across the organization to enhance customer experiences and streamline operations. The advent of GenAI in late 2022 prompted the bank to push its own digital boundaries further by incorporating the latest technology in DBS' business activities. Gupta saw this as an opportunity to realize what they set out to accomplish with Natural Language Processing (NLP) back in 2013, stating,

> With ChatGPT and GenAI, like everybody else, we thought that it could be quite a game changer. One is it takes NLP to a level where I think you could actually use unstructured data. All the progress we've made is mostly on structured data. So, my vision, which I had 10 years ago of plugging Watson into Bloomberg, is now realizable with the progress in NLP with GenAI. The second big thing is obviously the generative component.[40]

Bank employees saw the creation of powerful digital tools used internally that increased overall productivity and elevated customer experiences. Despite its promises, GenAI introduced new complexities and risks, necessitating DBS to adapt its existing operational processes and governance framework to effectively manage and leverage this emerging technology. Specifically, the bank had to supplement the existing PURE framework with increased human oversight to monitor the potential risks brought about by GenAI.

In the first few months of 2023, around twenty of DBS' key technology and business leaders convened during a one-day workshop to strategize on the future with GenAI. The approach towards GenAI experimentation would be more controlled, which Gupta termed 'one horizontal and three verticals'. The horizontal capability led to the development of DBS-GPT, the bank's proprietary GenAI-enabled digital assistant. Three vertical areas focused on using GenAI to augment call centre operations, relationship management, and internal system development processes like coding and user testing.

DBS has quantified the additional value generated by integrating AI into the bank's activities since 2021. They identified approximately SGD600 (US$444) million in economic value attributed to the use of AI alone in the period 2021–23, with a projected SGD700 (US$519) million for 2024. For 2025, DBS plans to focus on new revenue realization and new model development using GenAI.

Organizational Redesign—RenDanHeYi at Haier

From the time he ordered a public smashing of seventy-six defective refrigerators at Qingdao Home Appliance Company in 1984 to overseeing the company's ascent as the number one major appliances brand for fifteen consecutive years in 2024, Zhang Ruimin, the chairman emeritus of Haier, has heralded a hugely successful and large-scale experiment in organizational redesign and transformation.

Zhang likens himself to an architect or a designer of a ship, not its captain—as someone who can guide the company through ever-changing environments and help advance with times. In an interview with *McKinsey Quarterly*, he defines the RenDanHeYi organizational model, an antithesis to the traditional Western model of top-down hierarchy:

> Ren is a Chinese word that means people or person. We mainly use it to refer to employees within an organization. Dan means orders, and here it represents the needs or demand of users. HeYi means integration. So, we're talking about the fact that everyone, every employee, gets to create value for users. Whatever your value, it is mirrored in the value you create for users. For example, typically an R&D person works without worrying about the final sale [of

the product]. But in our model, everyone, including R&D people, must be responsible for the final sale—or lack of sales—of the product they develop. With 'RenDanHeYi', we're talking about a virtuous cycle built around creating value for users.[41]

This philosophy permeates the unique organizational models that have evolved at Haier. Traditional organizational structures such as functional departments and tiers are replaced with a network structure of small business project teams that operate like entrepreneurs—this has evolved from self-organizing work units called ZZJYTs (an abbreviation for *zi zhu jing ying ti*, which translates to independent operating unit)[42] to an ecosystem micro-community (EMC) comprising 4000 micro-enterprises (MEs).[43] Consider the origins of Haier's first ME, ThunderRobot. In 2013, three young employees, who were recent college graduates and inveterate gamers, approached the head of Haier's platform business with an idea of manufacturing a new kind of laptop. They had scoured online reviews of serious gamers and identified thirteen customer pain points, including lack of power, poor screen quality and lightweight, which made the laptop seem flimsy. With an initial investment of $270,000 from the company, the team went on to develop Haier's first gaming laptop with the help of third-party manufacturers within nine months. They set the Chinese online markets on fire with their success. Haier soon followed up with some more investments and, crucially, also allowed the founders of the idea to put in their own money to take up a 20 per cent stake in the venture. By 2017, ThunderRobot was listed on the National Equities Exchange and Quotation (and later Beijing Stock Exchange), with a valuation of $180M. It is today, just like Haier did to it, nurturing its own MEs in video streaming, e-sports and VR domains.[44] Think of a nested model of entrepreneurship.

In such a model, the employee role shifts from being a worker to becoming a business partner or an entrepreneur. The management mode shifts from one of control to empowerment. Each micro-enterprise is responsible for identifying customer needs, developing products to meet this need, marketing, recruiting people into the team and collaborating with third-party service providers. Zhang says,

> We do not have a human resources department, and we don't pay fixed salaries, so if I don't give you a fixed amount of money, then all I need is for you to create value for the user, and then, the higher the creativity, the more that you can share this. If you cannot create, then you need to disband.[45]

With EMCs, Haier is moving into the world of highly interconnected IoT-enabled ecosystems. Its COSMOPlat, an open industrial platform, focuses on achieving zero-distance interaction between users and corporate ecosystem resources. Other companies and industries can utilize COSMOPlat to enhance their manufacturing processes, enabling them to implement mass customization and smart manufacturing. The emphasis shifts away from products and industries to ecosystems that manage customer needs and scenarios. COSMOPlat efficiently processes vast amounts of customer data, rapidly converting it into detailed design specifications, which are then distributed to its extensive network of suppliers for bidding. COSMOPlat excels at making innovative connections, which can be probed and amplified by humans-in-the-loop. It leverages global ecosystem network capabilities while integrating regional knowledge and insight to both develop offerings and optimize distribution and logistics management.[46] For instance, Haier's Internet of Clothing (IoC), built on COSMOPlat, provides smart laundry and care solutions that meet customer needs in washing, maintenance, storage, matching and shopping, and in five major scenarios, including field, factory, store, home and recycling.[47] Haier's Internet of Food (IoF) service reimagined offerings beyond just a refrigerator to store food. IoF could fulfil customer needs of food purchase, storage and preparation. It connects their customers with farmer ecosystems for fresh produce and the dietitian ecosystem for healthy recipes.[48] As Zhang notes, Haier, like a self-adaptive 'rainforest,' should be able to bring complex interdependent ecosystems in the service of the particulars of every situation.[49]

One of the challenges of having highly decentralized entities attempt cross-sector partnerships is that the transaction costs of collaboration go up. Haier Workbench, a tool based on smart contracts and blockchain technology, was introduced in late 2019 to facilitate collaboration. In two years, over 400 EMCs have sprung up in Haier.[50] Zhang acknowledges that AI is one of the foundational technologies of the future. But he serves a note of caution when he says,

> AlphaGo can defeat the world chess champion; however, it cannot experience the joy of victory. Algorithms can solve a lot of problems, but they cannot reach out to people at an emotional or human level . . . if you bet everything on AI, you probably will not develop a very competitive business model.[51]

Enterprises can learn from Haier's motto of 'prioritizing people's value'. As Moore and Zhang note:

> A few thousand technology professionals in a few cities can't lead the transformation of life and lifestyles for nine billion. At the center, particularly in platforms as currently designed, there is limited intelligence and sensitivity to the human realities of people and how to help people make creative use of their lives, even with IoT and artificial intelligence everywhere.[52]

The examples of DBS and Haier illustrate the ongoing transformation of systems of management outside the tech sector, whether organizations are service-based (like DBS) or product-based (like Haier), evolving through phases of digitalized and AI-infused platforms in organizational ecosystems.

Organizations must also evolve their risk management, which undergoes a radical transformation in a world fuelled by co-intelligence-driven Life-Xverse innovation and value co-creation. Co-intelligence empowers organizations to shift from reactive firefighting to proactive risk mitigation. It facilitates continuous monitoring, identifying potential threats in real time. Additionally, it allows for the development of adaptive risk models that constantly refine predictions and optimize mitigation efforts. AI even fosters better preparedness by simulating various scenarios through powerful what-if analyses.

Risk Management in an Age of Co-Intelligence

Private sector organizations must navigate the balancing of shareholder and longer-term stakeholder impacts and value creation as they participate in coalitions with public (and plural) sector enterprises. At the same time, public (and plural sector) enterprises must also navigate collaborative coalitions with private-sector enterprises. Organizational risk management, whether anchored in the private or public (or plural) sector, undergoes a radical transformation in a co-intelligence world. All organizations must embrace cross-sectoral co-creative management of risk-value in a co-intelligence world, together with internal and external stakeholders.

Mark Frigo and Venkat Ramaswamy, combining their works on 'return driven strategy' and 'value co-creation', proposed a framework for sustainable wealth creation by private sector organizations that prioritizes *balanced risk-taking*. They noted that: 'Value co-creation with both external and internal stakeholders helps balance risk-return by mitigating different types of risks while enhancing return through an expanded engagement model that cuts across silos through engagement platforms that facilitate more co-creative interactions.'[53]

Let us first consider how traditional insurance companies, whose core expertise is in risk management, are embracing AI.

Managing Risk at Traditional Insurance Companies— CSAA Mobilitas and AXA

By integrating AI and leveraging cloud technologies (e.g., with Guidewire's insurance industry cloud), Mobilitas Insurance, a subsidiary of the century-old CSAA Insurance Group, is able to offer innovative, flexible, affordable and customer-centric insurance products that meet the demands of modern *mobility and gig economy sectors*. Initially focused on providing ride-sharing insurance, Mobilitas has broadened its scope to include several new insurance products tailored to the unique risks of these sectors. For instance, its Last Mile Delivery Insurance product is designed for small private contractors involved in the final stage of delivery, a growing sector fuelled by the rise of services like DoorDash, Grubhub and Instacart. This insurance offering helps protect against risks specific to short-distance, final-stage delivery activities. Similarly, its Downtime Protection for Gig Drivers compensates drivers who lose income due to an accident that prevents them from using their vehicle, reflecting the unpredictable nature of gig work. Mobilitas also plans to introduce insurance offerings that leverage telematics data to tailor coverage more closely to individual driving behaviours, offering a more personalized insurance experience.[54]

Established insurance companies are also, slowly but surely, transforming their existing flows in value-chain ecosystems, e.g., by enhancing interactions between underwriting and customer-facing entities and even 'risk-prevention' approaches with more sophisticated use of AI. For instance, AXA, a leading global insurance and asset management company of French origin, can analyse vast amounts of data collected from sensors, satellites and drones to predict and mitigate potential risks in real time. This capability allows AXA to offer more precise and dynamic underwriting and risk management services, enabling clients to anticipate and avoid adverse events before they occur. In partnership with Amazon Web Services (AWS), AXA has developed the Digital Commercial Platform (DCP), which leverages GenAI as a next-generation risk management tool and reimagines AI-infused engagement flows of data, content and service exchange. The DCP integrates geospatial analytics, environmental data and GenAI technologies to provide comprehensive risk insights. This helps maritime clients by generating real-time risk assessments that account for factors like weather patterns, geopolitical events and logistical challenges. This proactive approach allows AXA to provide its maritime clients with actionable insights and recommendations, helping them avoid or mitigate potential losses *before* they occur, in win-win fashion.[55]

Beyond just data analysis, AI tools enhance stakeholder engagement by fostering improved communication, collaboration and well-informed decision-making. Transparency and trust are bolstered through the integration of technology, such as blockchain, and the implementation of responsible AI, which must address issues like bias, privacy, fairness and explainability to ensure AI-driven practices remain ethical and socially responsible.

The National Institute of Standards and Technology (NIST), US, has identified three broad categories of potential harm related to AI systems: i) *harm to people*, which includes individual, group, and societal impacts on civil liberties, rights, safety and opportunities; ii) *harm to an organization*, affecting business operations, security, finances and reputation; and iii) *harm to an ecosystem*, impacting interconnected elements, global financial systems, supply chains, natural resources and the environment. Trustworthy AI systems have the following characteristics—*valid and reliable, safe, secure and resilient, accountable and transparent, explainable and interpretable, privacy-enhanced, and fair with harmful bias managed*. There is a need to balance each of these characteristics based on the AI system's context of use. Thus, trustworthy AI systems and their responsible use can mitigate negative risks related to people, organizations and ecosystems and contribute to their benefits.[56] NIST has also identified a set of twelve risks unique to or exacerbated by GenAI. It includes risks related to confabulations (commonly called 'hallucinations'), intellectual property violations (replication of copyrighted content), information integrity (fuelling misinformation) and Human–AI configuration (misalignment of goals and desired outcomes).[57]

At the same time, GenAI also takes risk management to a whole new level by fostering extreme collaboration and innovation. Imagine GenAI systems proposing entirely new risk mitigation strategies or facilitating discussions through interactive platforms where stakeholders can explore risks and co-create solutions. Personalized communication and engagement are also enhanced through GenAI, ensuring risk information resonates effectively with specific audiences. Also, GenAI's ability to continuously learn and adapt ensures risk management practices remain relevant in a dynamic environment. It refines strategies based on ongoing experiences and provides a wider range of options and insights to support informed decision-making. In this context, enterprises must navigate the balancing of shareholder and longer-term stakeholder impacts and value creation.

Private sector organizations must navigate collaborative coalitions across the public and plural sectors in their NEST ecosystems, with SWIs as a North Star. As noted by Venkat Ramaswamy and Kerimcan Ozcan in their book, *The Co-Creation Paradigm*:

> If the actual behaviour of human beings is affected by ethical considerations, then welfare-economic considerations must be allowed to have some impact on actual behaviour. And further, if wellbeing is considered to be the capability to achieve valuable human 'functionings,' then arguably wealth-welfare-wellbeing should be a basis of joint creation and evolution of value.

They go on to discuss how cross-sector value co-creation has 'the potential to balance the invisible hand of free markets with the visible hand of governments and civil society, together with stakeholder expectations of more responsible, responsive, and effective enterprises and coevolving better states of governance, infrastructure, development, and sustainability'.[58]

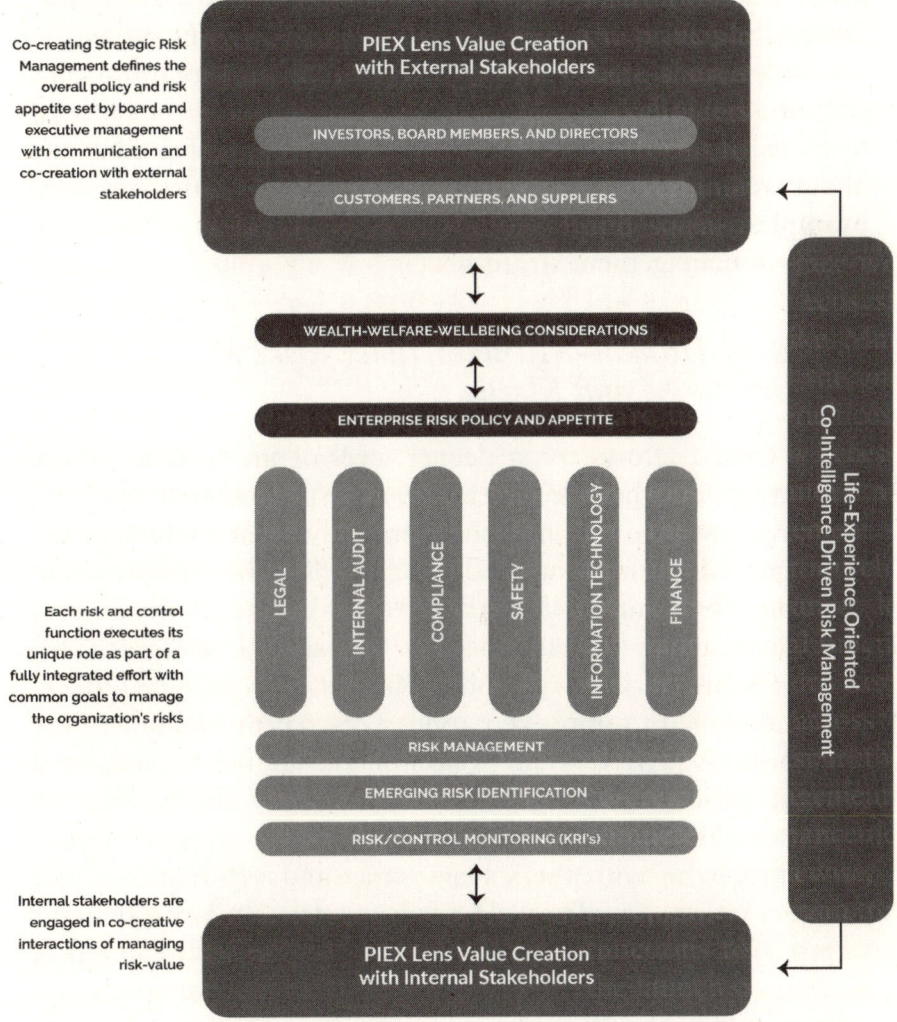

Figure 6-1: *Life-Experience-Oriented Co-Intelligence-Driven Risk Management (Source: Venkat Ramaswamy; adapted from Frigo and Ramaswamy 2009; Ramaswamy and Ozcan 2014).*

Figure 6-1 depicts an extended risk management framework that undergoes a radical transformation *with organizations in a co-intelligence world*. The November 2023 saga of Sam Altman's firing as CEO of OpenAI highlights the complexities of risk management in balancing value co-creation with internal and external stakeholders, especially in a co-intelligence world. The board's decision to terminate Altman, while intended to protect OpenAI's mission, disregarded the value employees placed on his leadership, creating a significant risk to the organization's stability. Ilya Sutskever's subsequent departure from OpenAI to focus on safe superintelligence reinforces growing concerns about responsible AI development. Let us consider some examples of how enterprises are framing and implementing their risk management strategies.

Managing Human–AI Interactivity Risks at Hippocratic AI and Klarna

While GenAI allows for a deeper level of interactivity, these interactions run the risk of being seen as superficial or synthetic if enterprises do not engineer them properly. That is why OpenAI leveraged AI-learning methods such as RLHF (reinforcement learning from human feedback) to make the chatbot seem more human-like in its responses. Consider *Hippocratic AI*, which focuses on developing *GenAI-powered healthcare agents* designed to improve patient experiences and outcomes. They address a wide range of non-diagnostic needs. Imagine a diabetic patient receiving personalized dietary and medication guidance through a friendly AI assistant or a post-surgical patient receiving empathetic reassurance and information about recovery milestones. These **AI nurse agents** are offered at a cost of just *$9 per hour*, around one-fifth the cost of a human nurse, making them a potentially cost-effective solution for healthcare providers facing staffing shortages. [59]

A healthcare agent based on generic LLMs is prone to hallucination and is even highly suggestible to erroneous inputs from patients. Hence, Hippocratic AI has been trained on evidence-based medicine and has incorporated an agentic-workflow-based architecture called Constellation. Munjal Shah, co-founder and CEO of Hippocratic AI, says,

> The architecture is not one model. It's actually twenty. So, we have one large language model that's doing most of the talking and we have 19 that are supervising it in different ways. One is supervising it on dosage, another on lab values and so on. That ensures it's safe.[60]

Consequently, the Constellation model helps it outperform real nurses in areas such as identifying a medication's impact on lab values (79 per cent vs 63 per cent) and pinpointing condition-specific, disallowed, over-the-counter medications (88 per cent vs 45 per cent).[61]

A key decision that Shah took was to keep Hippocratic voice-based and not text-based. It should engage in *real-time, natural conversations* with patients. In fact, their research showed that a half-second improvement in inference speed and response time increased the ability for patients to emotionally connect with AI healthcare agents by 5–10 per cent or more.[62] Hence, he forged a partnership with NVIDIA to develop *empathy inference*. It leverages NVIDIA H100 Tensor Core GPUs and its Avatar Cloud Engine suite of technologies to enable super-low-latency conversational interactions. The processing power and automatic speech recognition capabilities help Hippocratic **respond with human-like fluency and empathy**. This emotional connection is crucial for building trust and rapport with patients, ultimately leading to better adherence to treatment plans and improved overall health outcomes.

Hippocratic has not only baked in safety into its product architecture, but it has also adopted safety in its go-to-market process. Shah comments on the governance mechanisms in place:

One of the things we realized was that there's already a set of people that we trust, that's our nurses and doctors. We certify them, we license them, and they have to go through credentialing effectively. We had them assess the AI, and we only shipped the AI to patients when they said it was safe.[63]

Hippocratic's three-step approach to certifying the safety of its product involves—i) 50 nurses and physicians in phase 1; ii) over 1000 US-licensed nurses and 100 US-licensed doctors in phase 2; and iii) over forty health system and payor partners, over 5000 nurses and 500 doctors in Phase 3.

Or consider Klarna, a Swedish fintech company. Its CEO, Sebastian Siemiatkowski, acknowledges that deploying AI solutions, particularly in customer service, raises concerns about data privacy and compliance. Siemiatkowski ensured that they 'were GDPR compliant and that we could set the right structures around it since we're a bank'. He feels that Klarna's customer service team often has to act as a 'mini court' when resolving disputes between customers and merchants, a process that involves collecting evidence, communicating with both parties and making decisions about liability and cost coverage. It is complex and time-consuming.

Siemiatkowski, while enthusiastic about AI's potential here, acknowledges that 'this is actually having real-life business and real-life implications'. He foresees job displacement in roles like customer service, marketing and even translation. Klarna's AI-driven customer service already operates with the equivalent of 700 fewer full-time employees. Siemiatkowski also expresses concern that 'the amount of fraud and scams you're going to see will increase', especially with the rise of realistic AI-generated videos, and advocates for a global electronic identification system to combat this. While he believes AI can manage tasks like product descriptions, he cautions against over-reliance on it, especially in creative fields, stating that 'creativity is not the average' and AI, in its current form, tends to produce 'average' outputs, lacking the distinctive human touch. Klarna has also implemented a rule that customers should 'always know if they speak to AI or if they speak to a human'. But Siemiatkowski acknowledges that some individuals may prefer human interaction due to personal beliefs or past negative experiences with AI chatbots.[64] In February 2025, he said on X,

> We just had an epiphany: in a world of AI nothing will be as valuable as humans![65]

Let us next look at how Adobe manages intellectual property risks associated with GenAI.

Managing Risks of Intellectual Property Rights at Adobe

Adobe embeds AI ethics principles of accountability, responsibility and transparency into every stage, from design to deployment. This includes standardized training, testing and a diverse review board. For instance, its GenAI service, Firefly, is trained on datasets that are *carefully curated and licensed* to ensure they don't incorporate copyrighted material without permission. Shantanu Narayen, chair and CEO of Adobe, says,

> We took a very differentiated approach. We said we're only going to train our models with data that we have (a) license for. The other people chose to train it with data that they may or may not have had IP for . . . we were actually considerably differentiated because we said that for the creatives, we're going to stand up for what is licensed content with which we train the models.[66]

This ensures the AI-generated content is original and avoids legal issues. In contrast, OpenAI and even Microsoft have been sued in recent years for copyright infringement by multiple prominent US newspapers, including the *New York Times*.[67]

And which in turn has prompted them to consider content licensing agreements with publishers such as the *Financial Times*.[68] Adobe champions *responsible AI development* by providing artists with tools and workflows that promote **transparent attribution** of any source materials used by the AI in the generation process, likening it to nutrition labelling in the food industry. Another aspect of responsible AI is seen in Adobe's approach to the automation-augmentation question. Narayen says, 'Generative AI in the creative and in the art space is going to augment human ingenuity and not replace it.'[69]

Managing Commercial Risks at FedEx and Others

Let us consider value-chain integration risks at FedEx, the leader in global logistics. With a global presence spanning over 200 countries, its value chain comprises its customers, customs and border agencies, food and drug administrations, aviation authorities and other relevant organizations. It has embraced blockchain technology, whose secure and transparent record-keeping enables real-time tracking and verification of provenance throughout the value chain minimizes risks like fraud and counterfeiting. Rob Carter, their CIO, envisions a future where consumers can have complete confidence in the origin of their goods: 'Imagine knowing exactly where your (Thanksgiving) turkey came from, every step of the way, thanks to a secure and immutable blockchain record'.[70] FedEx has assumed a leadership role in fostering education and adoption of this technology in the global commerce industry. In 2023, in partnership with Don Tapscott's Blockchain Research Institute and the INSEAD business school, it began offering courses on Web 3.0 and blockchain on Coursera.[71]

AI hallucinations can pose other significant commercial risks. Air Canada was recently sued for providing misleading information through its AI-powered chatbot, which erroneously informed a customer that he could apply for bereavement fares retroactively, leading him to pay more for his ticket than necessary. Despite Air Canada's argument that the chatbot should be considered a separate entity, the British Columbia Civil Resolution Tribunal held the airline liable for the misinformation provided. They affirmed that enterprises have a duty of care to ensure the accuracy of their chatbot's information.[72]

In an increasingly data-rich but data-privacy-poor world, consumers face risks of identity theft, financial fraud, and targeted manipulation. India's Data Empowerment and Protection Architecture (DEPA) empowers individuals with control over their personal data. This framework prioritizes data privacy and security through a system based on explicit consent. Imagine someone needing a loan (borrower) approaching a small lending company (lender)—DEPA allows the borrower to securely share their data with lenders through trusted intermediaries called *consent managers*. These managers, like the company Sahamati, act as an account aggregator, i.e., a bridge between the borrower and the lender. When a lender requests the borrower's information, they contact the consent manager, who then facilitates the data transfer **only** with the borrower's explicit approval. Crucially, the consent manager cannot see this data, ensuring its confidentiality. Additionally, the bank, where the borrower's credit history and information exist, doesn't know the identity of the lender requesting the information, adding another layer of privacy. Rahul Matthan, commenting on a unique aspect of India's DPI story in *The Third Way*, says, 'Contained within these digital systems is a robust data governance framework that operates by embedding legal and regulatory objectives directly into code'.[73]

Another business model that follows Larry Lessig's maxim of 'Code is Law' is the *smart contract of the Web 3.0* world. It is a decentralized mechanism automating a variety of digital transactions. Consider Etherisc, a parametric blockchain insurance startup.[74] When a user purchases its flight-delay insurance, the terms are embedded in a smart contract on the Ethereum blockchain. The smart contract connects to real-time flight data sources and automatically triggers a payout if the flight is delayed beyond a specified threshold. This process eliminates the need for manual claims, ensures timely payouts and reduces administrative costs and disputes.

Managing Risks of GenAI Adoption at Enterprises— Bloomberg, Morgan Stanley and ING

How do enterprises go about adopting GenAI in a systematic way? They can either develop their *own proprietary AI models* and integrate them into end-user apps or products (internal or external users); or they can develop end-user apps without any proprietary AI models and instead *prompt-tune, finetune or distill existing AI models*, available as APIs or open-source checkpoints. Eventually, most of these enterprises will rely on infrastructure vendors, such as cloud platforms and hardware manufacturers, to run the training and inference workloads necessary for their GenAI models.

Consider how Bloomberg developed BloombergGPT from scratch to cater specifically to finance-related content. The model was trained using forty years of financial data, news, documents, financial filings and internet data, totalling 700 billion tokens, and utilized 1.3 million hours of GPU time. Given that it was meant to answer financial and investment-related queries, BloombergGPT was subject to strict evaluation. It was tested using publicly available financial data to see how well it performed tasks like recognizing specific names and entities, analysing sentiments (positive or negative tones) in financial news, and handling general language processing and reasoning tasks. Morgan Stanley, on the other hand, utilized prompt tuning to customize OpenAI's GPT-4 model, incorporating 100,000 documents with investing, business, and investment process knowledge. The system operates in a private cloud, accessible only to Morgan Stanley employees, ensuring data security. It uses 400 'golden questions' (to which it knows the correct answers) to test system changes.[75]

ING is a global bank of Dutch origin, with over 60,000 employees serving more than 38 million customers, corporate clients and financial institutions in over forty countries. ING collaborated with QuantumBlack, McKinsey's AI arm, to develop a GenAI chatbot aimed at enhancing customer support. The project involved a seven-week development period, during which they identified and addressed existing chatbot limitations. The joint team then explored how advanced GenAI chatbot technology could be used to improve the customer experience, giving customers the assistance they needed immediately. The final solution involved a multi-step process to generate the optimal answer for the customer, which included retrieving knowledge from available data stores and ranking potential answers by their helpfulness. When multiple helpful answers were found, the system would present several options to the customer, a method known as disambiguation.[76] Before sending any answer to the customer, a series of guardrails was applied. To achieve this, *ING risk stakeholders were involved from the beginning*, and ING-specific guardrails (such as avoiding advice on mortgages and investment products) were established.

The GenAI chatbot was tested with about 10 per cent of real customers in the Netherlands who were using the support chat function on the mobile app. It provided immediate, tailored responses, reducing the need for live agent intervention and significantly improving customer experience. This initiative allowed ING to assist 20 per cent more customers, decrease wait times and offer instant gratification. Since its launch in September 2023, thousands of customers have now interacted with the new chatbot. ING is now focused on a broader *capability-building* effort across fifty-plus support functions—in risk, contact centre, analytics office and technology—and building a scalable model that can be extended to all other ING countries.

In all these instances, it is evident that highly technical skills are required to effectively develop, fine-tune and maintain complex AI models, ensuring accuracy, reliability and ongoing improvements. This reliance on experts poses risks, such as increased costs for hiring and retaining skilled data scientists and engineers. There is a long way to go before GenAI model development becomes truly democratized as such.

Managing Cybersecurity Risks at Mandiant

Cybersecurity is a complex landscape encompassing various threats, from supply chain intrusions (such as the SolarWinds hack where attackers target a third-party service provider to gain access to its customers) through phishing (where attackers deceive individuals into providing sensitive information) to zero-day (targets vulnerabilities in software before developers have had a chance to patch them) and ransomware attacks (such as the WannaCry ransomware attack that exploited a zero-day vulnerability in Microsoft Windows). The evolving nature of these threats underscores the critical role of AI—it acts both as a powerful tool for defence and a potential threat.

Mandiant, a leading cybersecurity firm, was acquired by Google in 2022, bringing the former's expertise in threat intelligence and incident response together with the latter's robust cloud security infrastructure and shared-fate model. That meant working closely with customers to prevent security problems before they happen, unlike the usual approach of just sharing responsibilities. Mandiant CEO Kevin Mandia says,

> I am a proponent of Google Cloud's shared fate model. By taking an active stake in the security posture of customers, we can help organizations find and validate potential security issues before they become an incident.[77]

For instance, machine learning algorithms can analyse network traffic and user behaviour to detect deviations from established norms, such as unusual data access or transfer activities. Thanks to AI, the global median dwell time—the time between a breach occurring and its detection—has fallen from over 200 days a decade ago to sixteen days now. At the same time, malicious actors are also leveraging the very same technologies to enhance their attacks. For instance, GenAI enables the creation of highly personalized and convincing phishing emails by mimicking writing styles and using relevant context, making it harder for individuals to identify these as fraudulent. As Andrew Kopcienski, principal intelligence analyst at Google Mandiant, puts it, 'You don't need to break in if you can steal the keys'.[78]

Co-intelligence has to be leveraged proactively to manage the vast and complex data environments of modern organizations. Mandia says, 'How you leverage technology like AI and machine learning to learn (what's) normal for your organizations and identify the abnormal? . . . We're going to use AI to fix things. We're going to adapt better security technologies, technologies that think and learn.'[79]

Balancing Responsiveness and Risk at Amazon

During the Covid-19 pandemic, which induced lockdowns in cities and disruptions in supply chains across the world, Amazon had to rapidly reconfigure its systems and ecosystem processes to ensure that consumers did not face issues of unavailability or delivery delays. This not only involved understanding and predicting consumer demand but it also entailed a sophisticated logistics strategy driving retail supply chains towards a new end point: the consumer's home. Amazon CEO, Andy Jassy, in his 2022 letter to shareholders, explained: 'This meant that we had to double the fulfillment center footprint that we'd built over the prior 25 years and substantially accelerate building a last-mile transportation network that's now the size of UPS—all in the span of about two years.'[80]

Accordingly, Amazon invested heavily in programmes like Amazon Flex Drivers (who are gig workers hired as independent contractors) and Amazon Delivery Service Partners (DSP, who are small subcontracted parcel delivery firms that exclusively deliver packages for Amazon Prime customers). Amazon's acquisition of Whole Foods also improved its last-mile market position considerably—Amazon Flex Drivers started utilizing their stores to drop off and pick up packages at Amazon lockers.

Given its reliance on ecosystem partners for delivery, Amazon leveraged technology to monitor the operations and ensure better customer experience. Amazon provided each of its drivers (Flex as well as DSP) with an Android smartphone called Rabbit. It tracked a driver's movements in real time and provided information on the Prime customer and on each package delivery, such as package size, access codes to enter apartment buildings or notes on where to leave packages. The driver had to take a picture of the delivered package through Rabbit and upload it to the Amazon system to confirm delivery.[81]

As Amazon's emphasis shifted to interactive networked ecosystems of digitalized experiences, it found great success— by 2019, half of all Amazon Prime packages were delivered by these two programs (Flex and DSP). Its customers were happy too, with real-time visibility into their orders. But considering the life–experiences of its subcontracted delivery drivers, the outlook was not cheerful. Amazon's delivery drivers faced a lot of stress from a feeling of constant surveillance from their Rabbit device. Their movements were tracked by their formal employers (DSP), Amazon and Amazon's Prime customers. Jake Alimahomed–Wilson, a researcher, says,

> The Amazonification of logistics has created a new group of highly exploited contingent workers: delivery drivers. The working conditions facing Amazon's last-mile drivers are defined by a frantic pace of work, low wages, and relentless pressure to meet tight delivery deadlines established by Amazon. These jobs are also increasingly becoming defined as racialized-gendered jobs in the Los Angeles region.[82]

More generally, enterprises must contend with *new types of risks* they have to consciously manage across the Life-Xverse of organizational ecosystems. For instance, consider again the example of NIO (from Chapter 4) and its smart connected product engagement model of a community of owners in its offering ecosystem, which comes with its own risks. For instance, in August 2021, after a NIO driver died in a crash while using the NIO NOP (navigate on pilot) auto-driving function, two opposing groups of owners emerged online. One group, supported by over 500 users, accused NIO of misleading customers by promoting NOP as an autonomous driving system when it was merely an assisted driving feature requiring driver attention. A larger group of nearly 4000 owners disagreed, stating the joint statement did not represent them. These public disagreements from community engagements are a new form of enterprise risk that must be managed proactively. Although we have exemplified undesirable and, at times, unintended consequences in the contexts of Amazon and NIO, managing such risks apply to all enterprises.

The Co-Intelligent Enterprise

The traditional enterprise, with its rigid structures and constrained decision-making, is increasingly ill-suited to adapt to the dynamic and unpredictable environment of a co-intelligence world of individuals as creative-experiencers involved in Human–AI interactive engagement and co-creation of risk-managed value.[83] It calls for a symbiotic relationship between human flourishing and the socio-technical assemblages that we have formed collectively. Only through thoughtful, risk-managed co-intelligence value co-creation can we ensure that it empowers us, rather than extinguishes the very spark of humanity and life–experiences it seeks to amplify.

AI first needs to be seen as augmenting, and not just automating, human work.[84] Davenport and Kirby note the promise of augmentation in their 2016 book *Only Humans*

Need Apply: 'humans and computers combine their strengths to achieve more favorable outcomes than either could alone.'[85] As Nobel Prize-winning economist Daron Acemoglu argues, the focus on automation over augmentation is a choice and not a predetermined outcome of technological advancement. With the appropriate economic and non-economic incentives, such as tax policies and research emphasis, the right type of AI may be developed that supports employment and shared prosperity.[86]

Another important question that enterprises must ask themselves is what constitutes social responsibility in a business? They should find the right balance between a focus on maximizing profits for shareholders, solving social problems and improving society as a whole. Marjorie Kelly, a leading theorist in next-generation organizational design, suggests a way for profit-maximizing corporations to become living enterprises in a sustainable economy. She writes in *The Systems View of Life* (by Fritjof Capra and Pier Luigi Luisi): 'You don't start with the corporation and ask how to redesign it. You start with life, with human life and the life of the planet, and ask, how do we generate the conditions for life's flourishing?'[87,88]

As we have argued, we need a *Life-Xverse first* frame of reference in leveraging co-intelligence, one rooted in co-creating positive, valuable and emergent life–experiences with AI. Enterprises must co-design co-intelligence architectures steering organizational ecosystems with a life–experience orientation towards human and planetary wellbeing. *This calls for a new form of enterprise in leading the co-intelligence revolution powered by AI factories of the future.* Co-intelligence architectures must be configured to support offering, value-chain, management and NEST ecosystems, with organizations themselves seen as assemblages through which interactive agency takes place. In addition to the technical architecture, this requires paying attention to the *social architecture—the management structure, talent development, training, skills, beliefs, decision rights, performance metrics, rewards, and values of the organization*—to enable co-creative risk-managed value. Successful transformation rests on the co-creative capacities of organizational architectures to enable extended enterprise and open/social network-resourced capabilities to be harnessed effectively by the organization.[89]

We call this new form of enterprise a *co-intelligent enterprise*.

Building on our discussion of organizational management transformation and risk management in this chapter, co-intelligent enterprises are characterized by:

(i)   Harnessing Human–AI co-creation, leveraging tokens of digital intelligence (TDIs) through a risk-managed PIEX lens and co-innovating with stakeholders to build ecosystems of capabilities.

Additionally, as we will discuss in the next three chapters, they entail:

(ii) Designing organizations as *living-systems* that continuously learn and adapt through *'co-intelligence knowledge environments,'* where TDIs act as modular units of actionable intelligence, enabling managers—viewed as creative-experiencers—to engage dynamically with Nextgen AI systems and co-creating risk-managed value across individuals, communities, functions and sectors.

(iii) Co-Evolving SWIs at speed, scale and scope *across private, public and plural sectors*, with TDIs dynamically orchestrating feedback loops that iteratively align actions with SWI goals and enhance systemic resilience.

(iv) Cultivating *EcoAI literacy* and *lifelong learning*, leveraging TDIs as actionable bridges to integrate Nextgen AI literacy with eco-literacy, addressing environmental and societal concerns ethically, thereby steering organizational ecosystems towards a harmonious world of human development and planetary wellbeing.

7

Designing Co-Creative Living Organizations in a Co-Intelligence World

A Philosophy of Co-Creative Living Organization

A *living-system* organization is akin to a living organism. Ludwig von Bertalanffy pioneered the General Systems Theory, emphasizing the importance of studying systems as wholes (collections of interconnected parts) with emergent properties (where the whole is more than a sum of its parts). This applies across disciplines, from biology (living organisms) to sociology (societies).[1] In their book *The Systems View of Life*, Fritjof Capra and Pier Luigi Luisi suggest four characteristics of living-systems: i) they comprise *networks and structures*; ii) they are *regenerative*; iii) they are *creative* and allow for *emergence*; and iv) they are *intelligent, learning* systems.[2] Social networks are living-systems, just like biological networks, and are characterized by the exchange of information and ideas, culture and organizational boundaries. Human organizations possess a dual nature—they are designed for a particular purpose, i.e., they are legal and economic entities, and they are living-systems that nurture communities of people.[3] Capra sees living-systems as interconnected webs, where the relationships between parts are as important as the parts themselves. Life thrives on continuous cycles of renewal and *feedback loops*, with systems constantly adapting and rebuilding themselves. New properties and behaviours arise from the complex interactions within networks, not residing in any individual component. And intelligence in living-systems allows them to adapt, learn and *self-organize* for survival and growth.

As living-systems, enterprises *listen, cognize, synthesize, assist and act upon the world, constantly evolving and learning together with their stakeholders*. Leena Nair, CEO of the French luxury fashion house Chanel, says, 'The story of Chanel is about being supportive of women to be and become the best versions of themselves. To discover themselves.'[4] To accomplish this purpose, she has overseen Chanel's organizational and leadership redesign.

> One of my principles is about tapping into collective intelligence. I truly believe that the days of the superhero leader are well and truly behind us. World is so complex. There are crises at multiple levels. To imagine that one individual, no matter how bright and experienced they are, can have answers to all the questions, no chance. That's why I believe in collective intelligence, diverse perspectives, go around the room and listen to every voice, not just listening to the dominant voices in my meeting room.[5]

Organizational theorist Margaret Wheatley has emphasized the importance of distributed leadership within organizations and self-organizing systems. In her book, *Leadership and the New Science*, Wheatley says, 'Self-organizing systems demonstrate the ability of all life to organize into systems of relationships that increase capacity. These living-systems also demonstrate a different relationship between autonomy and control, showing a large system maintains itself and grows stronger only as it encourages great amounts of individual freedom.'[6] She emphasized the importance of 'recurring patterns of behaviour, what many call the culture of the organization'.

In addition to these perspectives of the systems view of life, co-intelligent enterprises as co-creative living-system organizations (CCLOs) also embody the notion of the *Life-Xverse*, which, as we have discussed entails emergent life–experiences in the lived-journeys of creative-experiencers (their lived experiences). This also aligns with Edmund Husserl's 'lifeworld', founded on everyday lived experiences upon which all knowledge and understanding are built.[7] Co-intelligent enterprises discern this *lifeworld* of their creative-experiencers and know how to navigate it, embed AI-infused interactivity through it, and then manage it. They also align with Jürgen Habermas's concept of the 'system', alongside and aiding the lifeworld through communicative actions. In flows of interactive engagements, communication is central, and actions are oriented towards reaching mutual understanding. However, following Habermas, a major concern is the potential for the system to 'colonize' the lifeworld. For example, social media can be a tool for social movements and citizen journalism, fostering a more informed public sphere. But it can also make our lifeworld shrink; it instrumentalizes our actions, turning our lives into a series of metrics to be achieved (e.g., time spent on social media and likes received), rather than the underlying sharing of rich experiences in the derivation of personal meaning.

How do we ground AI-infused engagement flows and the configuration of ecosystem platforms in the meaningful life–experiences of human *becoming*? Around 500 BCE, Greek philosopher Heraclitus wrote: 'Everything flows and nothing abides; everything gives way and nothing stays fixed. You cannot step twice into the same river, for other waters and yet others, go flowing on.'[8] For him, everything was in a state of flux, and change itself was fundamental. This mindset of 'becoming' applies as much to enterprise management as it does to individual life–experiences. It captures the idea of a shift from a static state of existence of traditional enterprises to a dynamic process of change and development in the co-intelligent enterprise.

Kerimcan Ozcan and Venkat Ramaswamy propose a *Dynamic Relationality Theory (DRT) of Creative*

Transformation, which 'emphasizes the fluidity, contingency, and interconnectedness of relations, offering a fresh perspective on the dynamics of complex systems'.[9] DRT posits networked entities as being defined by their relations. It introduces a visionary approach to understanding the evolving relationship between technology and human experiences, emphasizing co-creative, emergent life–experiences over mere digital platformization. It calls for a democratization of Life-Xverse innovation and value creation, which requires the weaving of a digital fabric across event-sensed flows of interactive engagements in the lived-journeys of creative-experiencers.[10] DRT provides a theoretical foundation for co-creative living organizations through Human–AI interactive engagement and creative transformation of organizational ecosystems.[11]

One of the critical aspects of a co-intelligent enterprise is co-intelligent perception, learning, actions and adaptation. This begins with recognizing *managers as creative-experiencers with AI*—and developing effective *co-intelligence knowledge environments* to support them, as discussed next.

Managers as Creative Experiencers Engaging with Nextgen AI

Real-Time Business through Palantir Foundry Ontology

In the landscape of co-intelligence architectures, Palantir Foundry Ontology stands out as a transformative platform that exemplifies the ability of shared digitalized infrastructures (SDIs) to model complex organizational data and provide actionable insights across ecosystems. Alex Karp, CEO of Palantir, says,

> People will pay for chips and ontology. You understand the chip's side . . . Ontology means you can actually use this raw resource (data) and process it into something that actually works.[12]

Foundry Ontology—a component of Palantir Foundry—offers organizations a way to unify, model and operationalize their data, enabling decision-making at an unprecedented level of precision.[13] This aligns well with the concept of co-intelligence architectures that allow organizations as living-systems to collaborate, adapt and co-create in real time.

A New Layer of Organizational Intelligence

Palantir Foundry is designed as a comprehensive platform to support data integration, transformation and analysis across different entities in an organization. Its ontology layer adds a distinct advantage: it provides a live, operational representation of the organization's data landscape, transforming the way data is understood and used. Unlike traditional data platforms that silo information into disconnected databases, Foundry Ontology brings data together in a relational model that mirrors the real-world entities and activities within an enterprise. This abstraction, called an 'operational ontology', is crucial for turning raw data into business insights and operational intelligence.

The ontology enables users to map operational entities—such as production lines, customer segments or assets—to their corresponding data sets, integrating them into a meaningful model that can be utilized by diverse stakeholders. By linking data points with the physical and logical assets they represent, Palantir Foundry empowers every stakeholder to access data in a contextually relevant manner, transforming raw information into actionable insights that reflect the reality of operations. Whether it's understanding the connections between manufacturing equipment, analysing customer transactions or optimizing logistics across supply chains, Foundry Ontology provides a 'digital twin' that allows organizations to react proactively and make data-driven decisions with high accuracy.

One of the major benefits of Palantir Foundry Ontology is its capacity to break down data silos and provide a unified view of the operational landscape. This holistic visibility creates new opportunities for collaboration among stakeholders across functions—including supply chain, finance, product development and more—within an organization. Foundry Ontology's interface allows users from different parts of an organization, even those without deep technical skills, to interact with data in ways that drive collaborative problem-solving. This is particularly relevant to the Life-Xverse concept, where ecosystems of co-intelligence involve the interactive engagement of individuals as creative-experiencers.

Palantir Foundry's ability to integrate various data sources—structured, semi-structured and unstructured—enables organizations to gain a comprehensive understanding of their value chain, identify bottlenecks and respond swiftly to dynamic changes in the environment. Karp says,

> The large language model is like a chemistry experiment that is useful when refined. And the refinement of that for your enterprise happens in what we call our ontology. This is where we impose the logic of your business on the large language model, in the security and intellectual logic of your business, and this is transformative.[14]

For example, in the healthcare sector, Foundry Ontology enables hospitals to link data on patients, beds, medical staff and equipment in real time, facilitating optimized workflows, efficient use of resources and ultimately better patient outcomes. In manufacturing, the ability to map production lines and identify anomalies in processes allows for predictive maintenance, minimizing downtime and enhancing operational efficiency.

Driving Collaborative Creation with Stakeholders

A key feature of Palantir Foundry is its emphasis on collaborative creation across an organization's ecosystem. Through Foundry Ontology, companies can create an operational representation of their environment that includes not only internal stakeholders but also external partners, customers, suppliers and even regulators. For instance, a company might utilize Foundry Ontology to engage in collaborative planning and forecasting with its suppliers. With real-time data on inventory, shipments and market demand, all parties can coordinate effectively, reducing inefficiencies and making proactive adjustments to ensure optimal outcomes for the entire value chain. Foundry Ontology's collaborative workspace environment allows different stakeholders to participate in data-driven discussions and contribute to shared goals—whether it's managing supply chain disruptions, predicting customer demand or optimizing resource allocation.

The ability to bring together various data contributors in a single, operational context promotes a culture of data-driven decision-making and collective intelligence. This emphasis on engagement flows of interactional creation—a core aspect of Life-Xverse innovation—facilitates not only operational improvements but also new avenues for innovation by identifying previously invisible relationships and opportunities.

Empowering Decision-Makers with Real-Time Analytics

Palantir Foundry Ontology is particularly powerful because it empowers both technical and non-technical decision-makers to interact with data in a meaningful way. The platform provides tools that allow users to query data and create actionable insights without needing specialized coding skills. Its user interface is intuitive, and decision-makers can visualize the complex relationships between different entities through dashboards, interactive graphs and AI-driven recommendations.

This democratization of access to intelligence is instrumental in making an organization agile and adaptive. In the Life-Xverse, where speed and the ability to adjust in real time are essential, Palantir Foundry enables decision-makers to act immediately on insights. The use of AI algorithms in Palantir Foundry also enhances the analytical capabilities of the platform, allowing for predictive insights that help managers anticipate changes before they occur. This predictive element is crucial in minimizing risks and optimizing performance across diverse domains, from financial planning to workforce management.

Risk Management and Compliance in the Life-Xverse

In addition to enhancing operational efficiency, Palantir Foundry Ontology places a strong emphasis on managing risks and compliance. In industries like finance, healthcare and government, where regulatory compliance is paramount, Foundry provides a robust mechanism to ensure that data usage is transparent, auditable and in line with regulatory standards. Foundry's Ontology allows organizations to embed compliance controls directly into their data models, ensuring that all data handling activities meet governance requirements.

This risk-managed approach resonates with the broader goals of co-intelligence, which emphasizes the importance of managing risks and ensuring ethical usage of AI-driven capabilities. By embedding compliance and governance into the operational framework, Palantir Foundry ensures that value creation in the Life-Xverse is both sustainable and ethically sound, fostering trust among all stakeholders involved.

Building the Managerial Foundation for a Co-Creative Living Organization

Ultimately, Palantir Foundry Ontology provides a foundation for organizations to become CCLOs. Its operational modelling capabilities enable a real-time representation of the organization's entire ecosystem, allowing stakeholders at every level—from front-line workers to executives—to interact with the data in meaningful ways. The emphasis on integrating diverse data sources and facilitating data-driven decision-making across teams supports the vision of a CCLO, where collective intelligence drives continual learning and adaptive value creation.

Through Palantir Foundry Ontology, organizations can create a living, breathing representation of their operations, continually fed with real-time data and accessible to all participants in the ecosystem. This forms a crucial basis for enhancing collective engagement, enabling interactional creation of value and fostering ongoing co-evolution in alignment with sustainable wellbeing impacts (SWIs).

Following the Palantir example, there are four basic requirements for managers as creative-experiencers of AI to effectively co-innovate ecosystems of life–experiences with stakeholders and co-create risk-managed value.

i) First, they must have access to as much real-time, event- or engagement-centric data as possible regarding the experiences of other creative-experiencers in interrelated ecosystems.

ii) Second, they need to understand and selectively intervene in individual experiencers' events or engagements while managing overall operations, balancing micro-level interactions with macro-level performance.

iii) Third, they must be able to respond quickly by mobilizing and reconfiguring resources as needed, ensuring agility and timely reactions to the dynamic demands of creative-experiencers.

iv) Fourth, they must become 'living-system leaders', i.e., emphasize adaptability, interconnectedness and holistic thinking, treating their organizations as dynamic, evolving entities. They must focus on sustainability, decentralized decision-making and continuous learning, empowering all stakeholders to contribute to collective success and value co-creation.

Organizations need to start with building AI-infused managerial environments. In a co-intelligence world, this involves leveraging AI/GenAI for rapid resource reconfiguration, shifting inventories, scaling production, reassigning personnel, modifying communication strategies, and other activities based on real-time data and predictive analytics. Managers need AI-driven insights contextualized to make informed decisions and coordinate actions efficiently. The environments must support real-time responses and seamless collaboration within the organization and with external partners, suppliers and customers. By infusing AI, the infrastructure becomes more dynamic and flexible, facilitating the continuous co-creation of value through agile and data-driven managerial actions. This flexibility in resource reconfiguration is essential for *experience quality management* (EQM) in a co-intelligence world, going beyond the traditional total quality management (TQM) of goods-services production-delivery.

We should recognize *managerial heterogeneity in AI utilization*, i.e., managers differ widely in their ability to access, interpret and utilize AI-generated insights. Effective AI systems must accommodate these differences by providing customizable interfaces and adaptive learning paths. Recognizing managerial heterogeneity involves understanding the *context of the moment* and how individual managers want to access, visualize and use information *in the flow* of their engagements. Some managers might quickly grasp and leverage AI insights, while others might require more time and support. Thus, AI systems should offer personalized experiences that cater to each manager's unique needs, enabling them to interact with AI tools at their own pace and according to their specific requirements. This recognition of heterogeneity ensures that the AI system is sensitive to the varying levels of sophistication and domain knowledge among managers.

An AI-infused managerial environment should also possess several key capabilities to *support diverse managerial behaviours*. Ensuring consistency in decentralized decision-making is crucial; while managers must have autonomy, AI systems should guide their actions to align with the organization's strategic goals. Visualization of AI-generated insights is also essential; managers need a visceral understanding of customer and other stakeholder experiences, facilitated through AI-enhanced data visualizations and simulations. These tools help managers refine their questions and respond effectively to real-time situations. Additionally, the environment should enable the creation and leverage of new knowledge by allowing managers to interact with AI systems, pose new questions and test hypotheses quickly. This capability supports rapid and effective decision-making, enhancing the organization's agility in responding to dynamic market conditions through the intelligent application of AI.

In a co-intelligence world, *experience-oriented operating rules and procedures* must evolve beyond traditional efficiency-centric frameworks to focus on enhancing performant co-creation opportunities, especially engendering SWIs with creative-experiencers. This involves creating business impact-based rules that prioritize real-time, context-specific interactions and dynamic adjustments based on experiencer feedback. Managers must develop and implement procedures that simultaneously drive revenue by enhancing valuable consumer experiences and reduce costs by eliminating inefficiencies that do not contribute to compelling experiences. The managerial environment must facilitate rapid consensus-building and agile resource reconfiguration to support these evolving procedures, ensuring that every action taken aligns with the goal of co-creating value in real time.

Thus, the concept of 'managers as creative-experiencers' in a co-intelligence world redefines the traditional managerial role by positioning them as active participants in the creative process with (Gen)AI, rather than merely as overseers or followers of a process. In a co-intelligence world, managers must engage directly with life–experience aspects of value co-creation. They need to gain access to as much real-time, event- or engagement-centric data at scale and scope as rapidly as possible to connect with and understand the life–experiences of other creative-experiencers and respond quickly by mobilizing and reconfiguring resources. This approach emphasizes building AI-infused managerial environments and recognizing managerial heterogeneity by understanding the context of the moment, enabling the workforce to foster creativity, innovation and SWIs within dynamic organizational ecosystems. We consider next examples of two consulting companies, Accenture and BCG, who are reskilling and upskilling their talent base with transformative learning experiences.

Workforce Transformation at Accenture and BCG

Accenture has developed a comprehensive and inclusive strategy to not only invest in AI but also in the continuous upskilling of its workforce to mitigate risks and maximize the benefits of AI integration. Julie Sweet, chair and CEO of Accenture, says,

> All strategies lead to technology—companies must reinvent all parts of the enterprise with data, AI and new ways of working to build resilience and find paths to new growth.[15]

In 2023, Accenture announced a $3 billion investment into AI over three years, with plans to double its AI workforce to 80,000. Sweet believes that this 'compressed transformation' due to GenAI is akin to the PC moment. 'It is like when we moved from typewriters to computers . . . It really is rewiring the way individuals work.' A key strategy to reduce the risk of skill gaps includes developing *technology quotient* (TQ) across the workforce, and Accenture has become an early adopter of Microsoft Copilot. Sweet says,

> I actually started with my most senior leaders because what we're telling all of our clients and we live what we say, which is that in order to make the right decisions as a CEO or in the C-suite, you have to understand the technology at a much deeper level.[16]

Sweet believes that not only does GenAI transform the business process, it also transforms the skills required in people managing these processes. For instance, a consumer goods company's salespeople traditionally needed to have good administrative skills. With GenAI automating administrative tasks, these employees can instead focus on new skills such as building deeper customer relationships and delivering strategic value.

There are risks associated with operating in a co-intelligence world. Accenture has articulated a responsible AI program and focuses on the ethical use of AI technologies while ensuring transparency, fairness and accountability.[17] The program emphasizes the importance of human-centric AI design while safeguarding privacy and data security. It is overseen by Accenture's audit committee and integrates responsible AI practices into every AI use case, addressing potential risks and challenges. Sweet says,

> What we say to CEOs in the C-suite is that every time you are looking at a use case for Gen AI, you should be asking the question, What are the risks and challenges potential in this use case? And how is our responsible AI program going to mitigate those risks and monitor them?[18]

Even BCG, a global management consulting firm, has begun experimenting with GenAI. A custom-developed enterprise GPT is available to all its consultants. In addition, over 3000 tailored GPTs for specific client engagements or optimizing administrative tasks have been created by the BCG consultants. They even have a leaderboard tracking the most popular GPTs. BCG undertook a scientific study to understand its impact— around 90 per cent of participants using GenAI improved their performance in tasks like creative product innovation, outperforming the control group by 40 per cent. However, for tasks like business problem-solving, which are beyond GenAI's current capabilities, their performance was 23 per cent worse than those who didn't use the tool. Further, they found that consultants mistrusted the tool where it could add significant value and trusted it too much in areas where it was incompetent.[19]

GenAI is a double-edged sword and needs to be risk-managed well to derive benefits. To maintain quality and nurture skill development of consultants amidst AI integration, BCG emphasizes 'purposeful toil'. It has put in guardrails by ensuring that human experts review and validate AI outputs, preventing full automation and fine-tuning models (such as constraining data ranges and outliers) for accurate results. Vlad Lukic, MD and senior partner at BCG, says,

> We put checks in the workflow that force the individual consultant to actually digest the materials (from AI), sanity check them and have an interaction with someone senior that can help them build intuition for sanity checking these materials. That's a new moment for all of us.[20]

As the Accenture and BCG examples suggest, effectively supporting managerial environments requires organizations to co-design broader Life-Xverse based-workforce environments for rapid knowledge co-creation that we call *co-intelligence knowledge environments* that foster *collective intelligence and rapid knowledge leverage across all levels of the organizational ecosystem*. Before we delve deeper into this latter concept, let us first explore two organizations in the healthcare domain that embrace its primitives.

Collective Intelligence at Project ECHO

Project ECHO (Extension for Community Healthcare Outcomes), developed by Sanjeev Arora in 2003, uses virtual mentoring to connect experts with remote healthcare workers, fostering collaborative learning and expanding access to specialized medical knowledge. This model has trained over 4 million professionals in nearly 200 countries, impacting over 200 million patients.

Project ECHO has partnered with Apurva.ai, an open co-creative innovation platform from India that 'enables change leaders to amplify the collective wisdom of their networks'. Such wisdom emerges during interactions among various stakeholders with diverse perspectives. ECHO's tele-mentoring sessions abound with such collective wisdom from the 'all teach, all learn' approach of problem solving. But this wisdom ceases once the meeting gets over, i.e., it is not readily accessible afterwards even to those who attended the meeting.

Apurva solves this challenge by transforming interactions into reusable building blocks that can be combined to generate succinct, synthesized summaries or longer, data-enriched insights. Think of Apurva as an intelligent agent that sits in meetings, either actively participating in conversations in real time and offering some insights (synchronous) or responding to queries later in different modes of text, audios and videos and in multiple languages (asynchronous). Kartik Dhar, CTO at Project ECHO, says,

> Our thinking has historically always been around communities of practice and building human connection. And it will continue to do so. That is the core of what Echo does. But this combination of human plus AI is something which can propel us on our mission to touch 1 billion lives much faster and much more efficiently.[21]

Project ECHO, powered by Apurva, serves as a powerful example of an organization that harnesses a co-intelligence knowledge environment. It fosters collaborative learning and knowledge sharing across global networks, *both outside-in and inside-out*, while enabling valuable impacts at scale.

We turn next to Infosys, a global IT, consulting and outsourcing major, and see how it is becoming a CCLO as an *AI-first live enterprise* in a co-intelligence world. Here, we will explore Infosys' transformation through the complete CCLO lens—a living-system organization harnessing the co-creative power of Human–AI interactive engagement, with continuous learning and adaptation and co-evolution of sustainable wellbeing impacts. We first examine how its co-founder, Nandan Nilekani, had a catalysing role as a *changemaker* not only at the company but also in the larger society and nation. Incidentally, one of us (KN) worked at Infosys for over a decade, and the other (VR) went on sabbatical with Nilekani's EkStep and Societal Thinking team (with the guidance of chief curator Sanjay Purohit) in 2017–18. We are grateful to the Infosys team for hosting us at their wonderful Bengaluru campus in August 2023 and sharing their digital transformation stories.[22]

AI-first Live Enterprise Transformation at Infosys

Nandan Nilekani as a Social Changemaker

Bill Drayton emphasizes the power of changemakers—individuals who see societal problems as opportunities and mobilize resources to effect positive change. One of Nandan Nilekani's most notable contributions is his leadership in the creation of Aadhaar, India's unique identification system, which we discussed in the first chapter. He remarks about how it brought about a transformational change in society:

> You can think about the progression from the basic requirements of life like 'roti, kapada, makaan' (food, clothing, housing) to infrastructure like 'bijli, sadak, pani' (electricity, roads, water) and to 'JAM—Jan Dhan (bank account), Aadhaar, mobile', the three digital numbers that are the basis for your future.' For instance, with Jan Dhan, 290 million women, including more than 100 million in rural communities, have gained financial empowerment as of 2024.[23]

Social changemakers harness the power of technology and innovation to drive the co-creation process. They create platforms and networks that enable seamless communication, knowledge sharing, and resource mobilization among stakeholders. Nilekani co-founded non-profit organizations such as iSPIRT (Indian Software Product Industry Round Table), which championed India's digital stack initiatives (as we saw in Chapters 1 and 2), and EkStep, which has created open digital platforms for education in India (e.g., DIKSHA, which we examine in Chapter 8).

In 2017, Nilekani, one of the co-founders of Infosys, returned to it as chairman over thirty years after it started. It was a period of some organizational challenges and a need for strategic rejuvenation, and Nilekani was there to offer a guiding light. He had just overseen the successful conceptualization and deployment of not one (Aadhaar) but two (UPI, which we discussed in Chapters 1 and 3) national-level digital transformation initiatives, together with the Indian government. Nilekani asked himself: 'Why not apply these learnings on transformation to global enterprises that are also large and complex and need to reinvent themselves to be like the digital natives? And why not start with Infosys to refine and demonstrate the model to the markets?'[24]

Infosys Live Enterprise

Inspired by these ideas, Infosys developed a framework, 'Live Enterprise Model'. Jeff Kavanaugh, global head of the Infosys Knowledge Institute, and Rafee Tarafdar, CTO of Infosys, describe the model in their book, *The Live Enterprise*. They view the enterprise as a living organism enabled by technology. They use metaphors inspired by nature and the human body, such as digital brain, sentience, and metabolism, to describe the model. The Infosys *digital brain* is pulsing with data, information, content and knowledge about different stakeholders in varied personas or groups, various entities, institutions, events, things, and systems related to the company. And each of these nodes in the network are interconnected. A digital brain *'is a center of intelligence that gives the enterprise higher cognition and makes every interaction a value-adding exercise'.*[25]

Now consider *decision-making* in a live enterprise. Digital brains, knowledge graphs and AI help in the development of a system-wide intuition. Kavanaugh says, 'Once the organization develops the ability to make decisions in an automated manner and has real-time visibility to everything in each of these ways, it becomes alive.'[26] Tarafdar talks about designing a 'sentient experience' in a live enterprise.

> Take the travel process. As a manager, how can I get information on what the cost impact is for approving this request and how many more travel requests can we do with the available budget? We want the system to provide information to users at the time that they are making the decision, based on context. Then, as an organization, we can complete that decision within the flow.[27]

A 'digital runway' enabled reimagination of employee experiences and new hire onboarding at Infosys, which was especially helpful during the Covid-19 pandemic when nearly the entire company operated remotely.

Nilekani, in his address at the Infosys AGM 2019, explains what embracing the 'live enterprise' vision has entailed:

> This has meant focusing on personal growth, nurturing zero-latency in processes, ensuring just in-time data for decision making, driving hyper productivity and facilitating continuous learning to instill new patterns of behaviour. For example, our InfyMe app is a mobile-first window into the world of Infosys that every employee can access with a simple tap on their phones. Lex is another app that is immensely popular among employees seeking to prepare themselves for emerging digital opportunities by developing corresponding skills. These are just early

manifestations of the connected, sentient digital world we are beginning to build for our people.[28]

Thanks to these efforts, Infosys saw its market capitalization more than double to $72 billion between 2017 and 2020.[29] As AI and GenAI became central to the digital transformation conversations with its clients, Infosys evolved its model to become an *AI-first live enterprise*—with its building blocks of AI-first experiences and processes (AI assistants and AI twins for better customer journeys); AI engineering excellence (AI platforms for engineering, testing, training and delivering products at speed and scale); responsible AI by design (right AI guardrails); and the AI operating model (new skills for an AI-first company of talent).[30] Infosys still uses the brain analogy to describe 'structurally ambidextrous' AI-first organizations, with AI assistants and in-the-flow tools helping deliver improved operations and near-term profits (enterprise left brain) and disruption, discontinuous growth and new forms of value (enterprise right brain). Nilekani says, 'As we go AI-first, we'll be giving each Infosys employee an AI-assistant. Through generative AI capabilities, the assistant will be a steady and empathetic human counterpart, well-versed in the day-to-day activities that employees have to do, while amplifying their creative and human potential in the process.'[31]

One key focus area was application development and maintenance, the core of Infosys' business model. It soon became one of the largest users of Microsoft Copilot. Tarafdar says,

In areas where nothing was available out of the box, we took largely open-source models and we fine-tuned these using the code and data we had. For example, we built a specialised model for our Finacle banking product, where, let's say we have a UI design, then looking at the UI design, it can automatically generate code end-to-end. We created fine-tuned models for Oracle, SAP implementation, for Cobol modernization.[32]

Infosys developed twelve other co-pilots for such specialized aspects of software engineering. In order to democratize innovation, it collaborated with NVIDIA and developed an internal AI cloud that provided easy access to GPUs. Infosys developers could quickly build, test and launch apps on this platform, with automation enabling completion in days instead of months. Let us now deep-dive into two other functions where the AI-first live enterprise model has had significant impact within Infosys—*sales* and *skill-development*.

Transformation of the Sales Experience

Catalyzed by the pandemic, and the disruptions to the sales process with the advent of newer technology-enabled channels and platforms, Infosys embraced the vision of the sales function as a live enterprise. It conducted multiple ideation workshops to map out a day in the life of an Infosys salesperson and identify micro changes to effect a transformation. Technology was leveraged to bring information in the flow of the sales process. Personalized dashboards highlighting key opportunities requiring follow-ups were presented. A sales enablement program called, Sales Excellence through Accelerated Learnings (SEALS), was created—top sales performers shared their insights with the rest of the salesforce; Infosys leadership created a virtual selling podcast series; and storytelling training programs were offered. Infosys also adopted a social selling programme leveraging LinkedIn Sales Navigator. Srividhya V.S., VP and global head of sales effectiveness and enablement at Infosys, says,

> We made sure every sales rep had a Sales Navigator license and ran month-long workshops and training sessions to ensure that they felt ready and equipped to use the sales intelligence platform. We used gamification tactics to clearly set out key milestones and paired these with reward and recognition. We recruited 'pro' Sales Navigator users as advocates . . . (Over two years) 93 per cent of our total

contract value and over $370 million in sales pipeline have been touched by Sales Navigator.[33]

Infosys created HINT, an internal knowledge search engine that scans over 65,000 assets, such as past deals, case studies and so on, to provide relevant inputs for new proposals. The InfyMe app enabled end-to-end sales process—helping the salespersons to understand client buying intent, discovering experts within the company to bring into a sales conversation and so on. These form part of the digital brain of a *sales* live enterprise. Technology development was a co-creative process, involving a cross-functional team of sales, sales effectiveness, and IT team members, collaborating in every development sprint. Adopting an agile blueprint borrowed from the development teams, the sales organization delivered, in sprints over twenty four months, long-lasting transformation through one micro change at a time. These efforts contributed to a total pipeline increase of 61 per cent in the 2021 fiscal year. The Sales Live Enterprise tools and techniques were applied successfully in Infosys' successful pursuit of its blockbuster deal (estimated to be over $1.5 billion[34]) with asset manager Vanguard.

In an AI-first world, Infosys has adopted co-pilots at scale to make its sales experience even more effective. Tarafdar says,[35]

In the past, our sales colleagues faced challenges when clients sought information on complex topics like ERP consolidation, for example. The conventional process involved reaching out to experts across different time zones, leading to time-consuming efforts in collecting and presenting information. However, with our Navi Sales assistant, an internal copilot, accessing 40 years of knowledge has become instantaneous. Sales colleagues can swiftly retrieve information on topics like ERP consolidation, identify experts, gather case studies, and seamlessly embed them into documents, significantly reducing turnaround time. Moreover, the Navi Sales assistant supports discussions with clients by providing on-the-spot information lookup, enhancing efficiency and client interactions.

Having established that the AI-first model was working well within its own organization—as 'client zero'—Infosys then offered this thinking and AI-infused solutions to all its global clients. It launched Infosys Topaz, a suite of AI-first tools, with over 150 pre-trained AI models, over ten AI platforms, AI talent and partner innovations. Salil Parekh, CEO of Infosys, says,

> When clients have knowledge-objects whether it is in, say a bank's credit department, in a manufacturing company in product elements, or what products to use, or in a telco in, say, pricing of their programmes . . . anywhere there are knowledge elements and objects and ways to leverage them in more efficiently . . . generative AI becomes very useful.[36]

Let us now consider how Infosys is leveraging its AI-first model externally with its clients and changing the game by co-innovating new offering ecosystems with its clients and transforming clients' value-chain and management ecosystems in the process, so they can, in turn, co-create better risk-managed value with their stakeholders.

Serving an AI Ace in the Tennis World

By infusing the age-old sport of tennis with AI, Infosys has catapulted the game into an unprecedented era of innovation and fan engagement. Sumit Virmani, EVP and global chief marketing officer of Infosys, says,

> Infosys has been associated with the world of tennis for over eight years now. We have a strategic partnership with the ATP (Association of Tennis Professionals), with Roland–

Garros, the Australian Open and the (International) Tennis Hall of Fame. This game has over a billion fans the world over, and they are passionate about consuming tennis in an immersive way . . . Tech keeps tennis at the cutting edge. Every single movement, from the time the ball leaves the player to the time it's received, is captured through millions of data points.[37]

The partnership with the ATP, the governing body responsible for men's professional tennis worldwide, began back in 2015 with the revamp of its player zone app. In just a month, Infosys built a comprehensive career hub for professional tennis players, offering features such as game analytics, appointment tracking and tournament logistics, all designed for ease of use. ATP already had a treasure trove of data—12 million data points on player performance, taken from the 85,000 games.[38] Interesting new insights revealed how athletes rated against their peers across playing surface, yearwise or career level on the ATP World Tour. Infosys also created interactive platforms like the ATP Leaderboards and the Second Screen, which provided fans, players, and coaches with in-depth insights and a more immersive experience. Massimo Calvelli, ATP CEO, says, 'The stats section is doing extremely well. 10 million views in 2022. Our interactive leaderboard is an incredible tool because it allowed us to organize and serve thirty-three years of match data to our fans. They could put our history to use and make it relevant today.'[39]

Infosys has since extended its technological innovations to Grand Slam tournaments. For instance, the Australian Open leveraged Infosys's AI-driven Virtual Hub to provide VIPs with exclusive virtual experiences, including 360-degree match viewing and interactive sessions with tennis legends and celebrity chefs during the Covid-19 restrictions. For the International Tennis Hall of Fame, Infosys created a metaverse-based digital twin of their museum, allowing fans worldwide to experience the rich history of tennis in an immersive virtual environment.

Let us now delve deeper into the collaboration between Fédération Française de Tennis (FFT) and Infosys and see how they enhanced the tennis fan experience and tournament operations through AI-driven innovations at Roland–Garros.

i.   *Match Beats:* Match Beats is an AI-driven feature developed to provide real-time updates and key moments from tennis matches, enabling fans to follow the action even if they cannot watch the live telecast. This tool continuously tracks and delivers crucial match highlights, scores and significant plays, ensuring fans remain engaged and informed regardless of their location.

ii. *Player and Coach Analytics:* AI is leveraged to provide real-time statistics and video analytics for players and coaches. This application allows them to review and analyse their performance almost immediately after a match, offering insights into their gameplay, strengths and areas for improvement. The system provides detailed data and visual feedback, which are critical for making strategic adjustments and enhancing performance. Florian Le Moigne, head of digital at FFT, says,

It was amazing because this population is really key for us. And providing them with almost live statistics and almost live videos that they can use just right after their match . . . they can analyse almost live and then try to enhance a little bit of some aspects of their game. I think they enjoy it. We received so many testimonies from them.[40]

iii. *AI-Assisted Journalism:* AI tools are utilized to assist the FFT editorial team in streamlining their content creation process. These tools generate insights and embed data directly into articles, making the journalism process more efficient. Moigne says,

The platform is really easy to use and understand. We published almost 100 stories thanks to this technology.

We are not only thinking about our fans, but we are also thinking about all the people who are building these tournaments year after year. This is a great example of how it can happen also for them.[41]

iv. *Automated Highlights and AI Shot of the Day:* AI technology is employed to automate the creation of match highlights and to select the best shot of the day. This process, traditionally handled by editors, involves reviewing extensive footage to compile engaging and concise highlight reels. AI takes over this task, efficiently sifting through match data and identifying the most exciting moments to feature. It is also interesting to see the different perspectives of the technologist and the business executive on this aspect—one wants the AI to behave like the human, while the other wants to amplify the potential of the human, given AI's benefits.

Raghavan Subramanian, AVP and head of Infosys Tennis Platform, says,

Typically automation does monotonous jobs. For us with Roland Garros, the challenge was to take up creative tasks and try AI on them. Creating highlights is a highly creative task. In one day, we have thirty-two men singles and thirty-two women singles. So, sixty-four matches and hundreds of winners to be able to go over all of them and sometimes even forcing shots and pick(ing) the best shot of the day was a wonderful challenge for us. Also, to be able to do that and run it against (the) past year's tournament and see whether it's producing results that are good for us.[42]

Moigne says,

From an organizer's perspective, what is interesting is AI is bringing this (productivity benefits) to us and it allows us to allocate our human resources differently. Technology is allowing us to think a little bit differently . . . and I think this is exactly the spirit of the partnership as well.[43]

Infosys too has thought similarly about its own employees: *how to leverage AI to train and make them ready to face the co-intelligence world?*

Development of AI-ready Talent and the Learning Experience

Infosys' training infrastructure, the Global Education Centre in Mysuru, is world-renowned for its scale, grandeur and ability to train over 14,000 employees in one go. The company also had significant investments in online training for its hundreds of thousands of employees the world over. The learning programme had stood Infosys in good stead all these years, but it required some rejuvenation. Thirumala Arohi, EVP and head of India business and platforms, group head—education, training and assessments at Infosys, says,

> Sadly, training in its current form is most often viewed as an 'interruption' to an employee's work. We must remember that learning has no impact unless it translates into successful employee engagement and change in learner behaviour, which, in turn, furthers an organization's business objectives. The need of the hour is therefore to bring learning into the workplace as a continuous process that is convenient, relevant, and appealing enough to inspire employees to be self-motivated lifelong learners.[44]

As part of its Infosys Live Enterprise strategy, Arohi and team completely reimagined the learning experience. They applied micro-change methods to redesign companywide reskilling. While previously, employees would be hesitant to take a day or two off to attend a training program, they were now spending thirty-five minutes every day on proactive skilling, aided by smaller online modules and individualized nudges.[45] The behavioural and attitudinal change towards skilling was supported and catalysed by an in-house developed digital learning platform, Lex.

Employees can access Lex anytime, anywhere and on any device. The content offered is aggregated from multiple sources, both internal and external. The learners can also virtually interact with the educators or experts at any given time. The Lex platform aims to pique the learner's curiosity and provide an immersive experience. Some of the engagement and platform capabilities include a flight simulator for participants to work on near real-life problems in a safe environment; adaptive learning powered by strong machine learning algorithms that understand employees' learning patterns, assessment results, production experience and manager feedback to provide proactive insights into learning that motivate learners to continue and complete their programme; gamification of learning in the form of leaderboards and badges for task completion;[46] and LexPrims, an application that enables content creators to make short videos.

Under the Future of Education project, Infosys reimagined the classroom experience powered with AI and mixed reality. Konnect, a Lex app used by trainers to run live quizzes and polls among course participants, is now available in an extended reality immersive world, Metaconnector, where learners can join and learn. Zoiee, the virtual assistant chatbot, is available in a personalized humanoid avatar. She can assist educators with content creation, translation and spotting plagiarism during evaluations while she acts as a guide answering queries and actively recommending relevant courses to learners.[47] Infosys offers a massive collection of learning materials (skills library) that acts like a roadmap. It shows employees exactly which courses to take (learning path) to develop a particular skill in a specific area (domain), whether they're just starting (beginner), building their knowledge (intermediate) or aiming to become an expert (advanced). AI-powered knowledge graphs help show how these skills connect to each other and to the broader related topics.

Having successfully implemented this change within the Infosys organization, it began offering the Lex platform to its clients under the name of Wingspan. Then, as part of its corporate social responsibility (CSR) charter, Infosys launched a community learning and reskilling programme/platform called Springboard, built on Lex/Wingspan. This caters to students from Class VI onwards to professionals, from educational institutions, NGOs and self-help groups. Infosys collaborates with external partners like Coursera and Learnship to develop specialized courses.[48] As part of its ESG Vision 2030, Infosys Springboard seeks to empower 10 million people globally with digital skills by 2025.[49] Arohi comments on their engagement with local communities:

> Infosys Springboard is democratizing digital learning, preparing more aspirants to explore emerging opportunities and equipping working professionals to flourish in the jobs of the future. The over 1.2 million, and still growing, learners benefiting from Infosys Springboard inspire us to redouble our efforts to help navigate India into the digital future.[50]

Sustainability Journey

John Elkington proposed a reboot of thinking from 'triple bottom line' to 'triple helix of value creation'—a shift from just an accounting mindset to a systems approach that was dynamic and interconnected. [51] The triple helix envisioned businesses as playing a regenerative role, fostering positive change for *people, planet and prosperity* simultaneously. Kavanaugh and Tarafdar, in *The Live Enterprise*, inspired by Elkington, assert that the 'live enterprise is a triple helix'.

Infosys began its sustainability journey in a formal way in 2008 and became *carbon neutral in 2020*, thirty years ahead of the timeline set by the Paris Agreement. To put this achievement in perspective—as of 2022, only 42 per cent of the Fortune Global 500 have delivered or are committed to delivering a significant climate milestone by 2030, while 37 per cent have not yet made any commitment at all.[52] How did Infosys get to be a decade ahead of most Fortune 500 companies in terms of its sustainability outcomes?

The answer is in how it built its *practical sustainability* capabilities. Corey Glickman and Jeff Kavanaugh, both senior leaders at Infosys, in their book, *Practical Sustainability: Circular Commerce, Smarter Spaces and Happier Humans,* present the themes of Infosys' Practical Sustainability framework:[53]

i.   *Regenerative Future*: Businesses evolve from extraction to sustainability to regeneration.
ii. *Circular Commerce*: Data, products and finance combine for innovative, eco-friendly business models (reuse over recycle).
iii. *Human Experience*: Sustainability requires a human-centred approach, leveraging technology to elevate people's work and wellbeing (with privacy and security).
iv. *System of Systems*: Complex problems like sustainability require a holistic view. They use interconnected systems to track, understand and improve.
v.   *Digital Twins*: Replicating the physical world digitally creates a single view for learning, optimizing and simulating a better future.

If the themes represent the 'what' of practical sustainability, Infosys' six-stage journey addresses the 'how' of it—i) create a sustainability plan; ii) create a business plan; iii) optimize digital and physical assets; iv) address the supply chain; v) develop a carbon-offset strategy; and vi) build a sustainability-first culture. The first step of creating a sustainability plan begins with identifying key focus areas. Infosys followed a consultative and data-driven process of identifying the most material issues related to a 'triple helix' of interactions among industry, academia and government. Infosys analysed external stakeholder perspectives such as investor viewpoints, peer benchmarks, global indices, insights unearthed by AI tools from media sources, regulatory landscape. It also conducted extensive internal discussions—belief audits with management and employee surveys—to come up with a materiality matrix that measures how much an issue impacts the organization's ability to sustain its business performance and how much the issue influences stakeholders' decisions and perceptions about the organization. For Infosys, i) enabling digital talent at scale, corporate governance, data privacy, information management, diversity and inclusion and climate change are critical issues with both high stakeholder influence and significant business impact; ii) 'tech for good' and water are highly influential but have a moderate business impact; and iii) employee wellness and experience, waste, energizing local communities have a moderate to high impact on business performance but are less influential to stakeholders as compared to the other issues.

Infosys leverages technology in a significant way to manage sustainability on its campuses. It designed Ecowatch, a software solution to track and improve its environmental performance. Built on Microsoft's Azure cloud platform, Ecowatch collects and analyses data on energy use, water consumption, waste generation and greenhouse gas emissions. This data is then used to identify areas for improvement, set sustainability goals and generate reports that comply with industry standards. At its Hyderabad campus, Infosys deployed a fleet of robots to autonomously navigate and manage solar panels. Additionally, Infosys leverages IoT sensors embedded in the solar panels to constantly monitor their performance. Infosys' ERWIN is an Internet of Things (IoT) device specifically designed for smart spaces. It acts as a comprehensive monitoring tool, gathering real-time data on various environmental parameters within a space, and an asset is viewed across historical, real-time and future horizons. At a digital command centre at the Bengaluru campus of Infosys, a team remotely manages these ERWIN boxes through a digital twin, leverages AI/ML to monitor and analyse data for utilities such as energy, water and air quality, space utilization, and asset-operating conditions.[54]

Thus, Infosys undertook a combination of energy efficiency initiatives, community-based projects and investments in renewables as it implemented its practical sustainability framework. The results have been spectacular. By 2020, against its 2008 baseline, Infosys saw a 43 per cent reduction in carbon emissions footprint, and a 55 per cent reduction in per capita energy usage (which translated to $225 million in energy savings). It constructed 25 million sq. ft. of highest-rated green buildings and campuses, and 44 per cent of their energy needs came from renewable sources.[55,56] The Infosys Lex and Wingspan examples we saw earlier power two of its 2030 ESG goals—enabling digital talent at scale (target of 10 million people including employees, clients, students, and others) and tech for good (target of 80 million lives via programs in e-governance, healthcare and education). Its 2030 ESG vision is integral to Infosys' sustainable business performance.

Taken as a whole, the Infosys example calls attention to the fundamental need for CCLOs in the Co-Intelligence Revolution to engage their managers and their work teams as creative-experiencers and rapidly leverage collective enterprise knowledge in a co-intelligence world across interconnected NEST ecosystems and value-chain, offering and management ecosystems. In the next section, we provide an architecture of such a *co-intelligence knowledge environment*.[57]

Rapid Knowledge Leverage at Scale and Scope

A *co-intelligence knowledge environment* must support the managerial environment as shown in **Figure 7-1**. The knowledge environment is fundamentally enhanced by integrating co-intelligence into the organization's *architecture* of knowledge access and leverage (e.g., recall the discussion of managerial ecosystems in the case of L'Oréal from Chapter 2), thus transforming each of its seven layers discussed below to support dynamic and real-time knowledge creation and sharing of insights and experiences.

There are seven layers and two foundational aspects of a co-intelligence knowledge environment.

i) *Skilling and Training*: The first layer, skilling and training, is crucial for building the skill base within an organization.

LAYER 7	**Co-creating Risk-Managed Value** Creating and evolving next practices
LAYER 6	**Facilitating Co-Discovery** Incorporating diverse insights
LAYER 5	**Mobilizing Action Teams** Creating new initiatives
LAYER 4	**Leveraging Sources of Competence** Ease of access, visibility, and dialogue
LAYER 3	**Using Information** Extracting contextual knowledge
LAYER 2	**Information Sharing** Knowing best practices within the firm
LAYER 1	**Skilling and Training** Building the skill base

Data Sovereignty, AI Ethics, and Governance — Ensuring Responsible AI use

Continuous Learning and Adaptation — Fostering a continuously learning organization

Figure 7-1: The Seven Layers of a Co-Intelligence Knowledge Environment (Source: Venkat Ramaswamy).

In a co-intelligence world, AI-driven skilling and training programs offer personalized experiences that adapt to each individual's learning pace and needs. Virtual mentors and AI simulations provide tailored support, making the learning process more effective and ensuring that employees acquire relevant skills efficiently (e.g., recall the Siemens industrial metaverse example from Chapter 2, which facilitates real-time learning on the job). This adaptability ensures that learning keeps pace with technological advancements and the evolving demands of the business environment.

ii) *Information Sharing*: The second layer, information sharing, involves the dissemination of best practices within the organization (e.g., recall the Airbnb example from Chapter 4 where Superhosts share their knowledge with new hosts). Advanced AI systems facilitate seamless information sharing across people and systems in the organization by synthesizing and grounding best practices for co-intelligence retrieval using data analytics and natural language processing. This technology ensures that valuable insights and knowledge are readily accessible to all employees, enhancing collaboration and operational efficiency. The accuracy of AI-driven information sharing helps convert tacit knowledge into actionable insights rapidly, promoting a culture of continuous engagement and improvement of practices.

iii) *Using Information*: The third layer focuses on extracting contextual knowledge from shared information. AI tools enable managers to contextualize data, providing real-time insights tailored to specific situations (e.g., recall from Chapter 4 the usage of AI at Shell to augment the capacity of the worker). This capability ensures that approved best practices are adapted appropriately for different markets and scenarios, improving decision-making accuracy. By offering contextualized information, AI helps managers respond more effectively to dynamic market conditions and emerging opportunities.

iv) *Leveraging Sources of Competence*: The fourth layer emphasizes the ease of access, visibility, and dialogue within the organization and its enhanced network (e.g., recall from Chapter 4 the coordination between AI Cooper and a human QA specialist at Lemonade). AI systems enhance the visibility of expertise and facilitate access to knowledgeable individuals across geographical and functional boundaries. By leveraging *knowledge graphs and AI-driven networks*, managers can quickly locate and engage with the right experts, ensuring that knowledge flows seamlessly throughout the organization. This interconnectedness fosters a collaborative environment where expertise is easily accessible, driving innovation and problem-solving.

v) *Mobilizing Action Teams*: The fifth layer involves creating and managing action teams for new initiatives. AI plays a crucial role in forming and managing these teams by analysing skill sets, project requirements and personal traits (e.g., recall from Chapter 4 how Airbnb Setup identifies the right Superhost for a host). This ensures that the most competent and synergistic teams are mobilized for new initiatives, enhancing project success and innovation. AI-driven team formation enables organizations to respond swiftly to new opportunities and challenges, maintaining agility and competitiveness.

vi) *Facilitating Co-discovery*: The sixth layer, facilitating co-discovery, is about incorporating diverse ecosystem insights to drive co-innovation. AI systems aggregate and analyse data from various sources in the organizational ecosystem, including customer feedback, market trends and internal data, helping managers co-discover new insights and opportunities (e.g., recall how Infosys' AI tools help its sales team discover new opportunities). This continuous co-discovery process fosters a culture of co-innovation and experimentation and allows organizations to stay ahead of the curve by identifying and capitalizing on emerging trends and technologies together with their partners. Recall also the example of Brazilian IdeiaGov from Chapter 4 with its engagement of workers and knowledge partners as creative-experiencers to co-discover and co-innovate customized AI-infused solutions suited to local geographic and cultural conditions and community contexts.

vii) *Co-Creating Risk-Managed Value*: The seventh layer, co-creating risk-managed value, focuses on developing and evolving next practices through interactional creation. As we saw in Chapters 3 and 5, co-intelligence empowers managers to co-create value with stakeholders by providing tools for real-time interactivity, collaboration and innovation. AI-driven decision-support platforms enable continuous dialogue, risk assessment, and transparency, fostering a dynamic environment where next practices are collectively developed, simulated and refined. This co-creative approach ensures that value creation is aligned with the needs and expectations of all creative-experiencers.

In the context of a co-intelligence world, there are two foundational aspects of co-intelligence architectures that act across all the seven layers of the knowledge environment.

i)   *Data Sovereignty, AI Ethics and Governance*: This crucial aspect involves establishing robust frameworks for data sovereignty, AI ethics and governance. Data sovereignty is critical to collaboration with shared digitalized infrastructures across the organizational ecosystem. Further, AI applications must be transparent, fair and aligned with organizational values and societal norms. Implementing ethical guidelines and governance structures is essential for maintaining trust and accountability in the use of AI technologies, especially in managing various forms of risk in co-creating unique value with customers, employees, partners, and other stakeholders.

ii) *Continuous Learning and Adaptation*: As we discussed in the Project ECHO and Apurva.ai example, the knowledge environment is itself continually learning from the actions of managers and other users, with its AI models being constantly updated and becoming more efficient. Recall **Figure 1-3** with 'humans-in-the-loop' and 'AI systems-in-the-loop' representing a co-creative paradigm of humans and AI systems actively participating in each other's knowledge-making processes. In the case of Apurva.ai, the collective wisdom of the organizational ecosystem is continuously nurtured and sustained. This self-improving system acts as a knowledge co-intelligence, facilitating ongoing learning. This layer promotes a culture of continuous improvement, ensuring that the organization remains competitive in a rapidly changing environment by leveraging the collective intelligence and evolving capabilities of the AI-infused knowledge environment. This not only drives the first layer of skilling and training but also competencies across all the other layers in fostering a continuously learning organization. Learning and adaptation are functions of being cognizant about and connecting with the lived experiences of individuals and co-designing Life-Xverse environments of human development, especially as organizations expand their locus of activities into the lived-journeys of individuals and the locus of performance into cross-sectoral SWI impacts.

Let us examine the case of Companhia Brasileira de Alumínio and see how it created a co-intelligence knowledge environment and built a co-creative learning community.

Companhia Brasileira de Alumínio—Building a Co-Creative Learning Community

In 2019, Companhia Brasileira de Alumínio (Brazilian Aluminium Company), an established leader in the aluminum industry with nearly seventy years of operational history, embarked on a transformative journey to become a CCLO. Recognizing the accelerating pace of technological advancements, it initiated this journey, branded **DigitALL**, to infuse its operations with AI, digital tools and co-creative learning, all while nurturing a workforce ready to innovate and adapt. Through DigitALL, the company aimed to build a digital-first culture that could dynamically adapt to evolving technologies while embedding co-intelligence in every layer of the organization. Early on, they identified a gap: the organization's existing learning models and culture were not prepared to absorb and scale new digital capabilities effectively.

In November 2022, the company launched its first co-creative learning community, Decoding Digital, designed to bridge digital skills gaps by fostering experiential, peer-driven learning. Decoding Digital evolved as an inclusive, ecosystem-oriented platform drawing on Human–AI interactions. The programme engaged leadership, in-house digital experts and employees as active participants, shifting the learning paradigm from traditional teacher–student structures to a co-created environment.

- *Human–AI Collaboration*: The learning community was led by Robert, an AI-generated avatar that served as a digital host, guiding participants through their learning journey. It placed AI as a co-facilitator in human learning and engagement.
- *Self-Learning and Peer-to-Peer Interaction*: Recognizing that 92 per cent of employees in similar contexts felt a greater sense of belonging through community-based learning, the company emphasized peer-to-peer interaction. This included a group of thirty volunteer 'decoders' who created content, led discussions and moderated experiences, fostering a culture where each participant was both learner and contributor.
- *Techbox Innovation*: A distinctive feature, the techbox—a suitcase of technological devices provided to employees—allowed employees to take digital tools home, experimenting with AI, VR and IoT devices. This approach extended learning to employees' families, reinforcing the company's commitment to a holistic life-Xverse of learning and innovation transcending organizational boundaries.

Building on the success of Decoding Digital, the company launched a second learning community in January 2024 focused on *AI and data*, supported by generative AI capabilities that empowered employees to co-create knowledge, experiment with AI-assisted tools and analyse data in real time. This community rapidly evolved into a metacommunity, blending experiential learning with practical AI applications, engaging 2500 employees (representing 50 per cent of the organization) in continuous interactive AI learning.

Through DigitALL and its subsequent communities, Companhia Brasileira de Alumínio demonstrates how a CCLO operates within an SDI, transforming traditional training and development into a co-intelligence architecture where knowledge flows across platforms and experiences. The results included:

- *Increased Digital Proficiency and Belonging*: Surveys indicated heightened confidence and readiness among employees to engage with digital tools, with a strong sense of commitment to the company's digital-first mission.
- *Data-Driven Insights*: Decoding Digital facilitated an internal study on digital skills gaps, allowing the company to identify internal experts, evaluate employee readiness and inform targeted development areas for future transformation.
- *Recognition and Impact*: The company's DigitALL program was recognized as one of Brazil's top transformation initiatives by Agile Trends in 2023 and 2024, underscoring its impact on organizational agility and innovation culture.

The Brazilian Aluminium Company's journey exemplifies a strategic shift towards becoming a CCLO, where AI and digital tools are co-intelligence partners, driving employee engagement, skill development and operational resilience. By embedding AI as a facilitator of learning and creating an adaptive, co-creative environment, the company is positioning itself as a future-ready organization, resilient in the face of continuous technological evolution.

* * *

Several prominent management thinkers' organizational observations and perspectives closely align with the spirit of CCLOs. Gary Hamel and Michele Zanini, in *Humanocracy*, advocate for dismantling bureaucracy to create resilient and daring organizations.[58] This resonates with our emphasis on managers as *living-system leaders* who prioritize adaptability and decentralization to empower stakeholders within dynamic ecosystems. Peter Senge's concept of a 'learning organization' in *The Fifth Discipline* mirrors our focus on continuous learning and adaptation within a co-intelligence knowledge environment, where organizations evolve through collective intelligence and holistic thinking.[59] Sumantra Ghoshal and Christopher Bartlett, in *The Individualized Corporation,* focus on fostering 'entrepreneurial energy' and individual creativity. This complements our emphasis on supporting diverse managerial behaviours and enhancing the capacities of managers as creative experiences.[60]

In *The Democratic Enterprise*, Lynda Gratton reimagines smarter working relationships based on free choice and shared purpose.[61] Linda Hill's approach to 'innovation leadership' through collaborative problem-solving, in *Collective Genius*, aligns with our idea of co-creating value in a dynamic, AI-infused managerial environment that supports collective intelligence and rapid innovation.[62] The concept of *ba* as a space of knowledge creation as described by Nonaka and Takeuchi in *The Knowledge-Creating Company*, and its dynamic nature and expansion for continuous innovation with practical organizational wisdom, as discussed in *The Wise Company,* reflects our notion of a co-intelligence knowledge environment where real-time knowledge creation and sharing are pivotal for continuous innovation.[63]

Susan Ashford's focus on the importance of 'small daily experiments' in *The Power of Flexing* parallels our emphasis on continuous learning and adaptation in response to real-time data and insights.[64] Arthur Yeung and Dave Ulrich's call for 'radical reinvention' in *Reinventing the Organization* aligns with our advocacy for rapid resource reconfiguration and agile decision-making in a co-intelligence world.[65, 66] Lastly, the Michigan Model of Leadership, which builds on the Competing Values Framework developed by Kim Cameron, Robert Quinn and others, highlights two 'tensions' that organizations face—'how to balance people (yellow) and performance (blue), and how to balance structure (red) and adaptation (green)'.[67] This aligns well with our notions of CCLO transformation.

Such a transformation requires the building of management systems in an intentional, principle-based manner to leverage the power of Human–AI interactive engagement in relational Life-Xverse ecosystems. It must empower the leaders, as proposed by Dutton and Spreitzer in *How to Be a Positive Leader*, who have 'the power of seeing possibilities and the awareness that small actions can have great impacts for bringing out the best in people and their organizations'.[68] CCLOs must co-design their living-systems for continuous learning and development, placing emphasis on reskilling and upskilling their talent base, even as they engage workers and managers as creative-experiencers and build co-intelligence capabilities to rapidly leverage ecosystemic/enterprise knowledge of value.[69, 70, 71] This necessitates continuous talent development in the workforce to adapt to rapidly evolving AI technologies and digital transformation initiatives, and equipping individuals with the necessary skills to thrive in a co-intelligence world.[72]

Reverse Prompt Engineering for Accelerating Scale and Scope of SWIs

GenAI brings a powerful strategic capability in external adaptation. SDI platforms can be purposefully built for co-creating life–experience-based insights. In the Project ECHO example, *Apurva.ai can prompt individuals* and gather continuous knowledge about lived experiences in real time. This is perhaps one of the biggest opportunities being 'missed' thus far in the evolution of GenAI applications, where an enterprise-centric mindset still lingers. While GenAI facilitates enterprise value co-creation experiences through the Life-Xverse, enhancing the quality of these co-creation experiences requires *proactive* rather than prevalent reactive reinforcement feedback loops. Recall the Jugalbandi example with which we opened this book. There is a massive opportunity for *elevating the efficient innovation of high-quality co-creation experiences* if the underlying system is designed for continuous learning and development in a proactive fashion. *Imagine if the system can prompt farmers about their actual lived experiences, learn from them, and share this knowledge base with managers so they can rapidly leverage insights in co-innovating enhanced Life-*

Xverse ecosystem environments that engender more valuable SWIs at speed, scale and scope. More generally, the talent base of CCLOs (from researchers and developers to workers and managers) can all benefit from 'collective societal and market insighting'. For instance, *People+AI* has built a population-scale user research studio focused on uncovering Indian consumer insights at the intersection of design, technology and culture. Individuals in CCLOs must be able to absorb such insights and act upon them.

Key Action Takeaways

In this chapter, we have seen how organizations must design themselves as CCLOs to thrive in a co-intelligence world with a life–experience orientation. Here are some key actionable takeaways:

1. Embrace Co-Intelligence Architectures Across the Organization

Develop co-intelligence architectures that allow for Human–AI interactive engagement in every aspect of the organization, from customer-facing offerings to internal value chains. These architectures should support multi-dimensional engagement across ecosystems, seamlessly integrating digital, physical and biological components.

- **Action:** Build platforms that enable stakeholders—employees, customers, partners—to collaborate in real time. For example, adopt SDIs that foster collaborative learning, enable data-driven decisions and facilitate stakeholder co-creation in product development and service delivery.

2. Prioritize Co-Creative Management Systems

Managers in CCLOs act as creative-experiencers who facilitate and drive co-creative engagement flows. This managerial role includes empowering employees as co-creators and enabling co-creation between internal and external stakeholders.

- **Action:** Shift the managerial focus from traditional supervision to facilitation of cross-functional teams, equipping managers to support dynamic, interaction-driven environments. Implement training programmes that enhance creative problem-solving and adaptive management to effectively engage with AI in decision-making.

3. Build Social Linkages and Culture for Continuous Growth

Develop an organizational culture that emphasizes interactive social linkages within human capital. CCLOs must align their internal and external ecosystems, supporting both unique customer experiences and employee experiences to foster continuous growth.

- **Action:** Enhance connectivity within teams and departments by using collaboration platforms and AI tools to support real-time communication and problem-solving. Focus on building a culture of co-learning and agile feedback, where employee experiences directly shape customer-facing innovations.

4. Empower Talent as Creative Experiencers through Lifelong Learning

Equip the workforce with ongoing reskilling and upskilling opportunities to navigate rapid technological changes. CCLOs prioritize ecosystems of lifelong learning, where employees continually adapt to new AI technologies and digital transformations.

- **Action:** Introduce learning paths that emphasize both technical skills (e.g., data analytics, AI literacy) and soft skills (e.g., collaborative innovation, adaptability). Partner with educational institutions or offer internal certifications to foster an adaptable, future-ready workforce.

5. Leverage Co-Intelligence Knowledge Environments

Create knowledge environments that facilitate collective learning and support co-creation by enabling access to internal and external knowledge sources. This structure supports continuous, agile responses to evolving opportunities and challenges.

- **Action:** Establish knowledge-sharing hubs and AI-driven insight platforms that provide employees and partners with on-demand data, predictive analytics, and scenario planning. These environments should support both strategic foresight and real-time decision-making, empowering stakeholders at every level.

6. Focus on Value Co-Creation at Scale through Stakeholder Engagement

Shift focus from isolated product or service outputs to networked, experience-centric ecosystems that integrate stakeholder input at every level. By involving stakeholders as creative-experiencers, CCLOs can scale personalized, AI-enhanced experiences tailored to individual and collective needs.

- **Action:** Utilize AI-driven tools for hyper-personalization, allowing customer and employee interactions to be continuously tailored and improved. For instance, co-develop product features or services with real-time user feedback loops to ensure alignment with evolving stakeholder expectations.

7. Embed SWIs into CCLO Metrics

Integrate SWIs into performance metrics, aligning organizational goals with societal and environmental value. This ensures that CCLOs contribute positively to broader ecosystems, driving sustainable and ethical value creation.

- **Action:** Adopt sustainability goals that align with global initiatives, such as reducing carbon footprint, supporting community wellbeing and ethical use of AI. Incorporate these goals into both strategic planning and daily operations, using AI to monitor and report progress transparently.

These steps position organizations to leverage AI not just as a tool but as a dynamic partner in co-creating adaptive, inclusive and impact-driven ecosystems that continuously engage and benefit all stakeholders. Co-creative living organization transformation requires the building of management systems in an intentional, principle-based manner to leverage the power of Human–AI interactivity in interconnected ecosystems. CCLOs must co-innovate ecosystems of lifelong learning, placing emphasis on reskilling and upskilling of their talent base, even as they engage workers and managers as creative-experiencers and build co-intelligence capabilities to rapidly leverage ecosystemic knowledge of value. All stakeholders have to be seen as creative-experiencers, and knowledge environments have to be built to support them and into their lived-journeys in the Life-Xverse. It necessitates continuous talent development in the workforce to adapt to rapidly evolving AI technologies and digital transformation initiatives and equipping individuals with the necessary skills to thrive in a co-intelligence world, to drive the *cross-sector co-evolution* of SWIs at speed, scale and scope.

8

Co-Evolving Sustainable Wellbeing Impacts Across Sectors

Recall our exploration at the end of *Chapter 3: Crafting and Leveraging Co-Intelligence Architectures* on how Sustainable Development Goals (SDGs) can guide sustainable wellbeing impacts (SWIs) as a North Star and the role of SDI platforms in doing so. In this concluding chapter, we explore the co-evolution of SWIs by leveraging shared digitalized infrastructures (SDIs) through cross-sector (private, public and plural) amplification of Human–AI co-creation (see **Figure 8-1**).

i) First, given the nature and complexity of sustainable development challenges, organizational initiatives must *go beyond incremental tendencies and bolt-on approaches* to a broader *SWI focus*. This requires a business commitment to people, planet, peace, and prosperity that has to become intrinsic to the purpose and strategic vision of the business. Otherwise, it can devolve into a failure of businesses to resonate with the ideals of sustainable development, such as those encapsulated under the UN SDGs.[1,2]

ii) Second, there is a need for Human–AI co-creation that leverages *SDI-based approaches* with a PIEX lens. The conventional point solution approaches to challenges do not tend to scale and are invariably limited in scope. SDI-based approaches are about offering a multiplicity of environments through which engaging actors as creative-experiencers can generate rapid unique solutions of value to them. It implies a variable outcome orientation, rather than a fixed output one.

iii) Third, it is not enough to just realize impactful outcomes of value to individuals but to also make the *value generated to individuals and communities of people more enduring.* Engendering SWIs at scale implies a focus on transforming the lives and livelihoods of and connecting with the lived experiences of people-communities as they engage across sectors in fashioning unique solutions and outcomes of value to them.

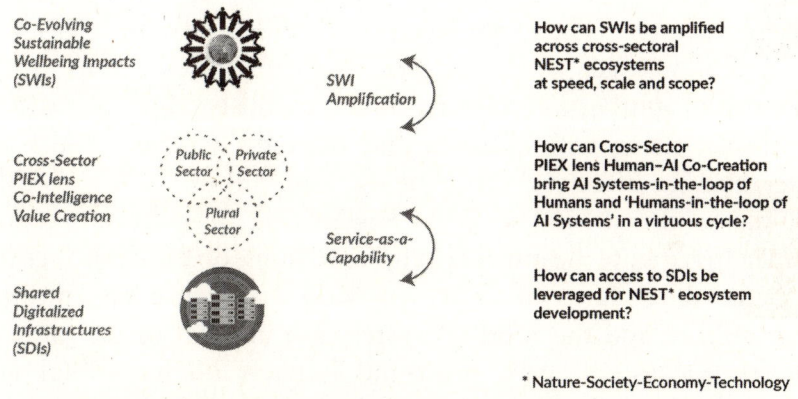

Figure 8-1: The Co-Intelligent Enterprise: Cross-Sector Co-Evolution of Sustainable Wellbeing Impacts at Speed, Scale and Scope (Source: Venkat Ramaswamy)

iv) Fourth, these shared-value and SWIs have to *co-evolve.* It draws inspiration from the interconnectedness of enterprises as living-systems. Businesses, social enterprises and communities can engage in a continuous learning process. This iterative approach allows all actors to adapt their strategies and actions based on new knowledge and evolving needs. This co-evolutionary process fosters a dynamic environment where sustainable development is not a fixed target but rather a continuously improving journey undertaken by a network of interconnected actors, expanding the planetary scope of SWIs.

Let us consider different examples involving organizations co-evolving SWIs as they innovate and co-create risk-managed value with stakeholders through their organizational ecosystems, across the private, public and plural sectors. We venture first into the Agriculture (Ag) Life-Xverse.

Into the Ag Life-Xverse

Let us first consider the dynamic relationality of agricultural and natural ecosystems. *Agriculture is both a driver and a victim of climate change.*[3] The sector is responsible for a substantial portion of greenhouse gas emissions, mainly through deforestation and the use of synthetic fertilizers. Simultaneously, shifting weather patterns, rising temperatures and extreme weather events are increasingly affecting crop yields. Agriculture is intrinsically linked to global food security. Sustainable agriculture practices can help mitigate the impact of climate change on food production, safeguarding the availability of food for future generations. Agriculture and the food ecosystem are integral to the modern health ecosystem, with profound impacts on individual and public wellbeing. The nutritional quality of food or the use of antibiotics in livestock influencing health, or the origins of pandemics in the food chain, illustrate the interconnectedness of these ecosystems. Mobility plays a crucial role in accessing healthcare, educational opportunities and agricultural markets. However, fossil-fuelled transportation systems contribute to air pollution and greenhouse gas emissions, exacerbating climate change and its associated health risks. Mobility challenges in rural areas hinder farmers' access to educational resources, so crucial in the understanding of sustainable agricultural practices, health promotion and environmental stewardship. These business ecosystems are intricately interconnected, and interventions in one will have cascading effects on the others.

For instance, promoting sustainable agricultural practices can improve environmental health, resulting in better air and water quality and, in turn, enhancing public health outcomes. Similarly, investing in education and mobility infrastructure can facilitate access to healthcare services and economic markets, enhancing overall societal wellbeing.

Digital technologies and AI are pivotal in advancing climate-resilient, sustainable agricultural practices and facilitating these relational interconnected ecosystems. For instance, precision agriculture leverages AI, satellite imagery and sensor technologies to optimize resource use, enhance crop monitoring and minimize environmental impact. There is also a need to foster innovation and research to develop climate-resilient and environmentally friendly agricultural practices. This includes promoting precision agriculture, water-efficient farming techniques and the use of climate-smart crop varieties. At the same time, farmers, and not just the tech-companies, should have a greater say in the adoption of technologies. Technology sovereignty includes the right of farmers (as food providers) to be co-creators of offerings of value to them to the extent they are willing and able, putting it at the centre of the agriculture, food science and technology policies.[4]

Consider the lived-journey experience of a farmer in India (see **Figure 8-2**). There, agriculture still offers employment to about 58 per cent of the population, like Ram, but suffers from low productivity and inefficiencies in the entire farming cycle, including pre-planting, planting, harvesting, selling and financing. About 86 per cent of all farmers in India are small and marginal landowners (with less than two hectares of land) while they own just 47 per cent of the crop area. The world over, agtech enterprises operate in complex environments. Jack, in this agricultural Life-Xverse vignette, belongs to one such enterprise. He can no longer adopt a business-as-usual approach of selling just his company's offerings to farmers. He aims to co-create greater value by operating across business ecosystems—agriculture, health, mobility and education. He aspires to increasing the size of the pie of value accruing to his enterprise by considering life–experiences and lived-journeys of his farmer-customers. He also feels the pressure to engender sustainable wellbeing impacts with them in the agricultural sector and beyond. Jack's private enterprise organization coexists with the public and plural sectors. Let us now consider a couple of forward-looking examples from the Ag Life-Xverse.

Ram stood on his two-acre farm, with a degree of pride and worry. The land was both his livelihood and his heritage, passed down from his ancestors who had tilled the same soil with hope and determination. At the same time, Ram, with his body weathered by the sun and the rains, his hands worn from years of toiling the land, and his eyes crinkled with concern at the dark clouds on the horizon, contemplated the harsh realities of life. Despite his deep connection to the land, Ram found himself at the mercy of forces beyond his control. The changing climate, unpredictable monsoon, and ever-present threat of pests and diseases posed constant hurdles. He found himself thinking about the allure of the new 'ag' (agricultural) company promising distribution efficiency and greater payout. Should he trust the local dealer's suggestions for seeds, fertilizers and pesticides? With every passing year, each transaction had become a high-stakes gamble, as he navigated through the labyrinth of clever marketing ploys, soaring prices and the fear of potential lock-in. Also, he did not understand the latest technologies—should he go for an electric tractor? What was this thing called AI all about? How could it on a phone know more about his land than he did? Despite his worries, Ram harboured a deep-seated desire to share the fruits of his labour with the common people.

But the farm was not his only concern. His young son, Rohit, showed no interest in agriculture. The allure of city life and the promise of opportunities beyond the agrarian landscape captivated him. What skills should he be learning to make a living? Ram also desired to provide his daughter, Pari, with quality education. But the village schools were not up to the mark. At the back of Ram's mind was the constant worry about the healthcare needs and costs of his aged parents. In this delicate dance between tradition and modernity, between heritage and survival, Ram stood as a solitary figure, grappling with the formidable forces that sought to shape his destiny. He offered a silent prayer to his village deity.

Thus, it was a rather pensive-looking Ram that Jack and Ravi encountered that morning. As VP of a global ag-solutions company, Jack, along with Ravi, his India sales manager, was keen to demonstrate their latest innovation. He was hopeful that Ram would see how game-changing their AI-powered farm advisory app was. Any farmer could converse with Sara, their ag-scientist bot agent, share details of their farm and receive customized recommendations. Very soon, Sara would be able to converse in Hindi too. Jack was confident of handling Ram, the crop advice-seeking farmer. But did he realize that he was also contending for a share of mind with Ram, a climate-concerned activist, an education-aspiring parent and a healthcare-obsessed son?

The story of Ram plays out across millions of farms in India. This could well be the narrative of Barry too, standing amidst his sprawling fields in America's heartland. The farm sizes and the agricultural corporations offering their services may be considerably bigger, but the plotline is the same with its life-experiences and impacts—the changing climate patterns, the looming threat of pests and diseases, the volatile fluctuations in market prices and the promises of AI and other technologies, all weighing heavily on Barry's mind as he contemplates the future of his modernized farm.

Figure 8-2: Into the Lived-Journey Experience of the Farmer
(*Source:* Venkat Ramaswamy and Krishnan Narayanan)

ITC's e-Choupal Ecosystem—Sustainable Co-Intelligence Value Co-Creation

ITC, a major Indian conglomerate with a significant agricultural division, launched its pioneering e-Choupal initiative in the late 1990s to address challenges faced by smallholder farmers in India, such as limited market access, low-quality inputs and unpredictable incomes. By establishing a digital infrastructure and engaging directly with farmers, ITC circumvented traditional mandis providing farmers with transparent pricing and a range of services designed to enhance productivity and incomes.

We (VR and KN) met S. Sivakumar, who conceptualized e-Choupal and is now a member of ITC's corporate management committee overseeing the company's agriculture and IT businesses, in Bengaluru in August 2023. He described e-Choupal's platform transformation as going

> from mass customized with a toolkit, through tech-enhanced personalization, to democratized personalization with GenAI.[5]

Initially, ITC set up e-Choupal kiosks in villages, each operated by a trusted local farmer known as a *sanchalak*. These kiosks served as information hubs, where farmers could access timely market prices, weather updates and best practices in crop management, all in their local language. By offering critical information and support, e-Choupal empowered farmers to make better decisions, negotiate fair prices and reduce dependence on intermediaries. This model provided the foundation for ITC's broader vision of building sustainable ecosystems for rural development and co-creating value with farmers.

Scaling Up with e-Choupal Hubs and Choupal Saagars

As e-Choupal gained traction, ITC expanded its reach by establishing regional hubs called Choupal Saagars. These hubs served as multipurpose centres where farmers could sell their produce directly to ITC, receive instant payments and purchase agricultural inputs such as seeds, fertilizers and pesticides. The Saagars also provided ITC with a window into rural consumer behaviour, as farmers often used their earnings to purchase ITC's branded goods. This dual function allowed ITC to streamline its supply chain while addressing rural consumption needs, creating a vibrant marketplace that fostered trust and efficiency.

Through partnerships with input providers and agricultural companies, ITC was able to diversify the offerings available at Choupal Saagars, giving farmers access to high-quality inputs that could increase crop yields and reduce costs. By aggregating demand at a local level, ITC could negotiate favourable terms with suppliers, extending the benefits of bulk purchasing to individual farmers. Additionally, ITC collaborated with organizations like Bayer and Nunhems to promote hybrid seeds and sustainable crop protection practices, helping farmers enhance both productivity and sustainability.

ITCMAARS—A Next-Generation Platform for Precision Agriculture

Building on the foundation of e-Choupal, ITC launched ITCMAARS (Metamarket for Advanced Agriculture and Rural Services), a comprehensive digital platform that deepens engagement with farmers and integrates precision agriculture practices. ITCMAARS offers a *phygital* (physical plus digital) model that supports over 250,000 farmers across seven states, anchored by farmer producer organizations (FPOs). This super app provides farmers with a range of AI-driven tools that facilitate informed, data-driven decision-making.

The platform's standout features include Crop Doctor, an AI-powered diagnostic tool that uses image recognition to identify pests and diseases, and Crop Calendar, a scheduling tool that offers customized guidance on planting, harvesting and post-harvest activities. ITCMAARS also provides personalized nutrient recommendations based on soil health analysis, remote sensing for real-time crop monitoring and sustainable practices guidance to enhance resilience and productivity. Farmers can access these services in their local languages via the Krishi Mitra chatbot, developed in collaboration with Microsoft, which provides region-specific advice on crop health, weather and market conditions.

ITCMAARS also benefits from partnerships with agtech startups and technology providers, which bring advanced tools like IoT sensors and drone-based fertilization to smallholders. This ecosystem approach enhances precision agriculture capabilities, allowing for targeted interventions and resource-efficient practices. With ITCMAARS, farmers receive not only direct support but also digital access to innovations like soil health diagnostics and crop advisory services, enabling more sustainable and productive farming.

Engendering SWIs

ITC's initiatives align with SDGs and prioritize creating SWIs by addressing key issues such as climate resilience, water conservation and livelihood diversification. Through its climate-smart agriculture programme, ITC has helped 450,000 farmers across 8000 villages adopt climate-resilient practices that reduce dependency on chemical inputs, improve soil health and adapt to changing environmental conditions.

Additionally, ITC's *Wellbeing Out of Waste* (WOW) program addresses waste management in urban areas, impacting over 5 million households and creating livelihoods for thousands of waste collectors. This program exemplifies ITC's commitment to environmental stewardship by tackling waste issues at the source, helping urban communities manage waste responsibly and providing job opportunities for marginalized groups.

To further support rural development, ITC launched Mission Sunehra Kal, a capacity-building programme that integrates water conservation, soil health management and agroforestry initiatives. This mission has greened over 950,000 acres, sequestered more than 6000 kilotons of CO2 and helped communities restore their natural resources. The project's holistic approach improves agricultural productivity, reduces environmental impact and promotes sustainable livelihoods by linking on-farm improvements with ecosystem restoration.

ITC's Sustainability 2.0 Vision and Strategic Partnerships

In line with its broader Sustainability 2.0 vision, ITC has set ambitious targets to create 10 million livelihoods while balancing social, environmental and economic goals. ITC's partnerships with stakeholders, including governmental bodies, NGOs and public-private coalitions, allow it to amplify the scale and impact of its initiatives. For example, ITC's recent collaboration with NITI Aayog in twenty-seven aspirational districts provided digital training to 2.5 million farmers, increasing incomes by nearly 60 per cent for certain crops. This partnership demonstrates ITC's commitment to advancing rural development through co-created, scalable solutions.

ITC's extensive public–private partnerships—over eighty-four in areas like water management, sustainable agriculture and waste reduction—enable it to address complex issues across sectors and create ecosystem-level change. By fostering a co-intelligence network that involves smallholder farmers, technology providers and policymakers, ITC creates shared value that aligns with SDG goals and advances sustainable development across rural and urban landscapes.

The Future of ITC's Co-Intelligence Ecosystem

ITC's evolution from an agricultural products company to a leader in digital rural development exemplifies the potential of co-intelligence ecosystems to generate significant social, environmental and economic impacts. Through platforms like ITCMAARS and the e-Choupal network, ITC has redefined the role of business in rural communities by co-creating value with farmers and stakeholders. ITC's approach illustrates how organizations can leverage co-intelligence and technology to build resilient, adaptive ecosystems that address both immediate needs and long-term challenges.

The ITC example highlights how co-intelligence, when integrated with a well-structured platform and partnership approach, can drive SWIs at scale. By blending digital and physical infrastructures, fostering extensive partnerships and committing to purpose-driven growth, ITC demonstrates a forward-looking, transformative approach that aligns business objectives with broader societal goals. This journey serves as a powerful illustration of how co-intelligence, enabled by Human–AI collaboration and innovative partnerships, can unlock sustainable value and drive impactful change in underserved communities.

Land O'Lakes—Co-Creating Value with the Farmer Community

Shifting our attention from Ram to Barry from our opening vignette, consider Land O'Lakes, a farmer-owned cooperative with a network spanning more than 300,000 producers and touching about half of America's harvested areas. It also owns the agtech company WinField United and the sustainability and stewardship-focused business TruTerra. The company believes that the success of a farming business revolves around forty mega decisions—about what and when to plant, when and how to fertilize, feed and harvest, doing all this sustainably, and how to market and sell—and these are areas where data and technology can help transform. Land O'Lakes is leveraging Microsoft's industry business cloud, Azure Data Manager for Agriculture (previously called Azure FarmBeats), in this endeavour.[6]

Its Digital Dairy solution helps farmers with a range of AI/ML-based analytics capabilities on data related to farm operations, soil, weather and more.[7] For instance, it can help assess farm health using vegetation index and water index based on satellite imagery, tracking farm conditions by visualizing ground data collected by various sensors and helping with the provision of farm health advisories. Farmers can photograph their cows, and their AI application can determine if the animal is underweight or not and suggest modifications in its feeding accordingly. Consumers of Land O'Lakes' milk, butter and cheese will be able to assuredly trace their products through the entire supply chain and know that they have been sustainably sourced.

Land O'Lakes' commitment to its farmer communities goes beyond just improving their agricultural productivity. It has an important focus on sustainability and natural resources stewardship to help farm fields become more resilient. Its Truterra Insights Engine utilizes soil, weather, economic and farm management data to analyse potential impacts of various stewardship practices at a field level and help track against both economic performance and conservation practices. In 2021, Truterra began a programme of making cash payments to farmers who sequestered carbon—in its first year, it paid $4 million to farmers who captured 200,000 metric tons of carbon.[8] With Microsoft, it is looking to develop capabilities to predict the carbon benefits of regenerative practices quickly and effectively, like no-till, precision nutrient management and planting of cover crops. Combining such capabilities with the real-time transparency from remote sensing and satellite data will make certification of these projects in global carbon markets easier, quicker and less expensive, ultimately maximizing the economic value for farmers.

Land O'Lakes is also adopting a holistic approach in its engagement with the rural communities in which their cooperatives exist. Its American Connection Project, in collaboration with Microsoft's Airband program and hospitals like Mayo Clinic, aims to close the digital divide by ensuring broadband services are accessible to rural communities along with other services such as telehealth, education and digital skilling.

Beth Ford, CEO of Land O'Lakes, reinforces the perspective that they must create valuable impacts across interconnected ecosystems for their members when she says,

> We discussed addressing water shortages, ensuring access to broadband and healthcare services, expanding economic vibrancy and revitalizing crumbling infrastructure by broadening availability of childcare and housing. We talked ag research funding and its necessity for innovation as we try to deliver improved production and feed a growing world population.[9]

This is an enterprise that knows how to create value, taking into consideration the lifeworld and life–experiences of its customers, which include the farms, farmers and their families, and the farming communities to which they belong.

Opening Up Development with Co-Intelligence

As noted by Nobel laureate Amartya Sen, 'human beings are not merely means of production (even though they excel in that capacity), but also the end of the exercise.[10] Development, as he has argued, is about capabilities to engage with freedom's processes and opportunities.[11] In alignment with this vision, opening up development with co-intelligence facilitates freedom-centric development through co-creation thinking and co-design of the human development experience.

Industree Foundation—Sustainable Livelihood Creation

In 1985, Neelam Chhiber had just graduated from India's premier design school, the National Institute of Design, Ahmedabad. Unlike the well-trodden career path taken by the other industrial designers, Chhiber was keen on exploring a world that existed in pre-Industrial Revolution India. After all, her project at NID was on the lost wax craft and traditional metal casting technique of the tribes of Bastar village in India. She saw a huge opportunity in India—there were millions of women in villages in subsistence living, tending to their smallholding farms or crafts, while the menfolk migrated to cities in search of jobs. This is true even today—India has 260 million women looking for work, of which 75 per cent are in the informal sector. Further, while co-ops constituted between 10 per cent and 18 per cent of Western economies in Europe and the US (think Etsy), in India it was less than 1 per cent, thus offering significant headroom for growth.[12] If only they became market-driven and their products were connected to national and international supply chains. She began working with rural Indian women and empowering them with skills and resources to start self-owned enterprises close to their homes.

In 2000, Chhiber and Jacob Mathew co-founded Industree Foundation, which pioneered a holistic, integrated approach to value-chain development and sustainable livelihood creation for women. Mathew says, 'The hardest problem is to understand the artisans and craftspersons you're trying to help . . . once you bring in a human dimension to the enterprise, it needs to become about fulfilling people's aspirations.'[13] Industree now works at the 'intersection of equity, climate and gender on nature-based solutions, using innovative finance.' Women, who depend on local natural resources for their livelihood, are more vulnerable to the effects of climate change. Industree empowers them as 'drivers of climate solutions' by enabling them to build a circular economy and curating regenerative value chains out of natural resources like bamboo, banana and sal leaves. Chhiber says,

> We now build women's collectives who plant regenerative material, like bamboo, which is also great at carbon sequestration. And then, we work on regenerative enterprise. That means value addition to the raw material

resources that surround the villages, which creates a lower carbon footprint, and which enables prosperity. The voice of the women in the community is heard. There is this long-standing discussion and discourse that when women earn, you see improved nutrition, improved health, improved education in the poorest families. So, we address a number of Sustainable Development Goals through this work.[14]

Industree's emphasis on environmentally conscious production methods and creating *climate-positive* value chains is a sign of its co-evolution with the times. It also taps into the global movement towards net zero and smart cities adopting low-carbon, lean-construction techniques. Industree's $15 million Regenerative Agriculture and Livelihoods (REAL) Fund is the first and largest of its kind in India to create sustainable bamboo value chains. They offer an environmentally and financially scalable model because communities can earn additional income through carbon credits, on top of what they earn from selling the raw materials they produce. Industree is planning to scale this bamboo model and replicate it in other value chains such as seaweed, another crop that has great potential for carbon capture and income generation in coastal communities. Over the last two decades, Industree has positively influenced almost 600,000 lives and generated a cumulative market value of $59.7 million.[15]

What makes Industree's business model different and so impactful? Chhiber says,

My approach to problem-solving is a lot of systems thinking because I realized that wicked problems, complex problems need systems solutions. It's not just about making a product to solve a problem. Like you make a safety pin, and it solves the problem of connecting two things together immediately.[16]

Indeed, there are no simple, silver safety pins. Industree's 6C framework provides an *ecosystemic model* to build and support sustainable and inclusive producer enterprises—*Create* (product design and technical innovation resources), *Construct* (aggregation, incubation and acceleration of enterprises), *Capital* (access to working capital and equity, both as social investment and philanthropy), *Capacity* (access to hard and soft skills), *Channel* (access to diverse markets and customers) and *Connect* (digital tools for enterprise management and network building).

For example, the Construct phase involves mobilizing and aggregating local women producers to form producer companies. A Mutual Benefit Trust is created to ensure that there is participatory ownership, called *distributed ownership*, in the companies—the women producers get a maximum share, along with an upside even to the professionals who offer their services to these producer-companies. For instance, Flourish, an ethical e-commerce platform is 90 per cent producer-owned and 10 per cent owned by the professionals. Industree realizes that women will not just automatically transform themselves into entrepreneurs with the formation of producer companies. Hence it provides *deep handholding* to these women and their collectives to ensure that they can cater to market needs in a professional and profitable manner. Capacity building focuses on enhancing the skills of women producers. This includes both hard skills, such as product making, tailoring and weaving, and soft skills, including financial inclusion training and social empowerment. The 6Y training program is a key element in this phase, encompassing training across six dimensions: *You* (producer*), Your Family, Your Work, Your Workmates, Your Community, Your World* and *Your Planet.* This programme aims to deepen producers' understanding of sustainable production, quality, timeliness and ownership, essential for becoming successful social entrepreneurs.

The adage 'it takes a village to raise a child' rings true for village producer companies as well. These fledgling businesses, born from the collective spirit of rural communities, require a multi-sectoral collaborative approach to flourish. For instance, channel development is about connecting producers to local and global markets and companies such as IKEA, H&M Home, Caravane and FabIndia. During the Covid-19 pandemic, Industree launched Creative Dignity, a movement comprising designers, grassroots organizations and artisanal entrepreneurs to provide relief and rehabilitation for artisans across India. Community Livelihood Coalition (CoLive) focuses on helping these vulnerable communities rebuild their lives post-pandemic. It is an active part of Catalyst 2030, a global movement to achieve the UN SDGs by 2030.

The Connect component leverages technology to link producers to a broader ecosystem. The tech intensity infused into Industree's business increased, especially post the pandemic. In 2020, it launched a *digital, first-mile, societal platform*, the Platform for Inclusive Entrepreneurship (PIE), in partnership with Vrutti (a non-profit in the social impact space) and the Platform Commons Foundation (a non-profit technology provider), inspired by the Societal Thinking method of EkStep Foundation. Sanjay Purohit, CEO and chief curator, Centre for Exponential Change (C4EC), says,

> By connecting them with the right support services via the PIE network, the aim is to aggregate producers into self-owned enterprises, help them build market connections, and access skills and capital. This design approach extends the current boundaries of leveraging technology to solve societal problems and calls for orchestrating co-creation between government, civil society and (the) private sector in PIE.[17]

The Industree PIE digital infrastructure includes a suite of applications, such as Collect App, Maker Management Portal, Co-create App and Enterprise Resource Management Tool, which addresses different areas such as onboarding, measurement and evaluation, compliance, orders and stock management. These apps create a digital space for connecting various entities involved in the value chains. PIE also offers online courses such as leadership training, gender training and entrepreneurship programmes to empower individuals with the right knowledge and skills necessary to run impact enterprises effectively. Such digital technologies facilitate scalability with traceability and transparency. For instance, on the Flourish platform, buyers will know which artisan made a product, and when it is bought, there is traceability in the money reaching the women producers' bank accounts. Chhiber says,

> We do believe if a bunch of tech tools are created, which tech is not going to solve the problem, but if communities are given access to more and more tech tools, a certain amount of standardization that is required in the global supply chain will be easier to make happen within the local context.[18]

Consider next, eGov Foundation, a private non-profit organization in India that is charting an impactful digital public infrastructure (DPI) journey in the societal and development Life-Xverse.

eGov Foundation—Samaaj-Sarkaar-Bazaar

Founded in 2003 to transform Indian urban government systems at scale, eGov Foundation began by building applications and products for urban local bodies (ULBs). Its eighteen modules offered a comprehensive suite of tools that catered to both citizens and government staff at municipalities. Citizens could leverage the platform to report issues like power outages, trash collection or public safety concerns. This fostered transparency as residents could track the progress of their grievances and hold municipal employees accountable. The municipal staff too benefitted from internal applications that streamlined tasks like financial management and property tax collection. These tools enabled better revenue tracking, helping identify potential leakages and analyse long-term trends.

In its formative years, eGov prioritized developing its suite of e-governance tools while establishing a strong presence within Andhra Pradesh (AP), the state where its platform achieved its most significant and widespread adoption. For instance, its case management technology implementation in AP during 2013–2018 saw a remarkable impact—over 55,000 citizen grievances were logged and addressed efficiently; grievance resolution time plummeted from fifty weeks to just ten weeks; and the number of grievances resolved within the promised timeframe doubled.[19] eGov functioned like any other ERP software product would—improve functionality with consistent in-house software development and also learn from its product implementations with customers. In fifteen years, it had achieved over 325 successful implementations across five states. While progress was made, the desired societal impact wasn't achieved as quickly as it had been envisioned or desired.

Thus, when Viraj Tyagi joined eGov as its CEO in 2016, he catalysed an organizational rethink: 'We realized building and implementing solutions by ourselves would exhaust us, with nowhere near the scale of impact we need. Instead, we started asking: how do we increase the capacity of the ecosystem to solve?'[20]

In this, eGov was inspired by philanthropist Rohini Nilekani's idea of *samaaj–sarkaar–bazaar* (society–state–markets). This is a model where value is created by taking a citizen-first and cross-sector approach.[21] Inspired by her extensive experience in Indian civil society, in organizations like Arghyam, Akshara Foundation, Pratham and EkStep, Nilekani emphasizes society (samaaj) as the foundation. Unlike traditional models that prioritize the state (sarkaar) or the market (bazaar), she argues that a strong and active citizenry is the bedrock for a well-functioning democracy and a thriving economy. She says,

> Civil society and its institutions will have to learn digitally to keep the bazaar and sarkaar of the digital age accountable to the larger public interest and to co-create better policies and

new rules of engagement in the virtual world. If they succeed,
I hope we can then move to a future which is technology-
enabled and not technology-led; where human destiny
remains in our hands, and not in the control of algorithms.[22]

For eGov Foundation, shifting focus from building everything
themselves to empowering the ecosystem to solve problems
led to its eGov2.0 strategy. It was like shifting from playing
the piano masterfully to orchestrating a perfect symphony.
DIGIT (Digital Infrastructure for Governance and Inclusive
Transformation) was conceived as an *open-source platform* of
digital public goods (DPGs) for transforming citizen services
and governance around sanitation, health and public finance
in the global south. eGov's government customers use the
DIGIT DPGs to create their own DPIs. For instance, during
the Covid-19 pandemic, the Indian government wanted its
CoWIN platform to issue tamper-proof digital vaccination
certificates for safe travel and work. Enter DIVOC (Digital
Infrastructure for Verifiable Open Credentialing), an eGov
DPG and societal ecosystem offering. Pramod Verma, former
chief architect of Aadhaar and co-chair of the Centre for Digital
Public Infrastructure, comments on an important architectural
principle they followed: 'When we designed DIVOC we were
very clear that we must adopt international specifications and
we have worked very closely with international authorities like
WHO. The power of a verifiable certificate which is printable,
multilingual and inclusive but natively digital in nature is quite
transformational.'[23]

Thanks to a compliance certification from the WHO, DIVOC
certificates were accepted in over 120 countries. Within a span
of eighteen months, DIVOC, as part of each country's app or
DPI, issued 2 billion certificates across five countries: India, Sri
Lanka, the Philippines, Indonesia and Jamaica. Given that DIGIT
comprises pre-built DPGs, the implementation process becomes
much simplified and cost-effective. The Punjab government,
which struggled to find a suitable e-governance solution for

its ULBs, found success with DIGIT. The cost of $1 million to implement across the entire state was a mere 4 per cent of previous quotations, and the rollout was swift, with 100 ULBs going online within ninety days and full coverage within a year. By December 2021, the Punjab government had handled over 1.5 million service requests and grievances and collected over $144 million in revenue. As a new capability, they integrated a WhatsApp chatbot onto DIGIT to create a public grievance redressal service to bring the government closer to citizens.[24]

eGov is also positively impacting governments in other countries. In August 2023, Mozambique launched Salama, the first DIGIT health DPI for public health campaigns. The Ministry of Health's Mozambique National Malaria Control Program (MNCP) used the DPI to coordinate their bed net campaigns under the Malaria Fora (malaria out) initiative. In Indonesia, the Ministry of Health has a medical waste management app, ME SMILE. They have integrated it with the DIGIT sanitation DPG so that garbage labelled in their system may be tracked through all phases of the life cycle till final processing. eGov is beginning to embrace co-intelligence into its architecture and creating a seamless experience for citizens, an integrated workbench for employees and comprehensive decision dashboards for administrators. Manish Srivastava, the CTO of eGov, says,

> We are leveraging GenAI to enhance public service accessibility, allowing citizens to interact in their preferred language via voice and chat interfaces. Additionally, GenAI bots will enable employees to perform their tasks more efficiently and intelligently. For administrators, GenAI will provide deeper insights into data, helping to identify and address areas for improvement.[25]

Thus, co-creating engagement-based platform ecosystem solutions as a coalition of plural-private-public sector partnerships together with served individuals as co-creators of wellbeing impacts has the enormous potential to enhance transformational impact by synergizing joint creational capacities.[26] The broad challenge is to continue evolving the relational dynamics of interconnected ecosystems through the involvements of different types of stakeholding individuals, with unique needs, motivations and desires for individual wellbeing, economic growth and collective welfare, while taking advantage of techno-social advances in a digitalized impact economy for co-creating unique value with them. This requires seeing stakeholders as not only entities that are affected by (and affect) enterprises but also going further by seeing them as possessing creational capabilities harnessed through SDG-infused ecosystem platforms. To borrow from Neil Armstrong, a small step by SDG-facilitating actors in such ecosystem platforms would be a giant step towards co-creating a better future for all.[27]

NEST Ecosystem Transformation

Co-creative living organizations should be seen as complex systems within ecosystems, strategically positioning themselves and collaborating with others to create positive SWIs. They exist within the broader systems of organizations (NEST assemblages), harmonizing technology with nature, society and economy (see **Figure 8-3**). While responding flexibly to changes, they also need to maintain a core identity in co-creative living organization transformation.

John Ehrenfeld and Andrew Hoffman's notions of flourishing, intergenerational equity and systems thinking in *Flourishing* and E.F. Schumacher's ideas of 'technology with a human face' and intermediate technology, which is 'conducive to decentralization and compatible with the laws of ecology', in *Small is Beautiful,* align well with our idea of NEST ecosystems. [28,29] Research by the Ellen MacArthur Foundation indicates that transitioning to renewable energy and improving energy efficiency addresses only 55 per cent of global greenhouse gas emissions. To achieve the net-zero goal, the remaining 45 per cent of emissions reduction must come from adopting a *circular economy*.[30]

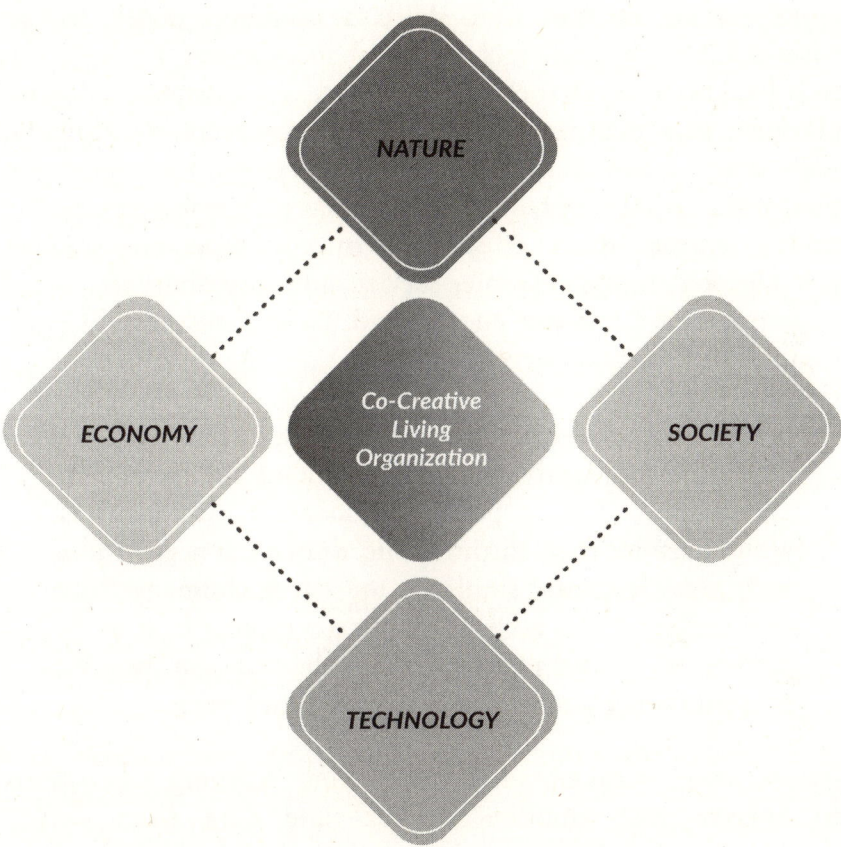

Figure 8-3: Harmonizing Technology with Nature, Society and Economy (Source: Venkat Ramaswamy)

We consider next the Kraken–Octopus partnership—where Octopus Energy's innovative approach to clean energy is powered by Kraken's advanced IT platform. Together, they are demonstrating how technology can be harnessed to build a more sustainable future.

Kraken–Octopus: A Powerful Duo for Sustainability

Kraken Technologies, an IT platform company, and Octopus Energy, the UK's most-awarded energy supplier, are two co-innovating entities that share a common goal—driving sustainability through technological innovation. Kraken, the tech backbone of Octopus' operations, is a complex software platform that manages millions of energy accounts globally, with unprecedented speed and efficiency. By leveraging the platform's capabilities, Octopus is able to harness renewable energy sources more effectively, offer competitive pricing, provide exceptional customer service, and contribute to a more sustainable and resilient energy grid. Greg Jackson, CEO and founder of Octopus Energy, says,

> I think it was like yin and yang, really. I think they both feed each other brilliantly, because controlling the technology allows us to drive a pace of innovation, to test ideas, without having to go through long, drawn-out negotiations with providers. And similarly, for a tech company to be able to have direct access to a huge consumer base in the market, to be able to tell you that the tech can do some magical things, and so they really feed each other.[31]

At its core, Kraken utilizes machine learning algorithms to analyse vast amounts of real-time data from energy consumption, generation and market conditions. This data-driven approach enables it to forecast energy demand and supply accurately, ensuring that renewable energy sources are utilized most efficiently. For instance, by predicting when wind or solar power will be abundant, Kraken can automatically adjust the charging schedules of electric vehicles and the operation of heat pumps, reducing reliance on fossil fuels and lowering energy costs for consumers.

Octopus Energy is able to offer innovative products to its customers. Consider its Zero Bill Homes project.[32] It aims to create self-sufficient homes that generate as much energy as they consume, eliminating utility bills. These homes utilize solar panels, energy storage solutions, and superior insulation to ensure continuous clean energy supply and minimal consumption. An advanced AI-driven energy management system can predict energy consumption patterns and adjust the energy flow accordingly. It optimizes real-time energy use, enhancing efficiency and sustainability. The project offers a practical solution for homeowners who want to live more sustainably without compromising on comfort or convenience.

Octopus' AI-infused platform forecasts weather patterns and energy usage trends, allowing for the intelligent allocation of stored energy to balance supply and demand across the grid. Jackson says:

> We take in billions of data points. If you've got a smart meter, several times per day, we'll do a two-year forecast at the half-hour level for your consumption. If you drive an electric car, and we've got the right APIs, we'll be forecasting how much you're going to use it every day. If you've got solar panels, we'll be working how much you're going to be generating, again, every half hour for as long as we can out. All of that, because what you want to be doing continually is optimizing.[33]

Consider its participation in National Grid's *demand response programmes*. During times of high energy demand, Octopus encourages customers to shift their energy usage to off-peak times. This collaborative effort helps balance the grid and provides financial incentives to customers. On one occasion, 420,000 customers shifted their demand by an hour, which was the equivalent of turning off all the power in Glasgow. Octopus' business model *turns its customers into partners*—it engages them as creative-experiencers. Intelligent Octopus is the UK's first 100 per cent flexible car charging tariff that offers drivers ultra-low-cost EV charging (at less than a third the price of standard plans) during off-peak hours. Alex Schoch, head of flexibility at Octopus Energy, commented: 'We urgently need to build flexible grid technology to turbocharge the green energy system. The tariff acts as a "virtual power plant", shifting demand out of peak times and therefore cutting bills for everyone.'[34]

As Octopus–Kraken expanded across multiple countries, their data volumes (for example, from smart meters) skyrocketed. It leveraged Databricks' Delta Sharing offering to streamline data processing and centralize data storage and management, thus reducing processing costs by eight times and cutting data load times by nine times.[35] In 2024, Databricks announced its Data Intelligence Platform for Energy, which helps energy companies like Octopus utilize GenAI to optimize operations, forecast energy production and support decarbonization efforts efficiently.[36]

Octopus excels in its customer engagement. During the 2022 energy crisis in Europe, it faced a surge in customer service inquiries. To address this challenge without compromising service quality, Octopus implemented a GenAI program in March 2023. This solution started by answering 5 per cent of customer emails and grew to handle 45 per cent by May 2023. The programme's success stemmed from its access to a comprehensive customer data set within Kraken, allowing for more accurate AI-generated responses. By the end of 2023, this GenAI solution wasn't just creating emails with an 80 per cent satisfaction rating (as compared to a 60 per cent rating if created by humans) but also taking actions like issuing refunds. Jackson remarks about how Octopus has benefitted from both automation and augmentation due to AI:

> We're now at the stage where, not much more than a year after the emergence of generative AI, almost half of the customer service emails for the UK's largest energy provider are being created by this AI. Increasingly, it's also doing the actions. And it's been a phenomenal help to our team because it's enabled each team member to put more of their time into looking after customers who need the

human support and take away some of the more tedious kind of typing repetitive tasks.[37]

Not only is Kraken transforming the way Octopus operates, but its technology is also available to other energy providers as well. EDF, Britain's biggest generator of zero-carbon electricity, has streamlined its operations with Kraken, reducing advisors' interfaces from twenty windows to just three. It has also undertaken an organizational and cultural shift in this transformation. Each team now manages a set of customers, with team leaders acting like mini CEOs responsible for their group's performance and customer satisfaction. Camilla McCorkle, residential operations director for EDF, says: 'Through our Early Adopters program, we actually seconded 200 of our people into Kraken to get used to the system, the operating model, the ways of working and then they could come back to EDF and be our kind of culture champions as we did our transformation.'[38]

Let us head to the US next and consider a different example of how Motorola Solutions is helping create public safety in a co-intelligence world.

Motorola Solutions—Enabling Public Safety

Motorola, which traces its roots to 1928, is a technology pioneer known for its car radios and first handheld cellular phone. In 2011, Motorola Solutions emerged as a focused entity specializing in mission-critical communication solutions for public safety, building on its legacy of technological leadership.

In a domain characterized by high-stress, time-critical situations, Motorola Solutions is employing AI to dramatically enhance response times and outcomes. Descriptive AI is being used to identify patterns in vast datasets, such as recognizing a stolen vehicle, while generative AI is transforming human–machine interaction. For instance, real-time translation and transcription of 911 calls are breaking language barriers and accelerating response. The staggering statistic of a one-minute reduction in 911 response time saving 10,000 lives underscores the life-or-death impact of this technology. Greg Brown, chairman and CEO of Motorola Solutions, says:

> We're not using AI to find a needle in a haystack. We're using AI to remove the haystack and find the needle. And in public safety, that means a lost child, an Amber Alert, a stolen vehicle, a perimeter breach, in the case of the school, a brandished weapon or an active shooter.[39]

Mahesh Saptharishi, executive vice president and CTO of Motorola Solutions, describes a notable example of how an AI-infused real-time crime centre in Yonkers, New York enabled the swift location of a missing autistic child within thirteen minutes:

> They were able to search this footage by description of the child—and within a matter of minutes, our system could tell them where the child wasn't. That way, they focused human attention on where the child could be. Effectively, AI removed the haystack and allowed humans to find the needle.[40]

Another example of using AI is in evidentiary management for body-worn cameras. This can expedite the process of redacting and blurring sensitive information, making it ten to fifteen times faster while maintaining accuracy. This not only improves productivity but also builds trust in the system by ensuring that humans verify AI-generated outcomes. It is also pioneering the use of AI in high-stakes scenarios like school shootings. By combining edge computing, video analytics, access control and sensor data, the company is developing solutions that can automatically detect threats, initiate lockdowns and guide first responders to victims. This level of real-time situational awareness has the potential to drastically reduce casualties. Brown says,

If you have the integrated ecosystem with blueprints, and you've got first responders connected with situational awareness with video, we could actually, during an active shooter, with sensors, light a green path, a physical green path, a light to safety. We can do that now. We don't need (the) cloud; we could put it right on the edge.[41]

While the transformative potential of AI is immense, Motorola Solutions is also acutely aware of the need for responsible AI development and deployment. It participates in initiatives such as the AI security initiative by the White House and the Coalition of Content Providence and Authenticity with Adobe, IBM and Google. These collaborations focus on ensuring the efficacy and reliability of AI technologies, especially concerning deep fakes and the watermarking of video and audio content. Motorola Solutions collaborates with local governments, school systems and private businesses to create integrated safety ecosystems. As we saw in the case at Yonkers, by linking private sector resources, such as video surveillance, with public safety operations, these public–private partnerships facilitate faster and more effective responses to emergencies.

Saptharishi highlights one important design principle that provides guardrails for their solutions—*high-velocity human factor* emphasizes the creation of AI tools that remain simple and effective for people under extreme stress: 'Folks in public safety say their jobs are hours of boredom punctuated by moments of terror. So, the same set of tools must serve this customer base, who are protecting our communities while they're relaxed—perhaps almost bored, fighting complacency—and then again when they're incredibly stressed.'[42]

Finally, dwelling on the usage of AI and other sophisticated technologies at a city/country level, let us now briefly consider smart city initiatives in Helsinki, Finland and Singapore and seek some Māori inspiration to measure SWIs at the national level in New Zealand.

Digital Twin Initiatives at Helsinki and Singapore

The 3D City Models of Helsinki is a comprehensive virtual model of the city, its digital twin. It combines information technology, open data and dynamic updates to create a detailed representation of the city's environment and infrastructure. The project includes two main models: the 3D mesh, which offers a realistic visualization based on aerial photographs, and the Urban data model, which provides detailed building and terrain information. These models support various applications, such as urban planning, energy analysis and public engagement, offering a versatile platform for exploring and managing city data. Helsinki monitors the implementation of its City Strategy through a comprehensive system of qualitative and quantitative indicators across thirteen priority areas. These areas include education, climate objectives, cultural activities, equality, safety and digitalization. Progress is tracked using two to eight specific indicators per area, with reports provided to the City Council at mid-term. A unique aspect of Helsinki's approach is the integration of data and digital tools, enhancing transparency and allowing for detailed monitoring and reporting on various strategic goals.[43]

One of the most impactful smart-city, digital-twin initiatives in the world is in Singapore, where the integration of AI and other emerging technologies has significantly improved urban management and efficiency. Virtual Singapore, a 3D digital model and collaborative data platform, aims to provide an authoritative virtual representation of Singapore, enabling users from various sectors and even citizens to simulate, test and plan urban solutions. It supports a wide range of applications, including urban planning, crowd management and environmental monitoring. Ronnie Lee, deputy director of GovTech's Geospatial Specialist Office, describes how simulations help in smart energy management:

> You could for example find all the roof surfaces for buildings of a certain height in a certain area or find all the wall surfaces orientated at a certain bearing and calculate

the amount of sunlight falling on them. The fact that the computer knows all this information means that more advanced simulation and analysis can be carried out.[44]

Living Standards Framework—Government of New Zealand

The Living Standards Framework (LSF) of the government of New Zealand is an exemplar of holistic sustainable wellbeing thinking and reporting.[45] At its heart is its focus on *kaitiakitanga* (guardianship, caring, protection, upkeep). In 2018, the Treasury released the LSF Dashboard, a tool to measure and track changes in wellbeing outcomes based on three sections: 'our people', 'our country' and 'our future'. *Our people* measures wellbeing distribution across nine domains for different population groups of New Zealanders (age, ethnicity, family type, etc.). *Our country* uses thirty-eight indicators to measure twelve wellbeing domains and describe the current wellbeing of New Zealanders, with comparisons to other OECD countries. *Our future* provides indicators on four resources (natural, human, social and financial/physical capitals) relevant to future wellbeing.

In 2023, the LSF included three levels: (i) *Our Individual and Collective Wellbeing*: This level captures the resources and aspects of people's lives that have been identified by research or public engagement as important for people's wellbeing as individuals, families, and *whānau* (extended families and communities); (ii) *Our Institutions and Governance*: This level captures the role that institutions and organizations play in facilitating the wellbeing of individuals and collectives, as well as safeguarding and building the national wealth and (iii) *The Wealth of Aotearoa New Zealand*: This captures how wealthy the nation is overall, including aspects of wealth not fully captured in the system of national accounts, such as the natural environment and human capability.

* * *

The next frontier in the co-intelligence revolution is facilitating valuable co-creation experiences with Nextgen AI in NEST ecosystems across the value-chain, offering and management ecosystems of organizations. It has the potential to make renewed progress towards the UN SDGs through co-evolution of SWIs at speed, scale and scope. But the promise of achieving the SDGs will not be realized unless the people, from scientists and business executives to political leaders and the common populus, gain deep appreciation for NEST systems through ecoAI literacy to guide Nextgen AI development towards sustainable practices. This would enable 'individuals and institutions to converge on the collective realization of human potential and enhance the growth, productivity, sustainability and resilience of the ecosystems in which we live, and the quality of peoples' lives'.[46]

In the next chapter, we examine the role of lifelong learning and development of people and the centrality of ecoAI literacy in co-intelligent enterprises.

9

Cultivating EcoAI-Literacy and Lifelong Learning

Co-intelligence-driven, life–experience-oriented ecosystemic transformation necessitates cultivating lifelong learning and development of people and talent in society and the economy, especially with respect to the ongoing sustainability and adaptability of organizations. We propose the idea of *ecoAI literacy*. It is an understanding of *how AI can be used to address environmental challenges and create more sustainable systems that emphasize the interconnectedness of human society with nature*. EcoAI literacy builds on the prevalent ideas on ecoliteracy and adapts it for the co-intelligence world. For instance, in *Ecoliterate,* Daniel Goleman, Lisa Benett and Zenobia Barlow propose a learning that 'prepares young people for the ecological challenges presented by this entirely unprecedented time in human history'.[1] EcoAI literacy is required for humanity to navigate the 'Co-Eaarth', our reimagined take on Bill McKibben's future, in an ethical manner.[2]

EcoAI Literacy

UNESCO, through its universities and the 2030 Agenda, emphasizes three strategies for educational institutions to become catalysts for a transition towards sustainability and embracing the UN Sustainable Development Goals (SDGs): i) A shift towards interdisciplinary and transdisciplinary approaches, i.e., integrating knowledge across disciplines in both education and research; ii) becoming more open, fostering dialogue around different ways of knowing and integrating diverse perspectives; and iii) demonstrating stronger societal engagement, direct involvement in experimental projects testing solutions, with student participation. Higher education institutions (HEIs) must also prioritize equipping both faculty and students with a deep understanding of sustainability and the SDGs by making them core requirements.[3]

UNESCO also advocates for public awareness and understanding of AI technologies and data value by promoting open and accessible education, civic engagement, digital skills, AI ethics training and media and information literacy. It recommends that countries should work with international organizations, educational institutions and private and non-governmental entities to provide AI literacy education to the public on all levels to empower people and reduce digital divides arising from the widespread adoption of AI systems.[4]

In the Co-Intelligence Era, as the world becomes increasingly complex to navigate, learning and development have become more important than ever. Equipping ourselves with ecoAI literacy is critical, whether it is at a university, enterprise or country level.

Sustainability Learning and Development Initiatives at Universities

Ohio State University (OSU) has been deeply involved in sustainability efforts, including committing to carbon neutrality by 2050 through the Presidents' Climate Leadership Commitment. OSU is part of Second Nature's University Climate Change Coalition (UC3), a group of leading North American research universities committed to accelerating climate solutions at local and regional levels. Its $15 million 2022 project tackles climate change with 'carbon farming'—to measure how much carbon dioxide soil can store, informing policies that reward farmers for these practices.[5] The University of Michigan's Planet Blue initiatives align with its broader educational and sustainability goals, emphasizing carbon neutrality, waste reduction, climate action, healthy environments and community engagement. It fosters interdisciplinary research that addresses pressing global challenges such as climate change, resource conservation and sustainable development. The research efforts are designed to create actionable solutions that can be implemented within communities and industries, further enhancing the university's impact on both local and global scales. This focus on sustainability research is tightly integrated with the university's educational programmes.

Humber College in Toronto and Siemens have partnered to achieve zero-net carbon emissions by 2050 and reduce energy and water usage by 2034. Key initiatives include building automation, HVAC optimization and the development of a campus microgrid with battery storage and EV charging. In 2023, they opened the Sustainable Microgrid and Renewable Technology Lab (SMART Lab) to provide students hands-on experience with microgrid technologies, turning its campus into a living lab for education and research.[6] The International Sustainable Campus Network's Campus as a Living Lab connects universities to share sustainability solutions. This fosters student engagement and empowers them to be eco-conscious consumers, influencing markets for good.[7] Villars Institute and Minerva Project have collaborated on a unique systems leadership course that combines intergenerational and interdisciplinary learning with practical systems thinking. The course aims to equip future leaders with the skills to address complex challenges by fostering creative and collaborative problem-solving.[8] One of us (KN) is now involved with the Global Learning Council and Villars Institute in exploring the development of an ecoAI literacy-based fellowship program.

In December 2023, scientists announced, via a *Nature* paper, a climate science GenAI assistant, ChatClimate. It has been trained on the Sixth Assessment Report from the Intergovernmental Panel on Climate Change (IPCC AR6), recognized as the most comprehensive and reliable resource in this field. By integrating this training with GPT-4's capabilities, ChatClimate delivers more accurate answers to users' questions. The researchers say, 'Our AI-powered tool makes climate information accessible to a broader community and may assist decision-makers and the public in understanding climate change-related issues. However, it is intended to complement, not replace, specialized local knowledge and custom solutions essential for effective decision-making.'[9]

While digital platforms and GenAI can turbocharge eco-literacy, population scale awareness creation also benefits from *grassroots movements*. Chetan Solanki, a professor from IIT Bombay and founder of the Energy Swaraj Foundation, has committed to living in a solar bus till 2030 and has earned the moniker 'Solar Gandhi'. Inspired by Mahatma Gandhi's teachings, he aims to make climate action a *jan andolan*, a mass movement. He says, 'Every user of energy and material, a poor or rich person, young or old, rural or urban, every person in every minute of their life is contributing to carbon emissions in one way or another.'[10] Solanki traverses the length and breadth of India, raising awareness and conducting online eco-literacy programmes about climate change, limiting consumption, promoting solar energy and localizing production.[11]

Triad of Intelligence at MIT and NTU Singapore

NEST assemblages also benefit from a co-evolution of intelligences. Subra Suresh, Vannevar Bush Professor of Engineering Emeritus at MIT and former director of the National Science Foundation, US, calls for drawing insights from *nature as well as humans and artificial intelligence*. He says,

The synergy of collective intelligence is fostering groundbreaking innovations and expanding the boundaries of knowledge. Human ingenuity complements these observations through rigorous experimentation and theoretical modelling, while AI accelerates discovery by processing vast datasets, identifying patterns and predicting outcomes that would be unattainable with conventional methods. This triad of intelligence not only deepens our understanding of complex systems but also drives sustainable and innovative solutions across various fields.[12]

Suresh's team of researchers has demonstrated success from this triad of intelligence: (i) by mimicking the hydromorphic properties of sunflower pollen, researchers at Nanyang Technological University (NTU) Singapore developed pollen-paper, a moisture-responsive material that can dynamically change shape and function. This groundbreaking material offers industries a potential 40 per cent energy reduction and enables courier companies to create more durable, weatherproof packaging; (ii) by utilizing the unique mechanical properties of diamond at the nanoscale, scientists at MIT and NTU demonstrated that diamond needles could bend significantly without fracturing, paving the way for advanced applications in electronics and thermal management through AI-driven simulations; (iii) by using AI and microfluidic devices to simulate the behaviour of red blood cells in diabetic and hereditary blood disorders, researchers at MIT and NTU demonstrated more precise diagnosis and treatment planning of disorders such as malaria, sickle cell anemia and elliptocytosis, offering a new level of personalized medical care.[13]

Beyond universities, ecoAI literacy and capability-building efforts are required at population scale. Next, we consider how AI literacy is being envisaged in the United Arab Emirates (UAE).

AI literacy in the United Arab Emirates

H.E. Omar Sultan Al Olama, the world's first minister of state for AI since 2017, has spearheaded the UAE's ambitious ascent in the technology and has transformed how the government and its citizens approach AI. He firmly believes that shying away from AI would be a grave mistake, akin to the Arab world's rejection of the printing press centuries ago, a decision that has had lasting repercussions.

> 'We are at a juncture in history, the same one that we as a region were in 600 years ago, and I think we do not want to make that mistake again,' he asserts, emphasizing the urgency of embracing AI rather than fearing its disruptive power.[14]

The UAE's journey is marked by a distinct focus on achieving AI sovereignty. This ambition has led to the development of Falcon, an open-source multilingual LLM, and Jais, a bilingual (English and Arabic) LLM. Al Olama positions the UAE as a potential hub for global AI development, capable of creating solutions that cater to a diverse range of languages and cultural contexts. 'The 200 nationalities that live in the UAE can help you localize your large language model or localize your software to many geographies without having to open offices all around the world.'[15] In April 2024, Microsoft announced a $1.5 billion investment in G42, the leading UAE-based AI technology holding company and creator of Jais.[16]

Beyond the technological focus, the UAE's AI strategy is rooted in the learning and development Life-Xverse of its government workforce and citizens. It has established the Mohammed Bin Zayed University of Artificial Intelligence (MBZUAI), the first university dedicated solely to AI and a collaborator in the development of Jais. Further, Al Olama's team collaborated with the University of Oxford to train over 420 senior government officials on AI ethics, deployment and regulation. These officials form what he calls the UAE's 'AI Army', ensuring that decision-making regarding AI is informed, strategic and devoid of ignorance.

Al Olama's vision also extends to democratizing AI knowledge among the public. One prominent example is the UAE AI Camp, a free programme offering AI training and awareness to people across the country, including those in rural areas and cities. The camp aims to demystify AI, making it more accessible and less intimidating for citizens. Another key initiative is the publication of practical guides, such as the *100 Practical Use Cases of Generative AI*, available in both Arabic and English. These guides provide citizens with concrete examples of how AI can be applied in various aspects of their lives and work, helping them understand its potential benefits. Additionally, the government utilizes UAE Codes Day, an annual event that encourages citizens to embark on their AI learning journey through accessible online platforms and resources. By sending push notifications via the telcos, the government has reached over 180,000 citizens in one day to begin their learning journey.

AI Literacy and Citizen Co-creation in Flanders

The Flemish government (the Dutch-speaking northern portion of Belgium) has demonstrated a strong commitment to AI literacy through its comprehensive AI Plan. Launched in 2019 with an annual budget of €32 million, the plan focuses on three core pillars: bolstering fundamental strategic research, encouraging AI adoption in businesses, enhancing general awareness and providing specialized training. Its AMAI! (wow in Flemish) programme, a collaboration between Scivil, the Flemish knowledge centre for citizen science, and KCDS (Knowledge Centre Data and Society), facilitates citizen co-creation in AI development.

Citizens are encouraged to submit their ideas for AI solutions to societal challenges. These ideas are then refined in co-creation workshops with AI experts and civil society representatives, leading to the formation of project proposals and consortia. Citizens also play a crucial role in selecting the projects that receive funding through online voting and participation in citizen panels. This collaborative approach ensures that AI initiatives address real-world needs and reflect the priorities of the community. The programme also fosters a sense of community among participants, encouraging knowledge sharing and collaborative problem-solving. Annelies Duerinckx, head of Scivil, says,

> Our two target groups, AI experts and civil society representatives, likely wouldn't have met without this type of program . . . One of my dreams is to create a similar program on climate change.[17]

Organizations also have to nurture lifelong learning. From a talent and skilling transformation perspective, we have seen several examples so far. For instance, in *Chapter 2*, we saw how *L'Oréal's* comprehensive approach to leveraging AI in human resources (with tools like Mya and Seedlink) streamlines recruitment while also ensuring a diverse and culturally fit workforce. Learning and development are deeply embedded in its management ecosystem to support its global strategy. In *Chapter 3*, we explored how tech-forward enterprises were transforming their own organizational ecosystems. For instance, how *SAP* has reinvented its enhanced competence base for a co-intelligence world. In *Chapter 4*, we saw how the *Commonwealth Bank of Australia* has transformed its customer-facing talent and internal development of AI-infused offerings with global talent capabilities. In *Chapter 5*, we considered how *Mahindra* developed a culture of co-creation. In *Chapter 6*, we saw how *ING* is facilitating new on-the-job employee support learning environments. In *Chapter 7*, we discussed how *Infosys* infuses its talent base with AI skills and how *Companhia Brasileira de Alumínio* is building a co-creative learning community. In *Chapter 8*, we saw how *ITC* upskills farmers from Indian villages and offers both digital and eco-literacy, and how *Industree* trains women in villages in building regenerative value chains and becoming drivers of climate solutions.

But what about *educational institutions*? How do they prepare individuals for lifelong learning and development in co-intelligent enterprises? How can universities and schools ensure that their students are trained appropriately for the future of work? How can these educational institutions transform *themselves* to become co-intelligent enterprises that thrive in a co-intelligence world? We turn to these questions next.

Into the Education Life-Xverse

Let us first visualize the *Education Life-Xverse* with a PIEX lens, where learning is now powered by industry clouds entailing datafication, softwarization and AI-infused innovation of new business configurations, offerings and value-chain activities. For instance, a university may augment its conventional systems of records, such as enterprise resource planning systems, with newer systems of engagement, such as a communication platform for students to collaborate and exchange ideas. This creates a new basis of operational efficiency for the university. In the education Life-Xverse, the co-intelligence ecosystem network may comprise a university campus and chatbot in the US, international campuses and chatbots in collaboration with partners in other countries, the university's own online engagement channels, and partnerships with Massive Open Online Courses (MOOCs) platforms and their chatbots. Such chatbot-based agentic co-intelligence ecosystems can reduce friction in switching services, use network effects to gain scale advantages and integrate data to create superior products and services. The digital fabric of such co-intelligence enterprise ecosystems is increasingly becoming part and parcel of the fabric of society itself.

However, in the education Life-Xverse, it is important to also pay attention to the lived-journeys of learners. Consider a student who may be learning about a given subject from several different sources—classroom, online, from personal tutors, virtual worlds, etc. How does the university help the student personalize a learning plan given this context? Further, while taking university courses, the student may also be running a startup. Does the university know this about that student? And how does it interactively engage in the ongoing lived-journeys of learners as entrepreneurs? How do learners want to engage? How do both educators and learners co-create mutual value? Finally, the performance metrics of a university include SWIs such as contributing to the growth of gross enrolment ratio (GER) of a nation, alignment to UN SDG Goal 4 on education, creating a sustainable campus, or ensuring the mental health of students, besides traditional measures of student enrolments, revenues and costs.

Second Nature has identified seven distinctives as key characteristics of higher education: knowledge creation, knowledge transfer, credentialing, trusted voice, trusted convener, living laboratory and loyal alumni.[18] HEIs are significant generators of new knowledge and innovation through research, and they play a critical role in transferring this knowledge to future generations through education and training programmes. Co-intelligence is allowing learning in new ways. Imagine real-time communication facilitated by GenAI between environmental monitoring systems and climate researchers, allowing for a more holistic understanding of ecological challenges. Further, a university's traditional roles of knowledge development (research) and knowledge dissemination (teaching) have expanded. Educational institutions have provided formal recognition of expertise through degrees and certifications, signalling the knowledge and skills held by graduates. Now, they are issued as tamper-proof, verifiable micro-credential badges on a blockchain. Historically, educational institutions have been trusted sources of information and expertise, influencing public understanding and policy. Universities and colleges often serve as neutral conveners, bringing together diverse stakeholders for discussions and collaborations on important issues. Co-intelligence now opens up Henry Etzkowitz's Triple Helix model, enabling real-time, global collaboration across diverse stakeholder groups that include universities, industries and the government. It can facilitate easier and more interactive participation of civil society, local communities or the users of innovations, thus facilitating a Quadruple Helix.[19]

Campus environments act as experimental grounds for testing and implementing innovative solutions, integrating academic research with practical applications. Universities can engage with partners (for example, VentureWell) and offer institutional access to resources and programmes on entrepreneurship and innovation for both faculty and students. VentureWell's programmes provide grants, mentorship and networks that empower creative entrepreneurs to develop solutions with significant social and environmental impacts. For instance, the E-Team Program, part of the VentureWell Accelerator, supports student ventures that develop scalable innovations that aim to solve a large social, health or environmental challenge. Since its inception, the programme has supported over 500 student teams, helping them raise more than $620 million to launch successful ventures across fifty countries.[20] Universities can also reimagine John Dewey's 'learning by doing' with AI, tailored simulations and feedback loops, accelerating skill development and optimizing the experience for each student.

Newer phrases have entered the education sector lexicon— once-novel terms like online education and lifelong learning are now commonplace, joined by phrases like personalized adaptive learning, modular pathways and stackable credentials. And the latest addition: the education co-pilot. Newer roles and tasks are being imagined in a co-intelligence classroom. Co-intelligence also opens up institutional opportunities with alumni. Traditionally, alumni networks have maintained strong ties to their institutions, supporting their missions and contributing resources, expertise, and advocacy. Imagine alumni seamlessly accessing a co-intelligence knowledge leverage system from their alma mater, for lifelong learning and industry-relevant problem-solving.

In the book *Co-Intelligence*, Mollick provides analogies from the mythical and sci-fi world—*centaur tasks* are those where humans and AI collaborate distinctly, leveraging each other's strengths for optimal outcomes, while *cyborg tasks* are those where humans and AI are tightly integrated, enhancing real-time performance.[21] What will be the centaur and cyborg tasks of lifelong learning and developmental impacts in the co-intelligence world?

We next consider an example of GenAI adoption in the private sector and examine Coursera, a global digital platform for university education and skill development.

Re-architecting Coursera with GenAI

Coursera is a global online platformized learning ecosystem that offers anyone, anywhere access to online courses and degrees from world-class universities and companies. When Coursera started in 2012, it offered digital educational content in the form of massively open online courses (MOOCs) directly to individuals. As of December 2023, it has created a learning ecosystem that includes over 140 million learners, 260,000 learners via social impact programmes, over 325 educator partners and over 1300 enterprise customers.[22]

Even before the GenAI wave, Coursera had been at the cutting edge of infusing AI into its products. Consider the situation just a couple of years ago. The platform allowed for a personalized discovery of courses, based on the learner's input on interests, location and so on. Skill Graph mapped skills to careers that the learners aspired to and helped them discover relevant course content. Its In-course Coach feature helped the learner stay motivated to learn and not drop off early from the course. The guided projects of Coursera Labs provided for hands-on learning online. Consequently, 81 per cent of learners gave its courses five-star ratings and 94 per cent of learners said they would recommend Coursera to a friend. For its university customers, its Course Match machine learning algorithm, fine-tuned on data from catalogues of over 1800 schools and over 2.6 million courses, helped match each of their on-campus courses with the most relevant online courses from Coursera's catalogue.[23]

All of this dramatically changed at the end of 2022. Jeff Maggioncalda, the former CEO, Coursera, says,

> On December 5, 2022, I received a Slack message from Coursera's VP of Product Management. It was a surprisingly precise recommendation outlining our approach to integrating Generative AI (GenAI) into Coursera. To my astonishment, he was able to draft this blueprint within seconds by entering a few prompts into ChatGPT, which led me to wonder how else large language models (LLMs) could be used as a thought partner for innovation and productivity. This was my GenAI awakening. I spent countless hours experimenting with ChatGPT. I was astounded by the many possibilities it could offer Coursera as an organization—and work as we know it.[24]

Maggioncalda swung into action. He put in place Project Genesis, comprising a cross-functional task force. But adoption of GenAI was not going to be just a product management challenge. It was also going to be a cultural transformation. Coursera was beginning its journey in becoming a co-creative living organization (CCLO).

The leadership team first devised five key principles for guiding its exploration of GenAI: positive impact, safety and security, fairness, transparency and accountability. Coursera launched the Generative AI Academy, bringing together carefully chosen content and practical exercises from leading AI minds at Microsoft, Google, Stanford Online and IBM, and soon launched a dedicated GenAI training program for its employees. Trena Minudri, Coursera's chief learning officer, says,

In GenAI Academy, you're learning from a professor or
an expert in the field through videos, content, or hands-
on exercises. We are then incorporating this training
into a hybrid approach within the organization where
the learning varies. We teach theories and concepts, and
then create a space where employees can apply it to their
work.[25]

They focused on driving employee adoption of GenAI, especially
the 'how' of it, i.e., 'How do I use GenAI to transform my job?'
And armed with this knowledge, how they could guide their
customers to adopt GenAI. Positive reinforcements boosted
Courserian engagement—they showcased LinkedIn praise,
highlighted top courses and celebrated early adopters in their
Slack channel, #customer-zero. Finally, the team also monitored
results—83 per cent of Courserians had completed a course by
the end of March 2024. Minduri says, 'This is not a one-and-
done type of game. It's not about finishing a program—this is
a journey.'

From a product perspective, Coursera achieved spectacular
success. Three significant product features were added: i)
language translation of courses, ii) Coursera Coach and iii)
Course Builder. Coursera leveraged machine learning to
translate 4000-plus courses, 600-plus specializations and 55-
plus professional certificates from partners like IBM, Meta and
Microsoft into seventeen languages.[26] This included translation
of course readings, lecture video subtitles, quizzes, assessments,
peer review instructions and discussion prompts. As a next step,
Coursera is looking into using GenAI to translate instructor
videos while cloning their voices.

Coursera offers learners a personalized learning experience
with Coursera Coach, an AI-powered companion. Learners
receive real-time answers, personalized feedback, and concise
video summaries to solidify their understanding of concepts.
Coursera Coach's impact on learning is promising. A pilot
study showed learners who engaged with Coach's pre-quiz

Q&A feature were 10 per cent more likely to pass quizzes on the first try.[27] Going beyond learning support, Coursera Coach is planning to leverage multi-nodal capabilities of GenAI to ensure academic integrity, i.e., detect potential cheating through methods like remote monitoring and analysing writing patterns. The third GenAI innovation, Course Builder, empowers universities to streamline course content creation. This AI-powered authoring tool eliminates the need to start from scratch by offering a curated library of world-class content from other university and industry leaders. It guides users through the process, automatically generating a flexible course outline that can be personalized with the university's specific materials.

Not only has GenAI transformed Coursera's products, but it has also transformed the demand for skills training on the platform. In 2023, Coursera saw a GenAI course enrolment every minute. By 2024, this rate had increased by four times. With an estimated 60 per cent of workers requiring retraining by 2027, Coursera is offering (through partnerships with leading universities and industry leaders) micro credentials for digital skills, including professional certificates.[28] Similarly, to address job-skill gap challenges at population scale, India is currently experimenting with the Open Network for Education Skilling Transaction (ONEST), designed along the lines of other digital public infrastructures (DPIs) like ONDC.[29]

Coursera's Course Builder is a powerful tool with which educators can co-create and develop new courses. Imagine if it allowed them to involve the students too in this co-creation process, i.e., assess the learning capabilities of each student, obtain their inputs on learning objectives and then create as many courses as there are students in a classroom, all in real time. This will shift algorithm-led personalization beyond human-led personalization and transform Coursera towards becoming a 'Learnera' if you will.

We next share some initiatives at the University of Michigan, with whom one of us is affiliated.[30]

University of Michigan—GenAI Strategy and Implementation

In November 2022, President Santa Ono announced plans to create a ten-year strategic vision for the University of Michigan, U-M Vision 2034. Around the same time when ChatGPT announced itself to the world. U-M, under the leadership of its Provost, Laurie McCauley and CIO, Ravi Pendse, convened the eighteen-member Generative Artificial Intelligence Advisory Committee to lead the charge in developing future-proof educational models. As part of a thoughtful way of architecting the GenAI strategy, the committee emphasized aspects like transparency, academic integrity, data privacy, security, bias mitigation, ethical AI research, equitable access and community engagement.

In August 2023, it became the first university in the world to provide custom GenAI services to its community—to all active U-M faculty, staff and students on the Ann Arbor, Flint and Dearborn campuses and Michigan Medicine. Three tools were created:

i)   *U-M GPT*: U-M's most accessible AI service, this tool grants users easy access to popular hosted AI models, including Azure OpenAI and U-M hosted open-source large language models. It functions similarly to ChatGPT, but one important difference is that the data received and produced by UMGPT is kept private by the university.

ii)   *U-M Maizey*: Users, by providing their own custom datasets, can leverage Maizey's powerful AI tools to extract valuable insights. Pendse says,

> It is a code-less platform. Anybody, (with) no programming or coding experience required, can take the Maizey platform, point it to their appropriate data source in their Google Drive or Dropbox, on the web or a bunch of videos. Maizey will ingest an index of all of that information

and then it's available to them as their own personal AI, assistant for them to query and ask questions.[31]

iii) *U-M GPT Toolkit*: Designed for advanced users, Toolkit is the most powerful and flexible AI service offered by U-M. It provides users with full control over their AI environments and models. Pendse says, 'Toolkit provides access to those researchers who are the AI experts who can understand building their own models.'

U-M's AI service attracts an average of 15,000 users a day.[32] President Ono says, 'And thousands are using those services every day. Members of our faculty have developed 24/7 AI tutors for their classes. Our tools are also being used to drive student- and faculty-led experiments exploring the responsible, legal, and ethical use of AI.'[33]

U-M has actively developed over 750 projects, ranging from classroom assistance tools to medical simulations and administrative streamlining solutions. The Wolverine Learning Assistant tackles complex academic subjects, making them easier to understand and more interesting for all students. LSA Newnan Academic Advising Center Maizey is designed for its 19,000 students seeking access to advice and guidance at their convenience.[34] For a course on Operations Management, U-M compared the performance of a Maizey Assistant (trained on the course material) with ChatGPT in answering student queries. Instructors later rated the answers of both language models. Maizey scored 20 per cent higher in providing answers that significantly enhanced student learning (on top of two-box ratings).[35] In another course, an AI coaching bot aims to enhance students' critical thinking and self-regulated learning. It helps students grasp the conceptual framework of problems, enabling them to solve similar issues independently, rather than just providing solutions to specific problems.[36] On the administrative front, an IT ticket handling system developed on Maizey has cut processing time from twenty to thirty minutes to just sixteen seconds per ticket, saving approximately 2.5 million minutes annually. Internal estimates suggest that U-M can potentially save costs significantly through reduced subscription expenses (upwards of $1 million annually) and productivity gains ($875,000 of annual labour costs saved per Maizey application).[37]

U-M's leadership role in harnessing the power of GenAI is not only benefitting its own community, but it is also creating a larger societal impact. U-M is in the process of enhancing a public-facing version of Maizey, which allows a student to easily discover eligible scholarships and grants. Pendse says,

> It will actually ingest and index all of the scholarships that are out there. Not just the Pell Grants (need-based financial aid provided by the US federal government to undergraduate students) . . . If you typed in 'I am a seventeen-year-old high-school student. I have this kind of GPA, and I'm interested in these areas. Can you identify scholarships for me?' In fifteen seconds, Maizey will find you all relevant scholarships. Even if twenty people are able to go to college because of this, it'd be worth it.[38]

Expanding its AI leadership further, U-M introduced the *Go Blue* AI app in February 2025—a mobile-first AI assistant available on iOS and Android. Go Blue AI provides U-M students, faculty, and staff with no-cost access to advanced AI-powered services enriched with university-specific data. Whether users need information on campus news, academic resources, dining menus, or event schedules, Go Blue serves as a personalized digital assistant, evolving weekly with new features. Unlike public AI models, *Go Blue* prioritizes data privacy, ensuring that all user interactions remain within the U-M ecosystem and are never used for AI training. 'No other university provides such deeply personalized AI tools while maintaining a commitment to privacy,' says Pendse.[39] In March 2025, U-M partnered with OpenAI and other educational institutions in the NextGenAI consortium, a broader $50 million effort by OpenAI to advance AI in research and education.[40]

Stepping back into the higher education Life-Xverse, educational institutions must grapple with several questions:

Students as co-creators

i) How can universities leverage education clouds and interactive GenAI platforms to improve communication and information flow with students?

ii) With students learning from everywhere—classes, online, chatbots—how can universities help them design personalized learning plans that leverage these options?

iii) Could universities create a connected learning ecosystem that integrates resources across campuses and online courses on contextual demand, making it easier for students to navigate and augment their education?

iv) Can universities track students' extracurricular activities, like startups, and invite them to co-teach an entrepreneurship course?

v) How can universities define success beyond traditional metrics like enrolment to encompass factors like alignment with UN SDGs (particularly Goal 4 on education) and student wellbeing?

Faculty as co-creators

i) How can we encourage *disciplinary specialization* to productively rub against *learning about and from other disciplines* with a growth mindset?

ii) How can we do so in an interconnected, interdependent textured world of co-created phenomena that we each subjectively experience?

iii) How can we harness the very power of GenAI in educating us about others' perceived realities of our shared world, bringing diverse perspectives into conversation with us?

iv) How can we co-evolve the systems thinking that is grounded in interdisciplinary perspectives of Life-Xverse ecosystems?

v) How do we ultimately evolve towards a more *holistic* education, one in wonder of humanity's co-existence and of the world and ourselves—where 'philosophy' and 'economy' converge to amplify our collective and individual human potential?

Voice-based Personalization at DIKSHA

Consider India's DIKSHA (Digital Infrastructure for Knowledge Sharing in India), an initiative for K-12 education built on a foundation of an open DPI. Sanjay Purohit, CEO and chief curator, Centre for Exponential Change (C4EC), says,

> DIKSHA has changed how education can be improved across 1.5 million schools with innovations that help students learn, empower teachers to improve, and nudge administrators to adapt best practices. Using simple ideas such as QR codes embedded in 600 million textbooks, teachers are now able to access updated digital learning content across 20 instruction mediums, a task that would have been tedious or impossible before.[41]

DIKSHA is a 'co-DPI' (see Chapter 3) that represents an advanced co-intelligence evolution of traditional DPI. It emphasizes Human–AI interactive engagement and co-intelligence flows within DPI systems to enable participatory, adaptive and sustainable value creation. Co-DPIs not only provide the technical backbone for inclusivity and large-scale services but also integrate co-creation as a foundational principle.

DIKSHA aspires to empower educators to create a truly personalized learning experience for every student. For instance, if it is to create unique lesson plans for each student, it should know the current state of learning and then determine specific learning pathways for every child. EkStep Foundation, a non-profit in the area of lifelong learning—particularly school education and a primary catalyst for DIKSHA, in collaboration with AI4Bharat Centre at IIT Madras, is now leveraging GenAI for this purpose. It is working with the Tamil Nadu state government's initiative Mozhigal (meaning language in Tamil), which has set up language labs in 6000 schools and is helping 1 million children by creating personalized, assisted language learning experiences. GenAI is leveraged to analyse the voice of a schoolchild to figure out what and how many syllables the child knows. Jagdish Babu, COO of Ekstep, says,

> I can do the same thing to a classroom what Google Maps does for us, i.e., they allow us to see journey time and the state of all roads in our path. For instance, in a grade three classroom, every child is expected to know 247 syllable combinations in Tamil. But how can a teacher find that out for every child? We use AI here. When a child reads into a microphone, based on speech recognition, the probabilities of their knowledge of Tamil are automatically derived, and then we can do speech diagnostics.[42]

Thus, DIKSHA is a co-DPI where AI curates personalized learning paths for students while teachers co-create content informed by AI-driven insights.

We are reminded of the story of 'Twin Sparrows' in Kai-Fu Lee's 2023 book, *AI 2041*, which evocatively explores a future of personalized AI tutors. AI Atoman drives competitive, goal-oriented learning, using rankings and rewards to motivate Golden Sparrow, while AI Solaris offers a more emotionally supportive, creative approach tailored to Silver Sparrow's introspective nature. Each AI companion adapts to the distinct learning styles of the twins.[43] Taking the Google Maps analogy at DIKSHA forward, imagine if the AI system further allowed students to communicate with it and share information about a 'blocked road', i.e., learning pathways that they found difficult. We turn next to Khanmigo, which unlocks just this.

Active Learning with Khanmigo

In July 2022, Sam Altman, CEO of OpenAI, reached out to Salman 'Sal' Khan, founder of Khan Academy, to explore a partnership. Khan describes the aha-moment he had from that meeting when GPT-4 (an early preview of the AI model) answered an AP biology question and gave detailed explanations for both the correct and the incorrect answers.

> In the back of my mind, I'm thinking about how much we invest in writing questions, solutions, and the rationales at Khan Academy. And so, I had it generate 10 more questions just like the first one, but on different topics, and it did it. And I thought, 'Oh, my God. The Young Ladies' Illustrated Primer could happen next year. This changes everything.[44]

The Primer is an interactive supercomputer from Neal Stephenson's novel, *The Diamond Age,* that educates and empowers young girls through personalized learning—an idea that had always inspired Khan. He decided to go all in and bet big on GenAI. In his book, *Brave New Words*, he articulates the one thing he sought from this transformation: 'At its best, an education-based AI platform can be the world's finest assistant and co-collaborator, objective in its assessments and thorough in its analytics, designed to do one thing and one thing only: to sharpen a student's skills.'[45]

That principle formed the basis of Khanmigo, Khan Academy's AI assistant. The word is a play on the Spanish phrase *conmigo*, meaning 'with me'. Kristen DiCerbo, chief learning officer at Khan Academy, ensured that rigorous pedagogical research guided Khanmigo's development.[46] Interactive engagement, the pinnacle of the active learning approach, involves discussions and debates with others, in a Socratic dialogue, which research suggests leads to the most significant learning gains. Unlike ChatGPT, which directly provides answers to questions, Khanmigo asks probing questions that encourage students to develop critical thinking skills and arrive at solutions on their own. The thoughtful design of Khanmigo is further reflected in the way it has implemented a number of guardrails. Khan provides a striking example of conversing with an AI bot of a historical figure, Harriet Tubman, an American abolitionist and social activist. He says,

> The simulations should engage only on issues in which the original figure would have had context. That is why the AI Tubman didn't engage on the modern notion of 'reparations' but did debate some of the more tangible related ideas about which the historical Tubman had a clear point of view.[47]

The primacy of the educators was kept in mind while designing Khanmigo. Khan says,

> AI can also keep the teacher in the loop as to what is going on, providing tips on how to better engage their students . . . the teacher can chat with the AI to understand how the students are interacting with each other . . . a teacher can have Khanmigo ask participants if they want to play a learning game together.[48]

Another instance is when users ask for a reference, a typical LLM might provide simply made-up links. Khanmigo addresses this challenge by cross-checking its output with Khan Academy's existing library of expert-developed content. It has also implemented moderation technology to detect inappropriate interactions and includes disclaimers about its limitations, reminding users not to input personal data.

The Khanmigo pilot project was launched in March 2023, initially involving over 400 participants and expanding to over 10,000 by July.[49] To students, Khanmigo offered personalized tutoring, helping them with math, science and humanities by guiding them through problems, generating practice questions and providing enrichment activities. Khanmigo helped teachers by creating lesson plans and practice tests and tracking student progress, serving as an automated assistant to reduce administrative workload. For Sal Khan himself, it represented 'educated bravery', the courage to face rapid technological advancements by understanding both the challenges and opportunities they present.[50] In May 2024, Khan Academy and Microsoft announced a partnership to provide US K-12 teachers free access to Khanmigo's AI tools, powered by Azure OpenAI, while also experimenting with Microsoft's Phi-3 'small language models' to scale affordable AI tutoring in math.[51]

The Khanmigo offering is illustrative of *co-intelligence* in action—a collaboration between human intelligence and a different kind of intelligence that is ChatGPT.[52] Educators, Ethan and Lilach Mollick, envisage seven roles such GenAI assistants can play: AI mentor, AI tutor, AI coach, AI teammate, AI student, AI simulator and AI tool.[53] AI mentors offer constructive feedback, guiding students to improve their work. As an AI tutor, it provides personalized instruction, helping students understand complex topics through tailored explanations. In the role of AI coach, it increases metacognition by encouraging students to reflect on their learning processes. As AI teammates, these models can enhance collaborative intelligence by presenting alternative viewpoints and supporting team dynamics. AI students enable peer teaching, where students can reinforce their understanding by explaining concepts to the AI. AI simulators create opportunities for practice, allowing students to apply their knowledge in simulated environments. Finally, AI tools assist students in accomplishing tasks more efficiently, extending their performance capabilities.

Khanmigo is an attempt to offer a Socratic method of learning at scale, which assumes a baseline of understanding that allows for deeper questioning, i.e., for a student to even 'know what they don't know'. In such instances, the AI system could do reverse prompt engineering, just like a human educator would do when a student is stuck. Most importantly, such reverse prompting can serve to develop and nurture lifelong learning ecosystems by equipping the next and future generations with the living-systems thinking, knowledge and skills they need to thrive in a co-intelligence world.

Navigating the Anthropocene

As the Co-Intelligence Revolution progresses, we are also witnessing the emergence of a new epoch, the *Anthropocene*, which, unlike past ones defined by natural forces, signifies an era where human activity has become the dominant influence on the planet. This influence is evident in everything from climate change and rising sea levels to widespread plastic pollution and mass extinctions to ubiquitous digital influence and the consequent e-waste. Unlike in previous eras, where human impact was relatively minor, co-intelligent enterprises in the Anthropocene must grapple with the reality that their actions significantly influence the very systems on which they rely. This necessitates a shift from a purely exploitative mindset to a more symbiotic one, the very essence of ecoAI literacy and NEST ecosystems.

A crucial question is the sustainability of AI systems. While it's clear that training AI models demands substantial energy due to the intensive computations involved in processing massive datasets, NVIDIA's Huang suggests that AI can be a powerful tool for enhancing energy efficiency and promoting sustainability. He points to the potential for situating AI centres near areas with surplus energy and leveraging renewable sources. Huang argues that AI can significantly improve energy efficiency—such as in weather and climate forecasting, where AI models can outperform supercomputers while using considerably less energy. Additionally, AI can optimize energy distribution by predicting and preventing grid failures, and it can assist in the discovery of new materials for sustainable energy solutions.[54] Microsoft's Nadella also underscores the importance of optimizing the 'performance per dollar per watt' of AI systems, believing that advances in hardware and software will drive exponential gains in cost-effectiveness and energy efficiency.[55]

Might Nextgen AI help us better navigate the Anthropocene, even as it threatens to upend humanity?

We conclude the book with a message—*Ad Astra per Aspera*, a timeless Latin maxim, which reminds us that the path to greatness is paved with challenges. It encapsulates the indomitable human spirit, urging us to reach for the stars.

Ad Astra

Imagine for a moment a grand cosmic timepiece, where each hour represents a staggering 10,000 years of human history. Our story, as Homo sapiens, began at 6 p.m. yesterday. For most of this journey, we tread the primordial path of hunter–gatherers, traversing the dark wilderness of the night, through the hopeful dawn and into the late evening the next day. At 11 p.m. today, our collective fate took an audacious turn. We embraced agriculture, the soil yielding to our dominion, allowing us to congregate in burgeoning communities, to erect cities and to forge intricate civilizations. Progress and innovation rushed forward, but with unforeseen challenges. As we approached 11:58:40 p.m., we entered the Industrial Revolution, where machines and technology cast aside the shackles of the past. The relentless gears of change propelled us into uncharted territory, into a modern age of industry and invention.

Then, at 11:59:36 p.m., artificial intelligence (AI) and digital technology made their grand entrance, a mere twenty-four seconds in the cosmic timescale that has transformed our world. This period also saw humans leave a pervasive and indelible signature on Earth—presence of manufactured materials in sediments, climate change, species extinctions, unsustainable resource extraction and so on—potentially creating a new epoch, that of the Anthropocene. We are the first advanced human society that has witnessed firsthand an epoch change that has stemmed from our own actions. Our present is now entangled with a Co-Intelligence Anthropocene, reshaping our reality and beckoning us into an uncertain future. As we near the second midnight of humanity, we stand at the brink of wonderment and worry. As our human saga unfolds, filled with uncharted realms, boundless potential and existential risks, what heights will we reach, what depths will we explore and will we even encounter another midnight?

Remember, the hands ticking the clock are ours. Welcome to the Co-Intelligence Revolution.

Key Concepts

Agentic AI: AI systems capable of autonomously executing specific action flows across applications and coordinating decisions proactively on behalf of users.

AI Factory: Advanced computational infrastructure that transforms data into 'tokens of intelligence' through deep learning and other AI techniques.

Co-Creative Living Organization (CCLO): A living-system organization enabling continuous learning and adaptation across interconnected ecosystems to co-create life–experiences of value.

Co-Intelligence: The creative synergy between human intelligence and machine intelligence, where AI augments and amplifies human capabilities through reciprocal interactions with *AI systems-in-the-loop-of-Humans* and *Humans-in-the-loop-of-AI systems*.

Co-Intelligence Architecture: A comprehensive framework enabling organizations to harness Human–AI interactive engagement for scalable value creation. It integrates systems, protocols, and platforms that facilitate co-creative synergy between humans and AI across interconnected organizational ecosystems.

Co-Intelligent Enterprise: An organization

- Harnessing Human–AI co-creation that leverages tokens of digital intelligence (TDIs) through a risk-managed PIEX lens and co-innovating with stakeholders to build ecosystems of capabilities.
- Designed as a *living-system* that continuously learns and adapts through *co-intelligence knowledge environments,* where TDIs act as modular units of actionable intelligence, enabling managers—viewed as creative-experiencers—to engage dynamically with Nextgen AI systems and co-creating risk-managed value across individuals, communities, functions and sectors.
- Co-evolving SWIs at speed, scale and scope *across private, public and plural sectors*, with TDIs dynamically orchestrating feedback loops that iteratively align actions with SWI goals and enhance systemic resilience.
- Cultivating 'EcoAI *literacy*' and *lifelong learning*, leveraging TDIs as actionable bridges to integrate Nextgen AI literacy with Ecoliteracy, addressing environmental and societal concerns ethically, thereby steering organizational ecosystems towards a harmonious world of human development and planetary wellbeing.

Co-Intelligence Knowledge Environment: A system that supports rapid knowledge creation and sharing across organizational ecosystems through Human–AI collaboration.

Creative-Experiencer: An individual (customer, employee, partner, etc.) who actively participates in co-creating value through interactive engagement rather than being a passive recipient.

Digital Twin: A virtual representation of physical assets, processes or systems that enables simulation, monitoring and optimization.

EcoAI Literacy: Understanding of how AI can be used to address environmental challenges ethically and foster sustainable systems, while recognizing interconnections between human society and nature.

Ecosystem Co-Innovation: Collaborative innovation across interconnected organizational ecosystems involving multiple stakeholders.

Generative AI (GenAI): AI systems capable of generating context-specific new content (text, images, code, etc.) and engaging in natural language interactions grounded in enterprise or domain contexts.

Human–AI Interactive Engagement: The dynamic interaction between humans and AI systems in co-creating value.

I2N2I Interactions: Individual-to-Networked AI-to-Individual flows of interactive engagements.

Life-Xverse: An interconnected realm of Nature, Society, Economy, and Technology (NEST) ecosystems across physical, digital, and virtual realities, dynamically fostering human and planetary wellbeing through co-intelligence flows and emergent life-experiences.

Lived-journey: The ongoing flow of life–experiences and engagements through which individuals derive value.

Management Ecosystem: The internal organizational systems, processes and capabilities that enable value creation.

NEST Ecosystems: Interconnected Nature–Society–Economy–Technology (NEST) ecosystems in which organizations operate and create impact.

Nextgen AI: The next generation of AI, spanning conventional analytical AI to Generative AI, Agentic AI, and Physical AI, incorporating evolving Neuro-Symbolic AI, Causal AI, and other advances in AI systems. It powers AI Factories producing Tokenized Digital Intelligence (TDIs) that drive real-time, adaptive intelligence outputs within co-intelligence ecosystems. Unlike past rule-based AI, Nextgen AI collaborates proactively with humans to enhance creativity, decision-making, and interactive experiences across digital, physical, and virtual realms.

N2I2N Interactions: Networked AI-to-Individual-to-Networked AI flows of interactive engagements.

Offering Ecosystem: The network of products, services and experience-environments an organization provides to customers.

Organizational Ecosystem: An interconnected system of platforms, interactive engagements, and environments through which an organization operates, comprising four interconnected ecosystem types: offering, value chain, management and NEST ecosystems.

PIEX Lens: An organizational lens comprising *P*latforms of *I*nteractive *E*ngagements driving *I*mpacts in *E*cosystems of life-e*X*periences.

Risk-Managed Value: Value created through co-intelligence (across individuals, communities, functions and sectors) while actively identifying and mitigating various forms of risk (technological, social, environmental, etc.).

Shared Digitalized Infrastructure (SDI): Technology platforms and capabilities that enable co-intelligence flows and support interconnected organizational ecosystems.

Sustainable Wellbeing Impacts (SWIs): Holistic impacts encompassing environmental, social, economic and human development outcomes that organizations aim to achieve.

Tokenized Digital Intelligence (TDI): A digital representation of knowledge, insights or actions created by AI systems. It is not a physical object but a modular and actionable unit that drives value in ecosystems by enabling adaptive, interactive, and personalized engagements.

Value-Chain Ecosystem: The network of activities, partners and resources involved in creating and delivering offerings of value.

Acknowledgements

We have benefited immensely from interactions with and insights from many individuals as co-creators. We owe a special debt to many who have given their time and energy, valuable perspectives, as well as their unstinted support over the years. In particular, we thank Kris Gopalakrishnan for his guidance and invaluable inputs; we would also like to recognize Jagadish Babu, P. Balasubramanian, N. Dayasindhu, Srilalitha Gopal, V. Kamakoti, Shankar Maruwada, N.R. Narayana Murthy, Nandan Nilekani, Sanjay Purohit, S. Sivakumar, Gopal Srinivasan, Subra Suresh and Pramod Varma. We also want to give a shout-out to Kulmeet Bawa, Naveen Chopra, André Ribeiro Coutinho, Vanessa Evers, Hagen Heubach, Karthik Jayaraman, Krishna Kumar, Ravi Pendse, Sapna Poti, Ramakrishna Srinivasan, Manish Srivastava, Rafee Tarafdar and Srividhya V.S., for their contributions to the book.

We are thankful to Manish Kumar, our editor, and Manali Das, our copy editor, and the entire team at Penguin Random House India for their wonderful support in making this book a reality. We also thank Vinith Kumar for his assistance with the design of the figures.

Venkat would like to especially thank Sharon Matusik, dean, Ross School of Business, and Roman Kapuscinski, senior associate dean for faculty and research, for the sabbatical and research support in writing this book. He also thanks Gretchen

Spreitzer, the Ross MAP Office of Action-based Learning and Ross Executive Education, for their continued support.

We also thank many people who have participated in the co-evolution of this book, from our students to faculty and colleagues (Ravi Anupindi, M.S. Krishnan, V.R. Muraleedharan, Kerimcan Ozcan, Amiyatosh Purnanandam, B. Ravindran, Ashley Roberts and P. Sudarsan). We are grateful to the support from itihaasa Research and Digital. Our heartfelt thanks go to everyone mentioned in this book and those we may have unintentionally omitted.

Notes

Preface

1 VR would like to thank Kirsten Sandberg, then editor at Harvard Business School Publishing, who had reached out to him on writing his first book, which she then helped as co-creator with the late C.K. Prahalad, in what became a bestselling book in several languages.
2 VR would like to thank Herb Schaffner and Emily Loose, then editor at Simon & Schuster Free Press, who helped shape his second book and market it internationally.
3 VR would like to thank Margo Beth Fleming, then editor at Stanford University Press, who helped in bringing to bear a scholarly yet practical third book expounding a new paradigm of co-creation.
4 VR would like to thank Subu Goparaju, then head of Infosys SET Labs, and Manjunatha Kukkuru, with whom he worked on Innovation Co-Creation.
5 KN would like to thank Manish Kumar, Penguin Random House India, and N. Maheshchandra, Indian Academy of Sciences, for their help in bringing out the books.

Chapter 1: Engaging with a New AI

1 Available at https://www.jugalbandi.ai/, accessed January 2024.

2   Available at Chen May Yee, 'With Help from Next-Generation AI, Indian Villagers Gain Easier Access to Government Services', Microsoft, 23 May 2023, https://news.microsoft. com/source/asia/features/with-help-from-next-generation-ai-indian-villagers-gain-easier-access-to-government-services/, accessed January 2024.

3   The demo involved coalition efforts between AI4Bharat, a research lab at IIT Madras working on developing open-source datasets, tools, models and applications for AI use cases in India; Bhashini, an Indian government mission to provide technology translation services in twenty-two scheduled Indian languages and OpenNyAI, a collaborative whose mission is to bring greater access to law and justice through AI. It was shown to Satya Nadella by Pratyush Kumar and team at AI4Bharat, affiliated with Microsoft Research India and now co-founder of startup Sarvam.ai (together with Vivek Raghavan and team, involved with OpenNyAI), with a developmental mission to democratize the impact of GenAI at population scale.

4   Available at Anna Tobin, 'Davos 23: Klaus Schwab in conversation with Satya Nadella, CEO of Microsoft', World Economic Forum, 10 September 2024, https://www. weforum.org/agenda/preview/8df5442d-17bb-49f7-a272-a8d86a69db5b/, accessed January 2024.

5   Available at Jordan Novet, 'Microsoft's $13 billion bet on OpenAI carries huge potential along with plenty of uncertainty', CNBC, 8 April 2023, https://www.cnbc.com/2023/04/08/ microsofts-complex-bet-on-openai-brings-potential-and-uncertainty.html, accessed February 2024.

6   Available at Satya Nadella, 'Annual Report 2023', Microsoft, April 2023, https://www.microsoft.com/investor/reports/ar23/ index.html, accessed February 2024.

7   Extracted from Satya Nadella's address, 'Microsoft Ignite 2024', Microsoft, 2024, https://news.microsoft.com/ ignite-2023/, accessed February 2024.

8   Available at Linda Lacina, 'Davos 2024: A conversation with Satya Nadella', World Economic Forum, 2024, https://www. weforum.org/podcasts/meet-the-leader/episodes/davos-2024-conversation-microsoft-satya-nadella/, accessed February 2024.

9 Extracted from the video: No Priors Ep. 13 | With Jensen Huang, Founder & CEO of Nvidia, No Priors: AI, Machine Learning, Tech, & Startups. https://www.youtube.com/watch?v=ZFtW3g1dbUU.

10 Extracted from Nvidia CEO Jensen Huang speech at GTC March 2024 Keynote. https://www.youtube.com/watch?v=Y2F8yisiS6E.

11 Available at 'NVIDIA CEO Delivers World's First AI Supercomputer in a Box to OpenAI', WebWire, 15 August 2016, https://www.webwire.com/ViewPressRel.asp?aId=204723, accessed March 2024.

12 Available at Jakob Uszkoreit, 'Transformer: A Novel Neural Network Architecture for Language Understanding', Google Research, 31 August 2017, https://blog.research.google/2017/08/transformer-novel-neural-network.html, accessed March 2024.

13 Charles Duhigg, 'The Optimists', *New Yorker*, 11 December 2023, Vol. 99, Issue 41, pp.28–39.

14 Available at Matt Hamblen, 'Update: ChatGPT runs 10K Nvidia training GPUs with potential for thousands more', FIERCE Electronics, 11 February 2023, https://www.fierceelectronics.com/sensors/chatgpt-runs-10k-nvidia-training-gpus-potential-thousands-more, which credits UBS research on ChatGPT, accessed March 2024.

15 Available at Bernard Marr, 'A Short History Of ChatGPT: How We Got To Where We Are Today', *Forbes*, 19 March 2023, https://www.forbes.com/sites/bernardmarr/2023/05/19/a-short-history-of-chatgpt-how-we-got-to-where-we-are-today/, accessed on 14 January 2024.

16 Available at Krystal Hu, 'ChatGPT sets record for fastest-growing user base – analyst note', *Reuters*, 2 February 2023, https://www.reuters.com/technology/chatgpt-sets-record-fastest-growing-user-base-analyst-note-2023-02-01/, accessed 14 January 2024.

17 https://www.msn.com/en-in/money/other/chatgpt-reaches-100-m-active-users-in-record-time-breaks-facebook-tiktok-s-record/ar-AA171wBP, accessed January 2024.

18 Available at Ministry of Agriculture & Farmers Welfare Press Release, https://pib.gov.in/PressReleasePage.aspx?PRID=1959461, accessed April 2024.

19 Available at 'Introducing the GPT Store', OpenAI, 10 January 2024, https://openai.com/blog/introducing-the-gpt-store, accessed January 2024.

20 Extracted and adapted from a Wall Street Journal podcast, available at Tim Higgins and Christopher Mims, 'Bold Names', Wall Street Journal, 2 February 2024, https://www.wsj.com/podcasts/wsj-the-future-of-everything, accessed March 2024.

21 Extracted from Nvidia CEO Jensen Huang speech at GTC March 2024 Keynote. https://www.youtube.com/watch?v=Y2F8yisiS6E.

22 Available at 'How Chinese AI Startup DeepSeek Made a Model that Rivals OpenAI', WIRED, https://www.wired.com/story/deepseek-china-model-ai/, accessed March 2025.

23 Available at 'DeepSeek Forces a Global Technology Reckoning', The New York Times, https://www.nytimes.com/2025/01/27/business/dealbook/deepseek-tech-stocks-reckoning.html, accessed March 2025.

24 Available at 'Chasing peak sugar: India's sugar cane farmers use AI to predict weather, fight pests and optimize harvests', https://news.microsoft.com/source/asia/features/chasing-peak-sugar-indias-sugar-cane-farmers-use-ai-to-predict-weather-fight-pests-and-optimize-harvests/, accessed March 2025.

25 Extracted from the video: Microsoft AI Tour keynote session by Satya Nadella | Bengaluru | January 7, 2025 | Microsoft India, https://www.youtube.com/watch?v=bYgP-tC5BFU&t=5s.

26 Klaus Schwab, *Shaping the Future of the Fourth Industrial Revolution* (New York: Currency, 2016).

27 Venkat Ramaswamy, 'Leading the experience ecosystem revolution - innovating offerings as interactive platforms', *Strategy & Leadership*, 48(3) (2020): 3–9.

28 M.E. Porter and J.E. Heppelmann, 'How Smart, Connected Products Are Transforming Competition', *Harvard Business Review*, 92(11) (2014): 11–64.

29 IDC Worldwide Black Book Live Edition (June 2023).

30 Marco Iansiti and Karim R. Lakhani, *Competing in the Age of AI: Strategy and Leadership When Algorithms and Networks*

Run the World (Boston, MA: Harvard Business Review Press, 2020).

31 Brynjolfsson, Erik, and Andrew McAfee. 2014. The Second Machine Age: Work, Progress, and Prosperity in a Time of Brilliant Technologies. New York: W.W. Norton & Company.

32 Tapscott, Don, and Alex Tapscott. 2016. Blockchain Revolution : How the Technology behind Bitcoin and Other Cryptocurrencies Is Changing the World. New York, New York: Portfolio/Penguin.

33 Available at Don Tapscott, 'Introducing the Trivergence: Transformation driven by blockchain, AI and the IoT', Magazine By Coin Telegraph, 29 December 2021, https://cointelegraph.com/magazine/introducing-trivergence-transformation-blockchain-ai-iot/, accessed February 2025.

34 Available at 'How COVID-19 has pushed companies over the technology tipping point—and transformed business forever', McKinsey, 5 October 2020, https://www.mckinsey.com/capabilities/strategy-and-corporate-finance/our-insights/how-covid-19-has-pushed-companies-over-the-technology-tipping-point-and-transformed-business-forever, accessed January 2024.

35 Available at 'Unlocking the Economic Impact of Digital Transformation in Asia Pacific and New Zealand', Microsoft, March 2018, https://news.microsoft.com/uploads/2018/03/Digital-Transformation-New-Zealand-presentation-.pdf, accessed January 2024.

36 Extracted from 'Microsoft Ignite: Satya Nadella', Microsoft, 22 September 2020, https://news.microsoft.com/wp-content/uploads/prod/prod/2020/09/09222020-Ignite-Satya-Nadella.pdf, accessed April 2024.

37 Available at 'The Intelligence Age', 23 September 2024, https://ia.samaltman.com/, accessed September 2024.

38 Extracted from Nvidia CEO Jensen Huang speech at GTC March 2024 Keynote. https://www.youtube.com/watch?v=Y2F8yisiS6E

39 Available at 'Market capitalization of NVIDIA (NVDA)', Companies Market Cap, https://companiesmarketcap.com/Nvidia/marketcap/, accessed November 2024.

40 Available at Juan David Campolargo, 'The $100 Trillion AI Industrial Revolution by NVIDIA's Jensen Huang', YouTube video, 13 June 2024, https://youtu.be/e5Zol4RYq2o?si=PIhYJR-d9PLCU3NS, accessed February 2025.

41 Available at Cliff Edwards, 'AI-Fueled Productivity: Generative AI Opens New Era of Efficiency Across Industries', NVIDIA, 13 July 2023, https://resources.nvidia.com/en-us-generative-ai-nurture-101/industry-blogs?ncid=em-nurt-150016&mkt_tok=MTU2LU9GTi03NDIAAAGWY2_sv4oIf40F1a-leK5e0CmvksFz2X1s3GTcbIq8GzX4KluChQTGoopQmuApT2HAjAO3ZwOjRQyEO4xnEET3g00eYE710laovAgI5v1A-RsxrRvGeK4&xs=555838, accessed February 2025.

42 In conversation with the authors.

43 Available at https://brainportal.humanbrain.in/publicview/index.html, accessed Feb 2025.

44 Available at Sindhu Hariharan, 'IIT-Madras' brain research work finds a mention in Nvidia GTC', *The Hindu Businessline*, 21 March 2024, https://www.thehindubusinessline.com/news/science/iit-madras-brain-research-work-finds-a-mention-in-Nvidia-gtc/article67975061.ece, accessed June 2024.

45 Available at Dr Nathan Baker, 'Unlocking a new era for scientific discovery with AI: How Microsoft's AI screened over 32 million candidates to find a better battery', Microsoft, 9 January 2024, https://cloudblogs.microsoft.com/quantum/2024/01/09/unlocking-a-new-era-for-scientific-discovery-with-ai-how-microsofts-ai-screened-over-32-million-candidates-to-find-a-better-battery/, accessed June 2024.

46 Extracted from YouTube video - The Future of AI: Leaders from TikTok, Google & More Weigh In (FII Panel) | EP #127, Peter H. Diamandis, accessed November 2024.

47 Available at 'AlphaFold', Google DeepMind, https://deepmind.google/technologies/alphafold/, accessed January 2024.

48 Available at 'Demis Hassabis Interview', The Nobel Prize, October 2024, https://www.nobelprize.org/prizes/chemistry/2024/hassabis/interview/, accessed October 2024.

49 Extracted from the video: Google DeepMind CEO: We Want To Build A Virtual Cell | Alex Kantrowitz, https://www.youtube.com/watch?v=CEOOMYxMvY4&t=7s.

50 Extracted from the video: Meet OpenEvidence, the 'ChatGPT' for verified doctors | CNBC Television, https://www.youtube.com/watch?v=FIWQ5yIPWto&t=673s.

51 Extracted from video, Nvidia's Jensen Huang speaks to Mukesh Ambani on AI reshaping industries, India's rise as AI leader, Moneycontrol, https://www.youtube.com/watch?v=uNkSfBI2vS8.

52 Available at Tom Simonite, 'Nvidia CEO: Software Is Eating the World, but AI Is Going to Eat Software', MIT Technology Review, 12 May 2017, https://www.technologyreview.com/2017/05/12/151722/Nvidia-ceo-software-is-eating-the-world-but-ai-is-going-to-eat-software/, accessed January 2024.

53 Ibid.

54 Extracted from the video: Keynote by Antonio Neri: Intelligence has no limits - HPE Discover Las Vegas 2024, HPE. https://www.youtube.com/watch?v=p28lHtjWn5k.

55 Available at Sean Kinney, 'Michael Dell on AI factories and the information revolution', RCRWirelessNews, 20 May 2024, https://www.rcrwireless.com/20240520/ai-ml/michael-dell-on-ai-factories-and-the-information-revolution#:~:text="Put%20all%20that%20together%20and,a%20lot%20of%20repeatable%20things., accessed February 2024.

56 Available at Naandika Tripathi, 'The inner workings of Asia's largest data centre, in Navi Mumbai', *Forbes* India, 8 May 2024, https://www.forbesindia.com/video/video/the-inner-workings-of-asias-largest-data-centre-in-navi-mumbai/92881

57 Available at 'Reliance And NVIDIA Partner To Advance AI In India, For India', NVIDIA, 8 September 2023, https://investor.nvidia.com/news/press-release-details/2023/Reliance-and-NVIDIA-Partner-to-Advance-AI-in-India-for-India/default.aspx, accessed November 2024.

58 Available at 'Denmark launches first supercomputer', The *Copenhagen Post*, 23 October 2024, https://cphpost.dk/2024-10-25/news/technology/denmark-launches-first-ai-supercomputer/., accessed February 2024.

59 Ibid.

60 Extracted from video: Jensen Huang Special Address from NVIDIA AI Summit Japan, NVIDIA, November 2024. https://www.youtube.com/watch?v=x8O6ChAWBxs.

61 Anil Ananthaswamy, *Why Machines Learn* (Penguin, 2024).

62 Available at 'What is generative AI?', McKinsey & Company, 2 April 2024, https://www.mckinsey.com/featured-insights/mckinsey-explainers/what-is-generative-ai, accessed May 2024.

63 Extracted from video: Jensen Huang Special Address from NVIDIA AI Summit Japan, NVIDIA, November 2024. https://www.youtube.com/watch?v=x8O6ChAWBxs.

64 Available at 'Gen AI: a cognitive industrial revolution', McKinsey Digital, 7 June 2024, https://www.mckinsey.com/capabilities/mckinsey-digital/our-insights/gen-ai-a-cognitive-industrial-revolution, accessed Februarty 2024.

65 Extracted from the video: A conversation with Nvidia's Jensen Huang, Stripe, 2024. https://www.youtube.com/watch?v=8Pfa8kPjUio.

66 Available at 'Accenture and NVIDIA Lead Enterprises into Era of AI', https://newsroom.accenture.com/news/2024/accenture-and-nvidia-lead-enterprises-into-era-of-ai, accessed March 2025.

67 Available at 'DeepMind co-founder: Everyone will have their 'own chief of staff' in the next five years', CNBC, 5 September 2023, https://www.cnbc.com/video/2023/09/05/deepmind-co-founder-everyone-will-have-their-own-chief-of-staff-in-the-next-five-years.html, accessed June 2024.

68 Available at M. Javaheripi, S. Bubeck et al., 'Phi-2: The surprising power of small language models', Microsoft, 12 December 2023, https://www.microsoft.com/en-us/research/blog/phi-2-the-surprising-power-of-small-language-models/, accessed February 2025.

69 Available at T. Schick and H. Schütze, 'It's Not Just Size That Matters: Small Language Models Are Also Few-Shot Learners', ACL Anthology, 1 June 2021, https://doi.org/10.18653/v1/2021.naacl-main.185, accessed February 2025.

70 Available at Harshjit Sethi and Vedant Trivedi, 'Sarvam's Mission to Build a UPI for AI', Peak XV Partners, 7 December

2023, https://www.peakxv.com/article/sarvams-mission-to-build-a-upi-for-ai/, accessed May 2024.

71 Available at https://www.sarvam.ai/blog/announcing-openhathi-series, accessed May 2024.

72 Available at Reuters, 'Nvidia Rolls Out Hindi-Language AI Model In India As CEO Huang Visits', NDTV, 24 October 2024, https://www.ndtv.com/india-ai/nvidia-rolls-out-hindi-language-ai-model-in-india-as-ceo-huang-visits-6862091#pfrom=home-ndtv_india_ai, accessed February 2025.

73 Available at 'Introducing Sarvam-2B, X, 13 August 2024, https://x.com/SarvamAI/status/1823300273118351688, accessed August 2024.

74 Available at Manish Singh, 'Why this AI startup is betting on voice-enabled bots to scale AI adoption in India', Yahoo! News, 13 August 2024, https://au.news.yahoo.com/why-ai-startup-betting-voice-111952947.html, accessed August 2024.

75 Available at https://www.sarvam.ai/blog/announcing-openhathi-series, accessed May 2024.

76 Available at 'Mapping the Mind of a Large Language Model', Anthropic, 21 May 2024, https://www.anthropic.com/news/mapping-mind-language-model, accessed July 2024.

77 For a discussion of category theory in machinic ecosystems, see Kerimcan Ozcan and Venkat Ramaswamy, *Dynamic Relationality Theory: Grounding Machinic Ecosystems in Life Experiences* (Elsevier, 2024).

78 Available at Brian Caulfield, 'GTC Wrap-Up: 'We Created a Processor for the Generative AI Era,' NVIDIA CEO Says,' NVIDIA, 18 March 2024, https://blogs.Nvidia.com/blog/2024-gtc-keynote/, accessed May 2024.

79 Extracted from the video: No Priors Ep. 13 | With Jensen Huang, Founder & CEO of Nvidia, No Priors: AI, Machine Learning, Tech, & Startups. https://www.youtube.com/watch?v=ZFtW3g1dbUU.

80 Extracted from the video: NVIDIA CEO Jensen Huang's Vision for the Future | Cleo Abram https://www.youtube.com/watch?v=7ARBJQn6QkM.

81 Pearl, J., & Mackenzie, D. (2018). *The book of why: the new science of cause and effect.* New York, Basic Books.

82 Extracted from Ark Invest, 'An Artificial Intelligence Conversation With Andrew Ng', YouTube video, 8 August 2024, https://www.youtube.com/watch?v=8lH1mUcxODw, accessed February 2025.

83 See also Daugherty, Paul R., and H. James Wilson (2018), *Human + Machine: Reimagining Work in the Age of AI* (Harvard Business Review Press).

84 Hoffman, Reid, and Greg Beato. 2025. *Superagency.* Simon and Schuster. https://www.superagency.ai.

Chapter 2: Into the Life-Xverse with Co-Intelligence

1   For a discussion of the 'plural' sector, in contrast to the private and public sectors, see Henry Mintzberg, 'It's Time for the Plural Sector', *Stanford Social Innovation Review*, 2015.

2   Available at 'CES 2024: Siemens delivers innovations in immersive engineering and artificial intelligence to enable the industrial metaverse', Siemens, 8 January 2024, https://press.siemens.com/global/en/pressrelease/ces-2024-siemens-delivers-innovations-immersive-engineering-and-artificial, accessed March 2024.

3   Extracted from Roland Busch, 'Siemen's Keynote', CES, 8 January 2024, https://videos.ces.tech/detail/videos/ces-keynotes/video/6344520939112/siemens-keynote, accessed April 2024.

4   Available at 'CES 2024: Siemens delivers innovations in immersive engineering and artificial intelligence to enable the industrial metaverse', Siemens, 8 January 2024, https://press.siemens.com/global/en/pressrelease/ces-2024-siemens-delivers-innovations-immersive-engineering-and-artificial, accessed April 2024.

5   Available at 'Alliance for OpenUSD Launches Materials & Geometry Working Groups, Forms New Liaison Relationship', AOUSD, 11 March 2024, https://aousd.org/news/alliance-for-openusd-introduces-new-working-groups-and-liaison/, accessed April 2024.

6   Extracted from the video: Siemens Launches AI and Ecommerce with Einstein 1 | Salesforce, Salesforce. https://www.youtube.com/watch?v=y2jyhwFd2VY.

7   Available at 'Siemens and AWS join forces to democratize generative AI in software development', Siemens, 8 January 2024, https://press.siemens.com/global/en/pressrelease/siemens-and-aws-join-forces-democratize-generative-ai, accessed April 2024.

8   Extracted from the video: Report by CEO Roland Busch at the Annual General Meeting 2024, Siemens, February 2024. https://www.youtube.com/watch?v=W2dQupQFv_U.

9   Available at 'Unlocking the Power of Generative AI: Siemens Industrial Copilot', Siemens, https://www.siemens.com/global/en/company/insights/unlocking-the-power-of-generative-ai-siemens-industrial-copilot.html, accessed April 2024.

10 Extracted from Roland Busch, 'Siemen's Keynote', CES, 8 January 2024, https://videos.ces.tech/detail/videos/ces-keynotes/video/6344520939112/siemens-keynote, accessed April 2024.

11 Extracted from the video: Report by CEO Roland Busch at the Annual General Meeting 2024, Siemens, February 2024. https://www.youtube.com/watch?v=W2dQupQFv_U.

12 Available at 'Digital simulations open up real-world possibilities', MIT Technology Review, 4 April 2023, https://www.technologyreview.com/2023/04/04/1070684/digital-simulations-open-up-real-world-possibilities/, accessed April 2024.

13 As of March 2025, Apple announced that the release of its more personalized Siri features will be delayed until 2026.

14 Available at 'Introducing Apple Intelligence, the personal intelligence system that puts powerful generative models at the core of iPhone, iPad, and Mac', Apple, 10 June 2024, https://www.apple.com/in/newsroom/2024/06/introducing-apple-intelligence-for-iphone-ipad-and-mac/, accessed August 2024.

15 Available at Salvador Rodriguez, 'Apple, Meta Have Discussed an AI Partnership', The *Wall Street Journal*, 23 June 2024, https://www.wsj.com/tech/ai/apple-meta-have-discussed-an-ai-partnership-cc57437e, accessed July 2024.

16 Available at 'Introducing Apple Vision Pro: Apple's first spatial computer', Apple, 5 June 2023, https://www.apple.com/newsroom/2023/06/introducing-apple-vision-pro/, accessed May 2024.

17 Available at https://www.msn.com/en-us/money/other/tim-cooks-aha-moment-with-apples-vision-pro-you-only-have-a-few-of-those-in-a-lifetime/ar-AA1hz2KM, accessed May 2024.

18 Available at https://ted2sub.org/talks/fei_fei_li_with_spatial_intelligence_ai_will_understand_the_real_world, accessed Mar 2025.

19 W. Saad, M. Bennis and M. Chen, 'A Vision of 6G Wireless Systems: Applications, Trends, Technologies, and Open Research Problems,' in *IEEE Network*, vol. 34, no. 3, pp. 134–142, May/June 2020, doi:10.1109/MNET.001.1900287.

20 Extracted from 'L'Oréal at CES® 2024', L'Oréal, January 2024, https://www.loreal.com/en/news/research-innovation/ces/, accessed January 2024.

21 Ibid.

22 Ibid.

23 Available at Sara Castellanos, 'L'Oréal Applies Digital Makeover to Sales Efforts', The Wall Street Journal, 10 November 2020, https://www.wsj.com/articles/loreal-applies-digital-makeover-to-sales-efforts-11605046234, accessed April 2024.

24 Available at 'L'Oréal unveils Perso, an AI-powered at-home system for skincare and cosmetics', L'Oréal, https://www.loreal.com/en/usa/news/science-and-technology/loreal-unveils-perso-an-aipowered-athome-system-for-skincare-and-cosmetics/, accessed April 2024.

25 Available at 'Beauty augmented by technology', 2022 Annual Report, L'Oréal Finance, https://www.loreal-finance.com/en/annual-report-2022/beauty-augmented-by-technology/, accessed April 2024.

26 Available at Ralf W. Seifert and Richard Markoff, 'L'Oréal: the beauty of supply chain digitization,' IMD, 13 July 2022, https://www.imd.org/ibyimd/innovation/loreal-the-beauty-of-supply-chain-digitalization/, accessed April 2024.

27 Extracted from Asmita Dubey, 'Augmented Marketing in Beauty with Generative AI', NVIDIA, March 2024, https://www.Nvidia.com/en-us/on-demand/session/gtc24-s62335/, accessed April 2024.

28 Available at 'Beauty augmented by technology', 2022 Annual Report, L'Oréal Finance, https://www.loreal-finance.com/en/annual-report-2022/beauty-augmented-by-technology/, accessed April 2024.

29 Available at 'L'Oréal creates unique beauty experiences with a data-driven approach', Salesforce, https://www.salesforce.com/resources/customer-stories/loreal-data-unique-beauty-experiences/, accessed April 2024.

30 Available at https://mediacenter.ibm.com/id/1_21xmh24k.

31 Available at 'Our Strategy: Universalization', L'Oréal, https://www.loreal.com/en/group/about-loreal/strategy-and-model/, accessed April 2024.

32 Available in 'Barbara Lavernos Appointed President Research, Innovation and Technologies', L'Oréal, https://www.loreal.com/en/news/group/barbara-lavernos-appointed-president-research-innovation-and-technologies/, accessed April 2024.

33 Available at 'L'Oréal Unveils New Research & Innovation Center In India', L'Oréal, 10 January 2013, https://www.loreal.com/en/press-release/research-and-innovation/loral-unveils-new-research--innovation-center-in-india/, accessed July 2024.

34 Available at Nell Lewis and Jenny Mark, 'Want to work for L'Oreal? Get ready to chat with an AI bot', CNN, 29 April 2019, https://edition.cnn.com/2019/04/29/tech/ai-recruitment-loreal/index.html, accessed July 2024.

35 Available at 'Niilesh Bhoite', LinkedIn, https://www.linkedin.com/posts/niileshsbhoite_leadership-culture-weareloreal-activity-6960453203683340289-sXD0/, accessed February 2025.

36 Extracted from the video: Transforming Talent Acquisition with AI—L'Oréal Case Study, PeopleMattersOnline.

37 Available at Austyn King, 'L'Oréal reveals AI chatbot with Mya Systems to help job candidates', Cosmetics Business, 25

October 2018, https://cosmeticsbusiness.com/l-or-al-reveals-ai-chatbot-with-mya-systems-to-help-job-candidates-148408, accessed February 2025.

38 Available at 'L'Oréal to Acquire Gjosa', L'Oréal, 9 January 2024, https://www.loreal.com/en/press-release/research-and-innovation/loreal-to-acquire-gjosa/, accessed April 2024.

39 Available at 'Social & environmental performance', 2023 Annual Report, L'Oréal https://www.loreal-finance.com/en/annual-report-2023/social-environmental-performance/, accessed February 2025.

40 Available at https://newsroom.ibm.com/2025-01-16-ibm-and-loreal-to-build-first-ai-model-to-advance-the-creation-of-sustainable-cosmetics.

41 See Kerimcan Ozcan and Venkat Ramaswamy, *Dynamic Relationality Theory: Grounding Machinic Ecosystems in Life Experiences* (Elsevier, 2024).

Chapter 3: Crafting and Leveraging Co-Intelligence Architectures

1 Available at 'Evolving the Databricks Brand', Databricks, 28 April 2020, https://www.databricks.com/blog/2020/04/29/evolving-the-databricks-brand.html, accessed August 2024.

2 Available at 'Data Intelligence Platforms', Databricks, 15 November 2023, https://www.databricks.com/blog/what-is-a-data-intelligence-platform, accessed August 2024.

3 Available at 'Introducing LakehouseIQ: The AI-Powered Engine that Uniquely Understands Your Business', Databricks, 27 June 2023, https://www.databricks.com/blog/introducing-lakehouseiq-ai-powered-engine-uniquely-understands-your-business, accessed August 2024.

4 Available at 'Accelerating Innovation at Jetblue Using Databricks', Databricks, 22 June 2023, https://www.databricks.com/blog/accelerating-innovation-jetblue-using-databricks, accessed August 2024.

5 Available at 'Fostering financial resilience through hyper-personalization', Databricks, https://www.databricks.com/customers/discovery-bank, accessed August 2024.

6 Available at HubSpot, 'Meet Breeze | INBOUND 2024', YouTube video, 23 September 2024, https://www.youtube.com/watch?v=QP0SHDV_7Ts&t=1242s, accessed February 2025.

7 Available at INBOUND, 'Easy, Fast, Unified Growth With Yamini Rangan | INBOUND 2024, YouTube video, 19 September 2024, https://www.youtube.com/watch?v=zbjqjm7Whn8&t=1467s, accessed February 2025.

8 Available at 'Marc Benioff's 2024 Letter to Stakeholders', Salesforce, 29 April, 2024, https://www.salesforce.com/in/news/2024-letter-to-stakeholders/, accessed July 2024.

9 Extracted from the video: Salesforce CEO Marc Benioff goes one-on-one with Jim Cramer, CNBC Television, August 2024. https://www.youtube.com/watch?v=zBacegvXVPw.

10 Available at Susan Galer, 'SAP CEO Christian Klein: Revolutionizing the Next 50 Years of Intelligent Sustainable Innovation, SAP, 11 May 2022, https://news.sap.com/2022/05/sap-sapphire-keynote-intelligent-sustainable-innovation/, accessed July 2024.

11 Available at Trung Van Tran, 'What is SAP Joule?', SAP Blog, https://blog.sap-press.com/what-is-sap-joule, accessed July 2024.

12 Available at 'SAP Announces New Generative AI Assistant Joule', SAP, 26 September 2023, https://news.sap.com/2023/09/joule-new-generative-ai-assistant/, accessed July 2024.

13 Extracted from the video: SAP Sapphire Opening Keynote: Bring Out the Best in Your Business | 2024, SAP. https://www.youtube.com/watch?v=gOVQhhm5yO0.

14 Extracted from the video: SAP Sapphire Innovation Keynote: The key to bringing out your best | 2024, SAP. https://www.youtube.com/live/4DP4RpPRlhQ.

15 Available at 'Databricks Announces Launch of SAP Databricks', https://www.databricks.com/company/newsroom/press-releases/databricks-announces-launch-sap-databricks, accessed March 2025.

16 Available at 'SAP and Databricks Open a Bold New Era of Data and AI', https://news.sap.com/2025/02/sap-databricks-open-bold-new-era-data-ai/, accessed March 2025.

17 Available at Julia White, 'SAP Cloud for Sustainable Enterprises: Taking Action Together', SAP, 11 January 2022, https://news. sap.com/2022/01/sap-cloud-for-sustainable-enterprises-take-action-together/, accessed July 2024.

18 Available at 'SAP India and Amul—Transforming Lives of 1.5 Million Indians, SAP, 5 April 2022, https://news.sap. com/india/2022/04/amul-sap-partnership/, accessed July 2024.

19 Extracted from the video: Google Cloud Next '24 Opening Keynote, Google Cloud. https://www.youtube.com/ watch?v=V6DJYGn2SFk.

20 Available at Sundar Pichai, 'Google I/O 2024: An I/O for a new generation', Google Blog, 14 May 2024, https://blog. google/intl/en-in/company-news/google-io-2024-keynote-sundar-pichai/#ai-agents, accessed July 2024.

21 'Vendor Rating: Amazon', Gartner, May 2022, https://www. gartner.com/document/4014709, accessed July 2024.

22 Extracted from the Video: Larry Ellison Keynote on Oracle's Vision and Strategy: Oracle CloudWorld 2024, Oracle, September 2024. https://www.youtube.com/ watch?v=1Nn8ADoWbKk.

23 Available at Bob Evans, 'Larry Ellison's Revolution: Every Customer 'Could Have Full Oracle Cloud in Their Data Center', Cloud Wars, 9 September 2024, https://accelerationeconomy. com/cloud-wars/larry-ellisons-revolution-every-customer-could-have-full-oracle-cloud-in-their-data-center/, accessed September 2024.

24 Extracted from video: Oracle's vision for the future—Larry Ellison keynote | Oracle CloudWorld 2023, Oracle, September 2023. https://www.youtube.com/watch?v=63DmgBN1rSI.

25 Available at Mark Zuckerberg, 'Open Source AI is the Path Forward', Meta, 23 July 2024, https://about.fb.com/ news/2024/07/open-source-ai-is-the-path-forward/, accessed August 2024.

26 Ibid.

27 Available at 'Transcript for Yann Lecun: Meta AI, Open Source, Limits of LLMs, AGI & the Future of AI | Lex Fridman

Podcast #416', Lex Fridman, https://lexfridman.com/yann-lecun-3-transcript, accessed August 2024.

28 Available at Satya Nadella, 'Annual Report 2023', Microsoft, https://www.microsoft.com/investor/reports/ar23/index.html, accessed August 2024.

29 Available at Stephen J. Dubner, 'Satya Nadella's Intelligence Is Not Artificial, Freakonomics, 21 June 2023, https://freakonomics.com/podcast/satya-nadellas-intelligence-is-not-artificial/, accessed February 2024.

30 Charles Duhigg, 'The Optimists', *New Yorker*, 11 December 2023, vol. 99 Issue 41, pp. 28–39.

31 Available at Shuyin Zhao, 'GitHub Copilot now has a better AI model and new capabilities', GitHub Blog, 14 February 2023, https://github.blog/2023-02-14-github-copilot-now-has-a-better-ai-model-and-new-capabilities/, accessed February 2024.

32 Available at 'Duolingo empowers its engineers to be force multipliers for expertise with GitHub Copilot', GitHub, https://github.com/customer-stories/duolingo, accessed February 2024.

33 Available at Yusuf Mehdi, 'Delivering Copilot for everyone', Microsoft Blog, 7 February 2024, https://blogs.microsoft.com/blog/2024/02/07/delivering-copilot-for-everyone/, accessed February 2024.

34 Available at Nilay Patel, 'Microsoft thinks AI can beat Google at search—CEO Satya Nadella explains why', The Verge, 8 February 2023, https://www.theverge.com/23589994/microsoft-ceo-satya-nadella-bing-chatgpt-google-search-ai, accessed February 2024.

35 Available at Jennifer Langston, 'From conversation to code: Microsoft introduces its first product features powered by GPT-3', Microsoft Blog, 25 May 2021, https://blogs.microsoft.com/ai/from-conversation-to-code-microsoft-introduces-its-first-product-features-powered-by-gpt-3/.

36 Available at John Roach, 'Microsoft outlines framework for building AI apps and copilots; expands AI plugin ecosystem', Microsoft, 23 May 2023, https://news.microsoft.com/source/features/ai/microsoft-outlines-framework-for-building-ai-

apps-and-copilots-expands-ai-plugin-ecosystem/,   accessed April 2024.

37 Available at Charles Lamanna, 'Unlocking autonomous agent capabilities with Microsoft Copilot Studio', Microsoft, 21 October 2024, https://www.microsoft.com/en-us/microsoft-copilot/blog/copilot-studio/unlocking-autonomous-agent-capabilities-with-microsoft-copilot-studio/, accessed February 2025.

38 Available at Microsoft, 'Satya Nadella AI Tour Keynote: London', YouTube video, 21 October 2024, https://www.youtube.com/watch?v=kOkDTvsUuWA&t=2s,   accessed February 2025.

39 Available at Stephen Levy, 'Microsoft's Satya Nadella Is Betting Everything on AI', *WIRED*, 13 July 2023, https://www.wired.com/story/microsofts-satya-nadella-is-betting-everything-on-ai/, accessed February 2024.

40 Available at Chen May Yee, 'India's schoolteachers are drafting better lesson plans faster, thanks to a copilot', Microsoft, 8 Beruary 2024, https://news.microsoft.com/source/asia/features/indias-schoolteachers-are-drafting-better-lesson-plans-faster-thanks-to-a-copilot/, accessed February 2024.

41 Available at PTI, 'India leapfrogged 40 yrs of development with DPI: G20 Sherpa Amitabh Kant', The *Economic Times*, 14 February 2023, https://economictimes.indiatimes.com/news/india/india-leapfrogged-40-yrs-of-development-with-dpi-g20-sherpa-amitabh-kant/articleshow/97925277.cms, accessed June 2024.

42 Krishnan Narayanan and Venkat Ramaswamy, 'Becoming a Co-Creative Living Enterprise in the Life X-verse', itihaasa Research and Digital report, December 2022, https://itihaasa.com/public/pdf/Becoming_a_Co_Creative_Living_Enterprise_in_the_X-verse_dec_2022_final.pdf, accessed January 2024.

43 Available at Rekha Gupta Menon, 'India's digital payments market looks beyond its borders', *The Banker*, 24 August 2023, https://www.thebanker.com/India-s-digital-payments-market-looks-beyond-its-borders-1692889695#:~:text=India%20accounts%20for%20nearly%2040,estimates%20from%20the%20Indian%20government, accessed March 2024.

44 In conversation with the authors.

45 Available at Dhirendra Kumar, 'India's startup growth to pave way to developed nation by 2047: PM Modi', *Mint*, 20 March 2024, https://www.livemint.com/news/india/indias-startup-growth-to-pave-way-to-developed-nation-by-2047-pm-modi-11710919187559.html#, accessed March 2024.

46 Available at MyGov, https://static.mygov.in/archive/8years/index.html, accessed January 2024.

47 Kris Gopalakrishnan, N. Dayasindhu and Krishnan Narayanan, *Against All Odds—The IT Story of India* (India: Penguin Random House, 2022).

48 Available at 'DPI reshaping India into "one mega economy": Nilekani', *Fortune*, 27 August 2023, https://www.fortuneindia.com/macro/dpi-reshaping-india-into-one-mega-economy-nilekani/113869, accessed May 2024.

49 Available at 'Report of India's G20 Task Force on Digital Public Infrastructure', PIB, 15 July 2024, https://www.pib.gov.in/PressReleaseIframePage.aspx?PRID=2033389, accessed July 2024.

50 Ibid.

51 Available at Sunainaa Chadha, 'At 48 billion, India accounts for largest number of real-time transactions in the world', *The Times of India*, 25 April 2022, https://timesofindia.indiatimes.com/business/india-business/exclusive-at-48-billion-india-accounts-for-largest-number-of-real-time-transactions-in-the-world/articleshow/91070124.cms, accessed March 2024.

52 Available at 'Report of India's G20 Task Force on Digital Public Infrastructure', RBI, 2 September 2024, https://rbi.org.in/scripts/BS_SpeechesView.aspx?Id=1460, accessed September 2024.

53 Available at https://openkochi.net/journey/, accessed February 2024.

54 Available at Aryaman Gupta, 'Ride-hailing app Namma Yatri begins operations in Chennai, plans expansion', *Business Standard*, 29 January 2024, https://www.business-standard.

com/companies/news/ride-hailing-app-namma-yatri-begins-operations-in-chennai-plans-expansion-124012900805_1. html, accessed February 2024.

55 Available at 'Hyderabad gets own homegrown ride-hailing app Yaary on ONDC', *The Economic Times*, 18 December 2023, https://economictimes.indiatimes.com/tech/ technology/hyderabad-gets-own-homegrown-ride-hailing-app-yaary-on-ondc/articleshow/106097776.cms, accessed February 2023.

56 Extracted from Moneycontrol, 'Live: Infosys Chairman Nandan Nilekani In Conversation With Uber CEO Dara Khosrowshahi', YouTube video, 22 February 2024, Available at https://www.youtube.com/watch?v=WulqSdCMj2w, accessed May 2024.

57 Ibid.

58 Available at 'Sustainable Development Goals Progress Chart 2023', UN Stats, https://unstats.un.org/sdgs/report/2023/ progress-chart/, accessed June 2024.

59 Available at https://www.undp.org/publications/accelerating-sdgs-through-digital-public-infrastructure-compendium-potential-digital-public-infrastructure, accessed June 2024.

60 Eaves, D., Rao, K., Pagliarini, G., & Vera, K. (2024). 'Global State of DPI', DPI Map. https://dpimap.org.

61 Bria/Timmers/Gernone (2025): EuroStack – A European Alternative for Digital Sovereignty. Bertelsmann Stiftung. Gütersloh. DOI 10.11586/2025006.

62 Agustín Carstens and Nandan Nilekani, 'Finternet: the financial system for the future', BIS, April 2024, https://www. bis.org/publ/work1178.pdf, accessed February 2025.

63 Extracted from the video: LIVE | Global Fintech Fest | Finternet: Transforming Financial Services Through Digital Innovation, CNBC-TV18, August 2024. https://www.youtube.com/ watch?v=kh0ba77r9nQ.

64 Available at Agustín Carstens and Nandan Nilekani, 'Finternet: the financial system for the future', BIS, April 2024, https://www.bis.org/publ/work1178.htm, accessed February 2025.

65 Michael E. Porter and James E. Heppelmann, 'How Smart, Connected Products Are Transforming Competition', *Harvard Business Review*, November 2014.

66 Shubham Singhal et al., 'The next wave of healthcare innovation: The evolution of ecosystems', McKinsey & Company, June 2020.

67 E. Schaeffer and D. Sovie, *Reinventing the Product* (Kogan Page Publishers, 2019).

68 See Van Alstyne, Marshall W., Geoffrey G. Parker and Sangeet Paul Choudary, 'Pipelines, Platforms, and the New Rules of Strategy', *Harvard Business Review*, April 2016.

69 Vijay Govindarajan and Venkat Venkatraman, 'The Next Great Digital Advantage', *Harvard Business Review* (May–June 2022), https://hbr.org/2022/05/the-next-great-digital-advantage, accessed February 2024.

70 Available at 'Our Microsoft Sustainability Journey,, Microsoft, https://www.microsoft.com/en-us/corporate-responsibility/sustainability-journey#:~:text=We're%20committed%20to%20being,we%20were%20founded%20in%201975, accessed February 2025.

Chapter 4: The PIEX Lens: Visualizing and Expanding Human–AI Co-Creation of Value

1 Kerimcan Ozcan and Venkat Ramaswamy, Dynamic Relationality Theory of Creative Transformation: Grounding Machinic Ecosystems in Life Experiences (Elsevier, 2024).

2 See 'The ecosystem playbook: Winning in a world of ecosystems', McKinsey & Company, April 2019.

3 C.K. Prahalad and Venkat Ramaswamy, The Future of Competition: Co-Creating Unique Value with Customers (Cambridge, MA: Harvard Business School Press, 2004).

4 See Venkat Ramaswamy and Kerimcan Ozcan, The Co-Creation Paradigm (California: Stanford University Press, 2014).

5 Available at 'Driving Farm Profitability and Planet Sustainabilty', Monarch Tractor, https://www.monarchtractor.com/, accessed February 2024.

6   Available at 'Monarch Tractor Identified as AG Unicorn by Forbes', Monarch Tractor, https://www.monarchtractor.com/news/identified-as-ag-unicorn-by-forbes, accessed February 2024.

7   Available at Scott Martin, 'Cheers to AI: Monarch Tractor Launches First Commercially Available Electric, 'Driver Optional' Smart Tractor', NVIDIA, 1 December 2022, https://blogs.Nvidia.com/blog/mondavi-monarch-smart-electric-jetson-tractor/, accessed February 2024.

8   Available at Nilay Patel, '"The Android of agriculture": Monarch Tractor CEO Praveen Penmetsa on the future of farming', The Verge, 30 September 2023, https://www.theverge.com/23895900/praveen-penmetsa-monarch-tractor-autonomous-ev-interview-decoder, accessed February 2024.

9   Available at 'New Holland expands into the metaverse with Microsoft and Touchcast', Highways Today, 16 January 2023, https://highways.today/2023/01/16/new-holland-metaverse/?utm_source=pocket_shared, accessed February 2025.

10 Adapted from Victor Hua and Xincheng Huan, 'NIO—User Enterprise, Report for New Products and Innovation Management course, Ross School of Business', 2022.

11 Available at Phate Zhang, 'Nio starts recruiting beta testers for AI-powered voice assistant NOMI GPT', CNEVPOST, 11 March 2024, https://cnevpost.com/2024/03/11/nio-starts-recruiting-beta-testers-for-nomi-gpt/, accessed March 2024.

12 Axel Schmidt et al., 'The automotive experience reimagined', Accenture, 2021.

13 Available at https://azure.microsoft.com/en-us/blog/converging-the-physical-and-digital-with-digital-twins-mixed-reality-and-metaverse-apps/, accessed January 2024.

14 Available at 'Reliance Retail set to foray into FMCG segment: Isha Ambani', Moneycontrol, 30 August 2022, https://www.moneycontrol.com/news/business/companies/reliance-retail-set-to-foray-into-fmcg-segmentisha-ambani-9102161.html, accessed January 2024.

15 Available at 'Introducing the First End-to-End Shopping Experience on WhatsApp With JioMart in India', Meta, 29

August 2022, https://about.fb.com/news/2022/08/shop-on-whatsapp-with-jiomart-in-india/, accessed January2024.

16 Available at https://peopleplus.ai/, accessed Mar 2025.

17 Available at '"India's CTO" Nilekani unveils AI strategy: Focus on use-cases, not "my model bigger than yours"', Monecontrol, 4 December 2023, https://www.moneycontrol.com/news/technology/indias-cto-nilekani-unveils-ai-strategy-focus-on-use-cases-not-my-model-bigger-than-yours-11853961.html, accessed March 2024.

18 Available at 'People+ai: Projects', Coda, https://coda.io/@peopleplusai/people-ai-projects, accessed March 2024.

19 Available at 'PeoplePlusAI/Sthaan', GitHub, https://github.com/PeoplePlusAI/Sthaan, accessed March 2024.

20 For an original discussion, see Venkat Ramaswamy, 'Embracing a Co-Creation Paradigm of Lived-Experience Ecosystem Value Creation',' in The Routledge Companion to Corporate Branding, ed. Oriol Iglesias, Nicholas Ind and Majken Schultz (2022), pp. 95–110.

21 C.K. Prahalad and Venkat Ramaswamy, *The Future of Competition: Co-Creating Unique Value with Customers* (Harvard Business School Publishing, 2004). Venkat Ramaswamy and Francis J. Gouillart, The Power of Co-Creation (Free Press, 2010).

22 See V. Ramaswamy and K. Ozcan, 'Offerings as Digitalized Interactive Platforms: A Conceptual Framework and Implications', *Journal of Marketing*, 82(4) (2018a), pp. 19–31.

23 Venkat Ramaswamy and Nicholas Ind, 'Company Brands as Purpose-driven Lived Experience Ecosystems,' *The European Business Review*, May–June, (2021).

24 Extracted from the video: Airbnb CEO Brian Chesky at Skift Global Forum 2022, Skift. https://www.youtube.com/watch?v=_a9XfJDYKYc

25 Extracted from the video: The Airbnb 2022 Summer Release: A new Airbnb for a new world of travel, Airbnb. https://www.youtube.com/watch?v=doczmXmQcP4

26 Available at Ryan Seow, 'Airbnb Rolls Out New AI Features and Introduces Exclusive "Icons" Category Vibranium,

13 May 2024, https://www.vibranium.sg/post/airbnb-rolls-out-new-ai-features-and-introduces-exclusive-icons-category, accessed February 2025.

27 Extracted from the video: Introducing the Airbnb 2022 Winter Release, Airbnb. https://www.youtube.com/watch?v=OaylI4a82T8.

28 Ibid.

29 Available at 'Preparing to host refugee guests with Airbnb.org', Airbnb, 29 August 2019, https://www.airbnb.com/resources/hosting-homes/a/preparing-to-host-refugee-guests-with-airbnborg-252, accessed February 2025.

30 Available at 'An Update on Our Work to Serve All Stakeholders', Airbnb Newsroom, 17 January 2020, https://news.airbnb.com/serving-all-stakeholders/, accessed February 2025.

31 Extracted from the video: Lemonade Investor Day - November 2022, Lemonade. https://www.youtube.com/watch?v=R07iUh78gMQ

32 Schreiber tends to anthropomorphize Lemonade's AI (Maya is a she and Jim is a he). We have retained these gender-identities as specified.

33 Ibid.

34 Ibid.

35 Available at Ilkhan Ozsevim, 'Lemonade sets world record with 2-second AI insurance claim', AI Magazine, 14 June 2023, https://aimagazine.com/articles/lemonade-sets-world-record-with-2-second-ai-insurance-claim, accessed February 2025.

36 Extracted from the podcast 'Disrupting the Insurance Industry with AI', HBR, 14 August 2019, https://hbr.org/podcast/2019/08/disrupting-the-insurance-industry-with-ai, accessed February 2025.

37 Extracted from the video: Lemonade Investor Day - November 2022, Lemonade. https://www.youtube.com/watch?v=R07iUh78gMQ.

38 Extracted from the podcast 'Disrupting the Insurance Industry with AI', HBR, 14 August 2019, https://hbr.org/

podcast/2019/08/disrupting-the-insurance-industry-with-ai, accessed February 2025.

39 Extracted from the presentation at Lemonade First Quarter 2024 Financial Results. https://investor.lemonade.com/news-and-events/events-and-presentations/default.aspx.

40 Available at 'Lemonade Shareholder Letter Q1 2023', https://s24.q4cdn.com/139015699/files/doc_financials/2023/q1/Shareholder-Letter-Q1-2023-FINAL-5-3-2023.pdf, accessed February 2025.

41 Available at 'CBA accelerates digital strategy to give customers global best technology', CommBank, https://www.commbank.com.au/articles/newsroom/2021/01/CBA-accelerates-digital-strategy.html, accessed May 2024.

42 Karim R. Lakhani, Yael Grushka–Cockayne, Jin Hyun Paik and Steven Randazzo, 'Customer-Centric Design with Artificial Intelligence: Commonwealth Bank', Harvard Business School Case 622–065, October 2021. (Revised December 2021.)

43 Extracted from Pete Steel and Andrew McMullan, 'A digital and analytics journey at the Commonwealth Bank of Australia (CBA)', McKinsey & Company, https://www.mckinsey.com/industries/financial-services/our-insights/banking-matters/a-digital-and-analytics-journey-at-the-commonwealth-bank-of-australia-cba, accessed May 2024.

44 Karim R. Lakhani, Yael Grushka–Cockayne, Jin Hyun Paik and Steven Randazzo, 'Customer-Centric Design with Artificial Intelligence: Commonwealth Bank', Harvard Business School Case 622–065, October 2021. (Revised December 2021.)

45 Ibid.

46 Available at 'Fireside Chat with Dr Andrew McMullan, CommBank & Sri Ambati', H2O.ai, 2023, https://h2o.ai/resources/video/fireside-chat-with-andrew-mcmullan/#h2o-ai, accessed September 2024.

47 Available at https://whatsnext.nuance.com/en-au/customer-engagement-en-au/financial-services-ai-au/major-au-bank-services-customers-with-ai-virtual-assistant/, accessed August 2024.

48 Available at Daniel Ferguson, 'CBA unveils new GenAI experiment at South by Southwest Sydney 2023', CommBank, 23 October 2023, https://www.commbank.com.au/articles/ newsroom/2023/10/generative-ai-synthetic-agents.html, accessed August 2024.

49 Available at 'In a world first, CBA shares its artificial intelligence model to help reduce technology-facilitated abuse', CommBank, 8 November 2023, https://www.commbank.com. au/articles/newsroom/2023/11/next-chapter-open-artificial-intelligence-model.html, accessed May 2024.

50 Available at 'CBA boosts the bank's AI capabilities to generate better customer and community outcomes, at greater pace and scale', H2O.ai, https://h2o.ai/case-studies/cba-boosts-the-banks-ai-capabilities-to-generate-better-customer-and-community-outcomes/, accessed May 2024.

51 M.R. Kramer, Thijs Geradts and B. Nadella, 'Philips Lighting: Light-as-a-Service', Harvard Business School case study, 2019.

52 Extracted from Signify, 'Schiphol Airport installs Philips Circular lighting in Lounge 2', YouTube video, 21 April 2017, https://www.youtube.com/watch?v=_11r0NYfIZk, accessed May 2024.

53 V. Ramaswamy and M.K. Pieters, 'How companies can learn to operate as co-creational, adaptive, 'living' enterprises', Strategy & Leadership, Vol. 49 No. 2 (2021), pp. 3–8. https://doi.org/10.1108/SL-01-2021-0009, accessed February 2025.

54 Available at 'Signify Annual Report 2023', Signify, https:// www.signify.com/static/2023/signify-annual-report-2023.pdf, accessed February 2025.

55 Available at 'Democratized AI using H2O Talk by AT&T at H2O World India', H2O.ai, https://h2o.ai/resources/ video/democratized-ai-using-h2o-talk-by-att-at-h2o-world-india/#what-does, accessed July 2024.

56 Extracted from the video: Foundry for Enterprise | AT&T at AIPCon 5, Palantir, September 2024. https://www.youtube. com/watch?v=jLYsw3z7IJA.

57 Available at 'AT&T Transformed into an AI Company with H2O.ai', https://h2o.ai/case-studies/att-transformed-into-an-ai-company-with-h2o-ai/?n=cs2, accessed July 2024.

58 Interview with Adrian Gore, interviewed by John D. Macomber, Boston, Massachusetts, USA, and Johannesburg, South Africa, 9 May 2022, Creating Emerging Markets Oral History Collection, Baker Library Special Collections, Harvard Business School.

59 Krishnan Narayanan and Venkat Ramaswamy, 'Healthcare X-verse Innovation: Applying the PIEX lens to digitalized health and insurance experiences', itihaasa Research and Digital, 2022.

60 Available at Cora Lydon, 'Vitality members benefit from AI-powered mental health support', Digital Health, 19 May 2023, https://www.digitalhealth.net/2023/05/vitality-members-benefit-from-ai-powered-mental-health-support/, accessed January 2024.

61 Available at Alec Hogg, 'Adrian Gore: Discovery's zip to R100bn journey has big lessons—here are the most important', BizNews, 21 September 2023, https://www.biznews.com/interviews/2023/09/21/adrian-gore-discoverys-shared-value-ip, accessed March 2024.

62 Available at 'What are the most valuable brands in South Africa?', Kantar, 1 September 2021, https://www.kantar.com/inspiration/brands/what-are-the-most-valuable-brands-in-south-africa-2021, accessed February 2024.

63 Extracted from the interview with Mark Wildon at C3 AI, 'Efficiency Redefined with AI: Optimized Industrial Operations with Lila Fridley | C3 Transform 2024', YouTube video, 14 March 2024, https://www.youtube.com/watch?v=1uV3GuE7rRI, accessed May 2024.

64 Available at Tracy Wang, 'NFT Artist Pplpleasr's New Project 'Shibuya' Brings Long-Form Animation to Web 3', CoinDesk, 11 May 2023, https://www.coindesk.com/business/2022/03/01/nft-artist-pplpleasrs-new-project-shibuya-brings-long-form-animation-to-web-3/, accessed February 2024.

65 Available at 'Fans are the New Creators', Li's Newsletter, 29 August 2022, https://www.lisnewsletter.com/p/fans-are-the-new-creators, accessed March 2024.

66 B. Leavy, 'Alibaba strategist Ming Zeng: "Smart business" in the era of business ecosystems', Strategy & Leadership, Vol. 47 No. 2 (2019), pp. 11–18. https://doi.org/10.1108/SL-01-2019-0006, accessed February 2025.

67 Available at Matthew Fulco, 'Down but not out: China's Alibaba looks towards challenging 2022', Al Jazeera, 18 January 2022, https://www.aljazeera.com/economy/2022/1/18/down-but-not-out-chinas-alibaba-looks-towards-challenging-2022, accessed January 2024.

68 Available at Goh Thean Eu, 'Dreams change the world, not technology: Jack Ma', Digital News Asia, 18 March 2015, https://www.digitalnewsasia.com/startups/dreams-change-the-world-not-technology-jack-ma, accessed March 2024.

69 Ming Zeng, 'Alibaba and the Future of Business—Lessons from China's innovative digital giant', *Harvard Business Review*, September–October 2018.

70 Available at Bernard Marr, 'The Amazing Ways Chinese Tech Giant Alibaba Uses Generative Artificial Intelligence', Forbes, 4 October 2023, https://www.forbes.com/sites/bernardmarr/2023/10/04/the-amazing-ways-chinese-tech-giant-alibaba-uses-generative-artificial-intelligence/, accessed February 2024.

71 Available at Reuters and Tony Monroe, 'China extends crackdown on Jack Ma's empire with enforced revamp of Ant Group', Reuters, 12 April 2021, https://www.reuters.com/business/chinas-ant-group-become-financial-holding-company-central-bank-2021-04-12/, accessed January 2024.

72 Available at 'Pursuing AI maturity in health', Novartis Foundation, https://www.novartisfoundation.org/news/media-library/pursuing-ai-maturity-health, accessed January 2024.

73 Available at 'Physicians (per 1,000 people)—Brazil, World Bank Group, https://data.worldbank.org/indicator/SH.MED.

PHYS.ZS?locations=br and 'Nurses and midwives (per 1,000 people)—Brazil, World Bank Group, https://data.worldbank.org/indicator/SH.MED.NUMW.P3?locations=br, accessed January 2024.

74 Available at 'Could AI transform life in developing countries?', The Economist, 25 January 2024, https://www.economist.com/briefing/2024/01/25/could-ai-transform-life-in-developing-countries, accessed January 2024.

75 See C.K. Prahalad and Venkat Ramaswamy, The Future of Competition: Co-Creating Unique Value with Customers (Cambridge, MA: Harvard Business School Press, 2004), p. 207.

76 Available at 'Cambridge Handbook of Strategy as Practice', Cambridge University Press, https://www.cambridge.org/core/books/cambridge-handbook-of-strategy-as-practice/1AAF572 D02EC804947E57322FC04567A, accessed February 2025.

77 W. Chan Kim and R. A. Mauborgne, Beyond Disruption (Cambridge, MA: Harvard Business Press, 2023).

78 W. Chan Kim, Renée Mauborgne and Mi Ji, 'Ping An Good Doctor: Creating a Nondisruptive Solution for China's Healthcare System', INSEAD Publishing, 25 February 2021.

79 Available at 'How a global components manufacturer built an ambitious carbon reduction roadmap', McKinsey & Company, 9 February 2023, https://www.mckinsey.com/capabilities/sustainability/how-we-help-clients/impact-stories/how-a-global-components-manufacturer-built-an-ambitious-carbon-reduction-roadmap, accessed August 2024.

80 Available at 'Danfoss and Google enter into a strategic partnership on AI and energy efficiency', Danfoss, 23 January 2023, https://www.danfoss.com/en/about-danfoss/news/cf/danfoss-and-google-enter-into-a-strategic-partnership-on-ai-and-energy-efficiency/, accessed August 2024.

81 Available at Inti Pacheco, 'How Nike Missed the Boom in Running Culture', The Wall Street Journal, 27 June 2024, https://www.wsj.com/business/nike-running-sneakers-competition-1d735fc8, accessed February 2025.

82 Available at Madeleine Schulz, 'Sport as our North Star': New Nike CEO unveils turnaround plan, Vogue Business, https://

www.voguebusiness.com/story/companies/sport-as-our-north-star-new-nike-ceo-unveils-turnaround-plan, accessed March 2025.

83 Vranica, Suzanne. 2025. "Exclusive | Nike Is Betting a Big Super Bowl Ad with Caitlin Clark, Rapper Doechii Can Help Reclaim Its Dominance." WSJ. The Wall Street Journal. February 9, 2025. https://www.wsj.com/business/media/nike-is-betting-a-big-super-bowl-ad-with-caitlin-clark-rapper-doechii-can-help-reclaim-its-dominance-8376b766.

84 Ibid.

85 Available at Nat Barker, 'Nike developing AI model as part of design "step change"', Dezeen, 7 May 2024, https://www.dezeen.com/2024/05/07/Nike-ai-model-john-hoke/, accessed July 2024.

Chapter 5: Ecosystem Co-Innovation with Stakeholders

1 Available at 'Electric car sales have surged in Europe—so why is adoption still slow?', World Economic Forum, 13 November 2023, https://www.weforum.org/agenda/2023/11/electric-car-sales-europe-barriers-ev-adoption/, accessed February 2025.

2 Available at 'A brief history of the electric car', Energy Saving Trust, 10 August 2021, https://energysavingtrust.org.uk/a-brief-history-of-the-electric-car/, accessed February 2025.

3 R.E. Freeman, *Strategic Management: A Stakeholder Approach* (Pitman, 1984).

4 Available at Uwe Winkelhake, 'The Digital Transformation of the Automotive Industry', *Springer*, 2022, https://doi.org/10.1007/978-3-030-83826-3, accessed February 2025.

5 Ibid.

6 Available at https://www.volkswagenag.com/en/news/stories/2019/03/automotive-cloud-volkswagen-and-microsoft-develop-mobility-ecosy.html#, accessed May 2024.

7 Available at 'We are CARIAD', CARIAD, https://cariad.technology/de/en/company.html#our-vision, accessed May 2024.

8 Available at 'BMW North America puts gen AI under the hood', Accenture, https://www.accenture.com/us-en/case-studies/automotive/bmw-puts-generative-ai-in-the-drivers-seat, accessed July 2024.

9 Available at 'Katana Studio Streamlines Automotive Marketing With Real-Time Application Built on NVIDIA Omniverse', NVIDIA, https://www.nvidia.com/en-us/case-studies/katana-studio-streamlines-automotive-marketing-with-real-time-application/, accessed November 2024.

10 Available at 'Weaving the Future', Toyota Woven City, https://www.woven-city.global/, accessed May 2024.

11 See Kerimcan Ozcan and Venkat Ramaswamy, *Dynamic Relationality Theory: Grounding Machinic Ecosystems in Life Experiences* (Elsevier, 1st edition, 2024).

12 Available at 'Master Plan Part 3', Tesla, 5 April 2023, https://www.tesla.com/blog/master-plan-part-3, accessed August 2024.

13 M.S. Krishnan et al., 'Tesla Motors—Software on Wheels: Digital Transformation of Auto OEM Business Model', University of Michigan's Ross School of Business.

14 Walter Isaacson, *Elon Musk* (Simon & Schuster, 2023).

15 Available at Elon Musk, X, 17 April 2024, https://x.com/elonmusk/status/1780376546148327690, accessed July 2024.

16 Available at Anissa Gardizy and Amir Efrati, "Why Musk's AI Rivals Are Alarmed by His New GPU Cluster', The Information, https://www.theinformation.com/articles/why-musks-ai-rivals-are-alarmed-by-his-new-gpu-cluster, accessed September 2024.

17 Extracted from the video 'The Hidden Autopilot Data That Reveals Why Teslas Crash', *Wall Street Journal*, 2024. https://www.youtube.com/watch?v=mPUGh0qAqWA.

18 Bruce Sinclair, IoT Inc: *How Your Company Can Use the Internet of Things to Win in the Outcome Economy* (McGraw Hill, 2017).

19 Available at 'Musk Says that Grok Will Be Integrated into Tesla (TSLA) Vehicles'. (2025). Nasdaq.com. https://www.

nasdaq.com/articles/musk-says-grok-will-be-integrated-tesla-tsla-vehicles.

20 Available at Kyle Field, 'Tesla Replaces Humans With Technology In New Touchless, Humanless Test Drives', Clean Technica, https://cleantechnica.com/2020/09/16/tesla-replaces-humans-with-technology-in-new-touchless-humanless-test-drives/, accessed May 2024.

21 V. Govindarajan and V. Venkatraman, *Fusion Strategy* (Cambridge, MA: Harvard Business Press, 2024).

22 Inma Martínez, *The Future of the Automotive Industry: The Disruptive Forces of AI, Data Analytics, and Digitization* (Apress, 2021).

23 Available at Lyle Adriano, 'Tesla rolls out new auto insurance product', Insurance Business, 18 October 2021, https://www.insurancebusinessmag.com/us/news/breaking-news/tesla-rolls-out-new-auto-insurance-product-313432.aspx

24 Michael Valentin, *The Tesla Way: The disruptive strategies and models of Teslism* (KoganPage, 2019).

25 Available at Fred Lambert, 'Tesla announces new $500 million Dojo supercomputer coming to New York', Electrek, 26 January 2024, https://electrek.co/2024/01/26/tesla-announces-dojo-supercomputer-new-york/, accessed May 2024.

26 Available at 'Samsung Announces Collaboration With Tesla at CES 2024 for SmartThings Energy', Samsung Newsroom, 5 January 2024, https://news.samsung.com/global/samsung-announces-collaboration-with-tesla-at-ces-2024-for-smartthings-energy, accessed May 2024.

27 Available at Jennifer Mossalogue, 'Panasonic to soon make new batteries for Tesla, could 'reduce' EV prices: report', Electrek, 15 January 2024, https://electrek.co/2024/01/15/panasonic-to-soon-make-new-batteries-for-tesla-could-reduce-ev-prices-report/, accessed May 2024.

28 Available at Mark Kane, 'Tesla Expanded Its Supercharging Network To Roughly 6,000 Stations', Inside EVs, 24 January 2024, https://insideevs.com/news/705972/tesla-supercharging-network-roughly-6000-stations/, accessed May 2024.

29 Available at Tesla Inc. form 10-K, United States Securities and Exchange Comission, https://www.sec.gov/Archives/edgar/data/1318605/000095017023001409/tsla-20221231.htm#business, accessed May 2024.

30 Available at Mark Kane, 'CCS1 To Tesla NACS Charging Connector Transition: Everything We Know', Inside EVs, 20 December 2023, https://insideevs.com/reviews/672485/ccs1-tesla-nacs-charging-connector-transition-info/, accessed May 2024.

31 Ford Integrated Sustainability and Financial Report Summary 2022.

32 Available at Thomais Zaremba, 'How a century-old brand is transforming the auto industry', Google Think, July 2021, https://www.thinkwithgoogle.com/future-of-marketing/digital-transformation/ford-business-transformation-case-study/, accessed February 2024.

33 Available at Iain Roberts, 'How Design is Driving Ford to Reimagine What a Car Company Can Be', Ideo, December 2019, https://www.ideo.com/journal/how-design-is-driving-ford-to-reimagine-what-a-car-company-can-be, accessed February 2025.

34 Available at 'Strategic Progress of Ford+ Growth Plan, Solid Financials in '21 Position Company for Connected EV Leadership in 2022, Beyond', 3 February 2022, https://media.ford.com/content/dam/fordmedia/North%20America/US/2022/02/03/financials-fy-ford-21.pdf, accessed February 2025.

35 Available at 'LG Energy Solution, Ford, and KOÇ Holding to Establish a Joint Venture to Produce Battery Cells as Ford Prepares to Bring More EVs to Customers in Europe', LG Energy Solution, 22 February 2023, https://news.lgensol.com/company-news/press-releases/1520/, accessed May 2024.

36 Available at 'Ford Pro Explained: Here's How Ford's New Commercial Business Will Work', https://fordauthority.com/2021/05/ford-pro-explained-heres-how-fords-new-commercial-business-will-work/, accessed May 2024.

37 Available at Joseph White, 'Ford has big goals for software sales to small business truck fleets', Yahoo! Finance, 14 March 2024, https://finance.yahoo.com/news/ford-big-goals-software-sales-100342697.html, accessed May 2024.

38 Available at 'Ford Pro Showcases Productivity-Accelerating Digital Solutions At Iaa Transportation Show 2022', Ford Media Center, 19 September 2022, https://media.ford.com/content/fordmedia/feu/en/news/2022/09/19/ford-pro-showcases-productivity-accelerating-digital-solutions-a.html, accessed February 2025.

39 Available at 'Strategic Progress of Ford+ Growth Plan, Solid Financials in '21 Position Company for Connected EV Leadership in 2022, Beyond', 3 February 2022, https://media.ford.com/content/dam/fordmedia/North%20America/US/2022/02/03/financials-fy-ford-21.pdf, accessed February 2025.

40 Available at Snapdragon, 'Snapdragon Summit 2024: Day 1 Keynote Livestream', YouTube video, 22 October 2024, https://www.youtube.com/watch?v=0e5zpV0NS50, accessed February 2025.

41 Available at Databricks, 'Building an Insights Factory at General Motors - Data + AI Summit 2024', YouTube video, 15 June 2024, https://www.youtube.com/watch?v=pKdZqKG9NPs, accessed February 2025.

42 Available at 'Radical change calls for even more radical collaboration', Catena-X, https://catena-x.net/en/, accessed February 2025.

43 In conversation with the authors.

44 Available at Bob Evans, 'How SAP and BMW Created the Catena-X Open Data Ecosystem for the Automotive Industry', Cloud Wars, 7 February 2025, https://accelerationeconomy.com/cloud-wars/how-sap-and-bmw-created-the-catena-x-open-data-ecosystem-for-the-automotive-industry/, accessed July 2024.

45 Available at 'CATENA-X: INNOVATION THROUGH COOPERATION', BMW Group, https://www.bmwgroup.com/en/news/general/2023/catenax.html, accessed February 2025.

46 Available at Hagen Huebach and Heiko Flohr, 'Enabling a Circular Economy Through Industry Network Collaboration', SAP News Center, 27 May 2022, https://news.sap.com/2022/05/circular-economy-automotive-industry-network-collaboration/, accessed May 2024.

47 Extracted from the video 'Circular Economy / Battery Pass', Catena-X, https://catena-x.net/en/offers/hmi-2023/circular-economy-1, accessed May 2024.

48 Ibid.

49 Catena-X Operating Model Version 2.1, released 16 October 2023.

50 Available at J. Parra–Moyano, K. Schmedders and A. 'Sandy', Pentland, 'How Data Collaboration Platforms Can Help Companies Build Better AI', *Harvard Business Review*, 26 January 2024, https://hbr.org/2024/01/how-data-collaboration-platforms-can-help-companies-build-better-ai, accessed February 2025.

51 Available at 'Governor Newsom Signs Executive Order to Prepare California for the Progress of Artificial Intelligence', Governor Gavin Newsom, https://www.gov.ca.gov/2023/09/06/governor-newsom-signs-executive-order-to-prepare-california-for-the-progress-of-artificial-intelligence/, accessed June 2024.

52 THE WHITE HOUSE. 2025. "Removing Barriers to American Leadership in Artificial Intelligence – the White House." The White House. January 23, 2025. https://www.whitehouse.gov/presidential-actions/2025/01/removing-barriers-to-american-leadership-in-artificial-intelligence/.

53 Extracted from the video Ola Källenius, 'We are the architects of our operating system', Mercedes-Benz Group, https://group.mercedes-benz.com/investors/events/2023-02-mercedes-benz-group-strategy-update.html, accessed May 2024.

54 Available at Ola Källenius, 'We are the architects of our operating system', Mercedes-Benz Group, https://group.mercedes-benz.com/investors/events/2023-02-mercedes-benz-group-strategy-update.html, accessed May 2024.

55 P. Hansen, 'The Hansen Report', ATZ Elektron 18, 37 (2023), https://doi.org/10.1007/s35658-023-1507-z, accessed February 2025.

56 Available at 'Cerence powers voice biometrics in Mercedes-Benz', Identity Week, 16 December 2020, https://identityweek.net/cerence-powers-voice-biometrics-in-mercedes-benz/, accessed May 2024.

57 Available at 'Mercedes-Benz takes in-car voice control to a new level with ChatGPT', Mercedes-Benz Group, https://group.mercedes-benz.com/innovation/digitalisation/connectivity/car-voice-control-with-chatgpt.html, accessed May 2024.

58 Extracted from Microsoft, 'The Industrial Metaverse', at CIO Connections by Judson Althoff, EVP and chief commercial officer of Microsoft, YouTube video, 11 February 2023, https://www.youtube.com/watch?v=wAlcX7QaWkc, accessed February 2025.

59 We are thankful to Gitakrishnan Ramadurai, professor at IIT Madras, and Ramakrishna Srinivasan for the invitation to the workshop.

60 Available at 'The Mobility and Intelligent Transportation Collaborative', MINT, https://www.themint.space/more/?page=how, accessed May 2024.

61 Available at UEI Alliance, https://ueialliance.org/, accessed September 2024.

62 Krishnan Narayanan and Venkat Ramaswamy, 'Automotive and Mobility Ecosystem X-verse Innovation: Applying the PIE X lens to digitalized automotive and smart mobility experiences', itihaasa Research and Digital, 2023; Mahindra-and-Mahindra-Annual-Report-2023-24; and Mahindra-and-Mahindra-Sustainability-Report-2024.

63 The co-creation movement at Mahindra builds on the article by Venkat Ramaswamy and Naveen Chopra, 'Building a Culture of Co-Creation at Mahindra', Strategy & Leadership, March, 2014.

64 The co-creation movement at Mahindra builds on the article by Venkat Ramaswamy and Naveen Chopra, 'Building a

Culture of Co-Creation at Mahindra', *Strategy & Leadership*, March, 2014.

65 Venkat Ramaswamy and Francis J. Gouillart, *The Power of Co-Creation* (Free Press, 2010).

Chapter 6: Becoming a Co-Intelligent Enterprise

1   C.K. Prahalad and Venkat Ramaswamy, *The Future of Competition: Co-Creating Unique Value With Customers* (Cambridge, MA: Harvard Business School Press, 2004). See also C.K. Prahalad and M.S. Krishnan, *The New Age of Innovation: Driving Co-Created Value through Business Networks* (McGraw Hill, 2008); Venkat Ramaswamy and Francis Gouillart, *The Power of Co-Creation: Build It With Them to Boost Growth, Productivity, and Profits* (Free Press, 2010); Venkat Ramaswamy and Kerimcan Ozcan, *The Co-Creation Paradigm* (California: Stanford Business Books, 2014).

2   See Gary Hamel with Bill Breen, *The Future of Management* (Boston, MA: Harvard Business Review Press, 2007); and the discussion on Management as a Co-Creation in Venkat Ramaswamy and Francis Gouillart, *The Power of Co-Creation: Build It With Them to Boost Growth, Productivity, and Profits* (Free Press, 2010).

3   Ibid.

4   Extracted from the video: On leadership | Jensen Huang and Joel Hellermark, Sana, 2023. https://www.youtube.com/watch?v=h5xY_kRKHxE.

5   Extracted from the video: No Priors Ep. 13 | With Jensen Huang, Founder & CEO of Nvidia, No Priors: AI, Machine Learning, Tech, & Startups. https://www.youtube.com/watch?v=ZFtW3g1dbUU.

6   Extracted from the video: On leadership | Jensen Huang and Joel Hellermark, Sana, 2023. https://www.youtube.com/watch?v=h5xY_kRKHxE.

7   Extracted from the video: A conversation with Nvidia's Jensen Huang, Stripe, 2024. https://www.youtube.com/watch?v=8Pfa8kPjUio.

8 Available at Rya Jetha, 'Being an Nvidia multimillionaire isn't as enjoyable as you may think', *Australian Financial Review*, 27 August 2024, https://www.afr.com/technology/being-an-nvidia-multimillionaire-isn-t-as-enjoyable-as-you-may-think-20240827-p5k5mq, accessed August 2024.

9 Available at Shareholder Letter, Microsoft, 2014, https://www.microsoft.com/investor/reports/ar14/index.html, accessed February 2024.

10 Available at Annual Report 2023, Microsoft, 2023, https://www.microsoft.com/investor/reports/ar23/index.html, accessed February 2024.

11 Available at 'Market capitalization of Microsoft (MSFT)', Companies Market Cap, https://companiesmarketcap.com/microsoft/marketcap/

12 Krishnan Narayanan and Venkat Ramaswamy, 'Digital India Innovation and the Experience-verse Revolution,' itihaasa Research and Digital Report, 2022.

13 Available at Shows, Learn Microsoft, https://learn.microsoft.com/en-us/events/ignite-mar-2021/general/key-segments/key11/, accessed February 2025.

14 Satya Nadella, Greg Shaw and Jill Tracie Nichols, *Hit Refresh: The Quest to Rediscover Microsoft's Soul and Imagine a Better Future for Everyone* (Harper Business, 2017).

15 Ibid.

16 Ibid.

17 Ibid.

18 Carol Dweck and Kathleen Hogan, 'How Microsoft Uses a Growth Mindset to Develop Leaders', *Harvard Business Review*, 7 October 2016.

19 Gino, Francesca, Allison Ciechanover, and Jeff Huizinga. 'Culture Transformation at Microsoft: From "Know It All" to "Learn It All"', Harvard Business School Case 921–004, September 2020. (Revised April 2022).

20 Available at Lindsay-Rae McIntyre, 'Microsoft's 2023 Diversity and Inclusion Report: A decade of transparency, commitment and progress', Microsoft Blog, 1 November 2023, https://blogs.microsoft.com/blog/2023/11/01/microsofts-2023-diversity-

and-inclusion-report-a-decade-of-transparency-commitment-and-progress/, accessed February 2024.

21 Rasmus Hougaard, Jacqueline Carter and Kathleen Hogan, 'How Microsoft Builds a Sense of Community Among 144,000 Employees', *Harvard Business Review*, 28 August 2019.

22 Available at Marco Insiati and Satya Nadella, 'Democratizing Transformation', *Harvard Business Review*, May–June 2022, https://hbr.org/2022/05/democratizing-transformation, accessed February 2025.

23 Available at Microsoft Inspire 2021, Microsoft, https://news.microsoft.com/inspire2021/, accessed February 2025.

24 A whitepaper on 'Reinventing the employee experience at Microsoft', Microsoft, February 2020.

25 Available at 'The Case for EXP', Microsoft, https://www.microsoft.com/en-us/worklab/the-case-for-exp,   accessed February 2024.

26 Doug J. Chung, 'Commercial Sales Transformation at Microsoft', Harvard Business School, 28 January 2019.

27 Available at Case study: Transforming global commercial sales with Microsoft Workplace Analytics, https://techcommunity.microsoft.com/blog/viva_insights_blog/case-study-transforming-global-commercial-sales-with-microsoft-workplace-analyti/3862392, accessed February 2025.

28 Available at Jordan Novet, 'Microsoft's sales overhaul a year ago has led to all-time high stock price and continuing cloud growth', CNBC, 16 July 2018, https://www.cnbc.com/2018/07/13/how-microsofts-sales-reorganization-has-impacted-its-business.html, accessed February 2025.

29 Available at https://www.delightfulcommunications.com/blog/storyteller-steve-clayton-microsoft-brand/, accessed February 2023.

30 Available at 'Watch Microsoft's "Empowering" ad from the Big Game', Microsoft Blog, 2 February 2014, https://blogs.microsoft.com/blog/2014/02/02/watch-microsofts-empowering-ad-from-the-big-game/, accessed February 2025.

31 Available at Carlsen Martin, 'We All Win: Microsoft's Super Bowl commercial made the news for all the right

reasons', Moneycontrol, 12 April 2019, https://www.moneycontrol.com/news/trends/we-all-win-microsofts-super-bowl-that-commercial-made-the-news-for-all-the-right-reasons-3501031.html, accessed February 2025.

32 C.K. Prahalad and Venkat Ramaswamy, *The Future of Competition: Co-Creating Unique Value With Customers* (Cambridge, MA: Harvard Business School Press, 2004). See also C.K. Prahalad and M.S. Krishnan, *The New Age of Innovation: Driving Co-Created Value through Business Networks* (McGraw Hill, 2008); Venkat Ramaswamy and Francis Gouillart, *The Power of Co-Creation: Build It With Them to Boost Growth, Productivity, and Profits* (Free Press, 2010); Venkat Ramaswamy and Kerimcan Ozcan, *The Co-Creation Paradigm* (California: Stanford Business Books, 2014).

33 Available at 'A Narrative for The Next Management by Richard Straub and Julia Kirby', Drucker Forum, 27 March 2024, https://www.druckerforum.org/blog/a-narrative-for-the-next-managementby-richard-straub-and-julia-kirby/, accessed February 2025.

34 Peter Ferdinand Drucker, *Landmarks of Tomorrow: A Report on the New 'Post-Modern' World* (Routledge, 2023).

35 Available at James F. Moore, 'Predators and Prey: A New Ecology of Competition', *Harvard Business Review*, May–June 1993, https://hbr.org/1993/05/predators-and-prey-a-new-ecology-of-competition, accessed May 2024.

36 Available at Eric Lamarre, Kate Smaje and Rodney Zemmel, 'Rewired to outcompete', McKinsey Digital, 20 June 2023, https://www.mckinsey.com/capabilities/mckinsey-digital/our-insights/rewired-to-outcompete, accessed July 2024.

37 Eric Lamarre, Kate Smaje and Rodney Zemmel, *Rewired: The McKinsey Guide to Outcompeting in the Age of Digital and AI* 1st edition (Wiley, 2023).

38 Available at Kelly Ng, 'Piyush Gupta counting on DBS' AI and data capabilities to pull ahead of peers', DBS, 31 October 2022, https://www.dbs.com/artificial-intelligence-machine-learning/artificial-intelligence/piyush-gupta-counting-on-dbs-

ai-and-data-capabilities-to-pull-ahead.html, accessed May 2024.

39 Available at 'DBS' AI-powered digital transformation', DBS, 7 August 2023, https://www.dbs.com/artificial-intelligence-machine-learning/artificial-intelligence/dbs-ai-powered-digital-transformation.html, accessed May 2024.

40 Available at Feng Zhu, Harold Zhu and Adina Wong, 'DBS' AI Journey', Harvard Business Publishing, 21 August 2024, https://hbsp.harvard.edu/product/625053-PDF-ENG?Ntt=DBS%20AI%20journey, accessed February 2025.

41 Available at 'Shattering the status quo: A conversation with Haier's Zhang Ruimin', McKinsey & Company, 27 July 2021, https://www.mckinsey.com/capabilities/people-and-organizational-performance/our-insights/shattering-the-status-quo-a-conversation-with-haiers-zhang-ruimin, accessed May 2024.

42 Available at 'The Haier Road to Growth', https://www.strategy-business.com/article/00323, accessed May 2024.

43 Available at Santiago Iñiguez, 'Management lessons from Haier's experience: An interview with Founder and Chairman Emeritus, Ruimin Zhang', Global Focus, 14 September 2022, https://www.globalfocusmagazine.com/management-lessons-from-haiers-experience-an-interview-with-founder-and-chairman-emeritus-ruimin-zhang/, accessed May 2024.

44 Gary Hamel and Michele Zanini, *Humanocracy: Creating organizations as amazing as the people inside them* (Boston, MA: Harvard Business Review Press, 2020).

45 Available at Santiago Iñiguez, 'Management lessons from Haier's experience: An interview with Founder and Chairman Emeritus, Ruimin Zhang', Global Focus, 14 September 2022, https://www.globalfocusmagazine.com/management-lessons-from-haiers-experience-an-interview-with-founder-and-chairman-emeritus-ruimin-zhang/, accessed May 2024.

46 Available at David Weinberger and Michele Zanini, 'AI Has a Revolutionary Ability to Parse Details. What Does That Mean for Business?', *Harvard Business Review*, 29 July 2022, https://hbr.org/2024/07/ai-has-a-revolutionary-

ability-to-parse-details-what-does-that-mean-for-business, accessed February 2025.

47 Available at 'Haier Internet of Clothing Opens the Chapter of the "Ecosystem Revolution" in the Cloud Era', Haier, 18 June 2020, https://www.haier.com/global/haier-ecosystem/list/20201021_149586.shtml, accessed May 2024.

48 Available at 'Haier IoF and XinHua Net Cooperation: IoF Products into Every Household', Haier, 18 June 2020, https://www.haier.com/global/haier-ecosystem/list/20201021_149587.shtml, accessed May 2024.

49 Available at 'Shattering the status quo: A conversation with Haier's Zhang Ruimin', McKinsey & Company, 27 July 2021, https://www.mckinsey.com/capabilities/people-and-organizational-performance/our-insights/shattering-the-status-quo-a-conversation-with-haiers-zhang-ruimin, accessed February 2025.

50 Available at Joost Minnaar, 'Organizing Based On Algorithms And Smart Contracts', Corporate Rebels, 22 October 2022, https://www.corporate-rebels.com/blog/haier-workbench, accessed May 2024.

51 Available at 'For Haier's Zhang Ruimin, Success Means Creating the Future', Knowledge at Wharton, 20 April 2018, https://knowledge.wharton.upenn.edu/podcast/knowledge-at-wharton-podcast/haiers-zhang-ruimin-success-means-creating-the-future/, accessed May 2024.

52 James F. Moore, Ke Rong and Ruimin Zhang, 'The Human Ecosystem', *Journal of Digital Economy*, Vol. 1, Issue 1, (2022), pp. 53–72, ISSN 2773-0670, https://doi.org/10.1016/j.jdec.2022.08.002, accessed February 2025.

53 Mark L. Frigo and Venkat Ramaswamy, 'Co-Creating Strategic Risk-Return Management', *Strategic Finance*, May, 2009, pp. 25–33.

54 Available at Mobilitas Insurance, https://mobilitasinsurance.com, accessed February 2025.

55 Available at 'Digitalization of the Insurance Industry: Trends and Innovations', AXA XL, https://axaxl.com/fast-fast-

forward/articles/digitalization-of-the-insurance-industry-trends-and-innovations, accessed February 2025.

56 Available at 'Artificial Intelligence Risk Management Framework (AI RMF 1.0)', National Institute of Standards and Technology, January 2023, https://doi.org/10.6028/NIST. AI.100-1, accessed May 2024.

57 Available at 'Artificial Intelligence Risk Management Framework: Generative Artificial Intelligence Profile', National Institute of Standards and Technology, April 2024, https://www.nist.gov/itl/ai-risk-management-framework, accessed May 2024.

58 See Venkat Ramaswamy and Kerimcan Ozcan, *The Co-Creation Paradigm* (California: Stanford University Press, 2014).

59 Available at Breck Dumass, 'Nvidia announces AI-powered healthcare 'agents' that outperform nurses — and cost $9 an hour', Fox Business, 21 March 2024, https://www.foxbusiness.com/technology/Nvidia-announces-ai-powered-health-care-agents-outperform-nurses-cost-9-hour, accessed May 2024.

60 Extracted from a conversation with Munjal Shah, co-founder and CEO of Hippocratic AI, 'Live from GTC: A Conversation with Hippocratic AI', NVIDIA, March 2024, https://www.Nvidia.com/en-us/on-demand/session/gtc24-ep64015/, accessed May 2024.

61 Available at Breck Dumass, 'Nvidia announces AI-powered healthcare 'agents' that outperform nurses — and cost $9 an hour', Fox Business, 21 March 2024, https://www.foxbusiness.com/technology/Nvidia-announces-ai-powered-health-care-agents-outperform-nurses-cost-9-hour, accessed May 2024.

62 Available at 'Hippocratic AI Announces Collaboration with NVIDIA to Develop Super-Low-Latency "Empathy Inference" for One of the World's First Generative AI-Powered Healthcare Agents', GlobeNewswire, 18 March 2024, https://www.globenewswire.com/news-release/2024/3/18/2848236/0/en/Hippocratic-AI-Announces-Collaboration-with-Nvidia-to-Develop-Super-Low-Latency-Empathy-Inference-for-One-of-

the-World-s-First-Generative-AI-Powered-Healthcare-Agents. html, accessed May 2024.

63 Extracted from a conversation with Munjal Shah, co-founder and CEO of Hippocratic AI, 'Live from GTC: A Conversation with Hippocratic AI', NVIDIA, March 2024, https://www. Nvidia.com/en-us/on-demand/session/gtc24-ep64015/, accessed May 2024.

64 Extracted from the video Klarna CEO Sebastian Siemiatkowski on Getting AI to Do the Work of 700 Customer Service Reps, Sequoia Capital, July 2024. https://www.youtube.com/ watch?v=m3niSE-8ZvE.

65 Available at https://x.com/klarnaseb/status/18903363134773 61862, accessed March 2025

66 Available at 'Transcript: The Path Forward: Artificial Intelligence with Shantanu Narayen', The *Washington Post*, 5 March 2024, https://www.washingtonpost.com/washington-post-live/2024/03/05/transcript-path-forward-artificial-intelligence-with-shantanu-narayen/, accessed May 2024.

67 Available at Sara Fischer, 'Major US newspapers sue OpenAI, Microsoft for copyright infringement', AXIOS, 30 April 2024, https://www.axios.com/2024/04/30/microsoft-openai-lawsuit-copyright-newspapers-alden-global, accessed June 2024.

68 Available at 'The Financial Times and OpenAI strike content licensing deal', *Financial Times*, https://www.ft.com/ content/33328743-ba3b-470f-a2e3-f41c3a366613, accessed August 2024.

69 Available at Jenny Luna, 'Shantanu Narayen: Generative AI Won't Replace Human Ingenuity', Stanford Business, 1 May 2023, https://www.gsb.stanford.edu/insights/shantanu-narayen-generative-ai-wont-replace-human-ingenuity, accessed May 2024.

70 Extracted from Jason Baker, 'Tech Minutes: Blockchain, FedEx, and the Future', Fedex, 29 May 2018, https://www.fedex.com/ en-us/about/policy/technology-innovation/blockchain.html, accessed May 2024.

71 Available at 'FedEx, Blockchain Research Institute and INSEAD Collaborate to Develop New Course Series on

Web3 in Global Commerce', Fedex Newsroom, 16 February 2023, https://newsroom.fedex.com/newsroom/global-english/fedex-blockchain-research-institute-and-insead-collaborate-to-develop-new-course-series-on-web3-in-global-commerce, accessed May 2024.

72 Available at 'Court Orders Air Canada to Pay Out for Chatbot's Bad Advice', CX Today, 19 February 2024, https://www.cxtoday.com/speech-analytics/court-orders-air-canada-to-pay-out-for-chatbots-bad-advice/, accessed May 2024.

73 Rahul Matthan, *The Third Way: India's Revolutionary Approach to Data Governance* (India: Juggernaut, 2023).

74 Available at 'About Us', Etherisc, https://etherisc.com/about, accessed May 2024.

75 Available at Tom Davenport and Maryam Alavi, 'How to Train Generative AI Using Your Company's Data', *Harvard Business Review*, 6 July 2023, https://hbr.org/2023/07/how-to-train-generative-ai-using-your-companys-data, accessed February 2025.

76 Available at 'Banking on innovation: How ING uses generative AI to put people first', McKinsey & Company, https://www.mckinsey.com/industries/financial-services/how-we-help-clients/banking-on-innovation-how-ing-uses-generative-ai-to-put-people-first?utm_source=pocket_shared, accessed August 2024.

77 Available at Kevin Mandia, 'Moving the Mission Forward: Mandiant Joins Google Cloud', Google Cloud, 12 September 2022, https://cloud.google.com/blog/products/identity-security/mandiant-joins-google-cloud/, accessed May 2024.

78 Extracted from the video: Cloud security threat briefing with Mandiant, YouTube, Google Cloud Tech. https://www.youtube.com/watch?v=PtUYzYTxq-k.

79 Extracted from the video: Keynote: Kevin Mandia, CEO, Mandiant, mWISE Conference. https://www.youtube.com/watch?v=9tWKkTagJZc.

80 Available at 'CEO Andy Jassy's 2022 Letter to Shareholders', Amazon, https://www.aboutamazon.com/news/company-news/amazon-ceo-andy-jassy-2022-letter-to-shareholders, accessed March 2024.

81 Jake Alimahomed–Wilson, 'The Amazonification of Logistics: E-Commerce, Labor, and Exploitation in the Last Mile', in *The Cost of Free Shipping—Amazon in the Global Economy* (Pluto Press, 2020).

82 Ibid.

83 G. Hamel and M. Zanini, *Humanocracy: Creating organizations as amazing as the people inside them* (Boston, MA: Harvard Business Review Press, 2020); Venkatram Ramaswamy and Kerimcan Ozcan, *The Co-Creation Paradigm* (California; Stanford University Press, 2014).

84 See Thomas H. Davenport and Julia Kirby, 'Beyond Automation', *Harvard Business Review*, June 2015, https://hbr.org/2015/06/beyond-automation, accessed February 2025.

85 Thomas H. Davenport and Julia Kirby, *Only Humans Need Apply* (Harper Business, 2016).

86 Available at Daron Acemoglu and Pascual Restrepo, 'The Wrong Kind of AI? Artificial Intelligence and the Future of Labor Demand', National Bureau of Economic Research, Working Paper 25682, March 2019, doi: 10.3386/w25682, http://www.nber.org/papers/w25682, accessed February 2025.

87 F. Capra and P. Luisi, *The Systems View of Life: A Unifying Vision* (Cambridge, MA: Cambridge University Press, 2014), doi:10.1017/CBO9780511895555.

88 Available at Marjorie Kelly, 'Journeys to the Generative Economy: five models of community ownership', Marjorie Kelly, https://marjoriekelly.org/wp-content/uploads/2021/12/WILPF-blog.pdf, accessed May 2024.

89 C.K. Prahalad and Venkat Ramaswamy, *The Future of Competition: Co-Creating Unique Value With Customers* (Cambridge, MA: Harvard Business School Press, 2004). See also C.K. Prahalad and M.S. Krishnan, *The New Age of Innovation: Driving Co-Created Value through Business Networks* (McGraw Hill, 2008); Venkat Ramaswamy and Francis Gouillart, *The Power of Co-Creation: Build It With Them to Boost Growth, Productivity, and Profits* (Free Press, 2010); Venkat Ramaswamy and Kerimcan Ozcan, *The Co-Creation Paradigm* (California: Stanford Business Books, 2014).

Chapter 7: Designing Co-Creative Living Organizations in a Co-Intelligence World

1   Ludwig von, Bertalanffy, *General System Theory: Foundations, Development, Applications* (New York: George Braziller, 1968).

2   F. Capra and P. Luisi, *The Systems View of Life: A Unifying Vision* (Cambridge, UK: Cambridge University Press, 2014), doi:10.1017/CBO9780511895555.

3   Adapted from Fritjof Capra's course at https://www.capracourse.net/, accessed May 2024.

4   Extracted from Bloomberg Television, 'Chanel CEO Leena Nair on her Leadership Style at the Luxury Fashion Brand', YouTube video, 25 April 2024, https://www.youtube.com/watch?v=LAIYfwkPphI, accessed May 2024.

5   Ibid.

6   Margaret J. Wheatley, *Leadership and the New Science: Discovering Order in a Chaotic World* Third edition (Berrett–Koehler Publishers, 2006).

7   Available at 'Edmund Husserl', *The Stanford Encyclopedia of Philosophy*, 28 February 2003 (revised 17 October 2022), https://plato.stanford.edu/entries/husserl/, accessed May 2024.

8   Steven Savitt, 'Being and Becoming in Modern Physics', *The Stanford Encyclopedia of Philosophy*, 11 July 2001 (revised 6 October 2021), ed. Edward N. Zalta, https://plato.stanford.edu/archives/win2021/entries/spacetime-bebecome, accessed February 2025.

9   See Kerimcan Ozcan and Venkat Ramaswamy, *Dynamic Relationality Theory: Grounding Machinic Ecosystems in Life Experiences* (Elsevier, 2024).

10 See also Marco Iansiti and Satya Nadella, 'Democratizing Transformation', *Harvard Business Review*, May–June 2022.

11 See also the additional two books by Kerimcan Ozcan and Venkat Ramaswamy in their DRT trilogy: *Creative Transformation of Organizational Ecosystems: A Fieldbook of Dynamic Relationality Theory* (DeGruyter) and *Machinic*

Life Experience Ecosystems: Creative Transformation through Human–AI Interactivity (Springer).

12 Extracted from the video: FULL Alex Karp Interview: June 2024! Palantir Vision. https://www.youtube.com/watch?v=P2A1iNPzS6c.

13 Available at 'The Ontology', Palantir, https://www.palantir.com/explore/platforms/foundry/ontology/, accessed October 2024.

14 Extracted from the video: FULL Alex Karp Interview: June 2024! Palantir Vision. https://www.youtube.com/watch?v=P2A1iNPzS6c.

15 Available at '360° value is at the heart of our business', Accenture, https://www.accenture.com/in-en/about/company-index, accessed July 2024.

16 Extracted from the video: 'Inside Accenture's AI Journey with CEO Julie Sweet', Microsoft. https://www.youtube.com/watch?v=4JXJEg5tcMQ.

17 Available at 'Accenture's blueprint for responsible AI', Accenture, https://www.accenture.com/mu-en/case-studies/data-ai/blueprint-responsible-ai, accessed July 2024.

18 Extracted from the video: 'Inside Accenture's AI Journey with CEO Julie Sweet', Microsoft. https://www.youtube.com/watch?v=4JXJEg5tcMQ.

19 Available at https://www.bcg.com/publications/2023/how-people-create-and-destroy-value-with-gen-ai, accessed August 2024.

20 Extracted from the video: Bernard Marr, 'The Amazing Ways Global Consulting Firm BCG Uses AI Internally', 2024. https://www.youtube.com/watch?v=lCG47inAITk.

21 Available at Anaga Sivaramakrishnan, 'How Project ECHO's knowledge hub is enhanced with Apurva.ai's roots in collective wisdom', Apurva.ai, 11 January 2024, https://apurva.ai/How-Project-ECHO%E2%80%99s-knowledge-hub-is-enhanced-with-Apurva.ai%E2%80%99s-roots-in-collective-wisdom.html, accessed May 2024.

22 Special thanks to Rafee Tarafdar, Srividhya V.S., Saikrishna Kaparthy, Ramesh N. and Ramachandran S.

23 Kris Gopalakrishnan, N. Dayasindhu and Krishnan Narayanan, *Against All Odds—The IT Story of India* (India; Penguin Random House, 2022).

24 Extracted from Nandan Nilekani's foreword in Jeff Kavanaugh and Rafee Tarafdar, *The Live Enterprise: Create a Continuously Evolving and Learning Organization* (McGraw Hill, 2021).

25 Rafee Tarafdar, Jeff Kavanaugh and Harry Keir Hughes, *Infosys Live Enterprise—A Continuously Evolving and Learning Organization* (Infosys Knowledge Institute, 2019).

26 Brian Leavy, 'Designed to evolve: digital transformation the Infosys way', *Strategy & Leadership*, Vol. 49 No. 4 (2021), pp. 16–24. https://doi.org/10.1108/SL-05-2021-0051, accessed February 2025.

27 Rafee Tarafdar, Jeff Kavanaugh and Harry Keir Hughes, *Infosys Live Enterprise—A Continuously Evolving and Learning Organization* (Infosys Knowledge Institute, 2019).

28 Extracted from Nandan Nilekani's address at the Infosys AGM 2019—https://www.infosys.com/investors/news-events/annual-general-meeting/2019/nandan-nilekani-speech.pdf, accessed May 2024.

29 Available at 'Market capitalization of Infosys (INFY)', Companies Market Cap, https://companiesmarketcap.com/infosys/marketcap/, accessed May 2024.

30 Available at 'Building the AI-First Organization', Infosys, https://www.infosys.com/iki/research/tech-navigator.html, accessed May 2024.

31 Tech Navigator: The AI-first Organization, Infosys Knowledge Institute, 2023.

32 Available at Sujith Jon, 'How to build an AI-first firm', MSN, https://www.msn.com/en-in/money/news/how-to-build-an-ai-first-firm/ar-AA1owgd5, accessed August 2024.

33 Available at Mimosa Basu, 'Creating Sellers of the Future: Infosys Shares its Transformation Journey', LinkedIn, 15 March 2023, https://www.linkedin.com/business/sales/blog/customer-stories/infosys-linkedin-sales-solutions-shares-transformation-journey, accessed May 2024.

34 Available at Shilpa Phadnis, 'Infosys' Vanguard deal pegged at $1.5 billion', The *Times of India*, 20 July 2020, https://timesofindia.indiatimes.com/business/india-business/infosys-vanguard-deal-value-pegged-at-1-5-billion/articleshow/77057344.cms, accessed May 2024.

35 Available at Harichandan Arakali, 'How generative AI is changing Infosys from within', *Forbes*, 5 March 2024, https://www.forbesindia.com/article/leadership/how-generative-ai-is-changing-infosys-from-within/91845/1, accessed May 2024.

36 Available at 'Creating Sellers of the Future: Infosys Shares its Transformation Journey', MSN, https://www.msn.com/en-in/money/news/strong-client-interest-on-genai-dont-foresee-layoffs-within-infosys-from-new-age-tech-ceo-salil-parekh/ar-AA1poCLr, accessed August 2024.

37 Extracted from the video: How AI is serving up data driven tennis, *Financial Times*. https://www.youtube.com/watch?v=xwN99F1dOcA.

38 Carlos Cordon and Franck Calleeuw, 'The journey to digitize tennis: Infosys (A), the past', IMD, October 2023.

39 Extracted from the video: How AI is serving up data driven tennis, *Financial Times*. https://www.youtube.com/watch?v=xwN99F1dOcA.

40 Extracted from the video: Experience the Next: Infosys and FFT reimagining tennis using Applied AI, Infosys. https://www.youtube.com/watch?v=KGFxjguJXwQ.

41 Ibid.

42 Ibid.

43 Ibid.

44 Available at Thirumala Arohi, 'How Impactful is Your Organization's Learning', Infosys, https://www.infosys.com/insights/human-potential/impactful-organization.html, accessed May 2024.

45 Jeff Kavanaugh and Rafee Tarafdar, 'Break Down Change Management into Small Steps', *Harvard Business Review*, 3 May 2021.

46 Available at Raghav Gupta, Ishan Gupta and Thirumala Arohi, ''Learning' to Succeed in a Dynamic World', https://

www.infosys.com/insights/disruptions/dynamic-world.html, accessed May 2024.

47 Mopia Kamdoum and Arnold Vogt, 'Shaping Corporate Learning and Reskilling With Infosys Wingspan', *PAC*, August 2023.

48 Available at 'Infosys launches digital skilling programme Springboard ', *The Economic Times*, 3 September 2021, https://economictimes.indiatimes.com/tech/information-tech/ infosys-launches-digital-skilling-programme-springboard/ articleshow/85886157.cms, accessed February 2025.

49 Available at 'Infosys launches digital skilling programme Springboard ', *The Economic Times*, 3 September 2021, https://economictimes.indiatimes.com/tech/information-tech/ infosys-launches-digital-skilling-programme-springboard/ articleshow/85886157.cms, accessed February 2025.

50 Available at 'In 100 days, Infosys Springboard onboards over 1.2 million digital learners across India', Infosys, 2 March 2022, https://www.infosys.com/newsroom/press-releases/2022/ springboard-onboards-digital-learners.html, accessed May 2024.

51 Available at John Elkington '25 Years Ago I Coined the Phrase "Triple Bottom Line." Here's Why It's Time to Rethink It', *Harvard Business Review*, 25 June 2018, https://hbr. org/2018/06/25-years-ago-i-coined-the-phrase-triple-bottom-line-heres-why-im-giving-up-on-it, accessed May 2024.

52 Available at 'Climate Impact Partners Releases Fourth Annual Report on the Climate Commitments of the Fortune Global 500', PR Newswire, 21 September 2022, https://www. prnewswire.com/news-releases/climate-impact-partners-releases-fourth-annual-report-on-the-climate-commitments-of-the-fortune-global-500-301629593.html, accessed May 2024.

53 Corey Glickman and Jeff Kavanaugh, *Practical Sustainability: Circular Commerce, Smarter Spaces and Happier Humans* (Houndstooth Press, February 2022).

54 Corey Glickman and Jeff Kavanaugh, *Practical Sustainability: Circular Commerce, Smarter Spaces and Happier Humans* (Houndstooth Press, 2022).

55 Available at 'Practical Sustainability', Infosys, https://www. infosys.com/services/engineering-services/service-offerings/ sustainability-practice.html, accessed May 2024.

56 Available at 'Infosys ESG Vision 2030', Infosys, https://www. infosys.com/about/corporate-responsibility/esg-vision-2030/ assets/docs/infosys-esg-vision-2030.pdf, accessed May 2024.

57 This builds on the concept of a knowledge environment that was originally motivated in the book by C.K. Prahalad and Venkat Ramaswamy on *The Future of Competition: Co-Creating Unique Value With Customers* (Cambridge, MA: Harvard Business School Press, 2004).

58 G. Hamel and M. Zanini, *Humanocracy: creating organizations as amazing as the people inside them* (Boston, MA: Harvard Business Review Press, 2020).

59 P.M. Senge, *The Fifth Discipline* (New York, NY: Doubleday, 1990).

60 Sumantra Ghoshal and C.A. Bartlett, *The Individualized Corporation: A fundamentally new approach to management; great companies are defined by purpose, process, and people* (New York, NY: Harper Business, 2004).

61 L. Gratton, *The Democratic Enterprise: Liberating your business with freedom, flexibility and commitment* (Pearson Education, 2004).

62 L.A. Hill, G. Brandeau, E. Truelove and K. Lineback, *Collective Genius: The Art and Practice of Leading Innovation* (Boston, MA: Harvard Business Review Press, 2014).

63 Ikujirō Nonaka and Hirotaka Takeuchi, *The Knowledge-Creating Company: How Japanese Companies Create the Dynamics of Innovation* (Oxford University Press, 1995) and *The Wise Company: How Companies Create Continuous Innovation* (Oxford University Press, 2020).

64 S.J. Ashford, *The Power of Flexing* (HarperCollins, 2021).

65 A.K. Yeung and D. Ulrich, *Reinventing the Organization* (Boston, MA: Harvard Business Review Press, 2019).

66 See also Charles-Edouard Bouée, *Light Footprint Management* (Bloombsury Publishing, 2018).

67 Available at 'What is the Michigan Model of Leadership?', Sanger10, https://sanger.umich.edu/our-model/, accessed September 2024.

68 J.E. Dutton and G.M. Spreitzer, *How to Be a Positive Leader: Small Actions, Big Impact* (Berrett–Koehler Publishers, 2014).

69 Nick Van Dam and E. Masie, *Elevating Learning & Development: Insights and Practical Guidance from the Field* (New York, NY: McKinsey & Company, 2018).

70 K. Palmer and D. Blake, *The Expertise Economy* (Nicholas Brealey, 2018).

71 R. Kegan, L.L. Lahey, M.L. Miller, A. Fleming and D. Helsing, *An Everyone Culture Becoming a Deliberately Developmental Organization* (Boston, MA: Harvard Business Review Press, 2016).

72 L. Prasad and S. Ramachandran, *Neoskilling for Digital Transformation and the Artificial Intelligence Revolution* (Wiley, 2018).

Chapter 8: Co-Evolving Sustainable Wellbeing Impacts Across Sectors

1 See R. Henderson, *Reimagining Capitalism in a World on Fire* (PublicAffairs, 2020), for a discussion on how to reimagine capitalism so that it achieves economic prosperity along with regard for the environment and social justice.

2 See H. Kissinger, E. Schmidt and D.P. Huttenlocher, *The Age of AI and Our Human Future* (Little Brown & Company, 2021), for a discussion on how AI is impacting knowledge creation, politics and human societies.

3 'Building a common vision for sustainable food and agriculture—Principles and approaches', Food and Agriculture Organization of the United Nations (FAO), 2014.

4 M. Montenegro de Wit, 'Can agroecology and CRISPR mix? The politics of complementarity and moving towards technology sovereignty', Agric Hum Values 39, 733–755 (2022). https://doi.org/10.1007/s10460-021-10284-0, accessed February 2025.

5   In conversation with the authors.
6   Available at Bill Briggs, 'How Land O'Lakes is cultivating ag-
    tech to help farmers harvest healthier profits', Microsoft, 15
    July 2020, https://news.microsoft.com/transform/how-land-
    o-lakes-cultivating-agriculture-tech-help-farmers-harvest-
    healthier-profits/, accessed November 2023.
7   Available at 'Azure Data Manager for Agriculture', Microsoft,
    https://azure.microsoft.com/en-us/products/data-manager-for-
    agriculture/, accessed November 2023.
8   Available at Alicia Wallace, 'As the CEO of Land O'Lakes, she's
    changing the rules of American farming', CNN, 21 November
    2023, https://edition.cnn.com/2023/11/21/economy/beth-
    ford-risk-taker/index.html, accessed February 2024.
9   Available   at   https://www.landolakesinc.com/Blog/
    November-2023/Showcasing-the-power-of-the-Land-O-
    Lakes-Coop, accessed February 2024.
10 Amartya Sen, 'Human Capital and Capability', in *World
    Development*, volume 25, issue 12 (1997).
11 Amartya Sen, *Development as Freedom* (New York, NY:
    Knopf, 1999).
12 Available at 'Neelam Chhiber on Creating an Ownership
    Based Ecosystem for Women in India', Catalyst 2030, 1 March
    2022, https://catalyst2030.net/neelam-chhiber-on-creating-an-
    ownership-based-ecosystem-for-women-in-india/,   accessed
    May 2024.
13 Available at S. Aijaz, 'Industree talks - Are dying handicraft arts
    worth saving?', YourStory, 26 June 2015, https://yourstory.
    com/2015/06/industree-foundation-jacob-mathew,   accessed
    May 2024.
14 Available at 'Interview with Neelam Chhiber (Industree
    Foundation)',   What's   Working   Solutions,   https://
    whatsworkingsolutions.org/resource/interview-with-neelam-
    chhibe-industree-foundation/, accessed May 2024.
15 Industree Foundation Annual Report 2022–23.
16 Available at 'Neelam Chhiber on Creating an Ownership
    Based Ecosystem for Women in India', Catalyst 2030, 1 March
    2022, https://catalyst2030.net/neelam-chhiber-on-creating-an-

ownership-based-ecosystem-for-women-in-india/, accessed May 2024.

17 Available at 'How platform know-how can drive social inclusion and empower billions', The *European Sting*, 1 April 2021, https://europeansting.com/2021/04/01/how-platform-know-how-can-drive-social-inclusion-and-empower-billions/, accessed May 2024.

18 Available at 'Interview with Neelam Chhibe (Industree Foundation)', What's Working Solutions, https://whatsworkingsolutions.org/resource/interview-with-neelam-chhibe-industree-foundation/, accessed May 2024.

19 D. Jonke, et al., MAP Final Report: eGovernments #301, University of Michigan, April 2018.

20 Available at Viraj Tyagi, 'How can we make citizen services transparent and easily accessible?', Societal Muse, https://muse.societalthinking.org/#/article?post=13&slug=how-can-we-make-governance-and-citizen-services-transparent-and-easily-accessible, accessed June 2024.

21 Available at Rohini Nilekani, *Samaaj, Sarkaar, Bazaar: A Citizen-First Approach*, 2022, https://www.samaajsarkaarbazaar.in/, accessed May 2024.

22 Rohini Nilekani, *Samaaj, Sarkaar, Bazaar: A Citizen-First Approach*, 2022.

23 Available at 'The Road to 2 Billion—An Overview', DIVOC, https://divoc.egov.org.in/, accessed June 2024.

24 Available at Viraj Tyagi, 'How can we make citizen services transparent and easily accessible?', Societal Muse, https://muse.societalthinking.org/#/article?post=13&slug=how-can-we-make-governance-and-citizen-services-transparent-and-easily-accessible, accessed June 2024.

25 In conversation with the authors.

26 Venkat Ramaswamy, 'Wealth-Welfare-Wellbeing, Private-Public-Social Ecosystem Innovation, and Co-Creation of Value,' *European Commission Report*, Open Innovation 2.0., 2014.

27 See Venkat Ramaswamy and Kerimcan Ozcan, *The Co-Creation Paradigm* (California: Stanford University Press, 2014).

28 J. Ehrenfeld and A.J. Hoffman, *Flourishing: A Frank Conversation About Sustainability* (California; Stanford Business Books, an imprint of Stanford University Press, 2013).

29 E.F. Schumacher and J. Porritt, *Small is Beautiful: A Study of Economics as if People Mattered* (Vintage, 1993).

30 Available at 'Fixing the economy to fix climate change', Ellen Macarthur Foundation, https://www.ellenmacarthurfoundation.org/topics/climate/overview, accessed June 2024.

31 Extracted from 'techUK talks with . . . Greg Jackson, CEO of Octopus Energy: Recording and Roundup', techUK, 13 February 2023, https://www.techuk.org/resource/techuk-talks-with-greg-jackson-ceo-of-octopus-energy-recording-and-roundup.html, accessed July 2024.

32 Available in the video: BBC StoryWorks 'The Human Component'—Kraken: The Smart Homes Eliminating Energy Bills.

33 Extracted from 'techUK talks with . . . Greg Jackson, CEO of Octopus Energy: Recording and Roundup', techUK, 13 February 2023, https://www.techuk.org/resource/techuk-talks-with-greg-jackson-ceo-of-octopus-energy-recording-and-roundup.html, accessed July 2024.

34 Available at 'Octopus Energy grows UK's largest virtual power plant', Octopus Energy, https://octopus.energy/press/octopus-energy-grows-uks-largest-virtual-power-plant/, accessed July 2024.

35 Available at 'Kraken sparks energy industry innovation with Databricks', Databricks, https://www.databricks.com/customers/kraken, accessed August 2024.

36 Available at 'Introducing the Data Intelligence Platform for Energy', Databricks, 19 July 2024, https://www.databricks.com/blog/introducing-data-intelligence-platform-energy, accessed August 2024.

37 Extracted from an Inside Octopus video 'How Kraken is powering a transformation at Octopus and beyond'. https://www.youtube.com/watch?v=UmmZxf6rFxc.

38 Extracted from the webinar 'Why a Decentralized Grid Requires a New Customer Experience', Industry Dive, https://resources.industrydive.com/technologys-role-in-turning-customers-into-partners, accessed July 2024.

39 Extracted from Greg Brown's talk at 'Leading in the Generative AI Revolution | Milken Institute Global Conference 2024' https://www.youtube.com/watch?v=x-uZ-Xk_Ah8.

40 Available at 'For AI to transform public safety, AI itself must also be safe', Fast Company, 26 June 2024, https://www.fastcompany.com/91137903/for-ai-to-transform-public-safety-ai-itself-must-also-be-safe, accessed July 2024.

41 Extracted from Greg Brown's talk at 'Leading in the Generative AI Revolution | Milken Institute Global Conference 2024' https://www.youtube.com/watch?v=x-uZ-Xk_Ah8.

42 Available at 'For AI to transform public safety, AI itself must also be safe', Fast Company, 26 June 2024, https://www.fastcompany.com/91137903/for-ai-to-transform-public-safety-ai-itself-must-also-be-safe, accessed July 2024.

43 Available at 'Helsinki 3D', Helsinki, https://www.hel.fi/en/decision-making/information-on-helsinki/maps-and-geospatial-data/helsinki-3d, accessed August 2024.

44 Available at '5 things to know about Virtual Singapore', Govtech Singapore, 28 March 2017, https://www.tech.gov.sg/media/technews/5-things-to-know-about-virtual-singapore/, accessed August 2024.

45 Available at 'The Living Standards Framework Dashboard', The Treasury, https://lsfdashboard.treasury.govt.nz/wellbeing/, accessed February 2024.

46 Venkat Ramaswamy, 'Co-Creating Development', *World Bank Outreach*, September, 2011.

Chapter 9: Cultivating EcoAI-Literacy and Lifelong Learning

1 D. Goleman, Z. Barlow and L. Bennett, *Ecoliterate: How Educators are Cultivating Emotional, Social, and Ecological Intelligence* (Wiley, 2012). See also https://www.ecoliteracy.org/

2   B. Mckibben, *Eaarth: Making a Life on a Tough New Planet* (Times Books, 2010).

3   Available at 'Knowledge-Driven Actions: Transforming Higher Education for Global Sustainability', UNESCO, 2022, https://doi.org/10.54675/ybtv1653, accessed February 2025.

4   'Recommendation on the Ethics of Artificial Intelligence', UNESCO, 2021.

5   Jayson Toweh and Tim Carter, 'Using the Distinctives of Higher Education to Accelerate Climate Action,' *Second Nature*, 2023.

6   Available at 'A truly sustainable partnership', Siemens Xcelerator, https://xcelerator.siemens.com/global/en/industries/higher-education/references/humber-college.html, accessed September 2024.

7   Available at 'Universities can be 'living labs' for sustainability', World Economic Forum, 15 July 2021, www.weforum.org/agenda/2021/07/universities-sustainability-hong-kong/, accessed June 2024.

8   Available at 'Learning to Become a Systems Leader in a Complex World', Villars Institute, 2 May 2024, https://villarsinstitute.org/posts/learning-to-become-a-systems-leader-in-a-complex-world, accessed August 2024.

9   S.A. Vaghefi, D. Stammbach, V. Muccione, et al. 'ChatClimate: Grounding Conversational AI in Climate Science', Commun Earth Environ 4, 480 (2023), https://doi.org/10.1038/s43247-023-01084-x, accessed February 2025.

10 In conversation with the authors.

11 See also D. Goleman, Z. Barlow and L. Bennett, *Ecoliterate: How Educators are Cultivating Emotional, Social, and Ecological Intelligence* (Wiley, 2012).

12 In conversation with the authors.

13 Extracted from Subra Suresh's speech at The 4th Villars Institute Distinguished Lecture; https://villarsinstitute.org/posts/villars-institute-distinguished-lecture-10-things-we-learned-from-subra-suresh.

14 Extracted from the video: UAE's Dynamic AI Journey: What Have We Learned? HE Omar Sultan AlOlama at GII 2024,

McKinsey & Company, May 2024. https://www.youtube.com/watch?v=gcotn5rMc1M.

15 Extracted from the video: UAE AI Minister Omar Al Olama on the era of artificial intelligence, AtlanticCouncil, Apr 2024. https://www.youtube.com/watch?v=3SwOCTaO4IM.

16 Available at 'Microsoft invests $1.5 billion in Abu Dhabi's G42 to accelerate AI development and global expansion', Microsoft, 15 April 2024, https://news.microsoft.com/2024/04/15/microsoft-invests-1-5-billion-in-abu-dhabis-g42-to-accelerate-ai-development-and-global-expansion/, accessed October 2024.

17 Available at amai, https://amai.vlaanderen/, accessed November 2024.

18 Jayson Toweh and Tim Carter, 'Using the Distinctives of Higher Education to Accelerate Climate Action,' *Second Nature*, 2023.

19 M. Roman, H. Varga, V. Cvijanovic and A. Reid, 'Quadruple Helix Models for Sustainable Regional Innovation: Engaging and Facilitating Civil Society Participation', Economies 2020, 8,48. www.doi.org/10.3390/economies8020048, accessed February 2025.

20 Available at 'The Impact of Angel Investing', VentureWell, https://venturewell.org/, accessed September 2024.

21 E. Mollick, *Co-Intelligence* (Penguin, 2024).

22 Coursera Annual Report, 10K SEC Filings, 22 February 2024.

23 Available at 'Coursera's Coronavirus Response Initiative', All India Council For Technical Education, https://www.aicte-india.org/sites/default/files/CIRCULAR_COURSERA.pdf, accessed June 2022.

24 Available at 'Navigating Generative AI Business Transformation', Coursera, 27 July 2024, https://www.coursera.org/enterprise/articles/generative-ai-business-transformation-cm, accessed June 2024.

25 Available at 'Generative AI In Practice: How Coursera Built and Implemented Its Foundational GenAI Learning Strategy', Coursera, 27 July 2024, https://www.coursera.org/enterprise/

articles/how-coursera-built-genai-learning-strategy-cm, accessed June 2024.

26 Ibid.

27 Srinivasan, Suraj, Michael Parzen, and Radhika Kak. 'Coursera's Foray into GenAI', Harvard Business School Case 124-089, March 2024 (Revised April 2024.)

28 Global Skills Report 2024, Coursera.

29 Available at ONEST, https://onest.network/, accessed August 2024.

30 Venkat Ramaswamy is a professor at the Ross School of Business at the University of Michigan, Ann Arbor. While affiliated with the University of Michigan, he was not involved with developing any of the initiatives discussed here.

31 Extracted from One Detroit, 'University of Michigan becomes first college to create AI tools for campus, students', YouTube video, 3 May 2024, https://www.youtube.com/watch?v=47FjlpWl8Og, accessed June 2024.

32 Available at https://er.educause.edu/articles/2024/2/how-and-why-the-university-of-michigan-built-its-own-closed-generative-ai-tools, accessed June 2024.

33 Extracted from University of Michigan, 'President Ono's Monthly Message—Generative AI', YouTube video, 19 March 2024, https://www.youtube.com/watch?v=DsN_dILsqs8, accessed June 2024.

34 Available at 'U-M Generative AI Use Cases', GenAI U-M, https://genai.umich.edu/use-cases, accessed June 2024.

35 Extracted from umichTECH, 'U-M Maizey Lets You Build a Teaching Assistant AI in Minutes', YouTube video, 22 November 2023, https://www.youtube.com/watch?v=Sn2bpp6kcU4, accessed June 2024.

36 Available at Ali Azhar, 'University of Michigan is Developing an AI Coaching Bot For Students', BIGDATAWIRE, 23 February 2024, https://www.datanami.com/2024/02/23/university-of-michigan-is-developing-an-ai-coaching-bot-for-students/, accessed June 2024.

37 Ben Causey et al., MAP Project—Azure Gen AI for Higher Education Final Report, Michigan Ross School of Business, 2024.

38 Extracted from University of Michigan, 'President Ono's Monthly Message—Generative AI', YouTube video, 19 March 2024, https://www.youtube.com/watch?v=DsN_dILsqs8, accessed June 2024.

39 In conversation with the authors.

40 Available at https://record.umich.edu/articles/u-m-openai-launch-partnership-to-expand-ai-research/, accessed March 2025.

41 Available at Sanjay Purohit, 'Towards a New Equilibrium', Societal Thinking, 15 November 2022, https://societalthinking.org/blog/towards-a-new-equilibrium/, accessed October 2024.

42 In conversation with the authors.

43 K.-F. Lee and Chen Qiufan, *AI 2041: Ten Visions for Our Future* (WH Allen, 2021).

44 Sahlman, William A., Allison M. Ciechanover, and Emily Grandjean. 'Khanmigo: Revolutionizing Learning with GenAI.' Harvard Business School Case 824-059, November 2023. (Revised April 2024).

45 Sal Khan, *Brave New Words* (Viking, 2024).

46 Available at 'How We Built AI Tutoring Tools', Khan Academy Blog, 7 March 2024, https://blog.khanacademy.org/how-we-built-ai-tutoring-tools/, accessed June 2024. Khan Academy's pedagogy is based on the ICAP (Interactive, Constructive, Active, Passive) framework developed by Micki Chi and Ruth Wylie.

47 Sal Khan, *Brave New Words* (Viking, 2024).

48 Ibid.

49 William A. Sahlman, Allison M. Ciechanover and Emily Grandjean, 'Khanmigo: Revolutionizing Learning with GenAI', Harvard Business School Case 824–059, November 2023 (revised April 2024).

50 Sal Khan, *Brave New Words* (Viking, 2024).

51 Available at Sally Beatty, 'Khan Academy and Microsoft partner to expand access to AI tools that personalize teaching and help make learning fun', Microsoft, 21 May 2024, https://news.microsoft.com/source/features/ai/khan-academy-and-microsoft-partner-to-expand-access-to-ai-tools/, accessed September 2024.